AT THE TOP

Books by Marylin Bender

THE BEAUTIFUL PEOPLE

AT THE TOP

Marylin Bender

AT THE TOP

Doubleday & Company, Inc.

Garden City, New York   1975

Library of Congress Cataloging in Publication Data

Bender, Marylin
At the top

"Most of the chapters . . . were published, in
somewhat different form, in the New York Times."
CONTENTS: The view at the top.—Avon, ding-dong-
down—Did success breed failure at General
Foods? [etc.]
1. Big business—United States—Addresses,
essays, lectures. I. Title.
HD2785.B43   338.6'44'0973
ISBN 0-385-01004-4
Library of Congress Catalog Card Number 74-33630

For Selig,
greatest of teachers, best of friends, and
dearest husband

AUTHOR'S NOTE

Fourteen of the chapters in this book are based on stories written for the New York *Times* over a period of four years from the early to the mid-1970s. They were years of crisis and unprecedented challenges for business and so it was both instructive and pleasurable for the writer (and, it is hoped, for the reader) to expand and update the stories, to find out (as one can never do in a Harvard Business School case study) the consequences of the decisions that were made and the confirmation or collapse of the assumptions and hopes accompanying those decisions.

All of the chapters except the first and last which are of a summary nature carry the date when they were first written for the newspaper as well as the date when they were brought to current status for this book early in 1975.

A majority of the stories were written for the Sunday business and finance section of the New York *Times* while John M. Lee was its editor. This reporter gratefully and respectfully acknowledges his encouragement and informed direction. For the editing of the other stories as well as for that constant mixture of leadership and approval that makes a reporter's craft a process of learning and joy, I give thanks to Richard E. Mooney, assistant financial news editor, to Robert E. Bedingfield, assistant to the financial news editor and, of course, to Thomas E. Mullaney, the financial news editor. Sydney Gruson, executive vice president of the New York *Times,* is hereby rendered appreciation for granting permission to use material published in the *Times.*

April 5, 1975.

CONTENTS

THE WHEELER-DEALERS

MINORITY REPORT

FINALE

INTRODUCTION

THE VIEW AT THE TOP

On the fourteenth floor of the eight-winged stone rectangle that is the headquarters of the General Motors Corporation in Detroit, the men who were once thought to be the most powerful in the industrial world huddle in splendid isolation, facing east.

From their windows they can look out upon Woodward Avenue, the city's main artery, over the blighted auto capital toward the airport from which they can escape to their offices on the twenty-fifth floor of the General Motors Building in New York.

The view from the fourteenth floor omits the harsher details of vacant buildings, human discards, and even the prices of gasoline at the pumps.

In New York, the scene is prettier. Central Park below is a constantly changing landscape, a Brueghel in summer and autumn, a Japanese pen-and-ink drawing in spring and winter.

The seats of power in American business are almost always at the tops of buildings as well as of organization charts. But the men on the fourteenth floor, or the twenty-fifth—or the third or fourth in the squat suburban complexes that so many corporations are gathering themselves into—invariably say that they don't look out. Their chairs are placed with the backs to the views or deep into the rooms. Besides, they are too busy to look out of windows.

Busyness is the dogma of American business management. The Indians demand more leisure in their union contracts while the chiefs stretch their working hours to fill the vacuum of the twenty-four-hour day, meanwhile worrying about new products to sell to the leisured population.

Gazing out of windows or into crystal balls and other seemingly idle acts are permissible for intellectuals and so-called creative people and it is possible for them to make a great deal of money from American business. But seldom as chief executives or business leaders.

Sages may be very well paid but as a rule they are not admitted to the pinnacle club of American business, that inner circle of corporation chairmen and presidents, of chief executive officers and chief operating officers, of directors of the board, of management consultants, investment bankers and corporation lawyers, any one of whom may be changing seats and titles with one or more of the others for any given time.

One of the innumerable ironies of American business is that although the best view from the office is one of the spoils of battle, the victors often let it go to waste. They don't know what they are missing.

There is a lot in this book about views and vision—both clear and faulty—and about opportunities exploited or squandered.

Scenic environment is the least of the reasons that men, and now at last some women, are driven to succeed in business. If one were to pay attention to the literature of this country or to what comes out of the mouths of babes, it is a despised occupation. Opinion polls are forever announcing the new low esteem in which business is held by the polled (presumably the same who, year in and year out place Mamie Eisenhower, Jackie Onassis, and now Pat Nixon on pedestals). Perhaps this indicates, among the polled, a profound distrust for power. Why do the pollsters continue the charade of asking them? So businessmen, in whose hire the opinion researchers survey, can lament how oppressed they are and ask the government to set them free?

No matter how many laws are passed or how the economic climate shifts, the power of business in the United States is not curbed. If checked in one direction, it veers to another.

Business remains the most accessible and the most versatile instrument for the exercise of personal power.

No fantasy of ambition is too outrageous to be played on the instrument of business. Young man, would you like to meet beautiful actresses, hobnob with pop stars, be a TV pioneer? Go into the funeral business, from there into parking lots, and transform yourself into the chairman of Warner Communications, Inc.

Obscure young housewife, would you dine with duchesses, be hostess to the woman for whom a king gave up his throne? Then make up some face creams and sell them to your friends. Give away your samples, be persistent with stores, work with your family seven days a week, and become the Estée Lauder of Estée Lauder, Inc.

Would you effect social change? If you are white, Anglo-Saxon, Protestant, and rich or if you are poor and black, do it through an international corporation based in the cornfields of Indiana, the Cummins Engine Company.

Would you be President of the United States? Maybe not, although a President most contemptuous of businessmen, John F. Kennedy, owed his motivation and the dollar power behind his campaign to his father's business interests in movies, whisky, and the stock market.

If not quite the presidency, there is the status of presidential hopeful acquired through the offices of governor or senator, as George W. Romney had from auto manufacturing and Charles H. Percy, by being a camera business prodigy.

Or one can be an adviser of Presidents. Nowhere as in America are businessmen taken so seriously. Where but in the United States could a bond trader, one of Wall Street's lesser callings, become Secretary of the Treasury as William Simon did and, by extension, world monetary marionetteer?

Being an organization man is safer than bond trading, a risky game for individualists, and, at the top of the corporate organization, the salary is so much better than that of a cabinet member and even that of the President.

Why should Fred G. Fusee be paid more than one and a half times as much as the President of the United States? Or Richard C. Gerstenberg and Harold S. Geneen four times as much?

Fusee is commander in chief of the bellringers who bring Avon cosmetics into the households of America. Gerstenberg, by virtue of his position, bore responsibility for what General Motors failed to provide in automobile safety, utility, and affordability, and indirectly for the security of some of the one in six jobs in the United States that depend on the auto industry.

A union leader suggested in the spring of 1974 that Geneen's sal-

ary of $814,299 may have been based on "his ability to walk in and
out of offices with hardly knocking." Geneen's attempts to arouse
the concern of the Nixon administration for the antitrust problems
of the International Telephone & Telegraph Corporation floated to
the surface before and during Watergate but no penalty was levied
on his efforts.

Other business leaders who were caught illegally sweetening the
campaign pot of Richard Nixon were chastised, fined ever so lightly,
and left to find other means of persuasion to the same end.

But the question of what these men do to deserve their breath-
taking salaries is only put once a year or so, when the magazines
publish their compensation lists for business executives or during
the seasonal shareholder meetings when the gadflies politely inquire.

It is sometimes said that chief executives earn their boodle that
one morning or afternoon of the year when the stockholders must be
faced. Relatively few stockholders, in fact, are present. The audience for these confrontations is controllable by cutting back on free
lunches and handouts of the products of the company or by holding
the meetings in the boondocks. The sessions are usually reported
superficially in the press and the corporate press attachés will ar-
range to erase prickly queries and revealing responses from the
postmeeting reports, which are adorned instead with photographs of
rapt listeners to the chairmen's remarks. Preferably, the photograph
should include one black, one young female, and several males with
moderately long hair.

A striking impression emerges from these rituals—how unexceptional the noblemen of corporate America are. One objective of
the feminist movement is to secure for women the same easy
triumph of mediocrity.

But if the wielders of power are ordinary, the power they wield is
singular. Business can build or destroy, gratify immediate mass
pleasures, and make long-range, world-significant plans. One man's
fancy, with the sanction of his peers, can create employment or
wipe out lifetime retirement funds.

Consider how many pensions evaporated in Avon fragrances and
the stocks of other companies judged to be nifty by the Wall Street
portfolio herd. Or try to quantify how much of the unemployment
statistic is traceable to the myopia of the men on the fourteenth
floor.

And always there is the confusion between private and public.

Business for private profit depends on public support. What then does it owe to the public?

There has been much propaganda in the business schools, the business press and in the councils where businessmen talk to each other, for the chief executives of corporations organized for profit to assume the role of statesmen, to be "the conscience of the corporations." The bigger the business, the bigger the possibilities for doing good (within self-selected definitions, of course). Benevolent paternalism on a global scale is an offer hard to refuse.

Only a few throwbacks to the eighteenth-century philosophers like Milton Friedman, the University of Chicago economist, maintain that the business of business is nothing else besides business.

Others of less extreme convictions doubt the omnipotence of the business executive. George Cabot Lodge, the professor who cultivates the ideological garden at the Harvard Graduate School of Business Administration, has spotted danger in business leaders prescribing for social needs. "It's a function of the political process," he has said.

In a more pungent and practical vein, Gaylord Freeman, chairman of the First Chicago Corporation, the midwest bank holding company, asserts that when the chief executive embraces the statesman's role entirely, "he will be a lousy chief executive."

C. W. ("Tex") Cook would have to agree. His excuse for General Foods Corporation losing millions in hamburger stands was that he, the chairman, was helping out with national matters such as minority employment and food industry standards.

Yet precisely because of the power inherent in the large business corporation, it is seen as a vehicle for social correction. An unusual concentration of black professionals, some drawn from the ministry, the civil rights movement, and the military have been attracted to the Cummins Engine Company because they believe it can do what in other times the Church and the government were expected to do—make economic opportunity color blind. Though they mention the corporation as the change agent, they acknowledge that it is the one man in control of the corporation who makes it likely to happen.

J. Irwin Miller is an example of an individual putting the stamp of his private social vision on a corporation which, by legal fiction, has public ownership. Miller is able to do this because he chose his ancestors wisely. They staked out positions in different businesses—milling, machine engines, banking, and real estate—so that he has had an instrument for change at his fingertips. Miller extends his benefactions to individuals and communities, through his family's private charitable foundations but also through the Cummins Engine Foundation. His influence is often invisible—his office is not at corporate headquarters in Columbus, Indiana—but nonetheless potent. Miller's use of the international corporation for social purposes generally wins praise.

Yet when another heir, Walter Beinecke, Jr., whose forebears struck gold in trading stamps, tries to impose his community vision on the island of Nantucket, he is attacked as a despot. Beinecke wants to preserve its historical heritage by making the island commercially viable. He speaks softly, using marketing terms, but he carries the club of real estate accumulation. He brooks no interference from little folk—small merchants and rooming house proprietors who don't share his vision. Beinecke does in miniature what those atop large corporations do sweepingly. Estopped from acting out his impulses through the Sperry & Hutchinson Company his grandfather founded, because another third-generation family member has the chief executive's seat, Walter Beinecke reverts to one-man entrepreneurship.

If Papa knows best, does Miller know better than Beinecke?

Paternalism is out of fashion, though, unless it is dressed in stylish new wrappings. Hiring a public relations firm as couturier, Herbert V. Kohler, Jr., of Kohler, Wisconsin, wants to cleanse the name of his family company, which had been more synonymous with industrial strife than with its contribution to the American bathroom culture. Family businesses such as the Kohler Company are a lively source of plot and counterplot. The conflicts and the power thrusts and parries are less hidden than in the impersonal corporate bureaucracies.

Brotherly love wears thin after a generation or two in business because sooner or later it becomes clear that there is room for but one at the top. The only reason the Pritzker family of Chicago financiers holds together, one of them admitted, is that they have so many irons in the fire.

When the family strength fades, professional managers take over as at International Business Machines Corporation when the sons of Thomas J. Watson retired or died. Or at Avon Products Inc., where Hays Clark, the founder's grandson, cheerfully sits off-center. If the company is publicly held, Wall Street and the business academicians usually approve of professionals holding the reins. But is it always a healthy indicator? Mightn't the company be better off if someone who cared were factoring his affections into the decision-making process?

Grant G. Simmons, chairman of the Simmons Company and great-grandson of the founding mattress maker, once said, "Someone like me can have a total preoccupation with the long-term health, growth and seaworthiness of the company for good times and bad.

"My successor will probably have a less benign attitude toward today's results. The bulk of my energies are connected with the Simmons Company down the road. It's like the difference between Eisenhower and Marshall, between deciding whether to invade the continent or deciding whether to win the war in the Pacific or the Atlantic first." Simmons saw himself as General Marshall.

"The professional manager is apt to be running against a short term," he said. "He has perhaps only ten years to make his mark. He's less relaxed. He may run a vessel with too much sail up for rough and stormy seas, figuring, 'I'm not going to be at the helm when it's struck.'"

Noting at that time that his father, his brother, and he had enough stock in the company to overshadow any other investor, Simmons declined to rate his own performance. He said it would be self-serving. Subsequently, Charles G. Bluhdorn, the conglomerateur, started buying Simmons stock for his Gulf & Western Industries, Inc. When he reached about 9 per cent of the common stock, he paused and those who admired what the Simmons Company had stood for for over a century sighed with relief.

For forty years, Revlon, Inc., was Charles H. Revson. Periodically, he would designate heirs-in-management (or they would imagine they had been anointed). Then he would cast them out. Just as the cosmetics industry and the investment community was reading Revson as King Lear, he played one of his intuitive hunches about the fragrance market. He contradicted common wisdom and he won. He also picked a chief executive who knew nothing about marketing beauty products but a lot about multinational management. Revson seemed to be getting the ship ready to sail on without him. Maybe he did know what was best for Revlon Inc. after all.

The nepotism theme in the sagas of business is never exhausted. Semon E. Knudsen, disappointed at not getting his father's presidential seat at General Motors, crossed into enemy territory to become president of the Ford Motor Company. He clashed with another princely ego and was fired by the chairman, Henry Ford's grandson.

Robert Lehman, the prince of Lehman Brothers, the venerable German-Jewish Wall Street investment banking firm, died leaving the succession unresolved. The barons fell to feuding. In desperation, they chose a knight from the outside, Peter G. Peterson, the son of a Greek restaurateur from Nebraska.

Pullman, Inc., a Chicago company with tired blood, had no more Pullmans in its midst. Out of Pittsburgh drove Samuel B. Casey, Jr., to become the chief conductor. Would Pullman have accepted him or would he have come at all if his stepfather, one of the company's directors and bankers, had not told Casey to get in there and do something?

Would Steven J. Ross have become chairman of a *Fortune*-500 company if he hadn't married an undertaker's daughter and found his father-in-law's business so uncharismatic?

The search for the successor may cause anguish, too, in businesses devoid of family members. Emotional currents can run deep beneath bureaucratic facades. According to management theory, the chief executive should choose and train his successor, preferably from within. Since almost one third of corporate presidents and chief executive officers have been coming from outside in recent years, it would seem that retiring sovereigns have problems doing so.

Harry Levinson is one of the more heeded business psychologists. A former lecturer at the Harvard Business School, now at the Harvard Medical School, he has discoursed on why the incumbent's search may be doomed to failure.

The chief executive, according to Levinson, may harbor unconscious feelings of rivalry toward anyone who might fill his shoes. He may be oblivious to changing business conditions that dictate a new kind of leader for the organization. He may be unaware of the qualities that made him a success, so he doesn't look for them in another. Obligations he feels to tradition may so circumscribe the selection process for him that innovators are not even considered for the job.

Or having chosen his crown prince, he turns on him and makes him the scapegoat.

Levinson's solution is to turn the choice of a successor over to a committee of corporate directors. He would even fill all management posts, not just that of the chief executive officer, by committee appointments. This, Levinson concludes, "can reconfirm the old truth of safety in numbers."

Without acknowledging it, Levinson has described the General Motors system. In 1974, after one of the worst profit drops in its history and after its top management failed to recognize the key factors that were bound to alter the course of the company and the national economy in which it plays so substantial a part, the GM committee of the board selected a chairman, a president, and a slate of back-up officers from the same short-sighted team. The most that could be said of them was that they had incredible staying power. They had outlasted all possible competitors including the innovators, whom GM rejects as though they were incompatible body transplants.

Levinson's faith in committees—in the light of the GM experience—gives credence to the suspicion that business is often a theater of the absurd.

But at least he makes it sound like a boffo melodrama. Business is generally considered boring by outsiders, and insiders propound the mistaken impression. The public relations departments labor to entomb the human qualities of business organizations in the clichés of press releases. Battered and bruised, the victims of corporate warfare take "early retirement for personal reasons," convincing no one and leaving evidence to the contrary dangling.

The lawyers bury the clues of corporate rape and plunder in the statements filed with the Securities and Exchange Commission that few outsiders see. The accountants perform their legerdemain in the footnotes of the financial reports. So, though much is disclosed, very little is found because not many stockholders have the stamina to locate and wade through the gory details.

An inkling of how grave crimes and Macbethian intrigue can be disguised under the lifeless language of the corporate memorandum was perceived during the Watergate hearings. The Nixon White House was administered by second-rate advertising and publicity men, corporate managers, and lawyers who, if the truth had not come out, would have probably retired to public affairs vice presidencies of major corporations. They may yet.

"What bothers me," said a corporate PR man in the summer of 1973, "is the bad name that this is giving to the public relations profession."

So the ad men were swept out of the White House with Richard M. Nixon and the spirit of Detroit was swept in with Gerald R. Ford. One of his first appointments to a labor-management committee on inflation was Richard C. Gerstenberg of GM.

The presence of a GM official at the President's side at least confirms the durability of the Horatio Alger legend. Starting out privileged would be a handicap to rising to the fourteenth floor at GM.

Horatio Alger is alive and well in the executive suites of American business. These days the hero may even be a girl from Youngstown, Ohio, who goes to New York, starts her own advertising agency, and marries a client—an airline chairman who had started working at the age of twelve. And then Mary Wells Lawrence is called to the summit by the same President of the United States to give her ideas on how to whip inflation, public enemy number one of that month. Get those government hands off business, she says.

So ingrained is the humble beginning in business lore that where lacking, it is invented. Casey, the president of Pullman, stresses his "ditchdigger" past, neglecting to clarify that his father and grandfather owned the companies for which he labored manually during school vacations.

It is a conceit of American business that country boys from Texas or farm boys from Wisconsin are nobler than Brahmins from Boston. In the movie business it's acceptable to be Brooklyn-born poor, just as in the cosmetics business it's permissible to flash a bit of zircon history.

Perhaps gritty antecedents are so valuable because they buttress the Puritan work ethic that is a password for the pinnacle club. The compulsion to toil can just as well be Irish Catholic or East European Jewish in origin, though.

Supposedly one works hard to earn milk and rent money until it gets to be a habit even when one has attained champagne and castles. The sons of the wealthy exert themselves as much or more if they want to succeed in business. As Jay Pritzker of the Chicago financier family said with artless candor, "What else are we going to do?"

For those who are not clansmen like the Pritzkers, some of that working time must be spent in corporate politics, finding a patron, taking credit when it is due (and sometimes when it is not), and publicizing one's light which never must be left under a bushel for long.

To be sure, the old-boy networks still prevail, but what is often overlooked is their number and variety. The Eastern Establishment gets a disproportionate share of the limelight. A Standard & Poor's corporation survey of 53,000 top executives finds that one in ten went to Harvard or Yale. It could just as well be reported that nine out of ten did not.

Despite a growing recognition of its shortcomings, the Harvard Business School still exerts a singular pull, especially on the gate-keepers of the business establishment.

Critics like Robert Townsend, former chief executive of Avis Rent-a-Car and author of *Up the Organization,* may scoff that the Harvard Business School gives training for only three posts—executive vice president, president, and board chairman. Townsend calls the graduates "a senior officer class, the non-playing Captains of Industry."

But in good times, the starting salaries for Harvard Masters of Business Administration are $1,000 or more above those offered to recipients of the same degree elsewhere. When times are tough, as they were in 1974 and 1975, job candidates from Harvard may net two or three instead of eight offers, but those from many other schools may have to scrounge for one.

So the $7,000 a year (of which $3,600 went for tuition in the 1974–75 academic year) that it costs one to attend the Harvard B-School factors out to a worthwhile investment for its 1,560 students. Most of them reasonably expect their first jobs to pay $15,000 to $20,000 a year.

Surely, much of the luster has been chipped away from the B-School myth. The image of the fair-haired decision maker who will save the corporation or win the war has shifted to one of the know-it-all with slide rule in hand. The dean of the whiz kids, Harvard B-School alumnus and teacher Robert S. McNamara has been side-lined to the World Bank. Coming from the Ford Motor Company to the awesome role as United States Secretary of Defense, McNamara's statistical controls were not equal to the problem of United States involvement in Southeast Asia.

Lesser Wunderkinder than McNamara made the figures sing of synergism in the 1950s and 1960s. Now they are tending their conglomerate shells or hanging out their consultants' shingles as they wait for their brothers in executive search or at McKinsey & Company, the management consulting firm with incestuous ties to the Harvard Business School, to find them other work.

Oddly enough, considering such legendary prowess at management controls, the Harvard B-School education is acknowledged to be relatively weak in quantitative and functional skills. The B-School supposedly creates generalist decision makers. Once out in the real world and climbing fast, they can rely on the M.B.A.s from the University of Chicago or Carnegie-Mellon University's Graduate School of Industrial Administration to do the analyses and run up the schedules and the computer programs. Or on the men and women of the University of Pennsylvania's Wharton School and New York University's Graduate School of Business Administration to explain the financial markets to them.

The Harvard Business School's academic training is probably held in least repute in its own backyard. The rest of the university regards it as a trade school. The B-School's geographic isolation from the arts and sciences is more than symbolic. It's just walking distance across the Charles River by the Anderson Bridge from the Harvard Yard in Cambridge to the B-School at Soldiers Field in Boston. Presidents of the United States—the Adamses, the Roosevelts, and Kennedy studied on the Cambridge side. Presidents of corporations—Stewart S. Cort of Bethlehem Steel, Howard J. Morgens of Procter & Gamble, and James L. Ferguson of General Foods—pored over their case studies in Boston.

The continuous replenishment of corporate executive peerages by Harvard Business School alumni perpetuates its myth and fulfills its prophecy. A 1974 survey by *MBA,* a magazine founded by graduates of the school, showed that it ranked first in "employment value" in a poll of 115 business school deans. They said, though, that Stanford's Graduate School of Business offers a better quality education.

Even if Harvard's invincibility may be pecked at here, the mystique spreads abroad through the multinational corporations and the B-School's alumni who are seizing the initiative in the newly rich Middle East.

Ghaith Pharaon, who bought control of the Commonwealth Bank of Detroit, is the son of an adviser to the late King Faisal of Saudi Arabia and a Harvard M.B.A. So is Roger Tamraz, who, while still in his twenties and not long out of the B-School, helped rescue the failing Intra Bank in Beirut on behalf of Kidder, Peabody, the Wall Street investment banking firm. When the petrodollar flood began in 1974, Tamraz cut loose from Kidder and set himself up as an independent conduit to the oil sheikhs.

In many foreign countries Harvard is the only known business school, the Coca-Cola of management expertise. The most distinctive parts of its training, apart from its value as a passport to the top, are the arrogance it inculcates, the determination it fosters to rise, and a willingness it encourages to do fast and fancy footwork.

As a member of the B-School class of 1949, a conglomerate founder and chairman said about a course in administrative practices at the school that he and his classmates had rated most helpful of all their studies: "It was about how to saw the rungs out of someone's ladder without his knowing it." The team spirit, holiest of business shibboleths, is not so important, after all.

The Harvard Business School, then, is where they teach Sammy to run gracefully.

The promotional talents of the B-School and its alumni are of incalculable help, too. An article in *Fortune* magazine in May 1974 called the class of 1949 "The Class the Dollars Fell On." It said that one fourth of the group are presidents or chairmen of corporations and 16 per cent are millionaires. The article was merely one fallout from the publicity campaigns waged by the reunion members every five years.

The class of 1949 is unusually adept at blowing its own horn. Looking back at the stories written about its twentieth anniversary, however, one sees that by 1974 some of the stars had changed jobs or figured in notable corporate shoot-outs.

William E. McKenna, one of the fading conglomerateurs, had been elbowed out of Norton Simon, Inc., and into problem-wracked Technicolor, Inc. Alan Wolfley had moved from Scovill Manufacturing Company to Cerro Corporation, then headed by another Harvard M.B.A., C. Gordon Murphy. Soon after the class of 1949's twenty-fifth reunion, the Pritzkers of Chicago paid Murphy to get out. Wolfley remained as a member of an executive committee with two of the Pritzkers. The Harvard Business School training, so often described as "boot camp," must be invaluable during such stressful contests.

The solid base for the school's unshakability is the symbiotic relationship that this oldest of the nation's graduate schools of management has with the business elite.

Its keen and affluent graduates contribute $1.2 million a year toward the school's annual operating budget of $20.5 million. Another $1.2 million is pumped in by its associates, the four hundred or so corporations whose recruiters seem to be convinced that the cream of the crop is to be found at the Harvard Business School.

Many of these corporations and others send their more promising executives to the Harvard Business School's Program for Management Development and the Advanced Management Program. These intensive, three-month hibernations on the banks of the Charles cost the corporations (or the military and nonprofit organizations that also subscribe) about $5,000 per student in tuition and fees plus transportation, the participant's salary, and that of his or her replacement at home base. The middle-aged students emerge from this polishing process more ardently imbued with their own manifest destiny and that of the school's than some of the younger generation with two years to spend being indoctrinated.

Another profitable arm of the B-School is the *Harvard Business Review,* an unillustrated, bimonthly that is the *Vogue* of the executive fringe. Industrialists like Henry Ford II and J. Irwin Miller of Cummins Engine Company use it as a platform for their pet ideas. Up-and-comers like Barbara Boyle, one of the first consultants on equal opportunity for women, prize it as a showcase for themselves and their businesses. The ability to ghost and place articles in the *Harvard Business Review* is a prerequisite for winning many financial public relations contracts.

Most enduring of all Harvard Business School products is the case-study method which it introduced after borrowing it from the academic disciplines of law and medicine. It is the primary teaching method at Harvard, which has disseminated it throughout the United States and now into the international circuit via the Intercollegiate Case Clearing House. Harvard operates the clearing house for the American Assembly of Collegiate Schools of Business.

The cases are usually written by faculty members from information supplied by co-operative corporations. Running from ten to forty pages long, they present a detailed and realistic body of facts about a business or management dilemma that urgently needs solving. Neither the decision nor the final outcome is divulged. The clearing house has forty thousand cases on file, of which nine thousand are in active inventory. Some nine hundred new cases flow in each year, of which nearly half are produced at the Harvard Business School.

A link to Harvard may be terribly useful for making it to the pinnacle club but it is by no means essential. A few things are. A devotion to money and no hesitancy about using other people's to get it are two requisites. For the first time, a craving for big bucks, self-earned, is becoming symbolically sexy for a woman—witness the admiring glances bestowed on Mary Wells Lawrence at the inflation summit meeting in Washington.

Though selflessness may be used for patina, a really significant career in business can't be achieved without a touch of greed. Those who tend to the social responsibility of corporations are in danger of being sidetracked. When G. Robert Truex, Jr., was made executive vice president for social policy at the Bank of America in California, civil rights activists hailed it as evidence the bank meant to atone for its past omissions. Realists said he had been taken out of the race for the presidency. In due course, Truex, an able banker and credible man of good will, moved north to become president and chief executive officer of the Rainier National Bank of Seattle.

However, it won't do to let lust for the dollar gleam too brightly. It must be softened by that Puritan ethic or stamped with a seal of ecclesiastic approval. Southern capitalists are the churchiest. Holiday Inns, as befits a Memphis-based company, has a corporate chaplain and Christian fellowship was voted as a business policy at its first board meeting. What with Billy Graham and Norman Vincent Peale to escort the rich men into the kingdom of heaven, despite what Matthew said, the Protestants would seem to have a corner on the corporate market. But then, they are the dominant national sect.

The Jews, only beginning to make a showing among the corporate elite, have concentrated their fund-raising efforts on obtaining contributions from corporate foundations and public relations budgets for those of their philanthropies which sponsor fights against social injustice. The corporations can claim a tax benefit or a necessary expense for what is in fact merely ingratiating itself with an ethnic market. As for the Roman Catholics, they finish a poor third in the open mixing of religious faith with corporate finance.

Besides monetary fervor, the rules for winning the business game are those that apply to other fields of endeavor: one needs a little bit of luck and at least one big patron.

Men advance in organizations by attracting the attention of powerful older men, and, office gossip notwithstanding, most women haven't learned to do that yet. Except for the fact that until now almost everyone at the top has been of the same gender, sex is only peripheral to getting there. Would Mary Wells have been an ad agency chairman if she had been born a boy? Probably. After all, Violet Wells kept whispering in her daughter's ear, "You can do anything you want to if you work hard enough." And don't studies show that behind most successful men is a confident parent or two?

Despite the fondness business displays for GOP elephants, political affiliation is as neutrally significant as sex. There is, over all, the principle of expediency. Even the *Wall Street Journal* carried an essay on its editorial page proposing that "the inclination toward expediency that permeated the Nixon White House was born in board rooms and country clubs."

Regardless of what party is in the White House or the executive suite, every corporation needs some ballast for both sides. Otherwise, how would so many good Democrats have sent money to the laundry in order to re-elect Richard Nixon. Business men are not too proud to change allegiance and political and economic principles. On with controls, off with controls, cut taxes (corporate), raise taxes (gasoline), balance the budget, let it bloat. All that matters is the bottom line.

So the more things change, the more things remain the same for making it in business, for thinking it's worth trying, and for going about it.

The entrepreneur spots a need and sets about filling it. The wheeler-dealer sees opportunity in misfortune—in the hospital wards and thrift shops of industry, the companies gone to ruin; he sniffs truffles in balance sheets. The professional manager succeeds to what the entrepreneur and the wheeler-dealer have created. He is the custodian and the beneficiary, taking the least risk for himself. And if he muffs it, the other members of the pinnacle club will assign him another seat.

THE OLD ORDER PASSETH

AVON: DING-DONG-DOWN

The officers and directors of Avon Products Inc., have learned how fickle the affections of Wall Street can be.

Avon had been one of the all-time glamour girls in the history of the New York Stock Exchange. The price of its common stock had appreciated 19,000 per cent in one postwar decade, thereby making paper millionaires out of numerous employees, executives, faithful friends and relatives, and other foresighted investors.

But in the summer of 1970 Avon's price sagged on the Big Board, down from its record high of 184½ the previous January. Like Xerox Corporation and International Business Machines Corporation, those other "vestal virgins," as the stocks unanimously adored by the managers of institutional funds were dubbed, it seemed a victim of its own success and the growth cult of the swinging sixties.

In the summer of 1971 Avon stock rebounded to 112, a record high for the year, but by November it slipped again to around 97. Its price/earnings ratio (or "multiple," as the term was used in Wall Street) was still around 50. This bothered some security analysts, especially those who had studied the principles of investing before the go-go era of the sixties and had been taught to beware of double-digit multiples.

Since summer, several analysts have been casting pessimistic glances at Avon stock, 10 per cent of which is held by institutional investors like pension funds, universities, foundations, and banks. They have been recommending it for sale or long-term hold but shooing away investors who were seeking "performance," that code word for large capital gain. Their warnings have been couched in almost apologetic terms, citing the excellence of Avon management and the company's robust health. Knocking Avon, after all, seems a little like repudiating an aunt who paid your way through college.

What the analysts have been doubting is Avon's future ability to maintain its spectacular growth rate of the past decade, a 16 per cent sales increase and 20 per cent in earnings compounded annually. During the last five years the profit spiral has slowed to 16 per cent.

In 1970 Avon had revenues of $759 million and net earnings of $99 million, or $1.72 a share. *Forbes* magazine ranked it the most consistently profitable company in the United States, first in average return on stockholder equity and on total capital (38.1 per cent) for the last five years.

But in July 1971 Wilbur Shook, the Avon treasurer, told analysts he was revising previous estimates for 1971 downward. He projected earnings at $1.85 to $1.90 a share against earlier hopes of $1.95 to $2.05. Nevertheless, Wayne Hicklin, the chairman, affirmed his faith in growth of 15 to 20 per cent in the 1970s.

During 1971 Avon encountered the first clouds on its horizon since its arrival on the New York Stock Exchange in 1964. Two of these were relatively minor from a financial standpoint.

First, it had to recall 106,000 jars of Prima Natura night cream and 14,800 cans of baby powder in which the Food and Drug Administration had found microbiological contamination. No cases of illness were reported, but for a company that boasted of quality of product and stringent controls, "our pride was hurt," acknowledged President Fred G. Fusee.

Second, Avon was charged with sex discrimination in a suit filed in New Jersey by a woman formerly employed as a products counselor. Her request for promotion to division sales manager had been turned down. Since 1969 the number of female division managers has risen from zero to thirteen, but there are no women officers or board members. Avon has always been a company that catered to women but was run by men.

Wall Street, however, paid more attention to other factors.

A company like Avon could be vulnerable to recession and consumer stand-offishness. So, in order to maintain sales increases and protect the earnings of the doorbell-ringing representatives on whom its marketing strategy was built, management decided to step up "specialing," as they called their continuous system of price discounts.

The Christmas selling season in 1971, traditionally the company's largest and very much under way by October, has been "good but could be better," David W. Mitchell, an executive vice president said. Nevertheless, he saw a sales increase of 15 to 16 per cent for 1971 over 1970 and domestic profit margins close to those of the previous year, or 31 per cent before taxes.

International sales, which represented the fastest growing segment of Avon's business in recent years (30 per cent of total sales in '69 and '70), have been showing lesser profit margins. Analysts are worried about threats of world-wide recession. Management dismissed their fears and predicted improved sales and profits as the kinks were ironed out in the fifteen countries Avon has entered since 1954.

Then there is the small but increasing presence of other door-to-door cosmetic companies such as Vanda Beauty Counselor Division of Dart Industries, and the Studio Girl Division of Helene Curtis Industries. For eighty-five years Avon has been unchallenged by direct competitors and is still the world's largest cosmetic manufacturer, with an estimated 15 per cent share of the United States cosmetics and toiletries market which itself has a projected growth rate of 10 per cent a year. But the name most often mentioned in competitive terms in the executive offices on the forty-seventh and forty-eighth floors of Thirty Rockefeller Plaza in New York City is Revlon, with 1970 record sales of $373.5 million and a price and packaging appeal for the Avon customer if she decided to leave her home to shop.

There is also the question mark of new ventures. Determined to diversify along careful guidelines of compatibility, similar profitability, and growth, Avon has opened six beauty salons in Denver as part of a twenty-month test of entry into a $4-billion industry. Sales and profits for the costume jewelry line also tried in 1971 have been encouraging, but the Christmas cards have flunked their Avon test and will be dropped.

While Wall Street ponders Avon's future, students at the Harvard Business School have been making initially negative prognoses for the company. But Professor Martin V. Marshall, who uses Avon's selling strategy as part of a case-method approach to marketing, forces them to reconsider.

"In the late fifties and part of the sixties the general tendency of most students was to be thoroughly critical of Avon's strategy being successful over the long term," he said in November 1971. "They felt other competitive mixes would be more powerful. It's amusing in a sense. When I asked, 'Would you buy the stock,' they said, 'No.'

"I used the case this fall and again the majority felt that during the seventies this company probably would not be able to compete against regular mixes. Students are mesmerized by the concept of youth. The young women in class said they wouldn't buy Avon.

"But I tell them the cosmetic and toiletries market has two segments. The hope market, which is the young woman after her man. The bigger market is the help market, or the older woman, and Avon is doing a wonderful job there. That company really understands the middle-aged woman.

"I try to get the students to be hardheaded in their thinking," Professor Marshall continued. "Is there anything unsound in Avon's strategy? No. They don't run the big risk of the innovator. They study the market. They have the test market built in without much risk. They have solid management doing careful thinking in everything. They give pretty good value in price and marvelous packaging.

"The students start off suspicious but when I force them to dig in and really understand Avon, they quickly develop a healthy respect for the company and change their minds," he concluded.

The strategy that turned skeptics into true believers is dazzling in its simplicity. It was conceived by David H. McConnell, a door-to-door book salesman from Oswego, New York, who might be called the Norman Vincent Peale of cold creams and colognes. Having discovered that the vials of fragrance he used in order to get his foot in the door were more appreciated than the books he was peddling, he abandoned literature and founded the California Perfume Company in 1886. (After several name changes it became Avon Products Inc. in 1950.)

His first envoy was Mrs. P. F. E. Albee, the patron saint of 450,000 Avon Ladies calling on households in the United States,

Canada, and fifteen other countries around the world. From Mrs. Albee on, the Avon Lady has been an independent sales representative, cajoled and otherwise tempted to sell on commission to friends and to strangers whom she is supposed to convert into friends. She also serves as a built-in test market.

McConnell died in 1937, a seventy-five-year-old Sunday school-teaching magnate, but his precepts lived on in a nearly billion-dollar company of 22,000 nonunionized employees and an eager, hungrily efficient team of twenty-eight officers, half of whom were wholly Avon-trained.

These executives, some of America's best paid (Chairman Hicklin drew down $369,578 in 1970), were not embarrassed to quote from *The Great Oak,* the little yellow booklet containing Founder McConnell's philosophy and formula for manufacturing and selling a line of goods direct from factory to consumer:

"Give others an opportunity to earn, in support of their happiness, betterment and welfare . . . helpfulness and courtesy . . . share with others the blessings of deserved growth and business success . . . cherish and retain the friendly spirit of Avon," it says in the booklet reprinted from a 1903 text.

"The Great Oak seems like corn," said James E. Clitter, forty-two-year-old senior vice president and marketing chief, using the word most often applied to Avon by baffled students of its success. "But direct selling has to operate according to the Golden Rule. No company can ignore it. You can't have a chintzy product and cheat and make a buck," he asserted.

Nor did Clitter apologize for the wholesome, unsophisticated style which permeated Avon from its product names ("To a Wild Rose," "Cotillion," "Rapture," and "Hana Gasa," for an Oriental note) to the immaculate kitsch of its skyscraper headquarters in Rockefeller Center with its dust-free plastic floral arrangements and its fragrance decanters used as bric-a-brac in the executive suite.

"In my mind, I start with—what does mid-America, average everybody want? What's comfortable at the PTA? Then you refine off from that. The average American is not the New York City swinger even today. But as you get to know us, you'll find we can swing with the best," said Clitter, whose race-track plaid suit and navy blue shirt lent him the sartorial image of *Guys and Dolls,* a jarring note in Avon's Babbitt-ish higher echelons.

"We've never been great crusaders in new product ideas because the average housewife who is our representative is not about to explain them to her customer," Clitter continued, confronting the noninnovator cliché about Avon.

False eyelashes didn't join the vast Avon line of five hundred individual items, 70 per cent of them for women and teen-agers, until 1970. Hair coloring was introduced in the spring of 1971 in fifteen shades. Sales were disappointing. Both products once bore mid-America connotations of sin and danger. "Before we introduce a product, the average woman has had to have used it. Psychologically, then, the Avon representative will not be afraid to offer it. The Avon representative feels disappointed if her customer isn't happy, because she's her friend," Clitter said.

"We allow the competition to change the mores," he said. And take the risks, he might have added. "When the woman knows the product is morally right and has learned through TV and her own daughter how to wear it, then our representative moves in to offer a quality product," he said.

Avon management moves cautiously. It took three and a half years to research and develop hair coloring, five years for a lipstick brush. In 1971 a skin-care line for 1974 was going through the research laboratories in Suffern, New York.

Letting others go first means, Clitter said, "that we've never had a major entry that has bombed." Some don't live up to expectations though. Avon Ladies begged for an extensive line of grooming aids for eight-to-twelve-year-old boys. It was cut back to four items "despite the hue and cry from representatives and mothers, because boys that age basically want to be dirty, not clean," Clitter explained.

Against a powerfully entrenched and advertised brand name, as in deodorants and hair coloring, Avon doesn't shine. It does relatively little product advertising and it doesn't look for sensation value in its product names because it is not competing on the drugstore shelf or department store counter.

Except for one unsuccessful attempt in the thirties by the late president David H. McConnell, Jr., against his father the founder's advice, to market an "Ambrosia line" of cosmetics and fragrances through variety stores, Avon's counter has been the Avon Lady's selling kit and the sales brochure issued twenty-six times a year is her display.

So it is that Avon spends a measly 2 per cent of sales on advertising (compared to some other cosmetic companies that spend 10 to 25 per cent). Dreher Advertising, Inc., which won the account in 1936 as a result of Monroe Dreher's locker-room friendship with David McConnell, Jr., at the Montclair (New Jersey) Golf Club, has hewed since then to an institutional pitch geared to opening the door for the Avon Lady and motivating her. Almost every ad contains at least an inset of a selling scene between two women who have the manner and fashion quotient of a pair of airline stewardesses graduated to suburban matronhood.

Starting in the late fifties, Dreher swung away from print media such as women's magazines and the *Christian Science Monitor* (chosen for its loyal readers and because Monroe Dreher was a Christian Scientist) toward an 80 per cent use of television spots in two hundred markets. Dreher created the unforgettable ding-dong "Avon Calling." Its one problem was in achieving sound fidelity for the chime which strikes A and C.

By 1970 black faces had begun to appear in Avon's advertising and a slightly interracial feeling had crept into all of its printed matter. About 10 per cent of its sales are to minorities. In 1970 the children's and teen's lines advertising were allotted to Ogilivy & Mather, Inc. The campaign planned for the adult lines for 1972 veers away from Avon's value-and-variety message and toward overcoming the resistance of noncustomers, who tend to congregate at the opposite end of the socioeconomic scale in hard-to-penetrate, high-rise urban structures. Apartment-house dwellers are reluctant to open their doors even when an Avon Lady is calling.

One of the criticisms of the Avon sales method made by former executives is that management never seriously tried to develop representative networks in factories and offices to offset the shrinkage of the accessible stay-at-home market.

Avon spends another 3 per cent of sales to promote its wares through the representatives. The main tool is the fifty-to-seventy page *Avon Catalog,* or booklet, produced by the in-house advertising department. Published every two weeks, its circulation rivals that of the top five national magazines. Projecting how many booklets the representatives will order is one of the derring-do feats of Avon's highly computerized operations. Each edition contains new temptations specially priced. The typical Avon customer is in the $7,000 to $15,000 annual income bracket, which would put her in the low to middle range. Avon products are priced accordingly.

Lipsticks sell for $1.50, a five-ounce bottle of nail polish for $1.10, and a three-ounce box of perfumed talc for $1.25.

Avon takes a back seat to no one in packaging. The booklets contain page after page of jars, bottles, and sculpted soaps that are the apogee of mid-American taste and have a second or alternative life as decorative objects and toys. The most expensive ($4.00 and $8.00 apiece) and most profitable are the fragrance decanters styled as automobile models, animal trophies, pitchers, and vases. They represent about 25 per cent of sales. "Even if the customers don't want the products, they want the bottles," said Mrs. Arline Donn, an Avon Lady from New City, New York.

About 250 new, redesigned, or reformulated products are introduced each year to make the representatives' selling job easier. For that Avon Lady—typically a middle-American housewife and mother in her mid-thirties with a yen to earn extra money—is the Atlas of the Avon world. On her status as an independent representative working on commission rather than as an employee rests Avon's enviable profit margins and low cost of sales. Considering that fringe benefits have been running 25 to 30 per cent of payrolls for many American businesses, a company that faces no such escalating costs from its sales force (or, for that matter, any threat of labor strife) is blessed indeed.

The Avon Lady is recruited from what heretofore has seemed to be an unlimited reservoir of housewives who would like to earn some money according to a tempo and schedule of their own choosing. "A job to fit your available hours," Avon tells them. They pay a one-time fee of $10 for a franchise, which means an exclusive territory of about two hundred families and a starter kit of products, supposedly worth $35 at list price. At $10 the company still makes a profit, even if the woman does no more than use the products herself which is precisely what happens with many candidates for representative.

To earn a 40 per cent commission, she must remit a minimum order of $100 every two weeks. Otherwise, her commission falls to 25 per cent. The commission is paid on suggested list price, but the representative decides what she will charge her customer. In a time of economic pinch, she may cut prices and work harder to make her minimum. She can return unsold merchandise to the company which backs her with an unconditional guarantee.

In 1966 the company raised the 40 per cent commission mini-

mum from $75 to $100 and shortened the selling campaign period
from three weeks to two. The disciplined procedure of the year-
round selling campaign had been established in 1932, and at that
time a regular three-week canvass by the representative was substituted for her previous once-a-month or so visits. That change from
the laxity of the early days has been credited with increasing Avon's
sales by 70 per cent in the acute depression years of 1931–36.

Some critics of the Avon method assert that the representative is
deprived of a customary industry discount since in effect she functions as a retail distributor, too, stocking merchandise as well as
selling it. Cosmetic companies that sell through retail outlets give
distributors and stores additional discounts above the sales commission they pay to saleswomen. Avon has no such middlepersons.

Avon makes it sound as though it pampers its representatives.
Their birthdays, their selling problems, and their credit habits are
stored in the computer. When the Avon Lady takes time off to give
birth, Avon mails her a baby card. If she sends word, to explain a
skipped selling cycle, that she has been to the hospital for surgery,
she receives a get-well card. She is encouraged with carrots, never
sticks, in the form of incentives that range from Savings Bonds to
sugar-and-creamer sets and color TV sets.

She is recruited, trained, and regularly pepped up by her district
sales manager, one of the eighteen hundred former Avon Ladies in
the United States who have been promoted to be salaried employees. The district manager reminds her that "Avon says the hardest
door to open is your own," an acknowledgment that courage to
leave home and ring doorbells is not easily mustered. But also that
an Avon Lady like Andrea Borgia from Somers, New York, has
decorated a bedroom a year with her Avon earnings, or that Arline
Donn of New City took a twenty-fifth wedding anniversary trip to
Europe with hers.

The representative is urged to be outgoing, but not too much.
"Don't make friends, don't have coffee. Don't take your coat off," a
district manager in Rockland County, New York, told a new recruit.

"Try not to spend more than twenty minutes in a home. Three
customers an hour, on an average of $5.00 a sale, is nice money," a
manager for northern Westchester cautioned.

Above all, representatives are warned when delivering previously
ordered goods not to depart without being paid. If the customer
begs credit for friendship's sake, they should leave behind only

half the order. "You get to know when pay day is in their family," a veteran Avon representative said, explaining how she times her deliveries.

A comparison of the training literature given to a white, middle-income Avon Lady and the versions given to her black counterparts shows a revealing stress on such "money management" tactics for minority representatives. The company makes arrangements to have their payments transmitted through a bank-deposit program.

At the end of each two-week selling cycle, the representative mails in her orders to branch headquarters. The company has been testing a telephone ordering system to speed deliveries. Within a week, the merchandise she ordered is delivered to her by outside trucking contractors and she takes it to her customers, is paid, and sends her check to Avon with her next cycle's orders.

Everything in the system, from computer-checked packing to the eye-catching containers is calculated to keep the Avon Lady happy and boost her earnings. However, despite the glowing tales of the district managers, a study of company revenues as well as its recruitment literature points to the average earnings of an Avon representative at $1,400 a year or $52 as an average commission earned every two weeks.

Whether that sum should be construed as found money or a subminimum wage depends on how many hours it takes the representative to earn it. It also depends on the size and nature of her territory. Is she ringing doorbells in an apartment building or driving across a prairie? How many doorbells must she ring to make a sale? How much time is she spending in bookkeeping, unwrapping, and stocking merchandise? How much time are family members spending who help her? What are the costs of gasoline and depreciation on her car?

What about the physical hardships? "They're like the mailmen. Neither snow nor rain stops them," the district manager in Rockland County said proudly. Considering that Avon is strongest in areas where housewives are least likely to get out to conventional shopping centers, it is a grim boast.

In a study of the company made in 1971 by the Corporate Information Center of the National Council of Churches, which did research on the social profiles of corporations, an Avon Lady from a Minnesota farming community earned $400 to $500 commission during a nine-month effort. This sum was reduced to $150 after she deducted her expenses.

"In addition to the expense of demonstration samples, the frequent blizzards and cold weather that accompany Minnesota winters make one wonder if a nine-month wage of $150 is indeed a wage," the report inquired. "It would seem reasonable for Avon to adjust commission rates to a range of factors in addition to that of the dollar amount of sales," the church group suggested.

Avon does not reimburse the representative for any of her expenses nor does it protect her in other ways. The sales dealer's contract she signs makes explicit how independent she is. Avon reserves the right to change the commission terms at any time by giving her ten days' notice. Though she is urged not to extend credit nor to push her customers to order more than they can afford, it is only through supersaleswomanship that she can earn her commission. The company is understandably touchy about the turnover statistic for representatives, which is more than 100 per cent a year.

Women's rights activists see the Avon Lady as a victim rather than the triumphant businesswoman of the company literature. They deplore the psychological pressure to which she is subjected. Since she is likely to be a woman who has no alternative path to earning money (because she lacks education, skills, or awakened consciousness), she can be intimidated by a district manager who signs her up and then keeps her reaching for more carrots.

As one former field operations manager recalled, "The district manager used to give short-range goals. 'You'd like to have your chair upholstered, wouldn't you? It'll cost $95,' she'd tell the representative. When she earned $90, the manager had to push her to have her couch redone, and when that was worked through, to do the rest of the living room, then the dining room, and then into the kitchen for a new icebox. Now they've gotten away from that into long-range reasons like a family vacation for $1,000. But there is a great disappointment when a woman signs up and earns only $12 the first week. That's why the $95 was the better philosophy."

The carrots get bigger and better. For the proficient there are competitions with prizes of appliances, automobiles, and government bonds. But as a feminist who was once an Avon district manager said, "When so many of those women fail, it becomes a kind of rejection. It's one more failure added to a life characterized by failure."

However, it can be argued that the Avon representative is no worse off than any male commission-salesman or free-lance operator. The critics could be seen as finding fault with the American Way of which Avon is only a distinctive example.

There are many jubilant, crackajack Avon saleswomen who think they've had their cake and eaten it, too. Some of them attend the annual meetings (having bought stock in the company with their earnings) and step up to a microphone on the floor to make constructive suggestions to the dais about increasing sales.

Some of them become district or field managers, the lowest level of salaried employees and the true workhorses of the organization.

It is the district manager's job to keep replenishing the supply of Avon representatives and to motivate them, or, as one said, "to help them over the bridge of fears and doubts."

As one Avon Lady said, with a grateful glance at her district manager, "A friend is what a district manager is. She wins your friendship to get your confidence up." She is also a psychiatrist, sales manager, trainer, administrator, and pitchwoman. These incredibly capable, driven women live, breathe, and involve their families with Avon since they work out of their homes. For this, some of them might earn as much as $17,000 a year, an extraordinary feat considering that all they receive is a subsistence base pay plus about 3 per cent commission tied to the increase of sales in their territories. Those sales typically range from $300,000 to $1 million.

Achievers are drawn into the "circle of leadership," an honorary society for district managers. They are further rewarded with annual meetings in Acapulco in Mexico, Lake Louise in the Canadian Rockies or seven glorious days of wining and dining in New York City plus rah-rah sales presentations from top executives who make them feel they are on the inside of corporate affairs.

They are then given further incentives—some say it's persecution—by having their territories split and redistricted so they can prove their mettle by building up new territories under tougher conditions.

Above every twelve to fifteen district managers is a division manager, then come the region managers, and above them, the branch managers.

In 1954 Avon started exporting its formula, first to Latin America, then to Europe and Asia. "There was no great master stroke. This is a rather parochial company and so we just followed an evolutionary course," said Hays Clark, an executive vice president and grandson of the founder. "Everyone was surprised" that the Avon Lady could be transplanted to a foreign culture, he said.

With some variations, of course. In Japan the permission of the woman's husband must be obtained before she will sign up to become a representative.

At home as well as abroad Avon has always behaved as a gentlemanly company, treating its women troops with deference and courtesy. "We love women," chairman Hicklin told the last stockholders' meeting, as usual an exercise in sweetness and light. On the executive office doors the names of secretaries appear in slightly smaller gold letters below their bosses'. So far, only four women have reached the level just below officer. They are called "directors," meaning heads of departments, not membership in the strictly stag board of directors of the corporation. In the field, most of the division and region managers and all of the branch managers are male. However, an urgent search for a female candidate for the board is being conducted.

As Avon has become a giant, its managers have tried to retain the personal contacts of a small, family-owned company. "We take great pride in dealing with people on an individual basis. I can't think of a personnel policy that says two and two make four," said Wesley Swigert, manager of the Suffern and Middletown, New York, manufacturing centers. From top to bottom, Avon pays its employees better than the going rate with handsome fringe benefits. Only the Avon Ladies, who are independent agents rather than employees, toil for pittances.

Its factories are humane for all their efficiency. Swigert abolished time clocks and put the assembly line workers on weekly rather than hourly pay without being asked to. The women on the packaging line were outfitted in pant suits with a choice of three colors.

Periodic management reorganizations, achieved peacefully and without outside consultants, have pushed a younger generation of technocrat tigers to the fore at Avon. The average age of corporate officers is forty-seven.

The literally fair-haired heir seems to be forty-three-year-old blond and blue-eyed David Mitchell. He started as an office boy in Pasadena in 1947, the same route taken by chairman Hicklin from Kansas City in 1928. Both claim to have swept floors. Mitchell became an executive vice president.

The other executive vice president, Hays Clark, gray-haired with "Man of Distinction" handsomeness, good-naturedly says his age disqualifies him from higher office. He is fifty-three. His family owns 14 per cent of Avon stock, two thirds of it in foundations named after his mother, Edna McConnell Clark, the daughter of Avon's founder.

Avon's notably stable though aggressive management style has been abetted by extraordinarily sound finances. Except at the outset, it appears never to have been starved for capital. Alexander Henderson, the chemist who produced the perfume vials for David McConnell, invested a modest sum to get the venture going. His son, Girard Henderson, an Avon multimillionaire, is still on the board. Avon's last loan, $6 million at 3⅜ per cent interest, was paid off in 1966. The more than $30 million in capital expenditures for 1972 (some for moving headquarters to a new skyscraper on West Fifty-seventh Street) will be internally financed.

To maintain its Wall Street reputation as a so-called growth company, Avon is bound on a course of diversification into other products and activities. Direct mail ordering for goods other than cosmetics and toiletries is being considered. A line of needlework will be test-marketed in 1972. The decision on owning and operating beauty salons will not be made until mid-1973.

In the fragmented beauty salon industry, two chains, Seligman & Latz, Inc., and the Glemby Company, Inc., do a mere 1.5 per cent of the $4-billion business. Avon has set a $100 million revenue target for itself within a dozen years. Its test salons are located in shopping centers and offer the latest twists in service and fashion haircutting at prices 25 cents to 50 cents higher than competitors. Some observers believe the usual Avon profit margins cannot be achieved in an industry that has labor costs as high as 60 per cent with 2 to 3 per cent return on sales. They question Avon's wisdom in entering a field that has been badly hurt in the last few years by social and fashion changes. Many women no longer go to beauty salons with any regularity.

"We welcome Avon because their professionalism can only help us if they succeed," said Paul Finkelstein, assistant to the president of the Glemby Company, which operates salons in department and specialty stores. "But I can't see how they can have the same after-tax return on sales as they do on cosmetics."

James A. Michaelsen, an Avon senior vice president replied, "If

we thought that, we wouldn't be there. We're shooting for an Avon-
type profit. If we recognize we can't have it, I'll recommend dropping out."

He said he believed labor could be held to 50 per cent of sales by
offering stylists Avon's fringe benefits and stability in return for
lower commissions and by generating traffic through the "synergis-
tic" carry-over from Avon representatives and their loyal customers.

As far as its main activity is concerned, Avon could be affected
by the economic picture at home and abroad, although less ad-
versely, perhaps than other industries. It can always counteract
price controls such as those President Nixon imposed last summer
by adjusting its "specialing" and by introducing new products.

"And if Phase Two works and consumer confidence is renewed,
it has to be good for us," chairman Hicklin said. "I just have a deep
conviction in the continued growth of this company."

Fall 1974

For a year AVP (the symbol for Avon Products Inc., on
the New York Stock Exchange) had been wasting away on the
ticker. By the fall of 1974, the glamour girl of the go-go sixties had
become the most talked about patient of the seventies bear market.
As it slipped below 20 in October, horrified investors kept being
reminded that the price of the common stock of the world's largest
cosmetic and fragrance company had declined from a high of 140 in
March 1973 and its multiple (ratio of its price in the marketplace to
its earnings per share) from 60 to 11.

The doubting Thomases of Wall Street in 1970 and 1971 had
been proven wrong in the stock market for more than a year. Avon
crossed the billion-dollar sales barrier in 1972. Its profits of $125
million that year still were impressive, though not by previous
growth-cult standards since they had only grown 7 per cent over the
earnings the year before. Yet the price of the stock and its multiple
had been climbing through 1972 and early 1973. Though the glamour girl didn't quite have the old spring in her step, her admirers still
looked at her with stars in their eyes. In mid-1973, a survey by
Vickers Associates Inc. showed it was thirteenth among cor-

porations whose stock was held in investment company portfolios, truly an institutional favorite.

Several changes at Avon had taken place since 1971, some superficial and others that merely deepened the questions asked then by the doubters. The company had become a little more worldly. In the fall of 1972 corporate headquarters had been moved to a new curved skyscraper on West Fifty-seventh Street designed by Gordon Bunshaft, the Establishment architect who was more and more lapsing into monumentalism. Inside, the decorative tone of Avon's offices was now more elegantly austere than soap-and-water folksy. The senior executives were sheltered behind wood paneled corridors in a cathedral quiet.

Three of the corporate officers in 1974 were women. In 1972 Phyllis Davis had been named vice president for advertising and sales promotion and Patricia Neighbors vice president for district management field operations. The latter post was not the "made work" for a woman some cynics suspected. As would become more and more evident, the recruitment and productivity of the Avon representative system needed bolstering.

In the fall of 1974 Alla O'Brien became the third woman with the title of vice president. She was given responsibility for advertising and public relations, Phyllis Davis having been reassigned to product management.

Avon had also taken two women to its board. One, elected in 1972, was Cecily Cannan Selby, executive director of the Girl Scouts of the U.S.A. and former headmistress of the Lenox School, a New York private school for girls. As if these qualifications were not appropriate enough for a company whose advertising had for years been played to the theme of "innocent freshness," the press release announcing Mrs. Selby's nomination disclosed that she had done her research for her Ph.D. from the Massachusetts Institute of Technology on cell structure of the skin. The other female addition to the board in 1974 was Ernesta G. Procope, president of E. G. Bowman Company, Inc., the largest black-owned insurance brokerage firm in the country.

Prodded by the tempo of the times as well as by a couple more sex-discrimination complaints filed against Avon by former employees, the company instituted an affirmative action program for women and minorities and began to promote members of these two groups from within as well as to hire them from without. While the number of blacks giving orders or occupying professional positions was still negligible, it could no longer be said absolutely that Avon was a company run by white men to make money through women.

In 1973 Avon signed a covenant valued at $59 million with the Reverend Jesse Jackson's Operation PUSH. The company agreed to hire more blacks, place some of its group life insurance with non-white-owned insurance companies, and take other steps to help minority businesses.

At the top, change had come as expected. Early in 1972 Wayne Hicklin, the sixty-one-year-old chairman, handed over his responsibilities as chief executive officer to fifty-five-year-old Fred Fusee, who had joined the company as a chemist in its Montreal facility in 1945. David Mitchell became president at the age of forty-four. Having started as an office boy and never attended college, the earnest, well-scrubbed-looking Mitchell properly conformed to Avon's legends of the self-made man. With the retirement of Hicklin, who had been one of the inventors in the 1930s of Avon's regular campaign-cycles sales techniques and who had been brought into the company by the founder David McConnell and his son, the last of the pioneer generation had gone. Avon was in the hands of the technocrats.

In 1973, both pioneers and technocrats damaged the company's pristine image somewhat. Mitchell, Fusee, senior vice president Clitter, and executive vice president Michaelsen, treasurer Shook, as well as retired chairman Hicklin, director and grandson of the founder W. Van Alan Clark, Jr., and Girard Henderson whose father had staked David McConnell long ago—in all, twenty-two top officers and directors of Avon—sold $10 million of Avon stock in the never-soon-to-be-seen-again price ranges of 102 to 140. The sales took place between January and August. On a Friday in September, after the Stock Exchange had closed and company spokesmen had become unavailable, an Avon statement was released. It confirmed rumors that had been circulating in the market since the big blocks of stock had been traded and after *Forbes* magazine had published a story saying that Avon was in a state of "well-preserved middle age to be sure, but the bulges and sags are beginning to show." The statement revealed that sales for the third quarter had been slowing down and earnings were flat.

It wasn't long before two stockholders brought derivative suits charging that the top officers and directors of Avon had improperly used inside information in connection with the sales of their stock. Chairman Fusee and treasurer Shook said whenever the subject was raised by investors or reporters, which it was frequently, that the sales had been made for their own personal financial reasons, such as having to repay bank loans to acquire the stock which some of them had bought through options offered to key executives. They denied that there was any impropriety on the part of the sellers.

At the annual stockholders' meeting in April 1974, one stockholder of fifteen years' standing took the microphone on the floor and announced, "I asked my stockbroker should I bail out and he said: 'No, it's an awfully good company. The officers don't have faith in it but I do.'"

The institutional investors must have shared his faith because there was every indication that they did not "bail out" even though profits kept contracting from one quarter to the next.

In September 1974, when the price of the stock had slipped to the low 20s because Avon's growth had come to a halt, a tabulation by Computer Directions Advisers Inc. showed that as of the previous June, fifty-nine mutual funds owned 3,498,000 shares, or 6 per cent, of Avon's common stock representing a market value of $166,175,000 (at $47.50 a share). One year earlier, sixty-four funds had owned 2,868,695 shares representing a market value of $354,284,000 (at $123.50 a share).

Two conclusions were inescapable. During the year of erosion, a few funds must have sold but others must have held and increased their holdings.

This was the case at the First National City Bank, which manages $15.7 billion of other people's money. In the year ended December 31, 1973, it had bought $49 million worth of Avon stock (Citibank's fifth largest equity purchase) and sold $28 million worth (its ninth largest equity sale). The bank's C Trust Investment Fund, a common stock portfolio in which a large number of individual trusts that it manages are pooled, had 20,000 shares of Avon for which it paid $2.1 million, an average price of $106 a share.

Not only Citibank but Morgan Guaranty Trust Company, Manufacturers Hanover Trust Company, and the Lilly Endowment—to name just a few—were loaded with Avon in their trust accounts.

If Avon was indeed lying shrunken in so many institutional accounts—in mutual funds, pension funds, trust and investment funds, foundation and university portfolios—then a great many individuals would suffer from the decline in Avon's value in the marketplace and from the obstinate attachment of professional money managers to the stock.

"Avon was such a faith stock," said Brenda Landry, a first vice president of the investment banking firm of White, Weld & Company and an analyst of the cosmetics and fragrance industry, trying to explain why the professionals overstayed.

It was also, in the parlance of the Street, a one-decision stock, which meant that the pros bought it and figured they'd never have to reappraise or sell it. In that case, one might ask, who needs a professional manager? Presumably, as Miss Landry would have it, the pros have now learned there is no such thing as a one-decision stock.

But there were no plaudits for the pro who was right all along. Abraham Karp, a veteran cosmetics analyst had been saying back in 1970 and 1971 that Avon was "an excellent company . . . but at this multiple, oversold." Then in the spring of 1973, when Avon was selling at 135, he told the institutional clients of Dominick & Dominick, the brokerage firm that then employed him, to get rid of their stock. He gave all of the reasons which everyone repeated after the stock was crashing down. "Nobody wanted to listen to me," he recalled, "and then later when everything I had said had come to pass, nobody came around to congratulate me." Karp left the firm some months later during one of the retrenchments that the Wall Street houses were taking. "Portfolio managers get fixations on stocks. And when you tell them to sell, they say 'What?' and shake their heads. Then later they don't come back to you because they feel foolish."

Characteristically, these who were caught with their portfolios packed with Avon stock accepted the company excuses. When it announced a 16 per cent earnings decline for the first six months of 1974 from the same period a year before, and all of this concurrent with a 10 per cent increase in sales, Avon attributed its woes to worldwide inflation and currency fluctuations.

The prices of the raw materials Avon used for its products had jumped wildly. Inflation had also affected consumer spending. When the housewife answered the ding-dong of the Avon Lady, she bought the less expensive staple items rather than the higher priced gift items like the decanters of fragrances. The Avon customer was in the income bracket that most felt the wallop of inflation on its household budget.

"The company had never experienced such inflationary pressure," chairman Fusee said.

Avon fought back by trying to put more steam behind its sales campaigns. It stepped up its "specials," another way of saying it slashed prices, increased the number of representatives (there were now 680,000 world-wide), and cut the territories of both the representatives and the district managers. More incentives were offered for selling and for recruiting representatives.

"This company has no experience dealing with recession plus inflation," Brenda Landry said. "They never had to discount their prices while their costs were increasing. It's a new phenomenon."

But there were other signs that the infallible Avon system might be a little winded. The decrease in size of the territories meant that everyone had to work harder, the representatives and those who had to keep them motivated.

All of the blame couldn't be laid at the door of economic downturn. Can a company keep growing as fast as Avon did before when the social premise on which it was founded is changing? Avon's strength had always been in the hinterlands where the housewife welcomed the friendly intrusion of the Avon Lady. In the 1970s more and more housewives were escaping from their nests into the work force, full or part time. When the Avon Lady called, they weren't there. And while they were away from home, they might have been buying cosmetics in a drugstore or department store.

Not only was it becoming harder to earn an Avon commission, but women who wanted to make money were becoming aware of the value of a dollar and the value of their efforts. It was foreseeable that fewer and fewer of them would choose the frustration and rigors of the Avon commission way.

President Mitchell was also dissatisfied with the commission system. He was testing variable commission rates as a means of making the merchandising of products more flexible in meeting competitive pricing. On a "special," the representative might only draw 30 per cent commission. On a high priced item, she might receive 50 per cent. Though Mitchell gave assurance that any new rate scale would not cut into the representative's earnings, it seemed inevitable that she would have to run harder to stay in place, especially if she were paying more for gasoline and the operation of her car.

Overseas, that old Avon profit magic hadn't developed quite as fast as had been hoped. With more representatives in the sixteen foreign markets (390,000 as against 290,000 in the United States), international sales of $414.6 million in 1973, or 36 per cent of the Avon total of $1.15 billion, produced only 27 per cent of net earnings.

Economic slowdown and currency fluctuations were not wholly responsible. There were also the cultural roadblocks that might have been anticipated in foreign countries. As any longtime American resident abroad or fairly perceptive tourist would know, the American openness about inviting strangers into the home is not matched in Europe and Asia. Even in some of the Western European countries that have become homogenized with American ways, the Avon representative is reluctant to venture past the circle of her friends.

In Japan, the market that every cosmetic company thought was irresistible, Avon misunderstood both the social and business climate and in 1974 was losing money after five years of trying. It ran into well-entrenched competitors—four top Japanese cosmetic companies and the wildly successful American firm Max Factor & Company, as well as the inhospitability of the Japanese Government toward newcomers from abroad wanting to do business there.

"It takes time," chairman Fusee said when questions were asked by investors.

Then there was the diversification program on which Avon had lost $3 million in 1973. More and more beauty salons had been opened and optimistic reports issued. President Mitchell disclosed that while the customers loved them, beauty salons "were not a sufficiently profitable operation to continue our commitment." The sixteen salons would be kept open at least for a year or so, he said, but no one in the company was saying how long after that Avon would be in the beauty salon business.

Optimism was re-directed toward two other test ventures. Family Fashions by Avon, a mail-order subsidiary for men's and women's apparel was positioned to compete with the higher end of the Sears, Roebuck line. Men's jeans were priced at two pairs for $11.98 and a woman's polyester double-knit dress at $17.98. Millions of names were being gathered from the Avon representatives and fed into the computer. Some of the representatives believed that apparel sales would reduce their customers' discretionary income for cosmetics and they became disgruntled and discouraged. Plastic housewares were being tried out in Canada. They were sold through the party-plan method in which the representative arranges for gatherings of friends and neighbors in homes. Refreshments are served and the product line is displayed. Hospitality is supposed to weaken sales resistance. But the cyclical nature of the mail-order and apparel businesses presented formidable problems. Was it time to remember that Avon's glory days had come when the company had no competitors? In 1974 Avon still held 85 per cent of the market for door-to-door cosmetics market and was twice as big as the second largest cosmetic company and leader in the retail field, Revlon, Incorporated.

"No one has ever written a book on how to go from a $1-billion to a $2-billion cosmetics company," one of the Avon executives had said. "We'll have to feel our way."

Clearly no one thought it could be done by leaps and bounds just by selling cosmetics. Even next-biggest Revlon was achieving some of its growth by a well-conceived diversification into pharmaceuticals.

The question being asked by concerned Avon-watchers was whether management really knew where it was going and whether Avon would ever be able to do anything as well as selling cosmetics to women in their own homes.

Chairman Fusee told the stockholders at the annual meeting in the spring of 1974, "This is not a sick company. There's nothing wrong with it." No one had said it was, but investors were wondering if it were still young and glamorous.

"Avon is a mature company," said analyst Brenda Landry, pronouncing the cruelest word of all. "They will be lucky if they attain a 10 per cent growth rate in the future. And it is unlikely that it will be rewarded again with a high multiple."

Chairman Fusee wouldn't quarrel with that. "It's questionable we'll ever see PEs in the stratosphere again," he said at the stockholders' meeting, using the Wall Street abbreviation for price-earnings ratio. He looked wistful and not fully comprehending.

DID SUCCESS BREED FAILURE
AT GENERAL FOODS?

July 1972

Another corporate god has stumbled on its feet of clay. Last January the General Foods Corporation, the nation's largest manufacturer of packaged "convenience foods," disclosed that it had lost $83 million, mostly on the Burger Chef fast-food chain it had acquired in 1968.

By the time the accountants had finished their KP duty, the extraordinary after-tax loss was pared to $46.8 million, of which $39 million was charged to the fast-food chain and $7.8 million to other extraordinary write-offs in domestic and overseas operations. Earnings on $2.4 billion sales declined to $1.32 a share from $2.38. But no matter how the auditors served it, that was a lot of money to lose on hamburgers in three years, especially on an original investment of $16 million.

Inevitably, the question is asked: How can a company so often described in business schools as one of the best-managed marketing companies make such a mistake?

And how many other mistakes can the company afford to make before its robust balance sheet, triple-A credit line, and impressive 15 per cent return on stockholder equity begin to weaken?

Some of those other mistakes are spotlighted by the 5 per cent earnings decline–even without the Burger Chef loss–that GF suffered on its 6.2 per cent sales increase for fiscal 1972. There would seem to be four areas of major marketing error.

With a dominant 39 per cent share of the domestic coffee market, and with coffee the most important part of its business—29 per cent, or $700 million—GF pioneered the technological achievement of freeze-dried instant coffee. It then let its first brand entry, Maxim, get trounced by Nestlé's Taster's Choice.

Long a leader in dessert through its Jell-O division, GF misjudged the importance of the new, individual portion, or snack, market in which Hunt-Wesson Foods carved a commanding—23 per cent—share with its Hunt's Snack Pack.

GF's pastry line that can be heated in toasters, Toast'em Pop-Ups, was also outdistanced by more aggressive competitors. The sale of the line to the Schulze & Burch Biscuit Company contributed to the $7.8-million write-off.

Late to enter the international zone, General Foods International had sales of $380 million last year but earnings of $3.5 million, well below the $8.1 million of the previous year. A $7 million write-off of good will in an Italian venture contributed to the loss.

"But Burger Chef was the event," said Arthur E. Larkin, Jr., in explaining his abrupt retirement last April at age fifty-five as GF's president and chief operating officer.

Larkin, who had held the post since 1966, was awarded a year's salary—$215,000—to be paid over two years.

During the next three years, he will also be receiving installments from the bonus pay of $110,000 he was awarded in fiscal 1971. No bonuses were given for fiscal 1972.

"General Foods is a proud company," Larkin observed. The scapegoat was sympathetic.

A tall, ruddy-faced man with a body going to paunch, Larkin was looking back at the wreckage of his career from his home in North Salem, New York, in northern Westchester County, a half-hour's drive from corporate headquarters in White Plains from which traces of his fourteen-year stay were being excised.

"The Burger Chef extraordinary loss was a shock to all of us," he said. "No man is indispensable," he added, in a voice devoid of rancor.

C. W. ("Tex") Cook, GF's persuasive and vigorous chairman and chief executive officer, who was turning sixty-three and was two years from mandatory retirement, took on the presidency and let it be known he was running the company again.

He had hired Larkin and groomed him to follow the path he had blazed on his own inexorable rise to the top.

Cook's success is of the sort that nourishes business school students' dreams. A medium-sized man, he conveys the impression of one much taller and younger by an almost military bearing. Oklahoma born and Texas trained, Cook had suppressed the names his parents had given him, Chauncey William Wallace in favor of the initials "C. W." and the jaunty nickname "Tex." With his engineering degree from the University of Texas, he made his mark over a dozen years in a series of production and plant engineering jobs with Procter & Gamble, the Cincinnati-based company with whom General Foods sometimes competes and always hallows for its marketing skills.

In 1942 General Foods hired Cook away from P&G to be its chief engineer. From 1948 until 1951 one of his main assignments was to supervise the development of the technology for an improved instant coffee. When the equipment was perfected and the product launched in 1951, Cook was told to learn marketing. He was appointed product manager for Instant Maxwell House. Its immediate success gained him the post of general manager of the Maxwell House division, GF's largest entity.

"I don't know whether I created instant or it created me," Cook once told *Fortune* magazine.

Cook had found his sponsor at General Foods in Charles G. Mortimer, the supersalesman under whom, in the late 1950s and early 1960s, General Foods had a golden age of profitability.

In 1963 *Fortune* advanced GF as a candidate for most successful billion-dollar company in the United States. From 1957 to 1962 its average annual return on invested capital had been 17.1 per cent, higher than that of International Business Machines or General Electric. The market value of GF's stock had quintupled in the previous decade. Mortimer brought Cook along behind him as executive vice president and then in 1962, when Mortimer became chairman, Cook succeeded him as president.

In 1958 Cook, in turn, had spotted Larkin, a marketing man at the George A. Hormel Company. Larkin was a hearty salesman type in contrast to Cook, the controlled engineer. Cook, who was then running Maxwell House, brought Larkin in as marketing manager. From then on, wherever Cook went, Larkin was sure to follow, first as general manager of Maxwell House, then executive vice president-operations and finally in 1966, when Cook became chairman a year after Mortimer retired, president and chief operating officer. They had been an inseparable team—"working in harness," both say—sharing the decisions that had, for nineteen years, presented investors with an unbroken string of annual earnings increases.

Last winter the decision was made to write down to realizable value some of the restaurant properties acquired in the pell-mell expansion.

"I, of course, participated importantly in that decision, although I didn't realize the personal implications," Larkin said.

"I believe the company's been knocked around in the financial market," he went on, sadly. "Any company that's had a long string of earnings increases is bound to be when it's broken.

"But if you press too hard to make it the year you shouldn't, you'll borrow real trouble. Yet that's what started the furor."

Wall Street analysts unanimously began issuing sell or hold-but-don't-buy recommendations. Or, as Tex Cook said bitterly, they started "all rushing to the same side of the boat."

Cook has said that "some of the adverse factors of the past" will continue well into fiscal 1973. However, he said, "We have identified the causes of softness in our performance and are taking steps to counteract them."

The financial community is persistently asking whether the new top-management team represents true change or a reshuffle and whether it can recharge GF's energy cells.

"We sense that management recognizes the scope of its task," said James A. Reavis, a food industry analyst with Eastman Dillon. "We believe that the proof of this, however, lies in the future.

"If it were to get its people going, GF could be a real steamroller," he added.

By sales, GF holds thirty-eighth place in *Fortune*'s 500 largest corporations. By its growth rate of 5.83 per cent for the last decade, it is two hundred fortieth on the list.

Cook named as his deputy Magnus R. Bohm, senior executive vice president, fifty-five, and a thirty-four-year GF veteran. Beneath him are three younger veterans and executive vice presidents: Joseph F. Abely, Jr., forty-three, chief financial officer; Robert P.

Bauman, forty-one, who directs nongrocery business and acquisitions; and James L. Ferguson, forty-six, who will supervise the five major grocery divisions. It is assumed that the trio will vie for Cook's place when he retires.

Both in corporate headquarters in White Plains, New York, and in North Salem, pains were taken to stress that no other executive paid for corporate errors with his job as Larkin had. But past mistakes of judgment are candidly acknowledged.

Take Burger Chef. Nudged to diversify by its long-range planners in 1967, GF saw in Burger Chef, an Indianapolis-based chain, a logical extension of its corporate expertise, as well as a chance to ride the growing trend toward eating away from home. The McDonald's hamburger chain was already a skyrocket in that realm.

In the boom year of 1968 $16 million was a reasonable price to pay for 700 owned and franchised fast-food units in what GF believed was a well-managed chain. One of the Burger Chef franchisees in Ohio had started a Jax roast beef network. General Foods bought it for $3 million and changed the name to Rix.

Just when the fast-food bandwagon was becoming crowded with hamburger, chicken, and roast beef optimists, GF eagerly expanded Rix and Burger Chef up to 1,200 outlets widely and thinly scattered across the United States. The Burger Chef founder left to pursue other interests. Another key executive of the fast-food chain had a heart attack, and other departures resulted in a management turnover that was nearly total within two years.

GF supplied the new management and, as Bauman now concedes, it had to learn that "the fast-food business is not like manufacturing a pound of coffee. Every one of those outlets must have a satisfying eating experience."

Furthermore, he recalled, "the economy started to suffer, and in the shakeout, roast beef was one of the first to go." The basic roast beef sandwich priced at 79 cents, in comparison with the 69-cent Jumbo Super Chef, did not offer "sufficiently broad appeal," he now realizes.

Inexperience with the real estate business—and fast food is almost as much real estate as it is a culinary service—led GF into inflated property commitments in weak marketing areas.

"We moved too far, too fast, under the pressures of the times," Larkin said. "It's wonderful what 20/20 hindsight will tell you. Had we been more deliberate in the face of other fast-food operators' bids for real estate, our problems would have been fewer. Had we been more deliberate, our problems would have been less," he added.

GF is now closing down and writing off all of the Rix roast beef units and consolidating Burger Chef into a regional chain. More than 100 units have been closed so far, and a net reduction of 25 per cent is planned during the next few years, even as capital spending continues to open new outlets and to modernize old ones.

Instead of trying to be a national franchise network like McDonald's, Burger Chef is being contained in size. It will concentrate on markets where it has strength, principally the Midwest. In Indianapolis, the city of its birth, for instance, Burger Chef is number one, even over McDonald's.

Improvements in quality and service are being made. Cook maintains that Burger Chef is already operating in the black. "We overestimated our ability to manage a business in which we had no direct experience," he admitted.

In the coffee business, on the other hand, GF has had more than forty years' experience, through its Maxwell House division. Over the last decade the $2 billion domestic coffee market has been declining about 2 per cent annually in per capita consumption, a trend that GF believes may be reversed as the population turns older. Last year GF increased its market share, although it paid dearly to defend itself against competitors.

The marketing strategy that led to what Larkin calls "the Taster's Choice-Maxim fiasco" will be endlessly debated in professional and academic circles, such as the Harvard Business School, where there are two case studies on Maxim out of sixty-seven based on GF files.

GF's relationship with the Harvard B-School is intimate. The company has been a steady recruiter of the school's graduates and, through its co-operation in the preparation of the case studies, an influence on the education of future managers.

Instant or soluble coffee had been patented a century ago. G. Washington had one on the market since 1909, but the significant development of the product didn't occur until World War II when a soluble coffee was needed for military rations. Earlier the Nestlé Company pioneered with its Nescafé. Both the G. Washington and Nescafé instants added "fillers" to their coffee content.

Instant Maxwell House, manufactured with a new technology

after World War II, was an all-coffee soluble. It was dried with warm air. After it was introduced, the consumption of soluble coffee soared to 35 per cent of the number of cups of coffee consumed in the United States.

Soluble coffee was more convenient to serve during the day other than at meals. From 1950 to 1963 the drinking of coffee between meals doubled while mealtime consumption remained static.

GF devoted the largest capital commitment in its history (a figure it refuses to divulge) to the development of freeze-dried instant coffee, which tastes more like brewed coffee than do spray-dried instants, and introduced it in the United States in 1964 through the brand Maxim. That year, Nestlé—the Swiss-based company that is also GF's neighbor in White Plains—sent a freeze-dried coffee into the German market, a coffee it would introduce in the United States two years later as Taster's Choice.

"General Foods' new coffee could have been positioned either as a brand-new category or as an evolution of a leading brand, Maxwell House," said a Harvard professor of marketing, Martin V. Marshall. "They tried to trade on their own coffee reputation but concurrently position the freeze-dried coffee as a really different product in the market. It was a perfectly plausible strategy."

The name, the packaging, and promotion clearly linked the higher-priced Maxim to Maxwell House. The label instructed the user to adjust the measurement to personal taste, possibly using less than the standard teaspoonful.

Teaching people to use less when selling something expensive is a flawed idea, psychologically, suggests a nonacademic market research consultant who prefers anonymity because of fear of offending corporate brass. "If you want people to enjoy the product, you don't tell them how to restrict its use," the consultant said.

Maxim's granules varied from crumb-size to fine and powdery. Without careful attention, there was no telling what distribution in granule size the user would collect in a spoonful. Taster's Choice had a more uniform granulation. "It's never as good as Maxim can be, but it's never quite as bad," a home economist said.

Relying on housewives' ability to follow explicit instructions was "running a big risk," according to Professor Marshall.

Nestlé's Taster's Choice took an opposite strategy from Maxim's. The consumer was never reminded of Nestlé's basic product, Nescafé spray-dried instant coffee, and was made only dimly aware of the manufacturer. The measurement was simple and exact, the jar distinctively square, and the marketing campaign was waged on an international front, but it concentrated first on areas of the United States with high instant coffee consumption.

Ohio was first. Then came the East in 1968, the South and West in 1969, and the rest of the country in 1972.

Coffee-drinking patterns vary throughout the United States. Westerners used to drink more cups of coffee a day than easterners. But the light coffee drinkers were the readiest converts to soluble coffee. That, plus its population density, made the East a high-acceptance market for instant coffee.

"The battle of the brands" wound up with each holding a 13 per cent share of the instant-coffee market. But the pre-eminent market share held by Instant Maxwell House, the older instant introduced twenty years ago with Tex Cook as product manager, had eroded. At the end of 1970 the combined market share held by Maxim and Instant Maxwell House was about the same as the share held by Instant Maxwell House alone in 1965, before Maxim was introduced.

Early in 1971 GF shifted to a marketing strategy that emphasized total instant market rather than just freeze-dried. It included price promotions and a new agglomerated form for Instant Maxwell House such as Nescafé already had. Another step in the production process gave the crystals more of the look of ground coffee. GF's total share of the instant coffee market perked up but the strategy was costly.

A decaffeinated Taster's Choice is now being marketed to challenge GF's predominant Sanka. The decaffeinated market seems to be the fertile side of the coffee business. Advertising is no longer beamed to insomniacs but to the larger throng of the tension-ridden. GF is countering with its freeze-dried version of Sanka and a new freeze-dried decaffeinated product, Brim.

Max-Pax, a ground coffee in disposable filter rings for the percolator, is in national distribution, an entry in the total domestic coffee arena where further competition looms from Procter & Gamble.

In 1963 P&G bought Folger's Coffee, an expanding midwestern company that has not yet reached the East. The industry speculates endlessly about its next stride. But GF is heartened by having won its latest confrontation with Folger's in the Cleveland area.

In packaged desserts, the error was in misjudging a new competitor. Last year, GF's Jell-O gelatin and pudding sales fell, although they still lead the field. In 1969 Hunt-Wesson introduced Snack Pack, a single-serving canned pudding.

The head of Hunt-Wesson at the time was Edward Gelsthorpe, an imaginative marketer who had been christened "Cranapple Ed" by the trade after "bringing cranberries into the twentieth century," as Jim Reavis of Eastman Dillon said. In his previous job with Ocean Spray Cranberries, Gelsthorpe had spurred the development of year-round products such as several cranberry juice cocktails.

After Larkin's exit, Gallagher's Report touted Gelsthorpe as just what the doctor prescribed for General Foods. White Plains paid no attention.

The concept of portion control (of which the single-serving pudding is an expression) had been used by General Foods in its institutional food services division. But there were packaging problems, involving children's cut fingers and taste quality. Canned pudding had an off-putting flavor unlike that prepared from ingredients packaged in a box.

GF, exercising legendary caution, tested, watched, and waited, while Del Monte and RJR Foods' My-T-Fine entered the contest against Snack Pack. About six months ago Jell-O Pudding Treats arrived.

"We didn't realize the potential of Snack Pack as quickly as we should," said Jim Ferguson. "Our testing didn't suggest they would be a lasting success. We were just wrong. Now we've gone into the market and are into it to stay.

"Cautious is better than not being cautious, when we are doing battle on as many fronts as we are," he said.

Professor Marshall concurred. "Given their wide product line, it's General Foods against all possible comers.

"From constantly observing the marketing management activities of consumer packaged-goods companies, I judge GF's skills to be good," he continued.

"GF has made mistakes as well as had successes. My general impression is that GF's mistakes are more publicly known than the mistakes of others who often discreetly bury theirs."

An executive of an advertising agency who had worked on GF accounts for fifteen years suggested other considerations.

"Being a late runner costs the division money, sure," he said. "But what if you think you'll have a better product if you wait? You bring out a product in a can even though you think you may have a better package in a year. Is that social responsibility?"

All the manufacturers were testing plastic cans which seemed to promise better taste quality.

The ad man went on. "General Foods is more concerned about social responsibility and what the Federal Trade Commission will think. Their oversensitivity about anticipating problems delays them. The smaller manufacturer doesn't give a damn. He figures he'll worry about the FTC later."

But Wall Street and other observers are not so tolerant. "Where are the new products, where are the new ideas?" they are crying.

The Post division, the nucleus of the GF empire, must reckon with a nearly static breakfast-cereal market caused by changing lifestyles. Grasping the straw of increased nutrition consciousness, GF is striving for a new nutritional cereal.

Kool-Aid, leader in powdered soft drinks—and probably the most profitable GF product—is recovering from the federal ban on cyclamate sweeteners in 1969. Initially, the edict caused about one fourth of the powdered soft drink market to evaporate and it has taken more than two years for Kool-Aid to rebuild anything near its former 75 per cent share. The substitution of sugar for cyclamates added to production costs.

Overseas, "we're Johnny-come-lately, and we're not yet getting the return we hope to," said Magnus Bohm. Eighteen acquisitions have been made in the fifteen years since GF decided that American convenience foods could not be marketed abroad without adapting to national tastes.

With coffee, the one exception, GF has been jousting with its more internationally savvy foe, Nestlé's. Competition and new-plant problems have been most acute in Italy, Japan, and Australia.

GF's product line abroad includes some items not marketed in the United States and Canada, such as ice cream, spices, soups, and bottled drinks. Candy and chewing gum are major franchises in Europe and Latin America. GF is the single most important presence in the French chewing gum market. In 1971 Chlorodont, a leading Dutch chewing gum company, and its associated Maple Leaf Chewing Gum Manufacturers of West Germany were acquired by General Foods. A Krema candy plant is being built at Reims in the French Champagne country. In England GF has the franchise for Kentucky Fried Chicken stores.

By what all insist is pure coincidence, the international division's last three chieftains have left GF in less than five years.

GF's recent dilemmas must be viewed against its history. It is the quintessential example of a giant that grew by acquisition.

Its forerunner was the Postum Cereal Company, organized in 1896 in a little white barn in Battle Creek, Michigan, to market a health drink. Charles William Post, the inventor of Postum, a cereal beverage, next concocted Grape-Nuts, one of the first ready-to-eat cold cereal products. A stream of other Post products followed. He called the corn flakes product, introduced in 1904, Elijah's Manna. Though a deeply religious man, like so many pillars of American business, he didn't foresee the widespread objections to the name. In 1907 he changed it to Post Toasties. Within two years of its debut in 1922 Post's 40% Bran Flakes became the world's best-selling bran cereal.

During the 1920s, under the stewardship of Edward F. Hutton, then the husband of Charles Post's daughter, Marjorie, the Postum Cereal Company started devouring other convenience-food companies. In 1925 Postum joined forces with the Jell-O Company, which Orator Francis Woodward had promoted to a household name from another man's gelatin dessert business he had bought for $450 a quarter century before. The next year, the Igleheart Brothers, makers of Swans Down Cake Flour, sold out to Postum. Minute Tapioca Company was also acquired in 1926 (during World War II, as a GF unit, it was to develop a precooked instant rice for the armed forces). The Franklin Baker Company (coconut) and the Walter Baker Company (chocolate) came aboard in 1927, along with Log Cabin Products (maple syrup).

And in 1928 the La France Company (makers of bluing for laundry and of Satina, an ironing aid), the Calumet Baking Powder Company, and the Cheek-Neal Company were taken into the GF fold.

Joel Cheek, the founder of Cheek-Neal, had coaxed the managers of the Maxwell House Hotel in Nashville, Tennessee, one of the South's better hostelries, into using a new blend of coffee he had developed. According to legend, it was Theodore Roosevelt who first said of Maxwell House Coffee, "It's good to the last drop."

In 1929 the diversified company took a more indicative name, General Foods. That year, it bought the 168 patents of Clarence

Birdseye, a fur trader and biologist from Gloucester, Massachusetts, who had developed a frozen-food process.

In 1933 the rights to a decaffeinated coffee developed by a German coffee merchant named Ludwig Roselius and named Sanka (a contraction of *sans caffeine,* the French phrase for without caffein) were acquired.

Under chief executives Colby M. Chester, Clarence Francis, and Austin Igleheart, GF went on buying companies in the 1940s and 1950s and continued to change its character from manufacturing to marketing.

Among the more significant acquisitions were the Gaines Food Company in 1943 and Perkins Products, makers of Kool-Aid beverages, in 1953.

Clarence Gaines was a miller and dog breeder who had scored a breakthrough with Gaines Dog Meal, a dry food for canines that could be stored in paper bags without spoiling. By 1958 the dog food market had grown and attracted other manufacturers. But 60 per cent of the market was in canned goods. Many dogs just didn't cotton to a dehydrated diet.

Gravy Train, a product of dry chunks with dehydrated gravy that could be made liquid with the addition of water was Gaines' response to that challenge and not a very successful one. Then, in 1960, technological improvements made possible the introduction of Gaines-burgers, a semimoist product containing hamburger that didn't have to be refrigerated and could be stored on shelves. Once it was put in the form of a patty and became a "hamburger for dogs," it encountered the resistance of dog lovers who did not believe that hamburger was a complete dog food. Nevertheless, GF is Number One in the $940 million-a-year dog food market.

By the 1950s it was obvious that antitrust laws would slow the acquisition pace in the processed food direction. So GF tried internal product development.

Under Charles G. Mortimer, as chairman, and his successor, Tex Cook, new-product budgets were more than doubled.

The United States was in its postwar growth cycle. Everything of vital interest to grocery manufacturers was on the increase—the population, consumer income, leisure time, and the supermarket chains, which were multiplying their retail outlets.

GF did battle against its competitors for space on supermarket shelves and in frozen-food bins. Not only did it have to inch out the name brands of other food processors but the growing incursion of the supermarkets' lesser-priced private label products as well. This year, for example, GF's ground coffee brands are priced on an average 20 per cent more and its instants 33⅓ per cent more than private label coffees in the same stores.

"Those stores don't have rubber walls," Tex Cook once said about the competition for the same turf of shelf space. To convince supermarkets to buy and display its products, GF has to invent new ones, distribute them more quickly and efficiently than other manufacturers through the food warehouses, and advertise them so skillfully that they practically walk off the shelves.

For many years GF has been the fourth largest advertiser in the nation, behind General Motors, Ford, and Procter & Gamble. It spent $136.8 million last year on advertising and promotion, mostly on television and in prime-time family shows and daytime soap operas. GF refuses to sponsor any program in which violence is a significant part. It would be counterproductive to have mayhem before the dessert commercial.

Freeze-dried coffee was one result of the Mortimer-Cook new-product push, which nevertheless had as one of its objectives the lessening of GF's dependence on coffee for sales and profits. There were less spectacular but durable successes such as Shake'nBake, a coating mix for meat, Cool Whip, a frozen, nondairy product, and Tang, an instant artificial orange drink. Tang received an assist from the national space program which sent it to the moon with the astronauts.

There were also monumental flops such as Birds Eye Gourmet food and frozen baby-food lines.

The acquisition of the S.O.S. Company in 1957 changed GF's destiny again. In a decision to which Cook still refers heatedly, the Federal Trade Commission forced GF to divest itself of the scouring-pad company in 1968 and laid down further strictures inhibiting acquisition.

The way Cook says GF's lawyers read the FTC's intent, the company cannot buy "a true leader in almost any field related to consumer-type goods."

So GF went shopping for foothold positions, such as Burger Chef. In 1970 it paid $38.9 million for the Viviane Woodard Corporation, a franchised cosmetic and skin care service sold in homes and, at the time, grossing $7 million a year; $7 million for the W.

Atlee Burpee Company, one of the best names in garden products, with a $10-million annual sales volume; and in an exchange of stock worth $8 million bought Kohner Brothers, a preschool toy company with sales of $6 million.

"What is General Foods doing in hamburgers, seeds, cosmetics, and toys and aren't these companies awfully small?" Bob Bauman posed the question often asked. "We spent quite a bit of time study- ing what General Foods is all about," he said, "and how it could move into areas that were growing rapidly and had sustained growth. All of these showed growth in line with disposable income for leisure time."

One of the acquisitions that was thought to meet the test was disposed of after a brief honeymoon. In 1970 GF sold Innkeepers Incorporated, a management service for hotels, motels, and clubs, back to its owners.

"It would have been ideal if we could have acquired larger com- panies," Bauman said. "But there are restrictions on our doing that. And it would be difficult to start from scratch.

"We had to find smaller companies with basic strength to use as a springboard to become a total factor and that would also give us av- enues to other things. To direct mail through Burpee, to door-to- door selling through Viviane Woodard. Through Burger Chef, we're learning about operating our own retail outlets."

A rival food giant had gone much the same acquisition route. General Mills Inc. of Minneapolis bought Lionel Trains, Play- Doh, and Parker Brothers games, and the mail-order crafts and outdoor equipment companies of Leewards and Eddie Bauer. But General Mills didn't panic when it appeared to have missed the fast-food train. It acquired a four-unit southern seafood chain called Red Lobster Inns and expanded it, calmly and profitably, to sixty- five restaurants.

Moreover, General Mills seems to have found the key to the new product spigot as well. On the other hand, though consumer groups and the FTC have been charging all of the cereal manufacturers with nutritional faults, it's General Mills and not General Foods that Michael Jacobson, co-director of the Center for Science in the Pub- lic Interest, has labeled a "junk food" producer.

There is still a sense of urgency about new-product development in White Plains.

"Everybody's in the game now," Tex Cook said. "It used to be that General Foods with its large development facilities was unique in its industries. But others came along.

"We have had a fair number of new products come out of the horn but not as big in contribution as some have been in the past. Instant coffee and Tang were blockbusters." Cook said that "corporate management is now deciding where the priority of effort on new-product development will be, instead of letting each division do its own thing. We are going to be sure that out of various lists the divisions have, we get corporate assessment of where priority lies. We've singled certain areas that can wait and will pick out those that seem most feasible, most promising."

Each division of GF will still have its own market research but demographic studies and surveys of what is happening to consumer habits will be made at the corporate level.

One trend of developing complexity and controversy that all food manufacturers must assess is natural foods.

"We read it as a fringe thing," Cook said. "We recognize there is some feeling about natural foods, but we don't see it as a major factor."

In the management of a billion-dollar corporation such as General Foods, who bears responsibility for success and failure?

Cook, the chairman, said, "I have ultimate responsibility as chief executive." Yet it was Art Larkin, his hand-picked president and chief operating officer, who paid with his job for decisions in which many shared.

Cook gave this explanation: the president has "the responsibility for literally running the business according to principles agreed upon, with obviously the obligation to counsel with and seek the advice of the chairman and chief executive."

Cook added that he had become increasingly occupied with outside affairs, such as hard-core unemployment and racial questions—activities for which he and GF have often been lauded—as well as grocery industry problems.

He had testified before Congress on nutrition, criticizing the bureaucracies of the Food and Drug Administration and the Agriculture Department.

Cook was a member of the President's Business Council and chairman of the Conference Board, the respected business research organization. He sat on the boards of the Whirlpool Corporation and the Chase Manhattan Bank, of Rockefeller University and Tuskegee Institute.

"I'm inclined to be on the conservative side. Art Larkin is very aggressive, a two-fisted man's man," he said. "In harness we worked well. I profited from his insights and aggressiveness. His aggressiveness in going after new products and new companies involved a certain amount of risks. Obviously before they were taken to the board, clearly I was involved.

"There's a tendency as you get within some period of mandatory retirement to say the younger men are going to live with some of the things they are proposing. On a couple of issues, I said, I have some concerns but the damn plant won't be built before I'm retired and if they feel strongly, I'm not going to buck it.

"With quite a number of things like Burger Chef, I would have to say the risk taking was more aggressive than warranted. A lot of this aggressiveness didn't pay off. Some go for broke—some don't. Some things might have mitigated the situation."

Becoming involved again last November, Cook assessed "how deep the surgery had to be." In January an extraordinary loss of $46.8 million was reported, and Cook "was back into operations."

"There were some things, if done short term, would have the year looking pretty good but I was not in agreement with some of those things," he said. "I mean not giving enough advertising support to some of the basic franchises."

At the April meeting of the board, from which Larkin was excluded, Cook said, "It was my recommendation I get back in and assume operating responsibility."

But why did the board of directors take so long to find out that trouble was brewing? Wilma Soss, the corporate gadfly, demanded to know why at the annual meeting always held in late July.

"It wasn't until April that they restructured this company? What made them take this long? Apparently this board has been had and we are supposed to re-elect this board?" Mrs. Soss asked.

She ran down the list of outside directors. John T. Connor, chairman of Allied Chemical Corporation (and, like Cook, a director of the Chase Manhattan Bank); B. R. Dorsey, president of Gulf Oil Corporation; William P. Tavoulareas, president of Mobil Oil Corporation; Elisha Gray II, chairman of the finance committee of Whirlpool Corporation (of which Cook is a director); Oveta Culp Hobby, chairman of the Houston Post Company; Frederick R. Kappel, retired chairman of American Telephone & Telegraph Company; William McChesney Martin, former president of the New York Stock Exchange and former chairman of the Federal Reserve Board; J. Wilson Newman, chairman of the finance committee of Dun & Bradstreet Incorporated; Henry R. Roberts, president of Connecticut General Insurance Company; Albert L. Williams, chairman of the finance committee of International Business Machines Corporation.

An august board it was, made up of heads of companies whose combined revenues form a torrent of billions and billions of dollars.

"There is doubt whether this board is tailored to a food business," Mrs. Soss said. "It seems to be a very repetitious board. Where is somebody who knows about food, about real estate? Something is wrong. Why don't you take a successful man who runs a grocery store? This board is too distinguished and too far away."

Cook assured her that a special committee of the board headed by Elisha Gray was working with him on "the total problem" of nominating a director to fill Larkin's vacant spot and of restructuring the organization.

Henceforth, Cook said, there will be more "participatory decision making, less one-on-one of decisive management . . . We were having too much of that"—and more chance for bright young men to have their opinions heard.

Larkin, who voiced only praise for Cook and GF, said, "In any one company, the one-man decisions are unusual. Most managers will do a lot of consulting with their confrères, and this was the case.

"Tex and I worked closely for fifteen years. He's the only boss I had. We said our strong points and weak points matched pretty well. Tex is a conservative Texan, a perfectly marvelous man. I'm a bit more aggressive and more of a risk taker than he. There are times for both—times to reach out and times to pull in horns. Over the years, I thought we did pretty well between us."

Compared to Procter & Gamble, GF is a fast-track company in which managers are often whisked from one assignment to another and across several divisions, rather than rising in one. The pressure to produce quick results is intense.

Victor Bonomo, now president of the Pepsi-Cola Company, had eleven jobs in twelve years at GF. He said, "I think it's a fair comment that not too many stay to reap the benefits or bear the blame for their mistakes." He indicated he had had successes "and a few failures, but I got out before they caught up with me." He declined to name them. "Maybe they are forgotten," he said.

Cook admitted, "We've made that mistake in a number of cases." He promised "There is going to be a change. A man will have to stay on the job long enough to make it clear he's not living on the momentum of his predecessor, seeing if it works. And if not, does he have the courage to pull it out and make it work?"

Two Years Later, Summer 1974

The new chairman of the General Foods Corporation received a visitor in his shirtsleeves. James L. Ferguson's shirt screamed yellow and blue stripes behind a somber maroon necktie.

Modish attire is no longer noteworthy in the executive suites of billion-dollar corporations. To the contrary, the white shirt and the crew cut sow suspicion of stagnation, especially in a marketing company.

But it tells a great deal about the nation's largest manufacturer of packaged convenience foods that on the third floor of its hilltop fortress in White Plains, where senior management has its lair, the informality of coatlessness is deemed significant in a chairman. Tex Cook, who has just gone into mandatory retirement at sixty-five and his predecessor, Charlie Mortimer, would never have appeared without their jackets, say those who knew them both.

The informality and Jim Ferguson's age are construed as hopeful signs that General Foods had been rejuvenated and set on course again. At forty-eight, the tall, solidly constructed, sandy-haired Ferguson is the youngest chairman in the company's history and he spent eleven years getting to the top, less time than previous chief executives.

Ferguson arrived in June 1963 as an assistant to the product manager of the Birds Eye frozen food division, from eleven years' apprenticeship at the Procter & Gamble Company (Tex Cook's alma mater), which he had joined after graduating from the Harvard Business School. Given that background, a computer could have picked Ferguson as model executive officer for General Foods.

Ferguson was lucky. He acknowledges that the divisions he was with seemed to "sail through" periods of difficulties elsewhere. At no point in his career at General Foods was he identified with the coffee division or tarred with the failure of the Maxim strategy.

He came to Birds Eye when the task was to develop products beyond the stage of basic vegetables and fruits. Under his direction at Birds Eye and then at the Jell-O division there had emanated Awake and Orange Plus, frozen breakfast-drink concentrates, Cool Whip, the dessert topping, and a line of international combination vegetables. His failures had been modest: Frozen Pizza sticks and Cool 'N Creamy frozen pudding.

In April 1972, when Art Larkin walked the plank for the $46.8 million extraordinary after-tax loss incurred mostly from a reckless expansion into fast food but to a lesser extent from a lack of marketing initiative, Ferguson was named executive vice president in charge of the grocery division.

He was positioned alongside two other bright, youngish executive vice presidents for the crucial lap. Joe Abely was given the same financial channels in which he had always swum while Bob Bauman was designated caretaker of the troublesome diversifications.

"It just so happened that I was in charge of the mainstream of the company and I was in as good a position as anybody to perform and commend myself. I was in the right place at the right time, and I was given a free hand by Tex to think of changes and improvements," Ferguson said.

Eight months later, Ferguson filled the presidency Larkin had left vacant. He had only nine months more to wait before Tex Cook gave him the title of chief executive as well. Becoming chairman in July, shortly before the 1974 annual meeting seemed almost anticlimactic.

One alumnus of General Foods pointed out, though, that Tex Cook has retained the title of chairman of the executive committee as did his predecessors when they reached mandatory retirement. And he won't have to relinquish that post until his seventy-first birthday.

"I remember Charlie Mortimer going up and down the halls of the third floor," the veteran said. Mortimer was chairman of the executive committee from 1965, the year he retired, until 1971.

"You cannot change the spots of a $3-billion company," said this former executive, who characterizes the elders of General Foods as "the dinosaurs."

The term may be unkind though not wholly uncalled for. Success such as General Foods enjoyed for almost twenty years—continuous earnings increases, to keep stockholders happy and Wall Street dissuaded from too much peeking in the closet—can breed pomposity and arrogance.

The GF headquarters in White Plains, to which the company moved in the 1950s, preceding the general corporate flight to the suburbs, has a slightly antiseptic, government-agency aura unrelieved by fanciful art or architecture as the newer corporate compounds have.

Nevertheless, there is no denying that during Jim Ferguson's tenure as president, General Foods returned to an upward profit trend for the first time in three years. For the fiscal year ended March 30, 1974, sales increased 13.5 per cent from year-earlier levels to $2.9 billion, and earnings increased 8.2 per cent to $119.5 million, or $2.40 a share.

Such performance did not come easy. Food manufacturers have been squeezed between the soaring prices of the commodities they use and restraints on raising their domestic profit margins, first from federal price controls and then from what Ferguson calls the "choking point" for inflation-battered consumers.

During the last year, there has been a 17.5 per cent increase in wholesale coffee prices, and the cost of sugar has nearly doubled. As over-all food prices leaped almost 20 per cent, housewives have been trading down, though not in a regular pattern, substituting lower-cost items for some higher-cost ones.

In a sudden twist of fortune, however, some of General Foods' lesser performers became lower-cost alternatives to menu items it doesn't make. Post cereals and Log Cabin Syrup, for example, are better breakfast buys than higher-priced bacon and eggs.

A major boost to profits has come from international sales, an arena the company was late in entering. General Foods is now the largest bubble-gum producer in the world, a depressing achievement in the eyes of students of American culture. In Brazil GF is the leading ice cream manufacturer.

Ferguson says the potential in international operations is not yet being fully exploited and that the brightest prospects for the company may, in the end, lie overseas. "Some decidedly parochial grocery peddlers have expanded their horizons quite a bit," he says. What top management has to do now is to develop "a true worldwide perspective and an instinctive world-wide attitude."

For at home, General Foods is somewhat handicapped by having a substantial amount of its business in mature, relatively static product categories such as coffee (the largest business GF is in, though now less than one third of the total), packaged desserts, and cereals. In others, such as frozen foods and dog food, where once it was unique, it is now one of the leaders.

But that doesn't mean there aren't opportunities to be seized. The drop in United States coffee consumption seems to have halted. Whether or not this means a long-term demographic turnaround as the postwar baby boom population reaches the prime coffee-drinking years, it is too soon to say. Furthermore, the decline in consumption has been all in traditional ground coffee. Soluble coffee drinking is stable or just barely increasing, decaffeinated up sharply.

In the last year or so, Maxim, the freeze-dried instant coffee on which General Foods lavished such high hopes and development costs, only to see it bested by Nestlé's Taster's Choice, has reclaimed about 7 per cent of the soluble market. Taster's Choice has 12 per cent.

"But we've regained our equilibrium and we have some plans to do more with Maxim," Ferguson said. Instant Maxwell House continues to grow.

"The most dynamic action in coffee has been the decaffeinated segment," Ferguson declared. General Foods blazed that trail with Sanka. The brand still holds a long lead while Brim, the new decaffeinated for the "caffein-conscious people who wanted an alternative to Sanka" has not been a disappointment. A new Instant Maxwell House Decaffeinated is in test market, further proof that a good brand doesn't die. It just goes on spawning others.

The Snack Pack episode would seem in the end to have vindicated the hesitancy of General Foods to jump into the individual-serving pudding contest. Almost every entry after Hunt-Wesson's, and there were several, was exhausted in a price war and the market turned out not to be big enough for more than one.

"We did a fair amount of research and it suggested the product was of relatively cyclical nature. But Hunt-Wesson did a pretty good job of establishing a franchise that looked good for a while," Ferguson said. "Sometimes research is not that definitive and we thought we ought to try to participate. Subsequent events showed we should not have bothered to begin with. But sometimes you know more in retrospect than you could have at the time. If we had been first in, we might have established a viable business over time, but we chose not to be."

Ferguson sounded tranquil though rather inconclusive about that product defeat, but this did not mean that the urgency of new products has diminished. In fact, in April of 1973 he reorganized GF for the purpose of sharpening that capability. Four of the five historic grocery products divisions, bearing venerable names such as Post, Birds Eye and Jell-O, were abolished.

Strategic business units—beverage, breakfast, main meal, desserts, and pet food—were put in their stead. These are supposed to reflect categories of consumer demand and should give "a better strategic focus against a given market segment." Maxwell House was not reorganized as its strategy focus seemed clear.

Last year GF's domestic grocery coffee sales were $884 million, or 41.3 per cent of the United States market, in which GF still holds its premier position.

One of the old-timers on the third floor remarked, "What a wrench to abolish the Post division. And Jell-O. Could Clare Francis or Charlie Mortimer or Tex Cook have done that?"

Ferguson said that the strategic business unit was an "outward and visible symbol" of a fundamental change in management approach and philosophy.

Operating responsibility was pushed down to the level of five group vice presidents and the title of "chief operating officer," formerly held by the president, was abandoned. The company is being managed by principles and policies.

Responsibility for strategy has moved upward into the hands of a senior management team headed by Ferguson. For example, the president of a division can no longer make a strategic decision such as taking money away from decaffeinated coffee and applying it to another product, if strategic company policy has established decaffeinated coffee as a major focus, as it has.

Out of earshot of Ferguson, a vice president expressed it succinctly: "Everybody has to pull out his drawer and look at the matrix before making a decision. It's management by established policy, with careful decision making, and it's all charted on matrices. It's as systemized as you can get."

More specifically on the sensitive issue of new development product ingenuity, Ferguson said, "We may not bring out and test the total number of products we have in the past. But hopefully, they will be ones that have more major potential."

After the reorganization was completed, the next ten months were spent examining strategic direction. When the strategists looked at the diversification program, they concluded, Ferguson said, "that it hadn't been as successful as we had hoped or as some of our competitors had been."

Burger Chef has been trimmed to 1,000 units and some have been modernized. Adding hostesses and condiment bars and a "Smiling Chef" logo seems to have increased sales volume by 40 or 50 per cent in some areas. "Burger Chef is profitable," Ferguson asserted without disclosing by what degree.

The other three diversifications still don't amount to quite $50 million in sales. Two of them, Viviane Woodard and Kohner Toys have been hard hit by inflation. Women are not inclined to buy expensive cosmetics in the one instance and the skyrocketing cost of plastics has eliminated the profitability of the other.

[In November 1974 General Foods arranged to sell Kohner to Gabriel Industries Inc. for about $5 million. In February 1975 the unprofitability of Viviane Woodard was conceded. General Foods announced it was withdrawing from the cosmetics business and would be selling Woodard at a loss of $22 million.]

Meanwhile, General Foods has been trying out the home sewing and needlework mail order business and a task force has been formed to work out guidelines for future acquisitions.

The reorganization of the company was based on recommendations from within and was widely supported, Ferguson said. Father of three, an Episcopal Church warden and a weekend Sunfish sailor, he would not want to be seen as an iconoclast. "Though I haven't been here my whole business career, I feel strong ties to the traditions of General Foods," he said. "Golly, I have a whole lot of respect for the people who preceded me and for the board that has a great deal of continuity and stature."

There are new faces in the board room. Jerome H. Holland, a former ambassador to Sweden and probably the most popular token black director in corporate America, and Peter G. Peterson, chairman of Lehman Brothers, the Wall Street investment banking firm, have become directors of General Foods. They are not exactly the food and real estate experts Wilma Soss had in mind.

Art Larkin, who was sent packing in 1972 to save face for the corporation and the board, shortly thereafter found a new home as president of Keebler Company, an Illinois cracker manufacturer, with sales of about $200 million a year. In April 1974, Keebler was taken over by United Biscuit Limited, a British company.

THE WHITE KNIGHT AT
LEHMAN BROTHERS

November 1973

Critics of capitalism have long accused Washington and Wall Street of intimate relations without really understanding the nuances of their enduring affair. Seldom, however, have the coughs and sneezes of the government had a more contagious effect on a single investment banking firm than they had on the venerable house of Lehman Brothers during 1973.

In its fiscal year ending September 30, Lehman Brothers Inc. sustained an $8-million loss, the worst in its 123-year history. Most of it was incurred during the three summer months when interest rates soared while the company held huge inventories of bonds, particularly government issues.

Lehman was forced to pay extremely high rates to finance these securities, which were yielding it relatively low return. This situation—Wall Street calls it a "negative carry"—was combined with rapid erosion of the market value of the inventories, and few buyers were to be found who might have helped extricate Lehman from its predicament.

Like many other Wall Street houses (including the seemingly invincible Salomon Brothers which posted a $6.6-million loss), Lehman was the victim of erratic government economic policy and its own mistaken financial hunches.

Peter G. Peterson, former Secretary of Commerce and international trade expert for the Nixon administration, joined Lehman Brothers in June as a partner and vice chairman. One month later, he emerged from a coup d'état, which he had not planned, as chairman and unifying force.

Curiously, the man elected to lead the company in its latest stage of evolution from family-centered investment banking to a professionally managed, "New Wave" Wall Street institution—whatever that may be—owed his meteoric ascent to the very forces that had terminated his Washington career.

If Lehman Brothers had gone on making money (it earned $32 million in fiscal 1971 and $18 million the following year), the revolt within the baroque palazzo at 1 William Street would probably have been postponed.

Dissension had been simmering below the surface for four years since the death of Robert Lehman, the princely banker and art collector who had left the succession unresolved. Today the only Lehman in the firm is his cousin, John, son of the late Governor Herbert Lehman. John Lehman's financial interest is minor.

Watergate and a crisis of economic confidence severely wounded an already troubled Wall Street. At Lehman Brothers the injury was sufficient to detonate a revolt.

If the forty-seven-year-old Peterson had not been eased from the Nixon Cabinet, presumably by his White House foes, H. R. Haldeman and John D. Ehrlichman, he would not have gone job hunting in Wall Street.

Common wisdom in Washington had Pete Peterson running afoul of the White House inner guard—specifically Haldeman and Ehrlichman—because of his popularity on the Georgetown party circuit where the dour, crew-cut Republicans were not invited.

"Mary McGrory, a very dear friend, said that one of my problems was that I wasn't a member of the home-movie set," said Peterson. McGrory was one of the newspaper columnists considered unfriendly to the Nixon regime. A keen cultivator of the press, Peterson was also chummy with Katharine Graham, publisher of the Washington *Post,* the Nixon Nemesis.

Once in New York, Peterson set about ingratiating himself with the New York *Times.* It just so happens that the dark-haired, owlish Peterson could almost be a double for A. M. Rosenthal, the managing editor of the *Times.*

Peterson and his wife, Sally, had achieved social standing in Georgetown by giving parties where the movies shown were professionally made and the guests were personages like Henry Kissinger. The Petersons' New York apartment, overlooking the East River at Gracie Square (and where they use the same elevator as Pan American World Airways' founder, Juan Trippe), is equipped for movie showings, too.

Another likely cause for his sudden fall from Nixon's favor was Peterson's lack of Prussian team spirit and proper humility before the arbiters. "I didn't click my heels fast enough," he said at a private dinner where his remarks were sure to be given public airing. He said that he had failed a loyalty test given to him by the White House "Germans" because his calves were too thick.

It was one of the glib phrases for which Peterson seems to have a knack, either by instinct or by advertising training. The press is delighted by wordsmiths and, if encouraged, will help make them pop-culture heroes and winning politicians.

To the further distaste of the Nixon guard, Peterson has always been extremely skillful in making sure that full credit for achievement is laid at his door. His favorite pronouns are the first person singular and the plural in distinguished company.

If the ability and willingness to drop the right names is a prime asset in investment banking, then Peterson is outstandingly endowed. "Henry and I talk frequently," he said, knowing the listener would take "Henry" to be Secretary of State Kissinger. As President Nixon's assistant for international economic affairs, Peterson meshed with Kissinger. "Al" Haig, Nixon's chief of staff, is another "close friend."

So is "Chuck," as in Charles Percy, the Republican senator from Illinois and a presidential hopeful. "I'd be pleased to support him," said Peterson, a protegé of Percy's whom he succeeded at Bell & Howell, the camera company. "I'm not that much of a partisan," he added, though identifying himself as at least a nominal Republican.

Like Percy, who became the whiz kid head of Bell & Howell at twenty-nine, Peterson was a business prodigy. Born in Nebraska in 1926 of Greek immigrant parents ("My ethnicity quotient is very low," he said), he graduated from Northwestern University and took his M.B.A. at the University of Chicago. At twenty-seven he was a vice president at McCann-Erickson. As general manager of its Chicago office he caught the attention of Percy, one of the advertis-

ing agency's clients. In 1958 Percy brought him over to Bell &
Howell as executive vice president. By the age of thirty-four Peterson was president of Bell & Howell. He was earning $125,000 a
year as its chairman and chief executive officer when he was called
to Washington in February 1971. In the twelve years he spent at
Bell & Howell, sales doubled and operating earnings quadrupled.

Percy's labeling of Peterson as a "brilliant and creative mind"
was repeated by President Nixon.

In the White House and as Secretary of Commerce, which he was
named in January 1972, Peterson labored tirelessly and effectively
for an aggressive United States stance in world markets and for economic co-operation with the East European Communist bloc. As a
presidential assistant for international economic affairs he produced
reports warning that the United States was losing its competitive
edge to Europe and Japan because of government neglect of foreign
economic policy.

When the trade accord between the United States and the Soviet
Union, containing both commercial and lend-lease settlement provisions, was signed in October 1972, Peterson could properly claim
as much credit as any one negotiator. He played an equally important part in the trade pact between the United States and Poland
concluded in November 1972.

Peterson's name had been dropped in several memos concerning
the International Telephone & Telegraph Corporation and its attempts to influence White House efforts in its behalf on antitrust
matters.

"There are voluminous records showing everyone Geneen saw
—Burns, McCracken, myself, Flanigan, congressmen," Peterson
has asserted in a reference to Harold S. Geneen, chairman and president of ITT, Arthur Burns, chairman of the Federal Reserve
Board, Paul McCracken, chairman of the President's Council of
Economic Advisers, and Peter Flanigan, a presidential assistant
for international economic affairs. "I had one meeting with
Geneen at the request of the President in which we discussed many
subjects having to do with international economic policy. Antitrust
was one of those. But I didn't contact anyone at the Justice Department. They asked Merriam [William R. Merriam, head of
ITT's Washington office] under oath and he said, 'Peterson
couldn't give us a break.' I did ask Ehrlichman whether I should

do anything and the response came back, 'Nothing. We've taken care of the matter.' "

Despite his activism that impressed businessmen and government leaders, Peterson was eased out of the Cabinet late in 1972 and offered an assignment as a roving trade envoy.

Though the job held attractions for him, he said he didn't want it because his powers were vaguely defined. Also it would have meant taking up residence in Europe which he believed was not in the best interests of his five children, one of whom is retarded.

From February to May, he roamed through Europe and Japan for Nixon and issued a report entitled "The Year of Our Friends." It encompassed security, political, trade, energy, and investment issues.

"My wife calls me an overachiever," Peterson said, after pointing out that his approach "was more comprehensive" than that of his "friends" Henry Kissinger and Secretary of the Treasury George Shultz. Their strategy had interrelated economic policy with security. He had done more than that and had predicted that the energy issue "would emerge as very important."

Meanwhile, he was looking for another job. He searched the usual corridors open to high-level businessmen who have tasted the power and made the contacts of Cabinet office.

He could return to industry, if not as a chief executive then as a consultant and director of many companies. He could take the safe and Olympian (though not so lucrative) route of the nonprofit institution, heading a major foundation or university.

Or there was investment banking which, he said, listing the opportunities it offered one-two-three, had lots of diversity, moving from problem to problem, and presented a new experience and a new frontier, which he was convinced was international.

In Lehman Brothers he saw "an excellent list of clients, an excellent name abroad, and a talented group of younger people."

What did Lehman Brothers see in him? One of the partners observed, "Call it a case of ten partners in search of a chairman."

"He fell into the role like a character in a Wagnerian opera," said Andrew G. C. Sage 2d, Lehman's forty-seven-year-old vice chairman, "ombudsman," and the one partner who could have held the firm together if he weren't determined to pursue other interests such as Wyoming real estate development.

Wall Street's investment banking and law firms have always been one of the caravan stops for the Establishment's political warriors and gray eminences of both major parties.

Currently, two Treasury Secretaries of previous Democratic administrations are parked at investment banking houses: C. Douglas Dillon at Dillon, Read & Company, the support base provided by the fortune his father made in Wall Street, and Henry H. Fowler at Goldman, Sachs & Company.

George W. Ball, a peripatetic figure of distinction had been in and out of Lehman Brothers since 1966 and was due to stay for a while. Certainly it was implausible to think he might return to Washington during a Nixon administration, inasmuch as the post of Secretary of State was the only one for which his pulse could still quicken.

Ball has the rare credentials of early opposition to United States involvement in Vietnam. From 1961 on, as Undersecretary of State for Economic Affairs under President Kennedy and later as Undersecretary of State under President Johnson, he warned against sending American troops to Southeast Asia and against escalating the war there. In the spring of 1968 Johnson plucked him for the thankless role of United States ambassador to the United Nations after Arthur Goldberg resigned.

At sixty-six the tall, white-haired Ball is a man of impressive intellect and energy, a corporation lawyer who is probably one of the few Americans who could really say he had a hand in structuring the Common Market (through his work for a client, Jean Monnet, father of the European Economic Community). A lieutenant of Adlai Stevenson in his two luckless campaigns for the presidency in the 1950s, Ball is one of the Democratic party's loyal operators, behind the scenes or just off center stage as the demands are made upon him. A midwesterner in whom the fires of internationalism burn deep, Ball is used to dealing on summit levels. As with so many of the deans of the party of the common people, Ball has never disavowed the advantages of being rich.

"I needed money," he said, giving the reason he had accepted Robert Lehman's invitation to become a partner in his firm. "Investment banking gives you a chance of making and keeping money. In the practice of law, a good deal of the money goes by."

At Lehman Brothers, he had carved a niche for himself as wise man of international business, an expert on Europe, of course, but also very familiar with Iran and Japan.

"Nothing impresses the president of XYZ Corporation of Emporia, Kansas, as much as coming to New York, being wined and dined in Lehman's private dining room, sitting next to George Ball, and telling the local Rotary about it when he gets home. It's a nifty trick," a Lehman competitor said enviously.

The provocative articles Ball wrote regularly for the New York *Times* and other respected forums of print served to advertise his wisdom and his new calling. Recently he had surrendered his day-to-day responsibility for international business to John R. Petty, a forty-three-year-old partner who had joined the firm in March of 1972 after resigning from a four-year stint as Nixon's Assistant Secretary of the Treasury for International Affairs. Lehman's public relations man, David Aldrich, referred to Petty in baritone stage whispers as "the architect of the first dollar devaluation." (Aldrich also insinuated into the dialogue a whisper of kinship between himself and Winthrop W. Aldrich, late chairman of the Chase Manhattan Bank and onetime ambassador to the Court of St. James's).

With Petty responsible for the administrative work, Ball was free to roam the world for his various purposes and to be able to say on the infrequent occasions when someone found him in his New York office, "I'm leaving tomorrow for Tokyo."

Though Petty had actually tendered the initial Lehman invitation to Peterson, Ball had been one of those charged with selling the firm to him. "We had a certain common background in foreign economic policy, a shared interest," Ball said. Peterson had been a candidate for other firms as well. "Whenever a man who is not too old and has considerable distinction and ability is leaving the government, the investment banking community considers him as a recruit.

"We saw him in various roles," Ball said. "I personally wanted someone who shared my views, who saw the future the same way, someone who had international experience. Some of the others saw him as a very competent man, available for new assignments, well known, and who had many friends."

So for an indeterminate time being, Pete Peterson is Lehman's glamorous leader and the Street's newest celebrity. As he whirls on the speechmaking circuit, delivering statesmanlike assertions about the energy crisis, the Middle East, the new Japan, Soviet trade, and other global economic matters, he sheds an international glow on the Lehman image.

Despite the skepticism of some economists, politicians, and diplomats about the merits of American financing of resource and industrial development in Communist countries, investment bankers are eager to establish Soviet and Chinese connections.

If the deals are imaginatively structured (which means if American investment bankers don't put up any of the money), they will collect their fees at the outset. If the deals turn sour, the lenders (notably American commercial banks and the Export-Import Bank) and the stockholders of participating American industrial companies will be left holding the bag.

Until now there has been no publicized evidence of Peterson's salesmanship, but Lehman's competitors are admiring of his presumed edge with the East European Communist bloc. Whether from envy or from the malice for which the Street is justifiably notorious, they are also predicting Peterson's downfall.

"Peterson's been snookered like Larry O'Brien was at McDonnell," said one cynic referring to the former Postmaster General and New Frontiersman who joined the brokerage firm of McDonnell & Company only to find it was doomed to bankruptcy.

"Peterson will be devoured by the wolves in the Street," said an investment banker, envisioning inevitable attempts of Lehman's competitors to steal its corporate clients by offering more than traditional underwriting services. In 1972 and the first half of 1973 Lehman's rank among underwriters of publicly offered corporate securities slipped to sixth place from third.

Such ominous forecasts fit Wall Street's current pessimism as well as its traditional suspicion of outsiders. They also feed on the rumors which are accepted as gospel in a secretive, inbred, and heretofore inefficiently managed industry like investment banking.

Lehman has never dealt directly with the public nor with the herd of small investors. Its brokerage customers have been institutions and very wealthy individuals. Lehman Brothers could afford the luxury of privacy and ignore the falsehoods. It had long been considered one of the proudest and wealthiest of Wall Street's German Jewish banking firms.

Three brothers from Bavaria, Henry, Emanuel, and Mayer Lehman founded a commodity business in Montgomery, Alabama, in 1850. After the Civil War, Emanuel and Mayer moved their operations to New York. A second generation of Lehmans, principally Mayer's sons, Sigmund, Arthur, and Herbert, and Emanuel's son, Philip, maneuvered the firm into investment banking.

In 1928 Herbert Lehman retired to public life for the next thirty years, serving as governor of and senator from New York and Democratic elder statesman. Through the friendship of Philip Lehman with Henry Goldman, Lehman Brothers entered into many joint ventures with the rival firm of Goldman, Sachs & Company.

Under the guidance of Bernard Berenson, the art scholar, Philip Lehman also started to amass the art collection which his Yale-educated son, Robert, was to shape into one of the world's finest. Berenson's cousin, Paul Mazur, now at eighty-one a limited partner, joined the firm as an economist and financier of retail companies. Among Lehman's clients over the years have been Sears, Roebuck & Company (whose stock Lehman and Goldman, Sachs successfully sold to the public in 1906 when other bankers disdained a mail-order company), Jewel Tea Company, Macy's, and Gimbels.

In 1925 Robert Lehman took over as principal partner and led the firm into its greatest ventures and prestige. He found the financing that enabled another Yale alumnus, Juan Trippe, to enlarge his tiny, flying service into Pan American World Airways. Because of Robert Lehman's avid interest in flying—he held a pilot's license—Lehman Brothers became a major banker for the airline industry. In 1929 he joined with W. Averell Harriman to lead the sale of $40 million in securities for the Aviation Corporation (AVCO), the holding company for a number of airlines that eventually were consolidated as American Airlines.

In 1941 Lehman Brothers underwrote the first public offering for Continental Air Lines so that Robert Six, a brash young pilot, could buy three fourteen-passenger Lockheed LodeStars for his fledgling southwestern airline. Since then Lehman has raised almost $1 billion for Continental. In January of 1973 the firm raised $75 million for Pan Am (which had become a very sick carrier) with a delayed-conversion debenture. The financing was construed at the time as a turn-around for Pan Am.

Indeed, Lehman Brothers has always arranged financing for new or risky industries and companies which many old-school-tie firms wouldn't touch. In the 1920s, when motion pictures were on the verge of sound, Lehman started financing the B. F. Keith Corporation, Radio-Keith Orpheum Corporation, and later Paramount Pictures Incorporated and Twentieth Century-Fox Film Corporation.

The firm was early in the broadcasting field, with the first public underwriting of a television company, the Allen B. Du Mont Laboratories, Incorporated, in the 1930s, then in financing for the Radio Corporation of America. For many years, a Lehman partner has sat on the board of RCA with a Lazard Frères partner.

In oil exploration Lehman financed a little known company named Kerr-McGee in 1948 and stayed with it through the bad years into the energy upturn. During the last three years Lehman raised $335 million for Pennzoil's oil and gas explorations.

It was partner Joseph A. Thomas who raised the $1.5 million for Charles ("Tex") Thornton to start Litton Industries in 1953. Lehman Brothers cleared a handsome profit for itself, too, by taking shares worth less than $1 that subsequently were traded at $150.

In February 1973, Lehman arranged the sale of Litton's subsidiary, the Stouffer Corporation to Nestlé, a Swiss client of Lehman. The $105 million cash sale took advantage of international currency revaluations. Lehman was also the banker for another conglomerate that was to spring a leak in the late 1960s, Ling-Temco-Vought, Inc.

Robert Lehman, the third generation of his family to run the firm, was the first to welcome nonfamily partners. He attracted a heterogeneous cast of entrepreneurs. There were those of WASP provenance like Joseph Thomas and the late Thomas Hitchcock, Jr., a famed socialite polo player. For though Lehman was a sportsman who kept polo ponies and racing stables and was a towering patron of the arts, as a Jew he was denied entrée to some of the clubs where Wall Street and the corporate establishments transact their business in social settings.

Besides partners with such unassailable social passports, Lehman Brothers had its contingent of elegant Jewish partners like the third- and fourth-generation Lehmans and Frederick L. Ehrman, a Californian who joined in 1928. He tried to run the firm after Robert Lehman's death but found his partners aligned against him. Peterson replaced him as chairman in the summer of 1973.

There were the self-made New Yorkers like Herman H. Kahn, who came to Lehman Brothers as an office boy in 1927 and grew rich through his wits and Robert Lehman's generosity.

Kahn, who developed the concept of private placement of corporate securities during the Depression, recalled how he was rewarded with a partnership in 1950.

"Bobby Lehman was a man of enormous generosity," said Kahn, a small, dapper sixty-four-year-old. Seated behind his green leather-topped desk in the walnut-paneled partners' room, he pointed to a desk placed catercorner to the window. "The vacated symbol of authority," he said. It was Robert Lehman's desk, which Robert took after the death of Philip (whose portrait hangs over the fireplace). When Robert died, Joe Thomas inherited it. Now Thomas was sixty-seven and ill from emphysema.

"I had absolutely nothing when I came," Kahn said. "I was earning $15 a week and I went to NYU at night. I got my degree in 1932. I was twenty-three and it was the Depression and I had no business being down in Wall Street. But many companies were in need of reorganization. So I figured if I can't make money in the maternity ward I'll make it in the funeral parlor." Many financiers of Kahn's generation extracted their first fortunes from bankrupt companies as the sixties' go-getters were to do from hot, new stock issues. "I made money in reorganization and recapitalization. I worked 'round the clock and brought in enormous volume. By the mid-thirties I was a one-man new business department. The market recovered and then in '38 the market went to hell. In '41 money rates were so low that there was opportunity for a lot of refinancing of high-coupon obligations.

"I started private placement. It was once a dirty word. I remember in '39, Elisha Walker, senior partner of Kuhn, Loeb & Company, called Arthur Lehman and said, 'There is this young man in your organization doing financing privately without using the distribution mechanism.' After Walker complained, Arthur called me in and said, 'Young man you keep on doing what you've been doing, but do it quietly.'

"You see, since the Securities Act, people feared making registration statements. They feared going to jail for public offerings. But at that time, insurance companies were big investors. So there was lots to be done directly with them. Equitable Life took a whole bond issue of Cuneo Press and I placed a bond issue for Jordan Marsh with the Prudential Life Insurance Company.

"The beauty of private placement was you didn't need capital. You had no unsold securities in inventory. The issues could move expeditiously and there was no market risk. And the fees were very nice. It turned out to be very prolific for us. It was like walking down a corridor studded with diamonds and no one there to compete with you.

"Since that time everybody in Wall Street has done private placement. We've done almost $10 billion in private placement.

"I made so much money they let me use the partners' bathroom.

"Late in 1949 Bobby Lehman said to me, 'We'll make you a partner. Your interest will be one fourth of one per cent.' Maybe that was worth $50,000. Then he said, 'But I will let you have another quarter of one per cent free.'

"I was forty years old. I was making $75,000 a year. I had stock market investments. All I bought was IBM. I said to Bobby, 'I don't have cash.' He lent me money to buy my capital interest. Later on, I wanted to buy a house. I was going to sell stock to do it. He lent me the money again. And I bought my five-bedroom house in Englewood.

"He was a father and friend to all of us. This was a family business. Bobby Lehman was its spiritual head. Now the head of the family is gone."

Robert Lehman also drew big names from government to his firm, public figures like George Ball and General Lucius D. Clay, organizer of the Berlin airlift. Such outsiders are prized as door openers to the corporate and government worlds. General Clay came to Lehman Brothers in 1963 at the age of sixty-six after an interim exposure to business as head of Continental Can Company following his retirement from the military in 1950.

"Lucius Clay is one of the greatest men in this country," said the deposed Fred Ehrman. "People crowd around just to say hello to him. And in a short period of time, he understood banking.

"Bobby Lehman had entrée to innumerable important people," Ehrman, an erect, white-haired man of sixty-seven, went on. "He was an important figure in art and as head of Lehman Brothers and he could communicate with anybody in the country anytime. André Meyer still has that entrée. André is the closest figure to Bobby Lehman in Wall Street." Meyer is senior partner of Lazard Frères & Company, the investment banking firm with an unrivaled reputation for merger-making of international scope and a list of celebrity clients such as the Kennedys, the Rockefellers, and the Agnellis of Italy.

At the age of seventy-five Meyer is doing exactly as Robert Lehman did—letting everyone guess who will take over when he dies.

Ehrman said he hoped that Peter Peterson would have some of the qualities of entrée that General Clay possessed. Ehrman had negotiated along with Petty and Ball in bringing Peterson into the firm. Now, less than a year later, Ehrman was preparing to leave it.

"I believed we should have someone who was young and aggressive and known in the industrial world to give us a presence which we were losing with all of us getting older. We'd been relatively successful in taking people from the outside," he said. For many of the old-line Wall Street investment banking firms, drawing from the outside was anathema. The ingrown, old-boy network reigned supreme. When the First Boston Corporation, the quintessence of clubby tradition, had taken Ralph S. Saul, former head of the American Stock Exchange, to its starchy bosom in 1971, everyone knew that the old era was gone forever.

"If you don't have people who are known throughout the country—known favorably—you can have all the hidden ability in the world and you don't have the same thing," Ehrman said. "Investment banking is a business of people. You're competing with other people. The Andrés and the Levys." He was referring to André Meyer of Lazard Frères and Gustave Levy, the managing partner of Goldman, Sachs, a Republican party fund raiser, a director of nearly two dozen corporations, and a corporate matchmaker.

In his time, Robert Lehman ruled the firm as a prince, in his personal lifestyle and in his Machiavellian management technique.

"No matter what, it always wound up that there was only one way to go. It was not the discussion, but what Bobby Lehman wanted to do," Ehrman said. "He was a very generous man but he ran this thing as his own firm."

Said Herman Kahn mournfully, "He had a canine personality. He was immediately responsive to people. Sure, we had disagreements. But I never saw a quarrel. We're all gentlemen, after all. We've all been wrong and stand to be corrected. This place was like a home."

Others describe Lehman Brothers as a collection of prima donnas kept in line by Robert Lehman. "He was a master of the pat and slap technique," Andy Sage said. "But he was lavish in his attention if he had been pleased."

Some remember how he pitted one partner or clique against another. When F. Warren Hellman, Ehrman's nephew and now, at thirty-nine, president of Lehman Brothers, protested that he thought Herman Kahn's son Sidney was being promoted to partner too soon, Robert Lehman told him his hands were tied and he asked

Hellman to keep the conversation a secret between them. Shortly thereafter, the senior Kahn called Hellman and said, "I understand you younger guys don't want Sidney, but we'll make it up to you."

It all worked just fine as long as Robert Lehman was providing the discipline and leadership. His quiet authoritarianism was exercised from what one partner called "his dinky little office" on the third floor. It was nine feet wide by fifteen feet long, with a Kees van Dongen painting of a racing scene over his desk. Since his death, it has been used as a conference room.

"His death left a real void at the top," said James W. Glanville, who had been a petroleum engineer with Humble Oil in Houston when Robert Lehman invited him to join the firm in 1959 to fortify its expertise in oil. "Many of my own clients are not prepared to face up to the ultimate problem of succession and Bobby Lehman wasn't either," the fifty-year-old Glanville said.

Ailing for the last four years of his life and unable or unwilling to grasp matters of consequence, Robert Lehman died in 1969 at the age of seventy-seven. With the succession up in the air, the prima donnas lunged for each others' throats and some moved to fill the vacuum that business, like nature, abhors.

The firm had changed during the last decade as it rushed to keep step with the unbridled growth of Wall Street in those mad years of the 1960s. The number of partners had doubled, its employee force multiplied by six. As with so many firms, size was commensurate with chaos. Lehman Brothers had its back-room mess, one of the worst in Wall Street, with clerical operations snarled, securities mislaid, and losses incurred.

Lehman Brothers pushed its way to the head of the line in the underwriting business. Raising money from the public through new issues of corporate stock or bonds is the standard function of investment banking. In the mid-sixties Lehman was second only to the First Boston Corporation as an underwriter of corporate securities.

Before 1960 the underwriting business was locked up by syndicates headed by the First Boston Corporation; Morgan Stanley; Kuhn, Loeb; Kidder, Peabody; and Dillon, Read. Then at the turn of the decade, a group of firms that came to be called "The Fearsome Foursome"—Lehman Brothers; Merrill Lynch, Pierce, Fenner & Smith; Blyth Eastman Dillon & Company; and Salomon Brothers—banded together to form their own syndicate and bid against the Establishment.

Out of the new ball game, Merrill Lynch and Salomon Brothers emerged as superpowers. Lehman increased its stature but it almost lost control of itself in the process.

Underwriting an issue isn't a one-way street to profit. It carries the risk of not being able to market the entire issue. The underwriter who is left with an inventory of securities may have to liquidate them at a loss. For this reason, the investment banker tries to build an extensive distribution network of other firms.

Lehman had never been a big retail broker, doing business with the public. Its following consisted of rich investors and some institutions, such as mutual funds and pension funds. Merrill Lynch, on the other hand, was broker to the mass market of small investors. It could easily dispose of an issue through its own retail offices and it also used the purchasing power of its customer masses to poach on the underwriting preserves of the firms that were once exclusively investment bankers. Merrill Lynch went around saying in effect to corporations, "We own 20 per cent of your stock through our clients and we'd like to be your investment banker. If you let us underwrite your next issue, we can distribute it broadly across the country."

So Lehman Brothers felt forced to build up its own distribution capability to ward off the Merrill Lynch threat. Besides relying on regional firms to distribute issues for them, Lehman opened its own offices in the South, Midwest, and West.

To maintain a position in the brutally competitive but increasingly significant segment of institutional business Lehman also went into block trading, an area pre-empted by Salomon Brothers. Lehman handled such single transactions as the sale of 5.5 million shares of American Motors Corporation and a $72.5-million trade of 206,000 shares of IBM.

Here again the risk is great because the block may not be successfully distributed. Block trading also requires substantial capital and operating overhead.

In 1963 Lewis L. Glucksman left A. G. Becker & Company, one of the leading commercial-paper houses, to put Lehman Brothers into this aging virgin territory of corporate finance.

Because of the insatiable appetite that corporations had for additional sources of capital in the expansionary sixties and because of the innovative skills of men like Glucksman, commercial paper became a new boom field. The pioneers created the two-way market in

short-term corporate notes. Previously these notes had been issued
for periods of ninety days or less and held. Now they are bought and
sold like government securities. Glucksman brought Lehman into
third place behind Goldman, Sachs and A. G. Becker.

The commercial-paper department is one of Lehman's most
profitable, with an annual turnover of $25 billion. It has managed to
avoid peddling lemons like Penn Central's commercial paper as
Goldman, Sachs did.

Apart from its profitability, commercial paper served to bind corporate clients more tightly to Lehman Brothers because the firm
could offer to get them money at a lesser cost by issuance of the
notes than the companies would have to pay through bank loans. A
contented client can be receptive to other services offered by such a
firm, for example, the arrangement of a merger or acquisition out of
which the investment banker gets a husky fee.

His phenomenal success with commercial paper and with deal
making gave the forty-seven-year-old Glucksman his clout and his
cockiness. Referring to the Litton-Nestlé deal, "I did it as a sideline
away from this shmeer," Glucksman said. "Making money in departments is the scorecard," he accurately observed.

Glucksman was named executive managing director of Lehman
Brothers in the spring of 1973. A graduate of DeWitt Clinton High
School, one of New York City's public schools, the College of William and Mary, and the New York University Graduate School of
Business Administration, Glucksman is cited as an example of the
"meritocracy of the sixties," when clever newcomers lacking connections or lineage were able to muscle their way into the power
structure of some of the older Wall Street firms with their brains and
money-making abilities.

A stockily built, round-faced, cigar smoker, Glucksman makes
sarcastic remarks about Harvard Business School degrees and ath-
letic trophies, which are interpreted as references to Warren Hellman and his patrician breed. The intensity of his competition with
Hellman and his dislike for Hellman's uncle Fred Ehrman provide
Wall Street with some of its choicest morsels of gossip.

On the wall of Glucksman's office hangs a framed quotation from
Alfred Lord Tennyson's *Ulysses*. It had a certain poignant application in Lehman's time of troubles:

Tho' much is taken, much abides: and tho'
We are not now that strength which in old days

Moved earth and heaven; that which we are, we are;
One equal temper of heroic hearts,
Made weak by time and fate, but strong in will
To strive, to seek, to find, and not to yield.

Glucksman said he had named his pleasure boat *Ulysses.*

In 1972 Glucksman had the firm set sail into the tempestuous seas of government securities. Others had ventured there and been forced to abandon ship.

The disaster for Lehman Brothers in government securities with the multimillion dollar losses sustained in the summer of 1973 has not visibly shaken Glucksman's confidence nor weakened his opposition to Ehrman, who had always been negative toward the firm's expansion beyond its traditional banking services.

"Without being vain about it, I'm expert in money. I'm as good at understanding money instruments as anybody in the country," Glucksman said, sketching what he saw to be his role in the firm. "I see us as purveyors of money to industries and governments."

He denied that Lehman would close its government securities operation as Wall Street believed would be the case following the publication of an anonymous advertisement in a banking journal offering to sell such a business. Inquisitive sources said it had been placed by Lehman. "It's another arm in our involvement in the money market," Glucksman said.

At the time of Robert Lehman's death, the ominous shape of the seventies, with recession, inflation, Watergate, and the "Grim Reaper" mood of Wall Street could not be divined. Glucksman rode high until the government securities mishap.

One of Robert Lehman's idiosyncrasies had been that he preferred not to have the nominal title of leader though, in fact, he was the most powerful member of the firm. He set up an executive committee with a rotating chairmanship held first by General Clay, then by Joe Thomas. "Bobby wasn't on the committee so there might as well not have been one," Andy Sage said.

Sage had joined the firm in 1948 at the age of twenty-two, having trained for a couple of years with his father, a specialist on the New York Stock Exchange. He was made a partner at thirty-three and, before Robert Lehman's death, managing partner, with Joe Thomas remaining as chairman of a somewhat reduced executive committee.

"This was Bobby's impression of succession. He didn't really plan. Maybe he preferred not to legislate posthumously," Sage said.

"Then he got sick, and after he died, Joe Thomas resigned as chairman. He had his emphysema and he went back to his deals. Everyone here has a disinterest in administration because it's a professional firm."

Fred Ehrman succeeded Thomas as chairman.

Robert Lehman had purposely reduced his interest in the firm to 12.5 per cent of the capital and 8.5 per cent of the partnership profits by selling and giving pieces to younger partners and newcomers. At his death, his interests were immediately liquidated. His only son, Robert Owen Lehman, offspring of the second of his three marriages, had no inclination toward Wall Street.

The Lehman Brothers firm was incorporated in October 1970 to preserve the partners' capital and limit their liability. The more hazardous underwriting and securities businesses went under the corporate umbrella while the less risky investment management and merger services remained in a partnership.

For example, such mergers as that of Helena Rubinstein, Incorporated, with Colgate-Palmolive Company and the acquisition of the Black & Decker Manufacturing Company by McCulloch Corporation which Lehman Brothers arranged in 1973, represented investments of time rather than capital. The income earned from such deals was earmarked for the partnership, which showed a profit in fiscal 1973.

The partnership also manages two large investment companies, The Lehman Corporation (organized in 1929 and one of the early "closed-end" investment funds) and One William Street, a mutual fund started in 1958. The latter's record of performance has been as woeful as that of any mutual fund and the quality of research and investment advice offered to the fund and other institutional clients of Lehman Brothers has brought no luster to the firm. "We've done terribly in investment research and money management," Jim Glanville said. "It started out as a few guys with green eyeshades watching Bobby Lehman's securities and that's not a very good background. We will do much better and clearly can do better in the future."

A third unit, also not incorporated, is Lehman Ventures—as its name suggests, a venture capital vehicle for the partners.

At the incorporation, Andy Sage became president and Fred Ehrman the chairman of Lehman Brothers. Though he was respected in the Street and by clients, Ehrman incurred the nearly unanimous resentment of his otherwise disunited partners. His contemporaries refused to follow his directives. The juniors chafed under his caution, which they considered nickel-and-dime shortsightedness. Among the younger partners who left the firm were Joe Thomas' son, Michael, Robert Lehman's cousin Robert Bernhard (who went to Abraham & Company and from there to Salomon Brothers), and Stephen M. DuBrul, Jr., a banker of promise who crossed over to Lazard Frères.

A man of enormous reserve, disinclined to exhibitions of personal warmth, Ehrman seemed mean-spirited at times even to those whose causes he backed. When his nephew Warren Hellman came to his office to report he had wrapped up a deal that would net the firm a $2.5 million fee, he nodded and changed the subject. Meeting others with whom he had less consanguineous bonds but with whom he had just worked on a deal, he pretended not to recognize them when they rode in the same elevator.

A measure of his insensitivity or perhaps of the moat he had dug around himself (and, some say, wanted to have around the firm) was his unawareness of the animosity accumulating against him. Partners were meeting in each others' offices. "Something must be done," they were saying to each other.

"When we were making money," one of them said, "there was a tendency to let things slide and say, 'Oh, well, he'll retire one of these years.' But when you're flat on your back, you have to do something."

In April of 1973 the firm was reorganized because Andy Sage was going off to do what he always said he wanted to do—run a land development company he had set up in the West.

Sage does not enjoy exercising his considerable administrative and conciliatory talents. He prefers "putting deals together, trouble shooting, or being helpful to people." So in April Sage resigned as president and took the "totally honorary designation" of vice chairman. Hellman became president and Glucksman succeeded Hellman as executive managing director.

"This firm lacked the imaginative leadership of a Robert Lehman to get us pulling together," Glucksman said in retrospect.

"I'm a fantastic leader," he said. "I'm the leader of one of the most specialized businesses in the country and that's very tough. More than a full time job." Glucksman conceded after prodding that he thought he "could have been a great leader" of the firm. He delivered this assessment of Hellman: "While the balance of power comes out of the presence of his uncle here, Warren Hellman has grown enormously and in my own feeling has done an incredible job since Peterson became chairman and since Ehrman left this firm." His gray eyes took on the chill of the Gulf of Finland as he uttered Ehrman's name, ignoring the fact that the former chairman was still physically present in his office at 1 William Street, tidying up his affairs as he took his money out of the firm.

Hellman, on the other hand, analyzed Glucksman as someone who needs "stroking, and Fred Ehrman couldn't give him any."

Hellman professed not to understand the reasons for Glucksman's feelings toward him, a measure, perhaps of the chasm in background and expectations that separates them.

No slouch as a warrior in the Wall Street jungle, Hellman was once described in an article titled "Warren Hellman's Race Against Himself" as one who "competes in business and in sports as if he were fighting his way up from the streets." (Some of those who have competed against Glucksman say "he knows how to play stickball.")

Hellman started out with a superabundance of the assets Glucksman had to struggle to acquire. His great-grandfather I. W. Hellman went West, became an investment banker and real estate investor, and bought his way into Wells Fargo. I.W.'s grandson, Warren Hellman's father, acquired a major interest in J. Barth, a West Coast brokerage firm that later merged with Dean Witter. I. W. Hellman's wife's sister had married Mayer Lehman and Wells Fargo maintained a relationship with Lehman Brothers. But Warren Hellman said, "that's not why I'm here." It was his kinship to Ehrman, on his paternal side, though, that was held against him by some members of the firm.

Hellman is a distressing competitor for self-made men to come up against. He has old, distinguished money and family connections, but he also has New Wave professional management training and that compulsion to be Number One that goes with a degree from the Harvard Business School (his M.B.A. is of 1959 minting, the year he came to Lehman Brothers at the age of twenty-five).

With his direct, blue-eyed gaze and trimly cut, side-parted brown hair, Hellman has the hungry-looking fitness that seems to accrue from generations of not worrying about food or rent. His sports—fixations, perhaps—are racing, skiing, and rock climbing.

Hellman's standards, whether in sports or business, begin at alpine level and he plays very hard to win. But in the ultimate crunch he has other alternatives to being Number One at Lehman Brothers. He can always be a ski schoolmaster in Vermont. Or so he says.

Hellman had definitely been his uncle's candidate to head the firm. Ehrman said it wasn't because he was his nephew but because he was the best qualified. And Hellman had many deals to his credit, such as the $113-million underwriting of the Chase Manhattan Mortgage and Realty Trust, which was successfully sold in June of 1970, a time of adverse market conditions, yielding a fee of close to $2 million to the firm. He was an effective leader of younger hustlers within the Lehman organization and a credible representative of the firm to the world outside.

But Hellman recognized his limitations. "It would have been totally improper for me to be chairman after Fred retired," he said. "I'm too young. I'm hardly a household word in American industry. I think I'm competent to be president but I prefer to spend several years under someone with more status. I've got time to get there."

Peterson arrived in June 1973 and took the title of vice chairman with the understanding he would probably become chairman in a year or so. "I was aware that management was not in perfect shape," he said. "There was an age gap. A generation gap between the older partners and a number of outstanding people between the ages of twenty-five and forty. I discussed these things openly."

Jim Glanville recalls Peterson saying to him when they met, "I understand you weren't too pleased." Glanville says he was "categorically opposed" to Peterson as the intended leader of the firm.

"I thought we needed to heal ourselves, to cleanse ourselves before we brought in a White Knight." Glanville didn't indicate whether he was sarcastically using the term in its proper literary reference to a bumbler or whether he really meant a knight in shining armor. In either case, Glanville didn't see himself in a position of over-all responsibility. "I would have done the job very poorly," he said.

Peterson said that "it was important to me that Warren Hellman and Lew Glucksman be enthused about my coming. But I didn't think I'd be chairman so soon."

The financial woes at Lehman multiplied. "Red ink shortened tempers," Sage said. The cabals regrouped.

"It was like sand dropping in an hourglass," Hellman said of his uncle's final downfall. "Suddenly, there was none at the top. It had all fallen down."

Only one member of the board, Paul L. Davies, had reservations about pushing Ehrman aside. The seventy-four-year-old Davies was one of the name-brand outsiders who had come to Lehman Brothers in 1966 after a long career as an industrialist. He had retired as a chairman of FMC Corporation.

Davies went into retirement with Ehrman and General Clay.

"We need a unifying force," Glanville said, expressing the sentiments of the board. Sage, with whom all felt comfortable pouring out their hearts, was unwilling to be "nursemaid to fifty prima donnas. . . . I couldn't be drafted," he said.

There was Peterson, a leader of men (Lehman has no female partners) and the only possible relief pitcher.

"He's the sort of guy you'd go to the wall for," Glucksman said.

"He's unbelievably hard-working. And you can't make him angry," Hellman said.

"He has come on the side of the angels. He's worked hard," Glanville had decided.

"He's the quickest way to bring political stability to the firm, to keep those characters at their knitting, rebuilding the momentum," Sage believed.

So one month after his arrival, Peterson was elected chairman, as of August 1, 1973.

The suddenness and vehemence of his partners' decision to oust him surprised Ehrman, but he accepted it with dignity and grace. "One of the things that's all important," he said the following November, "was that everyone should be happy with what he's doing and with his associates. Or to hell with it. Lehman Brothers was a way of life. I can see it one way and they saw it another. And you'll probably never know who's right."

Ehrman believed to the end that the real dispute was about the scope of the firm's activities—whether it should stick to its basic business of underwriting and mergers, as he said he contended—or branch further afield. He never saw his personality as a factor—or at least, he never indicated that he did. [He died unexpectedly, of a heart attack in December 1973.]

One of the rumors circulating in Wall Street has Lehman in a capital hemorrhage because Ehrman is withdrawing his major share. "If a guy doesn't run something, he shouldn't be party to the decisions," he said, conceding some "disenchantment" on his part.

But neither his departure nor that of Paul Davies or General Clay could cause a capital crisis because none of the fifty-one partners has more than a 6 per cent share of the firm's capital.

Unlike many firms dominated by one man or one family, Lehman Brothers has had a diffused ownership, which is likely to be maintained. A Peterson-initiated incentive compensation plan should reward younger, aggressive partners and give them the means to buy additional capital shares as they become available. A mandatory retirement age with withdrawal of capital is also in the planning stage.

If losses had continued in the magnitude of the summer Lehman would have been in serious trouble by March of 1974. But it went into the black in September of 1973 and was removed from the New York Stock Exchange's early warning list. Its capital-debt ratio is about five to one, safely below the Exchange's fifteen-to-one maximum. According to filings with the Securities and Exchange Commission, the firm has a total capital of $35 million. To be sure, this is far less than the $464-million net worth of Merrill Lynch, Pierce, Fenner & Smith. Salomon Brothers, a giant of block trading, the game Lehman tried and learned it couldn't play very well, has $131.7 million-capital.

Lehman has sufficient capital for its current needs and stated future objectives of being an international investment banker performing its traditional function of underwriting and privately placing corporate securities, arranging mergers and acquisitions, as well as offering new special services in equipment leasing and real estate development. All of these bring in fees in the millions of dollars but do not necessarily require large capital. Both the retail brokerage business because of its high overhead and block trading, which obliges the firm to hold positions in securities, are heavy consumers of capital.

Net worth can be a misleading indicator. Consider Lazard Frères, a powerful international firm with a stated capital of $17 million. However, Lazard can tap untold capital from the personal resources of its chieftain, André Meyer, as Loeb, Rhoades & Company could when John Loeb's daughter was married to Edgar Bronfman of the Distillers Corporation-Seagram's whisky empire and as Lehman Brothers could when Robert Lehman was alive.

"This is not a firm of wealthy people who could put up ten to fifteen million dollars apiece," said Hellman. A half a million to a million, perhaps, "but if we did a major deal, we do have access to tremendous amounts of capital from clients and institutions."

Contrary to another rumor, Lehman Brothers is not about to sell its eleven-story triangular edifice at 1 William Street (it is the last banking firm still in its own home) nor close the partners' gymnasium on the top floor.

Nor have standards been compromised much in the partners' dining rooms on the eighth floor, critically acclaimed as Wall Street's culinary best. The chef, who was an alumnus of Le Pavillon, that vanished shrine of French cuisine on Manhattan Island, retired three years ago. The incumbent served as a *sous-chef* at La Seine, one of the newer snob eateries. Lobster has disappeared from the menus because of its prohibitive price but French turbot and *escalopine de veau au citron* are regular fare. A staff of eleven waiters has been reduced to eight to serve an average of fifty lunches a day. The partners lunch together in their dining room around a Sheraton mahogany table that seats thirty-two or with guests in one of the four private dining rooms that are just cosy enough for deal making. Although bowls of fresh fruit have replaced fresh flowers on the table and lacquered place mats were substituted for linen tablecloths after a society decorator, Mrs. Henry ("Sister") Parish 2nd, redid the rooms two years ago, "We will never go to paper napkins, though," vowed William Proops, Lehman's director of food services. He is a graduate of a Swiss hotel school, and when he isn't running the dining rooms at 1 William Street, he does a little private catering for the partners uptown.

The loudest buzzing about Lehman Brothers in the Street has had the firm wasting away and cutting back. The number of employees has diminished by about 25 per cent to 955. The reductions have been mostly in the sales force, the government securities division, and other administrative categories. "They cut too much from the bottom and not enough from the top," Glanville said, bemoaning the slowness of the elevator service. Peterson has been busy recruiting "top management people from the industrial world" to work in New York and in Lehman's new Tokyo office.

One of Peterson's first acts was the appointment of task forces for each segment of the business. He listed his priorities as "defining who we are, where we want to be excellent, doing a few things excellently."

Lehman wasn't the only firm trying to reposition itself for a new era. Wall Street was undergoing the most radical change it had experienced since the 1930s. Among the irrevocable factors to be contended with: the abolition of fixed charges for brokerage transactions by the SEC which had mandated fully negotiated commission rates by 1975; the disappearance of the small investor from the market and the dominance of the large institutional customer; the intrusion of commercial banks in the investment advisory and investment banking functions. The old investment banking firm that hoped to survive in an arena with fewer and more savage gladiators would have to perfect its special skills.

"The more competitive the business gets, the higher the premium on excellence," Peterson said. "I'm putting so much emphasis on international because it's the trend of the future and we have the expertise of Ball, Petty, and myself."

He also asserted—as everyone has been saying since the air began leaking out of the Wall Street balloon in 1970—that professional management techniques must be applied to investment banking.

One of the changes borrowed from industry is the shifting of Lehman's compensation plan to performance-weighting and away from the traditional reflection of a partner's capital position in the firm. The salaries of top officers have been cut and an incentive program established to receive a significant part of the corporation's profits. From now on, younger partners who perform better may be drawing down more compensation than senior members, an overturning of Wall Street tradition which held that money begat power, which begat more money.

Cost-accounting procedures have been introduced. "What is our market? What is our share? What are our costs?" Peterson asked. "We already have made a study of our brokerage operation to find out how our costs compare with our competitors'. Another useful concept from industry is profitability accounting. Where are we losing money, making money? Wall Street does less cost accounting than it can do." Part of his job at Lehman Brothers, he indicated, is to see that it does more.

Wall Street's sidewalk superintendents continue to see Peterson's tasks as twofold: using his prestige, while it is still fresh, to lure big new business and to find new capital. Obtaining these would not only insure the firm's future but his own within the firm.

"If he can say, 'I am the financial adviser to the Politburo and they did two billion rubles of financing through us,' he can offset anything Hellman and Glucksman have to say," one investment banker said, delineating the plot. "And he can go out through his wealthy friends and bring in $20 million capital. But whatever he does, he has to do it fast or his image will be worn off."

What if Peterson should be summoned elsewhere—possibly through further unraveling on the Washington scene? Then the scenario will have to be rewritten, and Lehman Brothers will call for a play doctor.

Early in 1975

During 1974 Peter G. Peterson's good friend Henry Kissinger rose in influence as Secretary of State and his old enemies Haldeman and Ehrlichman were driven out of the White House and into the courtroom as Watergate culprits. A new flurry of rumors had the chairman of Lehman Brothers going back to Washington. The Petersons were reportedly seen househunting there. But Gerald R. Ford assumed the presidency, and as the new year of 1975 was rung in in a mood of economic despair, Peterson remained in Wall Street.

The gloom was thicker around the concrete canyons than at any time since the 1930s. Brokerage firms and investment banking firms disappeared through mergers and liquidations. Customers' men and security analysts moved as Bedouins from one firm to another or out of the business entirely. Though his tragic action was said to be unrelated to his work, one analyst dramatized the similarity to the Wall Street of the Great Depression by jumping to his death from his office window.

On January 3, 1975, President Ford signed the Trade Reform Act that was at last to give effect to the Soviet-American agreement of October 1972 that Peterson had helped design. But the issue of free emigration for Soviet Jews and other dissidents that Congress knitted into the law especially by imposing a $300 million ceiling on Eximbank credits caused the Russians to denounce the legislation. East-West trade went into the freezer.

Meanwhile, the scramble was on for Arab contacts as the oil-producing nations of the Middle East bubbled up billions of petrodollars that had to be invested somehow, somewhere.

Peterson and Ball were shuttling in and out of Teheran, Riyadh,

Beirut, and other petro capitals where they were bumping into their Wall Street competitors. Lehman Brothers was planning to open an office in Cairo.

The collapse of the Eurodollar market altered the European business scene after Peterson promulgated the international direction for the firm. United States dollars that had been hiding in Europe in the form of Eurodollars dried up as a source of capital. Financing had to be brought back to the United States or taken elsewhere, namely, to the Middle East.

Peterson and Ball had brought in some business to make good Lehman's international intentions. The firm was acting as an adviser to the national oil companies of Algeria and Indonesia and trying to help their governments with public financing. Lehman also was the intermediary in a proposed rescue of Pan Am by the government of Iran. The Iranians took an option to buy 13 per cent of the airline's stock, a controlling interest in its hotel chain, and were bargaining over making $245 million in direct loans to the carrier.

Peterson's Polish contacts from his government service had paid off in a deal whereby Lehman assembled a group of sixteen international banks to extend a $35-million credit line to Poland's foreign trade bank. Half a dozen other deals were pending in Eastern Europe.

In May of 1974 William Blackie, former chairman of the Caterpillar Tractor Company, joined the firm. He was seen as contributing, not only capital but valuable Far East contacts. Caterpillar had links with Mitsubishi, the Japanese trading entity.

On the domestic side, retrenching and remodeling went on at Lehman. The firm largely phased itself out as a dealer in government securities in 1974 and confined its operations to federal agency instruments and those guaranteed by the National Mortgage Administration. "Those have been just dandy," Peterson said. The firm withdrew from competitive bidding to underwrite public utility issues and corporate bonds. No longer a stalwart of the Fearsome Foursome, Lehman announced it would only bid for issues of its own investment banking clients. Its back offices were merged with those of Wertheim & Company in a new unit called Lewco Securities Corporation.

Peterson announced that Lehman had been in the black throughout 1974 and that January of 1975 had been the most profitable month in its history.

In September 1974 Lehman received a capital transfusion when two European banks invested $7 million in the firm. Banque Française et Italienne pour L'Amérique du Sud of Paris and Banca della Svizzera Italiana of Lugano acquired 7.5 per cent of the common stock of the Lehman Holding Company, Inc., a corporation formed to hold shares in Lehman Brothers.

The day after Christmas 1974 the banns were posted for the marriage of Lehman Brothers with Abraham & Company, a brokerage firm that had never accrued a loss in its sixty-year history. By this merger Lehman would gain a successful retail and institutional brokerage business as well as another $5 million capital; Abraham would win access to the investment banking business it had coveted and a 15 per cent profit participation in the consolidated firm which was to go by the name of Lehman Brothers.

Peterson had his fingers in every corner of the wedding pie as it was being baked. On Christmas Day he had been on the telephone to the reporters on the lonely holiday shifts at the *Wall Street Journal* and the New York *Times* telling them how to write the story and to be sure to include all of the names of the new top management.

Peter G. Peterson would continue as chairman of Lehman Brothers. Alexander Abraham, son of the founder of Abraham & Company would be vice chairman, George H. Heyman, Jr., Abraham's president, chairman of Lehman's investment committee, and F. Warren Hellman would be president of the merged firms.

The second week in January 1975 four men in their late twenties and late thirties were made Lehman partners. The firm's roster totaled fifty partners and 717 employees. A leaner army stood behind the White Knight on the battlefield.

PULLMAN'S JOURNEY TO THE EAST

Summer 1973

Since czarist days the Russian phrase for "sleeping car" has been *pullmanovskye spalnye vagony*. The Soviet Embassy in Washington is housed in the late George M. Pullman's mansion. Not entirely by coincidence, perhaps, Pullman, Inc., was one of the first two American industrial corporations accredited to do business in Moscow. That was in July 1972, just before the dawn of what was supposed to be a new era in Soviet-American trade.

In July 1973 Pullman's M. W. Kellogg division nailed down an assignment to design and construct three ammonia plants in the People's Republic of China, the first complete process plants awarded to an American company. But no one suspects that sentimental memories of Pullman sleeping cars had anything to do with that contract. Besides, Pullman has not made a sleeping car since 1956, and in recent years, the name hasn't exerted the generic magic of other corporate labels, such as Coca-Cola and Xerox, at least as far as Wall Street is concerned.

It was regarded as a widows'-and-orphans' stock, which had paid uninterrupted dividends for more than a century but was otherwise a "cyclical dog." (In 1970 the quarterly dividend was cut from 70 to 50 cents.) But suddenly, in the summer of 1973, Pullman the wallflower became the security analysts' darling. Its stock hit new highs. Mutual funds and banks started buying Pullman. Alas, the "little old lady from Dubuque," once its typical shareholder, had long ago sold her stock on the advice of her investment counselor.

Why did Pullman, in its 106th year, become glamorous? Because of record sales and earnings in the first half of the year—revenues of $458 million and net income of $17 million—the highest in its conservatively erratic history? Or its billion-dollar backlog of orders? Or the penchant of its forty-five-year-old president, Samuel Brown Casey, Jr., for describing Pullman as a growth company?

Casey also liked to repeat a Pullman officer's remark when he moved from the board room into the presidency in 1970: "Now Pullman has traded in her high-button shoes for a shillelagh."

"Pullman is psychologically right," said Gerard E. Manolovici, an analyst of special situations at Bear, Stearns & Company. "There's a good chance we'll have a whipcracking recession," he added, "but it won't affect Pullman's construction business."

Manolovici considered as "secondary reasons" the upswing in the railroad freight-car spending cycle and the potential business with the Soviet Union and China. In 1971 Pullman's Swindell-Dressler division signed a contract with the Soviet Union to build a $10-million foundry for the Kama River project which the Russians hope will be the world's largest truck plant and eighteen months later the Chinese deal was announced.

"It's a kicker," Manolovici said of the orders from the new Communist customers. "This economy is a mess, but it's going to have more gasoline capacity, so the real reason Pullman will do so well is that Kellogg will be building oil refineries." Kellogg was angling for contracts with petroleum companies to construct refining facilities both in the United States and overseas.

What Manolovici was saying in Wall Street argot was, "Don't think of Pullman as a transportation company because that category of stocks has been depressed. Think of it as a construction company in a position to benefit from the current energy situation. Energy stocks have performed outstandingly."

Stocks move up on expectations more than on current reality. By Manolovici's reckoning, Pullman was good for an energy "play."

Henry Livingston, a vice president and transportation analyst for Clark, Dodge & Company, Inc., was more upbeat in his enthusiasm for Pullman. "Now Pullman's story makes sense. Per share, they are responsive to crisis."

Indeed, it does seem as though Pullman is thriving on the problems of others.

For example, there's the world-wide grain shortage. The Pullman-Standard division, the world's largest railroad freight-car manufacturer, had been just crawling along since 1968. In mid-1973 it is swinging toward full capacity with orders for its new family of covered hopper cars, especially suited for transporting grain. Meanwhile, the Pullman Transport Leasing Company, the most profitable division, has been leasing the hoppers on long-term rentals to big grain shippers.

There's the energy crisis. M. W. Kellogg, a New Jersey company acquired in 1944 and one of the two engineering and construction divisions that have had mediocre earnings in recent years, can build those refineries Manolovici alluded to, if and when the oil companies decide to go ahead. Kellogg also has the technology for making gasoline out of coal which is attracting attention from those who view Old King Coal as a possible source of clean energy. Coal can be hauled on Pullman's open-top hoppers. Furthermore, Pullman has been mining coal from the Aloe Coal Mine in Pennsylvania that it acquired in 1970.

Then there's the environmental crisis. Kellogg has developed a catalytic cracking process to produce nonpolluting fuels from sulfur-contaminated feedstocks as well as other engineering expertise to help industrial companies meet new ecological requirements.

The urban mass-transit crisis, which could also be chalked up under the environmental crisis, offers the potential for "a real growth industry," Henry Livingston believes. A $210-million order for 745 subway cars from New York City's Transit Authority, as well as commuter-car business from the state of New Jersey, may have saved the Pullman Car Works on the South Side of Chicago. It could also help to steady the boom-or-bust cycle of Pullman-Standard's traditional dependency on the railroads.

As for the dollar crisis, Casey said the two devaluations of the dollar in 1971 and 1973 had enabled Pullman to compete successfully against Japanese consortia for the Soviet and Chinese contracts and should bolster its bargaining power in other international markets.

The economic controls in the United States caused much corporate breast beating. Many businessmen complained bitterly about them, but not the laissez-faireists at Pullman.

Most of its business is custom order—building specialized products such as chemical plants and railroad cars—and thus is exempt from price control. The one division that had to apply to the Cost of Living Council for a price increase was Trailmobile, the nation's second largest manufacturer of truck trailers and containers after Fruehauf Corporation. Trailmobile, a beneficiary of the trucking boom in the United States, makes a standardized product.

Its international units, such as Trailor, the French company that is its battering ram into the Common Market, are also immune.

Call it crisis, call it cycle, it appears as though the railroaders in Pullman's Chicago headquarters are justified in saying, "All the wheels are meshed and going."

It's been a long time since they could make that jubilant claim. The last feast year was 1966, when Pullman earned $5.72 per share mostly because the nation's railroads were on a freight-car buying spree, stimulated largely by the imminent suspension of the investment tax credit.

Two years later, the freight-car famine was on, and although the engineering and construction businesses were thriving, over-all revenues were slimmer, and earnings were nearly halved. Even in the turn-around year of 1972, when diversification efforts were hitting their stride, railroad cars represented 22 per cent of Pullman revenues, and their contribution to profits, a closely guarded secret, was minimal.

Until Sam Casey assumed the presidency late in the dismal year of 1970, Pullman had been a railroad-oriented company. It was founded on the strength of one man's vision. The Pullman Palace Car Company was incorporated in 1867 with forty-eight of its luxury sleeping wagons in operation on three railroad lines. They had been equipped to carry passengers on overnight journeys in the style to which they were accustomed when they stayed in grand hotels or their own homes.

George Mortimer Pullman was a cabinetmaker from Albion, New York, who had branched into the contracting business, moving buildings back from the edge of the Erie Canal.

In the early 1850s, obliged to travel by night on a train from Westfield to Buffalo, he bounced on a hard, springless bunk in a drafty, wooden railway car. In his sleepless misery, the dream of comfortable travel was born. Pullman nurtured it into the reality of an enterprise and an industry.

In 1857 Pullman was in the contracting business in the mid-continent boom town of Chicago. He hired a mechanic to help him reconstruct two railroad coaches. Using hand tools and wood, the two men outfitted them with plush-upholstered seats, washstands, oil lamps, and box stoves for heat. Suspended from the ceilings by ropes and pulleys were the "upper berths" for sleeping.

The first of the remodeled day coaches was christened "Old Number 9" and made its maiden journey on the Chicago and Alton Railroad from Chicago to Bloomington, Illinois, carrying George M. Pullman and ten passengers whose misgivings were allayed and boots removed by the nameless employee who was the first Pullman conductor.

Despite lack of enthusiasm from the railroads who were his potential customers, Pullman went ahead perfecting what had already been dubbed "Pullman's Folly." The Pioneer, a magnificent example of the cabinetmaker's craft that cost $20,000 to build, was completed at the end of the Civil War just in time to carry the body of President Abraham Lincoln on the last lap of its funeral trip in 1865 from Chicago to Springfield.

Pullman kept adding improvements to his sleeping cars. The first "hotel car" was named "The President." It had a kitchen at one end so that meals could be served at tables placed in the sections. The "parlor car" was furnished with upholstered chairs that could be adjusted on a roller device beneath the seats. The "vestibule car" allowed the passenger to move through the train as under the roof of a hotel.

As Pullman refined his product, it won hearty acceptance from travelers, particularly from the wealthy and famous whose presence aboard was well publicized in a series of inaugural trips that coincided with the opening up of the continent.

Every President of the United States from Ulysses S. Grant to Dwight D. Eisenhower traveled in a private Pullman. So did stars of stage (and later screen), politicians, foreign dignitaries, and native magnates. The just plain well-to-do had their measure of privacy in the ornate compartments of the hotels on wheels.

When George Pullman was invited to operate his sleeping cars in England, Queen Victoria became a stockholder in the company along with Marshall Field the first, Andrew Carnegie, Andrew Mellon, and Cornelius Vanderbilt the second.

The growth of the company paced the development of America

through its railroad transportation system. Lucius Beebe, the social historian, once theorized that the spectacle of grandeur that the railroads carried from one end of the vast new land to the other inculcated a national desire for the better things of life. Was George Pullman a missionary of the consumer society? In a way, perhaps. An industrial frontiersman more likely.

Pullman died in 1897, his name synonymous with both a luxurious mode of travel and labor strife. He had tried to build a monument to himself in an industrial town a dozen miles south of the center of Chicago, and later incorporated within the city, where his railroad cars were constructed and the workers who produced them lived as well.

In 1880 George Pullman designed and planned the town of Pullman with the aid of architects and landscape artists. It was laid out around a central arcade and market place, with elegant shops and a theater that attracted distinguished visitors. There were tidy rows of Dutch-looking houses, churches, grandstands, boathouses, a library, and a technical training school for children of employees. The company owned all of the property in the community.

Pullman, Illinois, had its cricket team and its annual bicycle race. It was a model of paternalism or, as some economists have concluded, of benevolent feudalism. Its pretty face won international awards for urban design. Its ugly side was visible during times of economic pinch, when workers were dismissed or had their wages slashed without corresponding alleviation of their obligations to keep up their rent payments. Or when company scouts sniffed out evidence of union organizing.

In May 1894 a worker protest against pay cuts led to a strike of historical consequence. The newly formed industrial union, the American Railway Union, instituted a boycott against the servicing of Pullman cars. Its founder and president, Eugene V. Debs, was eventually sent to prison for violating a court injunction obtained against the union trainmen. Over the objections of the governor of Illinois, John P. Altgeld, President Grover Cleveland dispatched federal troops to break the strike. It was while serving his six-month prison term that Debs became a socialist.

George M. Pullman's economic and political philosophy survived his death in 1897. Sewell Avery, the chairman of Montgomery Ward who in 1944 preferred to be carried out of his office still seated in his chair (and so photographed for posterity) rather than fulfill the terms of an agreement with the Congress of Industrial Organizations, was a director of Pullman. Until the recent era, many in Wall Street associated the company with Avery's reactionary spirit.

In an exquisite irony of corporate history, Samuel Casey, a devout Republican conservative, is taking the company into fond commercial embrace with the two Communist superpowers.

Pullman's Palace Car Company thrived not just from the manufacture of railway passenger cars but from the manufacture of street cars. The company's name was changed to the Pullman Company in 1899, and after World War I a number of acquisitions enlarged its position in the railroad equipment field. In 1921 Pullman bought the Haskell & Barker Car Company, freight-car manufacturers, of Michigan City, Indiana. In 1930 Pullman merged with Standard Steel Car Company, the freight-car manufacturer that once had "Diamond Jim" Brady as its vice president for sales, and with Osgood Bradley, a rival manufacturer of sleeping cars and street cars in Worcester, Massachusetts. Bradley had sold his sleeping cars directly to the railroads, whereas Pullman built and operated his cars for the railroads, an arrangement that resulted in a unified sleeping-car service in the United States.

In 1934 all of Pullman's car-building activities were consolidated in the Pullman Standard Car Manufacturing Company, while the Pullman Company operated the cars. Both companies were subsidiaries of Pullman, Inc., the holding company formed in 1927.

With two exceptions, President Lincoln's son Robert Todd Lincoln and W. Irving Osborne, Jr., who was chairman when Casey took over, Pullman's chief executives had grown up with Pullman or the car companies it acquired. Robert Todd Lincoln, a corporation lawyer, was the company's second president, serving from the death of George M. Pullman in 1897 until 1911.

Osborne's roots and wealth were in paper and meat packing. He had married A. Watson Armour's daughter, Elsa, and had been president of the Cornell Paperboard Products Company until he sold it to St. Regis Paper Company in 1959. He was beckoned to the Pullman board of directors in 1952 by his brother-in-law Champ Carry, to fill the seat vacated by the death of Morris W. Kellogg. Carry was president of Pullman from 1950 to 1961; a mechanical engineer, he liked to refer to his humble corporate beginnings as a shop hand for the Haskell & Barker Car Company, of which his uncle Edward F. Carry became president as it was being merged with Pullman. Carry passed the presidential seal to Osborne when he retired. There was, then, a Carry family regime at Pullman as there was to be a Casey family influence.

Pullman's corporate philosophy was summed up in the words "large capacity," which means idle plants in bad years and ready-set-go to make money when the railroad cycle changed.

The United States Government, in an antitrust decision, forced Pullman to give up operating sleeping cars and diners. It sold that business for $47 million to the railroads in 1947 to comply with the decree. In 1951 Pullman bought Trailmobile, a pioneer in containerization. "The end of the era of deluxe travel," lamented the old Pullmanites. "Dumb luck," said a more perceptive outsider.

Pullman kept its manufacturing operations for both passenger and freight cars, finally closing its obsolete facility in Michigan City, Indiana, in 1971. The modernization of other plants in Butler, Pennsylvania, and Bessemer, Alabama, have since reduced the break-even point to below 50 per cent of capacity.

Pullman was also tardy in seeing the glowing promise of leasing railroad freight cars. "It was neglect rather than resistance," said Arthur Berry, the Pullman veteran who heads Pullman Transport Leasing, Inc. Started in 1959, it is fifth among prosperous leasing companies, running swiftly behind the General American Transportation Corporation, the Union Tank Car Company, ACF Industries, and the North American Car Corporation.

According to trade sources, Pullman Transport Leasing's earnings during the last three years have been equal to three fourths of Pullman-Standard's. Obviously, the leasing and financing of transportation equipment is more lucrative than manufacturing, as the cash-gushing Trailmobile T/M Leasing division and the Trailmobile Finance Company also confirm. Pullman Transport Leasing's pretax profit margin amounts to 25 per cent of sales.

Pullman Transport Leasing has fulfilled both its goals: to offset the cycles in Pullman-Standard production and to market Pullman-Standard products. About 84 per cent of its fleet of 12,000 freight cars was manufactured by Pullman-Standard and sold to the leasing division at manufacturer's cost, a constant source of interdivisional dispute but a source of advantage to Pullman Transport Leasing in terms of the profits it makes on a lease.

The leasing company has realized benefits from arriving late on the scene. Its equipment is newer (average age four years) than many of its competitors' which means lower inventory replacement and repair charges and ample use of the 7 per cent investment tax credit.

That on-again off-again device of the federal government is aimed at stimulating the economy by encouraging business to make capital expenditures. It reduces a corporation's tax liability by granting as a tax credit a percentage of the amount spent on equipment. If the company doesn't have enough taxable income to make use of the credit, it can trade it off to a leasing company such as Pullman Transport Leasing for better terms on the rental of the equipment.

About 12 per cent of the leasing fleet is tank cars, so Pullman escaped the two-year slide from which the tank-car industry has just emerged. That decline caused pressure to reduce rental rates and shorten leases.

When Pullman entered the leasing field, it had no tank cars at all. General American Transportation Corporation, the pioneer of railroad car leasing, has the largest fleet of tank cars.

Within three years after the debut of the leasing venture, Pullman-Standard perfected its 4,500-cubic-foot covered hopper, an ideal car for transporting bulk grain in bins. Until then, grain shippers had never leased cars for this purpose. They had relied on forty-foot boxcars, which are much inferior to the covered hopper from the standpoint of cleanliness and leakage. The jumbo covered hoppers have 50 per cent greater capacity than the boxcars and can be loaded onto a ship five times as fast.

Pullman-Standard became the leading manufacturer of the covered hoppers, producing forty to fifty cars a day in its factory in Butler. Two thirds of Pullman Transport Leasing's fleet consists of these grain cars which are often subleased for a few months of the year to shippers of potash and other agricultural materials.

Though the railroads have been providing hoppers in increasing numbers, the total supply of the cars falls short of what is needed in periods of heavy grain shipments. The mammoth purchase of American grain by the Russians in 1972 was not only felt by the American consumer in wildly increased prices at the supermarket. It also resulted in one of the most serious shortages of freight cars in the nation's history, a heartwarming calamity for depressed manufacturers like Pullman-Standard. Furthermore, the big grain shippers like to be able to furnish some of their own cars since the points of origin of grain shipments skip around the country (say from Kansas to Texas) in contrast to coal shipments which tend to be fixed.

Pullman Transport Leasing's customers tend to be big, credit-worthy shippers, such as Cargill, Inc., the Pillsbury Company, and the Monsanto Company—the covered hoppers can be equipped to transport plastic pellets as well as grain—rather than the illness-prone railroads. "Thank God we didn't have any leases with the Penn Central," Berry said.

The fortunes of Pullman-Standard, on the other hand, still rise and fall with the railroads. In the Northeast the carriers are run down and bankrupt. Only the passage by Congress of a federal loan guarantee would give them the means to buy new equipment. Such legislation is being wrangled over, although desperate optimists are convinced that some form of surface transportation relief must be passed soon. It would also encourage purchases by the healthy railroads of the South and West through lower interest costs.

But nevertheless, cheer abounds at Pullman-Standard. Orders for 9,475 freight cars were received in the second quarter and the backlog of orders is six times larger than one year ago. "This is the year of the car knocker," the executives at Pullman, Inc. are saying. The term "car knocker" dates to prewelding days when rivets were knocked into place with sledgehammers if they didn't fit the holes.

Casey has always had doubts about the advisability of staying in railroad-equipment manufacturing. He considers himself a builder. Or, as he occasionally relishes announcing when pedigree-hunters attempt to identify his social ranking, "I come from the sewers of Pittsburgh. I'm a ditchdigger." His father, who preceded him on the Pullman board, also called himself a ditchdigger. The term is a habit of pride in a three-generation Pittsburgh construction family. The Caseys are a manifold Irish-American tribe with traditions not unlike those of the Kennedys. The Caseys' politics are strictly backroom Republican, however.

The patriarch John F. Casey, Samuel Casey's grandfather, left his Irish immigrant father's log home north of Toronto in the 1890s after a quarrel with his stepmother. He wended his way to Pittsburgh where he found work on the barges of a sand and gravel company. John F. Casey named one of his sons after his employer, Sam Brown.

Around the turn of the century John F. Casey moved into the construction business with a series of partners. The partnerships enabled him to bid on large projects such as the building of a dam in Columbus, Ohio. In 1904 the John F. Casey Company was formed. It was to become one of the prime contractors for the Pennsylvania Railroad and under the founder's guiding hand during the next forty years was to attain revenues of $5 or $6 million a year. His son and grandson would multiply those revenues thirty fold by the 1960s.

"If you're a contractor, you're in politics," Sam Casey, Jr., the president of Pullman said, explaining his grandfather's avocation. But John F. never ran for office. "He just ran the people who ran for office. He had responsibility for a county or two in Pennsylvania," his grandson said. "John F. felt strongly about Republican conservatism. If you didn't have money to buy it, you didn't buy it. That's the way Republicans used to think anyway," said Sam Casey, who took six months off from running the Casey company in 1964 to raise money to support Barry Goldwater's try for the presidency of the United States.

The interweaving of business and politics in John F. Casey's affairs is illustrated by one of many apocryphal chapters in the family legend. John F. sent an associate, Roger W. Rowland, to New Castle, Pennsylvania, to reorganize Lawrence County and recapture it for the Republican fold after it went Democratic in the 1928 election. While on this assignment, Rowland bought the New Castle Refractories Company for Casey and ran it as president for the next thirty-five years.

John F. Casey acquired a string of other companies—among them the Railway Maintenance Corporation, the Swindell Industrial Furnace Company, and the Dressler Tunnel Kiln Company. Swindell held the basic patents for open-hearth steel making while Dressler had patents for building kilns used to fire powdered metals, china, and clay. The two companies later merged.

All of the Casey acquisitions were tucked under the umbrella of his holding company, the John Lee Estate. John F. named his holding company after his father-in-law, a plasterer who, the story goes, preferred being supported by his daughter's husband to practicing his craft. John F. would seem to have had a great sense of humor or a greater sense of family solidarity.

The businesses were run by members of John F. Casey's extended-family blood relatives, relatives by marriage, and devoted retainers who came to feel as though they were relatives. The family gathered regularly for the quarterly meetings of the holding company in which they were shareholders. "As with so many Irish Catholic families, John F. believed that strength was in the pack," Sam Casey said.

"He let us know that the business was what would educate everybody and he had his children and grandchildren at those quarterly meetings listening to the affairs of the company. Business was responsible for putting bread on the table. We were all aware of where the dough was coming from. We were always talking business. John F. was a great people man. And he really picked great men for the companies," Sam Casey said. As the only male grandson living in Pittsburgh, he received the lion cub's share of the patriarch's companionship.

"John F. definitely had an impact on my comportment and my way of looking at things," Sam Casey acknowledges. There is the occasional side-of-the-mouth elocution and tough-sounding, though not more than mildly profane, vocabulary. Coming from a smallish man with an unlined face, bright blue eyes, and a full head of side-parted brown hair, these speech patterns give Casey more of the air of a parochial school valedictorian than a corporation president.

Like his grandfather, Casey conveys authority without raising the decibel count; male Caseys have iron convictions and gentle manners. The women in the family have the unaffected refinement and matriarchal convictions that seem to be the mark of attendance at the convent schools of the Religious of the Sacred Heart. The order was founded in France to teach the daughters of the displaced aristocracy after the 1789 Revolution. In the United States, the "Madames of the Sacred Heart," as they were called (with the accent on the first syllable) educated the female offspring of self-made men for citizenship in the upper middle class.

Sam Casey behaves in business with an old-fashioned courtesy not only to those with whom he deals on the outside but particularly to his older colleagues at Pullman. He is considerate of their seniority and solicitous of their infirmities. A chain-smoker himself, he won't let veterans of cardiac disease or emphysema touch cigarettes in his presence and he usually seizes the least comfortable seat in a taxi for himself.

Casey men feel compelled to remind the world and themselves of their Irishness and their humble beginnings. Sam Casey not only puts himself down in the ditches where the family fortune originated when making social conversation but he eschews the trappings of power in his corporate office. Lesser members of Pullman management have met Casey at airports, boarded airplanes with him, and taken their seats in the first-class section only to see the president marching back into economy class. "The back of the plane gets there just as fast as the front," he remarks. If careful with company money, he is circumspectly generous with his own. He likes good wine and fine restaurants for which he likes to pay with crisp cash. John F. and Sam Jr. traveled together often, making such ritual pilgrimages as the August journey to Saratoga, New York, where Sam Casey remembers meeting John F.'s business and political pals, some of them exalted figures like James A. Farley of New York, the former Democratic National chairman and Postmaster General in Franklin Delano Roosevelt's first administration who had broken in 1940 with FDR over his third-term campaign.

Sam Casey did, in fact, start his working days as a laborer. "There was a rule in the family that I knew when I was ten. We called it playing with the bucket and it meant I would start when I was sixteen and that I'd never stop working," he said. When he was sixteen and on summer vacation from Georgetown Preparatory School, a Jesuit school near Washington, D.C., he was a shop laborer in the Railway Maintenance Corporation. The next summer he worked as a construction hand on the building of the Elizabeth Bridge across the Monongahela River. The third summer he was a lineman on the construction of the bridge at Edgewood, Pennsylvania, and became attracted to the engineering side of the business. He enrolled in engineering studies at Pennsylvania State University after he returned from two years' service in the U. S. Army Air Force. But his university career was spotted with mediocre grades and several crises. He finally graduated in 1950 with a degree in business administration.

There are two versions of Casey in academe. His mother says, "He's not the brightest of my children. My two girls are. But Sam's a plugger and he loves people and he could charm the paper off the wall." He is her only son. One daughter, Thérèse, died at twenty-one. Daughters Joan and Rosemary made socially prominent marriages and have produced, respectively, four and six children each.

According to his mother, Sam was allowed to remain at Penn State by her tugging at the heartstrings of the deans who wanted to expel him. "His father was very ill when they called me the first time," she relates. "I said, 'You can't. It would kill his father.' The dean asked, 'What would you suggest?' And I said, 'Why don't you put him in so-and-so school.' Three months later, he called me again. I had a big house and I had to do this terrible maneuvering to take the telephone call and not be heard. 'There's the business school,' I said. 'Why don't you put him in that?' And that's where he graduated from. I can still see myself conniving in the back hall."

Sam Casey doesn't sound quite as amused as his mother as he presents his recollection. "Mother always said I was the dumbest. That's really a kind of Irish thing with mother. She thought I had a lack of humility. But I wasn't that damn bad a student. The facts of the case are that through high school I did really very well.

"Studies did not come easy to me but I worked hard. After I got to college, I asked to lay out a semester because I fell in love with a pretty girl from St. Peter's Parish and I was cutting my engineering classes."

There is no dispute about Casey's unwillingness to go into the family business after graduation. He had a job offer from the Armstrong Cork Company at $275 a month.

His grandfather had died two years before at the age of seventy-six. Samuel Casey, Sr., had succeeded to his powers and responsibilities in 1945, which included the presidency of the John F. Casey Construction Company. That year Sam Senior had the first of many heart attacks that were to impair his health for the next eighteen years.

He offered to top the Armstrong offer by $5.00 if his son would go with Swindell-Dressler as a draftsman. "I felt that was far enough away from the family," Sam Casey, Jr., remembers. "It didn't have the name, and whereas dad's background was in construction supply, Swindell-Dressler was in engineering construction which was much more attractive to me in view of the education I'd had."

He had risen to product manager when his father sold Swindell-Dressler to Pullman in the fall of 1959 in an exchange of stock. "Dad had me over for dinner with my wife, Peggy, and he chopped me up. For me, everything stopped at the Fourth Commandment." Honoring his father, he agreed to accept the presidency of the Casey Construction Company. He was then thirty-two. "He did it as a favor," his mother says. In 1969, he became chairman.

In 1963 Sam Senior died and most of his Pullman holdings were liquidated to pay estate taxes. Sam Junior also reduced his stock to 690 shares. However, he received options for 10,000 shares of stock at $48.31 when he became president. Altogether the Casey family and their associates now own about 2 per cent of Pullman common stock.

Shortly after the Caseys received Pullman stock in payment for Swindell-Dressler, it split two for one. But as Casey said, "We went through the soaring '60s and the stock didn't do a helluva lot, and that's as much reason as any why I'm here."

In 1965 his mother, Constance Connelly Casey, had married Frank R. Denton, the sixty-six-year-old vice chairman and chief executive officer of the Mellon National Bank and Trust Company. Both had been widowed within the two previous years. Their families' business and social bonds were exceptionally secure. John F. Casey had been a friend of Andrew W. Mellon. Frank Denton had been the closest adviser of Mellon's nephew, Richard King Mellon, chairman of the Mellon Bank and steward of the vast Mellon financial empire. Among the directorships Denton held was a seat on the Pullman board.

"He's a working man, too," Constance Denton says of her Kansas-born second husband. She refers to the three Casey men she admires most, her father-in-law, her first husband and her son, as "prodigious workers."

Though Constance Denton has never held a paying job ("heavens, I'm the dumbest thing you ever met," she says), she is a woman of formidable energy and business interest. An early riser, she regularly telephones her children at 5:30 A.M., forgetting that they may be in different time zones from Pittsburgh. After attending one five-and-a-half-hour annual meeting of Gulf Oil Corporation of which Frank Denton is a director, she telephoned Sam Casey to announce that she would henceforth be voting against management inasmuch as "they aren't doing things right."

Sam Casey calls his stepfather "The General," in deference to the rank of brigadier general he held in World War II.

"He's had a terrific impact on my life largely because he married Mom, though I'd known him since I was in short pants," Casey says. "He was my father's absolute best friend and Mrs. Denton and mother were close as six is to seven. For twenty years he was running the biggest thing in Pittsburgh and it's been said that Pittsburgh should be renamed Mellonburg."

Dismayed by Pullman's lethargic performance, as all the Caseys were, the General told Sam Casey, Jr. to "get in there," first by claiming a seat on the board in 1964. Then, in 1970, with the urging of three other directors, Murray Shields, an economist, William C. Bolenius, vice chairman of American Telephone & Telegraph Company, and John T. Pirie, Jr., chairman of the executive committee of Carson, Pirie Scott & Company, the Chicago department store, Casey was persuaded to take the presidency.

Later, as president of Pullman, he was invited to join the board of the Mellon Bank. Now that Denton is well into his retirement, another Mellon officer, Silas Keehn, senior vice president of the bank, sits on Pullman's board. The Mellon Bank is one of Pullman's primary financial sources.

Constance Denton said she thought her son should "stay home. A lot of people were dependent on the Casey Company." But the General prevailed and her son moved to Chicago.

On December 1, 1970, ten weeks after he was installed in Pullman's headquarters in the Loop, Casey submitted his resignation—to take effect December 1, 1980. It was his way of motivating younger executives.

"I do hope you'll never stop your own rush toward the top," he told them at a staff meeting. "If you aim high, then you're with the right company—and at the right time. If I am reluctant to yield this pleasant job to you today, I can still offer you, in the meantime, a clear shot at a million dollars."

The resignation gesture also served to highlight his blueprint for Pullman. "I've dedicated myself for the next ten years to giving this company greater breadth and diversity, increased depth of management and resources, and a better return on invested capital for the owners of this business," he said.

Within the first few months of his arrival, the Michigan City freight-car building plant was shut down. Pullman, Inc.'s quarterly dividend was cut from 70 cents to 50 cents. Four divisional presidents were appointed and each was made personally responsible for an earnings growth over the next five years of at least 9 per cent compounded annually in his division. If any missed his goal, he would be replaced.

Casey also closed the New York office of the M. W. Kellogg

division, which had been registering a loss, and transferred the operation to Houston, the hub of the oil-drilling market.

The reason for these prompt actions became evident in February 1971 when Pullman reported its 1970 results. Net income had withered to $9.9 million from $19.8 million in 1969. Sales and operating revenues had decreased to $711.5 million from $751.4 million.

His role, Casey said, was to be "doubting Thomas." Certainly, he added, "Nothing in my experience would lead me to expect anything good about the car manufacturing business."

Elwyn Ahnquist, who had become president of the Pullman-Standard division shortly after the Casey take-over, persuaded him and the board to allow two years before closing the Pullman Car Works, the original plant of the founder, George M. Pullman. The $210-million New York subway-car order, the biggest order ever placed for rolling stock, came through in 1972. That and other mass transit orders could help smooth out those railroad cyclical bumps.

But there are risks, too. Urban transit is strewn with financial and technical disasters. Ahnquist denies that Pullman underbid to get the New York order, as some have suggested. Although he is confident that the deal will be profitable, he will not guarantee it. And inevitable though it may seem in an energy-conscious era for such cities as Los Angeles and Houston to build mass transit, that market has still to materialize. "The jury is still out on the decision," Casey said, "but we're going to stay in the business."

He demonstrated he meant what he said when, early in his administration, the General Electric Company won a contract that Pullman had wanted—to build rapid transit cars for the Philadelphia area. Pullman believed it had been unfairly treated in the method of bidding. Casey ratified Ahnquist's decision to sue the United States Secretary of Transportation, the Southeastern Pennsylvania Transportation Authority, and the New Jersey Commissioner of Transportation.

Pullman lost the case but Ahnquist and Casey believe it may have helped them win the New York contract because it showed Washington and the industry that Pullman was not going to sit back and be stamped on.

There are other imponderables in Pullman's future, Casey admitted.

The Soviet and Chinese deals are both toeholds on frontiers and the most striking proofs of Casey's determination to have Pullman take a multinational stance.

Getting the Soviet contract was a fifteen-month saga that might fittingly be titled "Perils of Pullman." The executives of Swindell-Dressler who sweated out the signing of the $10-million contract to design a foundry for the Kama River project like to think it "broke the log jam" on U.S.-Soviet trade.

It all began, as most dealings with the Russians do, seemingly by happenstance. In September 1970 E. Stanley Haynes, head of Swindell's foundry department, met two Russians at a cocktail party at the International Foundry Congress being held at the English seaside resort of Brighton. They questioned him about the new auto foundry at Flat Rock, Michigan, that Swindell had designed for the Ford Motor Company. The previous spring Henry Ford had discussed with the Russians the possibility of becoming the over-all contractor for the Kama River project. Then Secretary of Defense Melvin R. Laird raised the specter of the Soviets using the acquired truck technology to supply the North Vietnamese on the Ho Chi Minh Trail. After that heavy-handed hint, Ford terminated the talks.

Haynes's conversations with the Russians at Brighton were to be followed by rounds and rounds of meetings in London, Zurich, Stuttgart, Moscow, Pittsburgh, and Washington, D.C., involving top Pullman people such as Donald J. Morfee, president of Swindell-Dressler and Samuel Casey.

The strains of trying to do business with the Russians were matched by the subtleties of obtaining an export license from the United States Government in the face of Pentagon objections to an American contribution to the Kama River complex.

The Swindell engineers were not allowed by the Soviet Government to visit the site for the project, 550 miles east of Moscow. They had to rely entirely on data supplied by the Russians, and everything had to be screened through the many layers of Soviet bureaucracy. The Pittsburghers knew they had both domestic and foreign competitors for the contract. For a while, the Jervis B. Webb Company, a Detroit engineering concern, was thought to have nailed it down.

There were also many linguistic misunderstandings, which complicated the intricacies of price-setting. At one point the Americans thought they were selling engineering designs only for the foundry process while the Russians seemed to be asking for designs for the support buildings as well.

On the Washington front, Swindell and its lawyers tried to bypass the Pentagon and concentrate their persuasive powers on the Departments of Commerce, State, and Treasury as well as on key members of Congress. They argued that trade with the Soviet Union could mean improvement in the balance of payments and more jobs for Americans. Casey enunciated the gospel himself to Secretary of State William P. Rogers at a Washington cocktail party one evening.

By the time the application for the export license reached the White House, late in the fall of 1971, the way had been paved by Peter G. Peterson, then President Nixon's assistant for international economic affairs and an architect of the U.S.-Soviet trade agreement that was eventually signed a year later. The agreement was for Swindell to design the foundry and was signed in Moscow just before Christmas 1971. Early in 1972, negotiations were resumed toward a second contract to supply equipment for the foundry. It was the first deal clinched by an American company in the Kama River project.

The profit potential in a $40-million sale of electric-arc furnaces was far more meaningful to Swindell (whose annual sales run about $100 million) than the engineering design contract. "Russian business is the toughest business in the world," Casey said. "The Russian is the finest technician and the toughest buyer. But a deal is a deal with them and we are excited about this market."

The Soviet relationship rubbed off on other East European business. The Russians told Swindell executives they had won a contract from Poland to design a $43-million iron foundry before the Poles notified them. The Swindell men hadn't known that the Russians were aware of their discussions with the Poles.

More Soviet business was forthcoming for other Pullman subsidiaries. Through its French subsidiary, Trailor, Trailmobile arranged to sell fifty refrigerated truck trailers. Pullman-Standard was asked to quote prices for freight cars for the Soviet railways.

Credit was not extended, however. The Russians have been kept to forward payment schedules with terms of net thirty days on the engineering contract. Ninety per cent of the purchase price of the equipment is paid before it is shipped from Montreal, 5 per cent on arrival at Kama, and the balance, as one Pullman executive said, "when we catch 'em."

In July of 1972, Pullman, Inc., was accredited by the Soviet

Government to do business in the Soviet Union. Simultaneously, permission was given to the Occidental Petroleum Corporation, whose chairman, Dr. Armand Hammer, had been cultivating Soviet relationships since Lenin's time. Pullman opened an office in an apartment building in Moscow, staffed it with two representatives, three Russian secretary-interpreters, and three drivers, and covered its overhead by acting as a 5-per-center, or agent, for twenty-eight other deal-bent American companies.

The Kama River foundry project was retarded four months by further misunderstanding of Soviet and American engineering design customs. "The cause of delay," Casey said, "was that 25 per cent of the project is standard Soviet-produced. They had 10,000 tons of bearing pile we have to drive. They wanted the drawing for a bearing pile. They needed drawings for 2,000 tons of fasteners, for panes of glass, tar paper, corrugated sheeting for the foundry. That was eighty-seven acres' worth. They wanted the drawings. We said, 'It's your problem.' They said, 'It has to be engineered and designed.' We said, 'It's a standard.'

"It's a pioneer effort and as such a very difficult thing," he said, as if bolstering his spirits. "This is the biggest structure the world has ever known."

Doing business with the People's Republic of China is another matter. M. W. Kellogg's order for the three 1,100-ton-a-day ammonia plants evolved into $300 million in orders for eight ammonia and eight urea plants plus the purchase of design know-how for two ammonia plants through Japanese licensees. First payments were made in guilders through Kellogg's Dutch subsidiary.

"We'll do fine with China. Their type of socialism is most exciting to us," said Casey solemnly. "Under Mao what you do for one province, you do for all twenty-seven. We have a great conviction that the PRC [People's Republic of China] has a greater profit potential than the Soviet. We had what the PRC wanted. Their big problem is agriculture and our ammonia works for agriculture. One fourth of the world's supply of ammonia comes from Kellogg-designed plants."

M. W. Kellogg also had orders on its books for fertilizer plants from Mexico, Pakistan, and Cameroon.

"American companies that have the technology in the agricultural part of the world are in an enviable spot," Casey crowed. "By virtue of the devaluation, we're nose to nose with any Japanese consortium and they can't cut their prices."

Not surprisingly, Casey is acquisition-minded. "A big acquisition is important to Pullman, and more so every day," he said. Its stock price is rising and its approximate 40 per cent premium over book value would grease the acquisition route.

"It should be something that would be anticyclical, in an allied field. It doesn't necessarily have to be an American company," he added. "An investment in the foreign market catering to the European Economic Community is the most attractive to us. But we need a big acquisition. We need stability in this company."

Epilogue: Spring 1975

Sam Casey had beaten his own timetable of having Pullman, Inc., in the billion-dollar league by 1975. In 1973 the company had revenues of $1,059 billion compared to $800.5 million in 1972. Its net income of $36.5 million was double that of the previous year though the earnings per share of $5.06 still fell short of the sacred $5.72 of 1966.

The billion-dollar backlog of orders at midyear had snowballed to $1.6 billion, more than twice that of a year ago. Pullman's freight-car plants were booked solid for the next two years. In the fall of 1973 stockholders received a 12.5 per cent increase in the quarterly dividend rate and the common stock was split, with one new share given for each two held.

Casey didn't get his big acquisition in 1973 or 1974 but an important step was taken to facilitate the possibility of one or more in the European Common Market. Trailor, the French subsidiary of Trailmobile, was launched on the Paris Bourse in November 1973, not the best of times since Western Europe had just been dealt the blow of the Arab oil embargo. The rationale for the step was that a publicly listed French company could more easily buy and develop companies in other European countries.

To accomplish the listing, Pullman sold as stock to the public 15 per cent of its 80 per cent interest in Trailor and received a $5.5-million pretax profit from the sale which boosted corporate earnings.

Jean-Marie Tiné, general manager of Banque Française de Dépôts & de Titres (a Paris investment banking firm affiliated with White, Weld & Company in New York) and president and director-general of Trailor, went on Pullman's board.

Tiné was a natural choice to captain Pullman's European strategy. One of that generation of middle-aged French financiers with fresh, multinational viewpoints, he had negotiated the granting of permission by the French Government for Pullman's purchase of Trailor.

In 1969, Compagnie Industrielle de Matériel de Transports (CIMT-Lorraine), a nearly bankrupt manufacturer of railroad cars and truck trailers and a Pullman licensee, had asked Tiné's help in finding a solution to its problems. Tiné approached Pullman which said it was interested only in the trailer part of the business. The railroad-car operations were sold to the French subsidiary of a Swiss concern. The plan that won government approval for the American take-over was a reorganization of the trailer segment with French minority partners and with the objective of European expansion.

The matter reached the desk of Valéry Giscard d'Estaing, then the Minister of Finance in the cabinet of President Georges Pompidou (Giscard would be elected President of France in 1974), where it was affirmatively decided in behalf of Pullman. The Chicago company abandoned its licensing policy in Europe for one of ownership.

Trailor, as the new company was named, had had neither an effective management team, an efficient plant, nor a significant share of market. Pullman turned it over to young French managers imbued with American management methods. (The same philosophy of local talent trained in American ways was used in the acquisition of Peak Commercial Vehicles, a small and unprofitable British company that became Trailor U.K. Limited, and will be used wherever Trailor expands in Europe, growing as modern highways tie the cities of the Continent together.) Since 1970 Trailor has tripled its sales and made money. It is now the leading truck trailer manufacturer in Europe in volume and profits.

All through 1974, storm clouds kept drifting across Pullman's multinational course. In Europe worsening economies aggravated political instability, particularly in Italy and Britain. Qualms were felt about business policies based on Common Market unity. Russian business had been grinding nearly to a standstill as the U.S.-Soviet trade pact became entangled in Congress with political issues such as the emigration of Soviet Jews. M. W. Kellogg had negotiated a joint project with a Japanese firm to build five ammonia plants in the Soviet Union each worth about $25 million. But the Russians wanted to pay for the American technology with loans from the Export-Import Bank. The Pullman representatives had to tell the Russians to be patient and, if they really wanted Kellogg's ammonia process, to wait. Otherwise, to go to the competition.

Meanwhile, Casey and Pullman lobbyists were active on the Washington scene. They addressed their exhortations about the merits of East-West trade to congressional leaders like Speaker of the House Carl Albert and Senate Majority Leader Mike Mansfield. They cited figures to Jewish groups that indicated a rising tide of emigration of Jews from the Soviet Union.

It had been much easier the first time around when Peter Peterson was at the White House and then at the Commerce Department proselytizing for economic détente or when George Shultz was carrying the cause in his pocket over at the Treasury. In the late spring of 1974 Casey was saying hopefully, "Nixon is absolutely devoted to free trade." He was even wondering if it just might be possible that an organized Communist effort had triggered the media attack on the President. After all, Casey was just back from France where it had been revealed that Communist party money had been funneled into the camp of the Socialist candidate, François Mitterand, during the presidential election. Though he didn't say so, Casey's craving for Communist business was sticking in his conservative craw.

A few months later, the Watergate denouement had driven Nixon from the White House and Republican conservatives like Casey were free to acknowledge that he had betrayed their principles.

When Congress finally passed a trade reform act at the end of 1974, it linked the extension of trade benefits to freer emigration from the Soviet Union. The ceiling of $300 million over four years set on Eximbank credits irked the Russians. Nevertheless, early in 1975 M. W. Kellogg, in tandem with a French firm received an order to build another four ammonia plants in the Soviet Union.

Pullman was gaining international ground elsewhere. Swindell-Dressler won a $60-million contract from the government of Iraq for two sponge iron plants. Kellogg was building oil refineries in Abu Dhabi, selling its catalytic-cracking technology in Brazil and

Mexico, and building liquefied natural gas receiving terminals on the East and Gulf coasts of the United States.

Casey had revised his outlook on coal and decided that mining operations were not consistent with long range corporate objectives. Options were granted to the minority owners of Aloe Coal Company to buy Pullman's 80 per cent interest. Pullman's stake in coal would be through selling gondolas (open freight cars with low sides) and hoppers for railroads to haul the coal and in Kellogg's coal gasification research and development.

Late in 1974 Casey was able to announce that the over-all corporate backlog had reached $3 billion, twice the amount of a year before and that the quarterly dividend was being increased by another 13½ per cent.

At the same time, he had to revise his earnings predictions for the year downward, to an estimate of $5.50 to $6.00 a share from an earlier one of $6.00 to $7.00 a share. When the final accounting was made for 1974, Pullman had net income of $41.3 million or $5.69 a share on revenues of $1.4 billion. Though the per-share figure was 3 cents below the 1966 peak, 1974 was the best year for sales and profits in Pullman history.

The security analyst's guess of "a whipcracking recession" had been fulfilled, but it was a peculiar economic slump, attended by inflation and shortages of materials. Congress hadn't passed the loan guarantee for railroad equipment, but Pullman wasn't showing any ill effects from that disappointment. The cause of Pullman-Standard's having to shut down two assembly-line tracks and slow the delivery of its freight car orders was a shortage of steel. Shortages and inflation were affecting Trailmobile and the engineering and construction divisions, too.

But Casey wasn't glum. Even in the depths of the Wall Street despair, analysts were recommending Pullman as an "energy play," though some were emphasizing coal freight more than oil refineries.

Then in March the first of the 745 subway cars were shipped to New York City and it was revealed that the dream order of 1972 might be Pullman's nightmare of 1975.

Sam Casey had the disagreeable chore of acknowledging to the financial community that not only unforeseen inflation but a contract drawn with predictable disadvantage to Pullman-Standard had ordained substantial losses on the order. Industry sources estimated that the write-downs would be around $10 million.

The contract was written without an escalator clause. It set a fixed price of $210 million, or about $282,000 for each subway car. In the three years since the contract was signed, manufacturing costs had more than doubled.

Furthermore, under the 1972 agreement, Pullman had to advance more than $50 million in tooling and initial inventory and labor costs before it could collect its first installment of payment from the New York City Transit Authority. Pullman's ready cash was thereby sucked into the subway-car order at a time of high interest rates and tight money.

Casey admitted to *Business Week* magazine that someone at Pullman should have seen the potential cash-flow problems and hoisted a warning flag. "We just didn't have that smart fellow come along and say, 'If those are the terms they insist upon, we should walk away from the business.' We thought we could make a profit even with the cash-flow situation."

Sometime during 1975 decisions would have to be made about Pullman-Standard continuing with passenger-car production. It was quite probable that the division would not only stay with it but would expand capacity. Early in April Pullman-Standard obtained a $167-million order for 235 double-deck coaches from the National Railroad Passenger Corporation (Amtrak). Increasing demand from urban transit systems seemed more certain than ever, too. The New York subway-car deal had been a "learning experience," a Pullman executive said.

If 1975 seemed to be shaping up as a year of new crises, Casey and the company had never been in more fit condition to cope with them. Pullman, Inc., was a much more glamorous, younger, and stronger company than when Casey arrived five years before. In 1974 a former astronaut joined its board. James A. McDivitt had retired from the Apollo program into civilian life as an executive vice president of Consumers Power Company of Jackson, Michigan. Early in 1975 Casey hired him away from the utility company to become a vice president of Pullman, Inc.

One of the last vestiges of the Carry family administration had gone in 1974 when W. Irving Osborne, Jr., took official retirement.

George M. Pullman's company was unmistakably in its Casey era. For a while, at least. At forty-seven Sam Casey had five years to go before his announced retirement in 1980. His only son, Samuel B. Casey III, was twenty-four and a second-year law student in San Francisco.

"I'd love for him to be associated with a family business," the president of Pullman said. "But if he doesn't come in, then maybe I'll go into another business with him."

For, as Sam Casey said whenever he was in an introspective mood, "The business of life can be art. It can be religion. It can be business. The business of my life is business."

FOUNDERS STILL IN CHARGE

"THAT MAN" REVSON LEADS,
BUT WHO WILL FOLLOW?

October 1974

In the spring and summer of 1974 Charles Revson, undisputed king and grand curmudgeon of the American beauty industry, released two lightning bolts. Without the slightest forewarning, he divorced his wife and hired a president for Revlon, Inc.

As months went by and speculation was fed by Revson's usual failure to clarify, some wondered whether the two events were in some way connected. The only visible link was a hospital stay between the two abrupt announcements. In April, doctors for the sixty-seven-year-old chairman and chief executive officer of the nation's second largest cosmetic and fragrance company issued a statement that he had undergone gall bladder surgery. After he emerged from the hospital, reports of his ill health continued to circulate. Skeptics recalled his legendary hypochondria and habitual air of malaise. But others saw a recognition of mortality as the only plausible reason for Charles Revson's behavior.

In February he had celebrated the tenth anniversary of his marriage to his third wife, Lyn Fisher Sheresky, a wide-eyed divorcée more than twenty years his junior. He had reportedly bestowed upon her valuable jewels in commemoration of the alliance which friends and associates said had slightly mellowed his tyrannical spirit.

Or perhaps it was more a case of the marriage providing another outlet for his authoritarianism. Charles Revson had chosen Lyn Revson's clothes—keeping her hemlines dowdily below the knee even when the mini wave had converted grandmothers, and outfitting her in yachting shirts and pants that matched his. No details of her grooming escaped him. He had personally telephoned to discuss the performance of a Revlon shampoo with the woman who washed Mrs. Revson's hair at the Monsieur Marc salon.

Then, a few weeks after the anniversary celebration, Revson had his lawyer notify his wife by telephone one morning after he had left for the office that he was filing for divorce. Neither the terms nor the cause of the divorce settlement were publicly disclosed.

In July he announced that the post of president and chief operating officer of Revlon, Inc., vacant since 1969, was to be filled by forty-two-year-old Michel C. Bergerac, president of ITT-Europe and an executive vice president of its parent company, International Telephone & Telegraph Company. Analysts who followed the Byzantine history of that conglomerate which, though twenty times larger in revenues than Revlon, suffered from the same case of one-man rule, had been speculating that the French-born Bergerac would succeed Harold S. Geneen, chairman of ITT, if he ever agreed it was time to step down.

To woo Bergerac away from ITT Revson had dangled terms that broke previous records of executive indulgence. "It was an interesting romance," Bergerac said with corporate noblesse oblige. "The offer was extremely attractive, and I wanted the chance to run my own business." In addition to a five-year contract at $325,000 a year, there were "substantial other benefits." They included an unprecedented $1.5-million lump sum payment just to take the job as of September 1974, plus options for 70,000 shares of Revlon common stock at $41 a share. There was the usual reimbursement of expenses incurred in moving from Brussels to New York as well as the right to sell to Revlon for $400,000 a co-operative apartment in New York that Bergerac bought for $425,000. Most significant, however, was a proviso that if he were not named chief executive officer within a year, Bergerac could resign and still draw his base salary of $325,000 for two years. Another clause provided for the two-year salary continuation if the contract were not renewed in 1979.

Revson said he had been "enormously impressed" by Bergerac's financial capability and his experience in mergers and acquisitions on an international scale. These talents would not only make up for his lack of consumer-product marketing experience but would be just what a management consultant might prescribe for a company headed in the direction in which Revson has been steering Revlon, Inc., for the last decade.

The nail polish company that Charles Revson, one of his brothers, and a friend started forty-two years ago with a $300 capital base is now a diversified international corporation that dominates the cosmetic and fragrance markets of the world. Its sales of $506 million in 1973 exceeded those of any other manufacturer of beauty products distributing through retail outlets, and only door-to-door Avon Products Inc. had a larger share of the $5-billion industry. But nearly one fourth of Revlon's revenues (and slightly more than one fourth of its $43-million earnings) were derived from drugs and health services.

The diversification had been achieved entirely by buying outside companies, the most significant one being the purchase of the United States Vitamin & Pharmaceutical Corporation in 1966. Other acquisitive ventures by Revson had been thwarted or come a cropper.

So it made great good sense as well as constituting a corporate raiding coup of some magnitude to have Revson hire a man of Bergerac's stature. But the high dollar value of the assurance given Bergerac that he would run Revlon, Inc., seemed the really fascinating turn of events.

To some it indicated that Charles Haskell Revson, the creator, guiding light, occasionally benevolent dictator, chief product manager, marketing strategist, and corporate planner of Revlon, had finally chosen his successor. Was it possible at last, others wondered, that the half-billion dollar corporation would stop being Charles Revson's one-man band?

The importation of an honor-laden professional manager not in the least beholden to the founder for his medals could only serve to bolster Revlon's stock in Wall Street. For although Revlon had always had a warm place in the affections of the mostly female security analysts who chart the cosmetics industry, institutional investors had long been concerned about what would happen to the company when Charles Revson departed.

There had been peaks and valleys of concern stimulated quite naturally, by events such as his hospitalization in April of 1974 or, in 1971, the approach of his sixty-fifth birthday. In most publicly held corporations with a cherished Big Board listing, that milestone in the history of a founder and chief executive is usually treated as a time for sentimental farewells and a changing of command along carefully planned lines of succession. That is, if the commander hasn't already cashed in his stock options and sailed away into retirement. But Revlon's management style and structure had never resembled that of most major corporations. So it was that on October 11, 1971, Charles Revson celebrated his sixty-fifth birthday quietly with his wife, Lyn.

The only memento of the event on his office desk was a solid gold miniature of his 257-foot yacht, the *Ultima II,* which he had bought five years before from the secretive billionaire shipbuilder, Daniel K. Ludwig. Revson had it redecorated as the last word in whispering luxury and rechristened after Revlon's prestige cosmetic line. (Lloyd's Register lists the boat's owner as the "Ultima II Corp. or Charles Revson," its home port as Monrovia, Liberia.)

Revson never cruised aboard the *Ultima II* without taking along his doctor and a cholesterol-measuring device. He made daily telephone calls to his office and his beloved Revlon research center in the Bronx from the boat.

During the summer of 1971 there had been a power confrontation on the yacht. A group of Revlon's top executives had converged on Charles Revson as the boat put into a Mediterranean port to wrest additional operating responsibilities from him.

As a result of that meeting, the Cosmetic Operating Committee had been named. The members were: Joseph Anderer, then president of the Revlon Cosmetic and Fragrance Division: Paul P. Woolard, then executive vice president of that division; Robert W. Armstrong, chairman of the International Division; Sol Levine, executive vice president for operations, and Victor J. Barnett, executive vice president for administration.

Wall Street and industry Revlonologists scrutinized the committee as though it were the praesidium of the Central Committee of the Soviet Communist party on May Day.

A few months after it was formed, Anderer resigned to become president of M. Lowenstein, the textile concern. According to one observer, "he thereby violated the Revson rule of 'you can't resign, you're fired.'"

That left four rivals on the committee until the Bergerac appointment eliminated them from the presidential race. Two piqued the interest of outside bettors. Paul Woolard, who also bore the nickname of "the golden goy" because he was the only non-Jewish candidate for fair-haired boy of the moment, had been named to succeed Anderer as head of cosmetics and fragrances. Victor Barnett was the son-in-law of Harry Meresman, Revlon's outside accountant and director of long standing, as well as the nephew of Sir Isaac Wolfson, a British retail magnate.

Barnett was thought by some to have slipped into the seat which had been vacated by E. William Mandel. In that eventful year of 1971 Mandel had resigned as president of the Revlon Development Corporation, an empty title he had held for two years while waiting for his sizable stock options to ripen.

Regarded by many as a whiz-bang advertising and marketing man, Mandel had sat at the right hand of the sovereign. Twice passed over for corporate president, he contested Revson on corporate philosophy and, predictably, lost.

Mandel had signed on with Revlon as advertising manager in 1955 at the age of twenty-nine and developed the techniques for creative television advertising.

Advertising was one area Revson could never keep his hands off. In one three-year period in the 1950s he changed advertising agencies seven times. "Creative people," he reportedly once said, "are like a wet towel. You wring them out and pick up another one." In 1958 Mandel asked for and received the job of Charles Revson's assistant, an assignment he was sure he could survive although no one else, Revson included, believed he could stand the torture.

Mandel had supervised Revlon's sponsorship of the television quiz shows "$64,000 Question" and the "$64,000 Challenge" from 1955 to 1958. The shows had helped to triple Revlon's sales and more than double the price of its common stock, which had been offered to the public at $12 a share on December 7, 1955, and flared to $30 in the next three months. It was subsequently revealed that the shows had been rigged. Revson dumfounded the congressional subcommittee that investigated the rigging in 1959 (but even more so those who knew his meddling tendencies) when he testified that he had no part in it. "I was flabbergasted," he declared.

The link between Revson and Mandel grew to resemble one of

those surrogate father-and-son relationships that so often determine corporate destinies. Mandel preferred to think of it more as Damon and Pythias, or of himself as a replacement for Revson's younger brother, Martin. (The brothers had been estranged in 1960 after Martin sued Charles for fraud, misrepresentation, and breach of agreement in a stock deal.)

When Mandel became his assistant, Charles Revson promised he would make him a millionaire. The promise would have been realized if the price of Revlon stock had hit 100. It reached the high seventies just before the 1970 bear markets set in. Mandel has also said that he was promised the presidency. Some of those who had been in attendance at the Revson court are uncertain about whether King Charles regularly went back on his word to favorites of a given period or simply led them to entertain visions of themselves as his heir.

Mandel first saw George H. Murphy brought in from a subsidiary of Johnson & Johnson as president in 1962. That move was intended to establish a credibility heretofore lacking for Revlon with Wall Street.

The corporate image of disingenuousness had stemmed as much from its high officers' secretiveness as from its complicated balance sheets. There was also the lingering whiff of past scandals like the fixed TV shows and another revelation of the 1950s that the company had tapped employees' telephones. Murphy was a man of suavity as well as financial *sagesse*. He lasted four years, withdrawing in stages, as his options matured, into retirement.

He was followed in 1966 by Dan Rodgers, who came from American Home Products Corporation. Rodgers resigned "amicably" three years later. After he left, the presidential slot was unfilled for nearly five years until Bergerac was discovered.

Mandel, who was chafing through all of this as executive vice president for marketing, had received offers from other cosmetic companies over the years, and after Rodgers was installed in the corporate presidency he thought was rightfully his, he went ahead and made a deal with Helena Rubinstein Inc.

Revson persuaded Mandel to cancel it but did not give him the signed manifesto Mandel asked for, according him undisputed authority in certain areas. Obviously, Mandel had lost his patron and he was allowed to go, eventually, with bruised heart and ego and his stock into the green pastures of retirement.

He remained a Revlon director until 1972 and kept a certain following among some of his fellow board members who possibly might have brought him back if the leadership had suddenly fallen vacant at that time. But as Mandel had learned once before when he had tried to instigate a board revolt against the chairman, a majority of the board would not contradict Charles Revson as long as he was alive, well, and the largest single stockholder. He currently holds 10.33 per cent, a controlling amount of the common stock.

As time passed and changes took place on the board, Mandel's star dimmed further. Two new directors were especially obligated to Charles Revson. Aileen Mehle, better known under the pen name of Suzy, was a columnist whose society gossip was syndicated through the Chicago *Tribune*. A frequent guest on the Revson yacht and inflater of his social standing in her column, she was regarded as Revson's token nod to the movement to put women on corporate boards. "She is erudite and *au courant* in her fine feminine taste," he told stockholders at the annual meeting in the spring of 1972. "We're in the feminine business in a great measure and her contribution to our activities should be helpful."

In 1974 Jay I. Bennett joined the board. As vice president for personnel and industrial relations since 1965, he had earned the sobriquet of "director of the Central Intelligence Agency" for his extensive files, usually kept under lock and key.

As if management history, particularly in the case of Mandel, did not prophesy the future of the Cosmetic Operating Committee, Revson made it obvious in his inimitable way during an interview with a reporter for the New York *Times* early in 1972. It was held in his office at corporate headquarters on the top four floors of the General Motors Building on Fifth Avenue where Revlon, Inc., surmounted its competitors, Estée Lauder Inc. on the thirty-seventh and thirty-eighth floors, and Helena Rubinstein Inc. on the thirty-second floor. The proximity of the foes caused one wag to say, "Even the olives in the martinis are bugged."

The Revlon offices were decorated by Ellen Lehman McCluskey Associates in what a press release said was "traditional, classic comfort and permanence." But the unmistakable hand of Charles Revson was seen in the somber wood paneling and heavy monochrome quiet bespeaking his notion of mannerly taste.

"The management committee is a help and an aid. It gives a lot of experience, it helps solve everyday problems," Revson said, alluding to the Cosmetic Operating Committee, but not for long. "We're taking young men and bringing them along. John was just made a vice president. He's a young boy of twenty-eight," he added. John Revson, his older son by his second marriage had just been promoted to vice president and general manager of Etherea/Fine Fragrances, a department that embraced a new, still unprofitable hypoallergenic line and an expanding group of fragrances that included both triumphs and tribulations. Charles H. Revson, Jr., twenty-five, his younger son, was made marketing director of Ultima II.

The senior Revson hastened to mention other youngsters. "Dan Schneider [recently promoted to vice president, general manager of Ultima II], Tony Liebler, Gerry Simmons from IBM, a wonderful piece of talent. We're looking to develop these people. A lot of thirty- to forty-year-olds are getting responsible positions." In less than three years these three were gone from Revlon's employ. "Paul Woolard, Victor Barnett, we just made Sam Kalish president of International. He's in his very early forties. That's all young stuff, not too young, but young," he went on.

He leaned his slight frame back against his chair, closing his eyes in one of his nerve-wracking habits that leaves those in attendance unsure if he has dismissed them or fallen asleep. "Everyone knows one of these days," he said, opening his eyes, and pausing. "It doesn't mean for the rest of my life I'm going to be the cat's meow, because there are times and days . . ." He hesitated. "It may not be right now."

The gray eyes, hooded under bushy gray eyebrows, turned radiant.

"All of these young men—like John—have a monkey on their back all the way to Dixie. Why, John, he's a profit center all by his lonesome. I'm not mothering him."

The recent elevation of John Revson, a chip off the old block down to the eye-closing gambit, had unsettled the Revlon-watchers once more. It also reshuffled the deck in what Robert W. Armstrong, international chairman (who once left Revlon for six years to become president of Wertheimer Frères, the French owners of Chanel perfumes, and then returned), candidly acknowledged as "one of the great guessing games"—the management succession of Revlon, Incorporated.

"This is one of the few major companies where the founder is still chief executive," Armstrong said. "This company has no hierarchal structure. But it's one of the few companies that has corporate charisma. Charles built this company and he personally attracted some tremendous talent. Charles is one of the greatest recruiters of all time," he said.

As a talent wooer, Revson put no dollar limits to his courtships. The contract with Bergerac was merely the latest example of his corporate largesse. In 1969 he had lured Sol Levine from the presidency of Del Laboratories (which was controlled by his alienated brother, Martin Revson) to straighten out chaos in the Revlon factories. Levine was given a nonrecourse loan secured by his 165,200 shares of Del stock that could net him no less than $2.2 million but possibly up to $4.5 million during the next three years.

"The factories were in such a mess they could have come to a halt if it had gone on another year," said Theodore Boutis, then Revlon's treasurer. Boutis left a year later to join Joseph Anderer at M. Lowenstein. "The loan has paid for itself already. We're pleased with the job he's done."

Boutis discounted any motive in the loan to take over Del, a cosmetic and drug company in the variety-store price category Charles Revson has always avoided. Revlon would be holding 13.7 per cent of Del's stock, however.

Martin Revson, four years younger than Charles, is a marketing man once described as someone who could sell iceboxes to Eskimos. He acquired his position in Del in 1963 after settling out of court the stock fraud suit against his brother.

Martin and Charles Revson were reconciled in 1971 after the death of their eldest brother, Joseph, who had helped Charles and Charles R. Lachman, a chemist, establish the Revlon Nail Enamel Corporation. Lachman, long since affluently retired, supplied the "L" in the corporate name.

Indeed, many executives have made fortunes, small and large, from their associations with Charles Revson, an educational experience said to combine the rigorous disciplines of the Talmudic *cheder* and the brainwashing of Chairman Mao.

"Charles thinks of himself as a great teacher and he is a great teacher but he never thinks it's time for graduation," said one alumnus now consigned in financial ease to a limbo where Revson never refers to him or, if he must, refers to him as "what's his name."

There are so many Revlon veterans in the cosmetics industry (such as Stanley Kohlenberg, president of Coty, John Malcolm, executive vice president of Elizabeth Arden, and Suzanne Grayson, marketing consultant and founder of the Face Factory stores), that the company is properly called the Macy's and Procter & Gamble of the beauty business. Revlon seems to be the beauty training school for success elsewhere that Macy's and P&G are in retailing and consumer product marketing.

Yet a number of key Revlon executives such as Messrs. Armstrong, Woolard, Sanford Buchsbaum (senior vice president for advertising), Lawrence Wechsler (executive vice president for marketing), and Irving Bottner (president of the professional products division) have lasted ten to fifteen years.

According to some witnesses, survivors must endure not only the whiplash of Revson's perfectionism ("he demands and he demands but he can never say thank you," a Revlon refugee said) but also the intrigues of his courtiers who vie for his favor and emulate his idiosyncrasies, from his scathing sarcasm to a penchant he had in 1972 for lavender shirts and green ties.

Proximity to the throne inevitably transforms many able, decent human beings into sycophants with instincts for the jugular. The only alternative may be flight. "Charles Revson humiliates people in front of others though he doesn't have to raise his voice," said a female drop-out from Revlon who, like most women employees, allude to his charm and human qualities. "They in turn scream at you when others are around, and the poor secretaries beat up the mail boys."

An executive of an advertising agency that had the Revlon account for several years explained how Revson crushes executive morale. "It's a typical meeting to present new product ideas that have been worked over for weeks. The meeting is finally scheduled for 3 P.M. Friday. It is held at 7 P.M. and opened by Charles saying, 'You ruined my nap with this meeting. Now don't show me any of this crap that doesn't sell.' The president of the division interrupts. 'But Charles, you haven't seen anything.' Charles looks for a while and then he interrupts with, 'You know no woman will buy yellow.'

"Of course," the ad man said, "I've laundered the language in telling this. Charles spent one year trying to clean up his language but he had an awfully hard time."

Furthermore, the courtiers conceal or delay presenting matters for Revson's decision or awareness. Their deceptions enhance his tendency to forget what he doesn't wish to acknowledge.

The president of another ad agency wrote Revson a letter one year before the termination of their contract, telling him in a friendly way that he wanted to be relieved of the fragrance accounts so that he could go after a larger piece of business from a pharmaceutical company. Because of its toiletries products and Revlon's drug division, the new account would have presented a conflict of interest for the agency. He received no reply to that letter or several others except for a mumbled greeting from Revson when he collided with him in the lobby of the GM building. Shortly after that encounter, the ad man was called by a Revson subaltern who said, "You're really trying to rub it into Charles, aren't you?" To protect himself, the agency head then sent a legal notice of termination by registered mail and never heard another word from anyone at Revlon.

On another occasion Revson attended a farewell party for a woman executive who had told others in top management that she was going into the consulting business and would have another cosmetics company as one of her clients. They had not dared to tell Revson, however, and when she mentioned it at the party, he acted as though he had been betrayed.

Revson's erratic memory, particularly manifested in the omission or misuse of names, is one of those flaws he'd rather not admit. Seated next to the wife of an associate at a dinner party, he kept calling her "Evelyn." Her name is Vivian. She responded by calling him "Meyer." At the end of the evening, he asked her in troubled tones, "Why do you call me 'Meyer'?"

Despite the efforts of subordinates at dissimulation and secrecy, no one doubts that all major decisions are made by one man, Charles Revson. He has no compunction about reaching down through several layers of management to learn the return rate from a single department store on one product promotion, or to offer to send a medical specialist to an employee's ill child on a weekend, or to prod a small, snobbish specialty store in Palm Beach to carry Revlon products. Palm Beach is considered the turf of his archrival, Estée Lauder, whose privately owned company cultivates a high fashion image and distributes only through specialty and department stores.

And of course, it was Charles Revson who in 1973 made Lauren Hutton the highest paid model in American history (and therefore a celebrity and news magazine cover girl). A similar fate had befallen Dorian Leigh, the Revlon Fire and Ice girl in the fifties. After photographer Richard Avedon overcame his doubts about Miss Hutton's unexceptional looks and gap-toothed smile, Revson signed her to a contract that nets her nearly $200,000 a year for modeling no other products but Charles Revson's Ultima II line in advertisements. She is free to take on editorial assignments for magazines or to act in movies. She had the feminine lead in the 1974 film *The Gambler.* In the Ultima II ads she is photographed to convey a slightly sluttish, girl-next-door quality that seems to be Revlon's (or Revson's) feminine ideal. In one ad she posed in the buff, hands awkwardly shielding part of her breasts. The photograph was cropped slightly below the navel. The expression on Miss Hutton's face was quizzical.

Stick-to-it-iveness, gutsiness, patience, daring, and unflagging competitiveness. These are Revson attributes to which foes and friends pay tribute. Or as he put it, "You make mistakes, you pick yourself up, you come back. Pride. Pride to win. That's important. You don't cry in your beer."

He confessed that this was his personal creed although at the time (during the interview early in 1972) he had in fact been referring to Valentino, the Roman couturier publicized as a favorite of Jacqueline Onassis. Revson had decided to buy the rights to market a perfume under Valentino's name; the scent was being tested for introduction in 1973.

Revson was explaining why he had chosen Valentino, just a few years ago a dark horse compared to the front runners of the Paris couture and perfume world. "He's solid Jackson," he said, hammering a table on which a butler had just served 6:45 P.M. tea. "He makes a fine, highly tailored coat or suit." Revson, a fastidious dresser, had sold dresses on Seventh Avenue before going into nail polish.

"He knows who he's making clothes for, what sex they are. They're for people who have money. He'd never pose in the nude like what's his name," he said, meaning Yves Saint Laurent, the Paris designer who was then a property of Squibb through its acquisition of Lanvin-Charles of the Ritz, Saint Laurent's backer. The frail-looking designer had been photographed in his bare skin for a male fragrance ad. "You wouldn't catch Valentino posing in his shorts. And those others. What's his name? Courrèges. What's his name?"—he left it to an underling to supply the name of Ungaro, whom Estée Lauder had signed up—"Where did they all go? They all went South," he finished with unconcealed glee.

The Lauder-Ungaro deal lapsed, but as it turned out, Revson never brought Valentino to the fragrance market either.

In the meantime, one of Revson's earlier impulses—to market a made-in-America, expensive ($50 an ounce) perfume called Norell—has been recognized as the "instant success" of recent fragrance history. Introduced in 1968 via a lavish social and promotional event at Bonwit Teller, Norell perfume grossed $1 million sales the first year.

In 1974 Norell perfume sales were running at $10 million a year and "the most expensive lipstick in the market" was introduced that fall under the Norell name at $7.50 (a refill cost $3.75). Norell's death in 1972 at the age of seventy-two had not slowed the momentum in the least.

Associates had opposed Revson's selection of an aging designer like Norman Norell, whose audience had been limited to women willing and able to pay from about $800 to $4,000 apiece for his dresses. But Lyn Revson liked and wore his clothes, and Charles Revson thought they epitomized good taste.

Norell was given authority over the packaging of the perfume named for him but Charles Revson masterminded the scent. He is justifiably proud of his "nose." Impressive numbers of upper-middle-class American women have been buying Norell perfume for themselves year round, instead of waiting to receive it as Christmas gifts, and using it up unstintingly.

With Norell the first American fragrance to achieve prestige and profits, Revson scored another victory in February 1973 by bringing out another fragrance line for younger, breezier women. It sold at $6.50 for a half ounce of concentrated perfume oil. He named it Charlie—an obvious example of competitive egocentricity after Lauder's introduction of her perfume, Estée—although an apparel manufacturer, Charlie's Girls Inc., instituted suit against Revlon for trademark infringement. Within one year, Charlie fragrances had attained a volume of $10 million a year, which industry sources estimated was probably the largest single fragrance introduction ever. A cosmetics and treatment line was then introduced under the Charlie brand.

Revlon's best-selling fragrance is Intimate at $25 an ounce. In 1965 its lagging sales were given a 26 per cent boost through the "What Makes a Shy Girl Get Intimate" advertising campaign developed by Leber, Katz Partners. Revson halted it six months later after someone told him the advertising was obscene.

Two years later it was reinstated when he learned that a survey of college students showed it was the fragrance advertising they remembered best. Sales grew another 12 per cent. Then Intimate sales leveled off at about $20 million a year. For some time, Revlon's fragrance people have been adjusting Intimate to make it more long-lasting, according to Revson's instructions. Estée Lauder's Youth-Dew proved the profitability of scented staying power.

During the last decade some of Revson's executives tangled with him on the issue of direction. Mass versus class: should Revlon concentrate its forces more on the battlefield of middle America where Avon, the only bigger cosmetic company had 15 per cent of the market or should it increasingly pursue prestige and high fashion through lines like Ultima II, Norell, and Bill Blass for men? Revson's admirers say the latter tactic, which is costly and slow to pay off (Ultima II turned into the profit column after eight years), provides a launching pad for extra revenues. It also sheds some fall-out on basic Revlon, the company's medium-priced, quality mass market line sold in drug and department stores and the largest contributor to Revlon, Inc.'s beauty revenues. Dissenters attributed the prestige pursuit to Revson's ego and a personal preference for elegance and opulence.

His lugubrious and rigid style of dressing and interior decoration hinted, some said, monumental social insecurity. Close associates believed that the winner of the 1950 Horatio Alger Award, given to former poor boys who struggled to the top in business, dreaded being thought gauche or being caught committing a faux pas. For years Revson wore only dark blue or banker's gray custom-tailored suits, blue shirts, and black neckties, and though he shifted into slightly brighter shades during the sixties era of peacockery, he soon returned to solemn tones.

Visitors to the thirty-room Park Avenue triplex apartment formerly inhabited by the late Helena Rubinstein, which he bought for $392,000, felt overpowered by beige. Some were jolted by the contrast with the former owner's riotous eclecticism. Madame Rubinstein had never hesitated to combine great art with bewitching junk. Revson employed two decorators, Edward Benesch and McMillen, Incorporated, to create an aura so tranquil that one could hear a false eyelash drop.

Similarly, when he acquired Daniel K. Ludwig's yacht he had it refurbished in a superluxurious monotony that was like a roar for silence. Oceangoing palaces beg for guests, and for several years, the *Ultima II*'s cabins and decks were filled with the titled and famous hangers-on of Earl Blackwell, the owner of Celebrity Service, party stager, organizer, and arranger of social quotient lifting for needy tycoons.

The *Ultima II*'s arrival in Acapulco or Monte Carlo was chronicled by Blackwell's allies, Aileen Mehle and Eugenia Sheppard, the fashion-cum-society columnist. The Revsons joined Raffles, an eating club in the Sherry-Netherland Hotel and appeared at the Nine O'Clocks, a social dancing circle both of which Blackwell had helped to organize.

Then William J. Levitt, the realty magnate, built a rival yacht and had it decorated by John Gerald to suit the eighteenth-century French inclinations of Levitt's wife, Simone. When the yacht, *La Belle Simone* docked on the French Riviera that summer, the Blackwell coterie transferred aboard her, leaving the Revsons alone in the same harbor.

Even before the Levitt rout, Estée Lauder had captured the French Riviera, scoring another win in her comic and vehement feud with Revson. Strictly on her own and with no use for the services of an Earl Blackwell, Mrs. Lauder had become a social celebrity, with guests both royal and rich in her villas in Cap Ferrat, Palm Beach, and her Manhattan town house.

The social rivalry was extended to the fields of philanthropy as well, and here Revson kept ahead. The Lauder foundations built children's playgrounds in Central Park, but Revson paid for a fountain in Lincoln Center and a plaza at Columbia University. A Lauder son became identified with the Museum of Modern Art, but Charles Revson's name is inscribed as a major donor at Albert Einstein Medical College and Brandeis University.

More important from a business standpoint, however, were the Lauder-Revson skirmishes in specialty and department stores, where Lauder products maintained a lead.

There had also been a certain switching of allegiance of key personnel, perhaps more common in the cosmetic industry than some others. The gossips had special fun with a Lauder-Revson exchange, though. Robert Nielsen, a marketing man, had moved from Lauder to an executive vice presidency at Revlon but only after an interim job—some called it laundering—with an ill-fated Zsa Zsa Gabor cosmetics venture.

Then, a year before his employment contract was up, Revlon's chief research chemist, Joseph Gubernick gave notice that he was going with Lauder. Since research is the heart of product development and, besides, research was Revson's professional passion, the news was treated as though it were a defection from the KGB to the CIA.

Revson had had the last word in earlier vendettas with beauty empresses. The late Elizabeth Arden called him "that man" and he so named one of his men's fragrances. The late Helena Rubinstein referred to him as "the nail man" and he wound up residing in her apartment.

Some industry insiders say that Revlon had been at a disadvantage at the counter because it had no celebrity authority like Lauder, Arden, and Rubinstein backing its products. Therefore, they maintained it was sound business judgment which justified his apparent ego when Charles Revson introduced the Braggi men's line with a Revlon-paid advertising campaign that teamed himself with Andrew Goodman, the dapper president of the carriage-trade specialty store Bergdorf Goodman.

Subsequently, Revson's name began to encroach on the Ultima II label until it became Ultima II-Charles Revson. A CHR Treatment Collection and CHR Face Makeup System were added to the line. The chairman's sayings dominated the advertising. In 1973, when a new fragrance, Ciara, was introduced, as "the thoroughly female fragrance by Charles Revson," its brand parent, Ultima II, did not appear in the ads. Instead, this statement was carried, "This is the fragrance I've always wanted to create—very elegant and unlike anything you've ever worn before Charles Revson." For the debut of the fragrance Cerissa one year later, the full-page advertisements were dominated by a sketch of Charles Revson. It was a flattering likeness of the Revson of twenty years ago, but still easily recognizable by the luxuriant eyebrows.

"It's not done for glory on my part," Revson had insisted the year before when questioned about his growing intrusiveness. "The decision is not founded on Charlie's Folly. Ultima will henceforth have a separate marketing organization from Revlon. The ultimate dream," he said, not intending a pun, "is to have a group of separate companies run on their own with separate profit centers."

Bowing to the major tenant in his office building, Revson compared his company with GM. Ultima II would be his Cadillac and basic Revlon the Pontiac. There is no Chevrolet (or variety store line) in Revson's garage.

Thus far, Revlon, Inc., has had a highly centralized organization based on franchised or controlled distribution and a broad-scale vertical penetration.

The Revlon Domestic Division has six distinct cosmetic lines, or "houses," each intended to meet the needs of a particular segment of the consumer market in terms of age, lifestyle, and income. They are: Revlon, Moon Drops (a treatment line, one of the most profitable parts of the beauty business), Natural Wonder for the youth market, Ultima II-Charles Revson, Etherea/Fine Fragrances (which combines products for allergy-sensitive skins, women's fragrances, and men's grooming aids in a single division), and Marcella Borghese, a premium-price line.

The first three, medium-priced lines are sold in one out of five of the nation's drugstores, a deliberately restricted retail distribution, as well as in some department and specialty stores. The prestige lines were developed for and sold in specialty and department stores which account for only 18 per cent of the $5 billion cosmetic and fragrance sales in the United States.

Fragrances, another potentially high-profit category, had been an "underdeveloped" part of Revlon until recent years, Paul Woolard said. His aim was to bring it up to 30 per cent of an expanding total cosmetic business.

The beauty industry, long regarded as depression-proof, has not been immune to rising costs and consumer resistance in the "stagflation" economy of the 1970s.

Nevertheless, in 1973 and 1974 Revlon, Inc., was able to widen the profit margins on its bounding sales of cosmetics and fragrances, recovering nicely from a contraction in operating profits in 1970 and 1971.

Operating profit margins ran to 14.9 per cent of the $230.6 million in domestic sales of cosmetics and fragrances in 1973 and 16.3 per cent of the $140.8 million in international sales.

Revson's foresight had taken the company into one hundred foreign markets in the past seventeen years, with wholly controlled manufacturing facilities for cosmetics and fragrance products in eleven countries, even in Japan which has tended to restrict operations of foreign enterprises. A Brazilian plant was opened in 1974, to take advantage of that newest of dynamic consumer markets.

Still, beauty has been a purposefully shrinking share of Revlon, Inc.'s sales and profits. In 1967 cosmetics and fragrances accounted for 84 per cent of sales and 91 per cent of earnings; in 1973, 77 per cent of its $506 million in sales and 72 per cent of its earnings of $43.4 million came from these sources.

The balance and growing share was represented by health products and services. It is more than coincidence perhaps that Charles Revson, a health zealot who offered medication when his employees sneezed and sent portly friends' meat dishes back to restaurant kitchens for leaner slices, focused his company's diversification program on pharmaceuticals and proprietary drugs.

American consumers spent more than $9 billion on pharmaceutical products in 1973. In the same period, when Revson was striking into this lucrative territory, drug companies were buying up once great cosmetic companies. Eli Lilly's acquisition of Elizabeth Arden and Squibb's purchase of Lanvin-Charles of the Ritz were notable examples. But whereas the drug giants achieved lackluster results with their glamour properties and seemed unsure about cosmetics, Revson's health businesses flourished under the Revlon umbrella.

Revson had floundered with diversification in the early 1960s, making some unprofitable "fashion" acquisitions such as the Evan-Picone women's sportswear company and an artificial flower business.

Then in 1966, against the advice of most of his associates, he paid $66 million for a sleepy company, United States Vitamin & Pharmaceutical Corporation, doing $18 million in annual sales. It gave him his entrée to the drug field. By 1973 Revlon's USV division had sales of $110 million here and abroad.

Another $25 million in sales was produced from the Mitchum-Thayer Division, which resulted from the merger of a personal-care products company with a proprietary drug and toiletries company. Revson added to his health nucleus in USV with smaller acquisitions such as a British pharmaceutical company and a small medical testing laboratory.

However, he did not succeed in his efforts to acquire other important pharmaceutical houses like Norwich Pharmacal, Parke-Davis (which went to Warner-Lambert after government antitrust scrutiny), and Calbiochem.

For Revlon's destiny in the drug field, 1971 was a significant year. In the spring, USV's oral antidiabetic product, phenformin, marketed as DBI and DBI-TD, was threatened by a statement from the University Group Diabetes Program, financed by the National Institutes of Health, that the drug was no more effective than diet in prolonging life. The research methods as well as the findings of the study were widely disputed, but the American Medical Association recommended oral antidiabetic drugs be used only as a third resort after diet and insulin, and the Food and Drug Administration required labeling changes for phenformin.

More important, though, was the tax-free swap of drug products between USV and Ciba-Geigy Corporation, which took effect in December of 1971. USV acquired seventeen prescription drugs for the treatment of arthritis, high blood pressure, and mental illness from Ciba-Geigy in exchange for domestic rights to market DBI and DBI-TD. USV received the right to market phenformin in the United States under another brand name and under DBI abroad.

Within the next two years, USV was manufacturing and selling ethical pharmaceutical products in fourteen out of twenty major therapeutic categories and ranked twenty-fourth among drug companies on the basis of purchases by hospitals and drugstores in the United States. Revlon, Incorporated, was thus on its way to becoming what one Wall Street security analyst had euphorically labeled "a drug company with a cosmetic side."

Such enthusiasts reasoned that Revlon's marketing aggressiveness, or what one of its executives termed "the attitude that nothing is impossible," can more successfully be transferred to the drug field than vice versa. The drug companies that acquired cosmetic companies seemed to have bought headaches mostly because they lacked the intuition, creativity, and willingness to turn on a dime while hedging losses for short-term risk. "They don't understand that this is a 'touch' business," a Revlon cosmetic executive asserted. The drug business, Theodore T. Boutis once said, before he resigned the treasurer's post at Revlon, "is a license to steal because the person with a prescription needs that medicine. But you have to get out and sell that lipstick because there are a hundred others the customer could buy."

A former director of Revlon suggested however that the most optimistic forecast that could be made about USV was that its executives had managed to hold Revson at bay. His nagging interference in the health side of his company has so far been minimal.

Disparaging remarks of this sort are made about Charles Revson all the time. His detractors are legion, but many of his employees tend to soften their judgments once they escape his clutches. More often than not they give credit where credit is due. It would be rewriting history to deny his influence on an industry and on the fortunes of many individuals who worked for him. Some collapsed in harness. Others escaped to thrive in freedom.

Born in Boston in 1906, reared in Manchester, New Hampshire, Revson, a cigarmaker's son, went to work in a Seventh Avenue dress house at the age of seventeen. At twenty-four he was selling nail polish for a distributor. At that time there were only three shades of transparent polish, old rose, pink, and red, and they invariably streaked when applied. Polishes with a creamy base that went on smoothly were just being developed. On March 1, 1932, half a year before his twenty-sixth birthday, Revson, his older brother Joseph, and a chemist named Charles Lachman went into business to market opaque nail enamels in a tempting array of colors. The experimental batches were heated over a Bunsen burner in the one-room loft on West Forty-fourth Street that they rented.

The Revlon colors were christened with exotic names like Tropic Sky and Windsor Rose. At first they were sold in the beauty salons that were burgeoning since the improvements in the permanent-wave machine. Later the nail enamels were distributed through department and drug stores, but Revlon never lost its lock on the salon business.

Revson had translated the fashion concepts of the garment center to one beauty care product, selling it as style rather than necessity. In 1939 he extended the strategy by matching nail polish to lipsticks and co-ordinating those colors to fashion trends in clothes, with suggestive and ever changing themes. "Theme is my religion," he said. Old comrades from the early days remember him walking around with splashes of lipstick and nail colors on his hands.

"In the factory we make cosmetics, in the drugstore we sell hope," was another Revson *bon mot*.

In the 1950s Revlon added make-up, creams, and lotions to its product lines and used advertising to the hilt to sell them. The TV quiz shows made Revlon and Revson part of mass culture. "The $64,000 Question" became an overused metaphor.

In 1955 Revlon, Inc., went public, and within a few years Charles Lachman, older brother Joseph Revson, and younger brother, Martin Revson (who had come aboard in 1935) took their stock and left Charles Revson in sole command.

Martin invested in Maradel Products, which evolved into Del Laboratories. Both of his sons were killed in auto racing crashes, Douglas in Denmark in 1967 and Peter, a racing hero, in South Africa in 1974.

Charles' two sons went to work for him. Some have suspected that the mystery quiz game of the Revson succession was their father's delaying tactic until the older son, John, could be groomed for the job.

In the meantime, only "that man" knew the answer.

Postscript: May 1975

Charles Revson did not appear at Revlon's offices after October 1974. He was in and out of the hospital and confined to his home. Bergerac was running the company, which posted banner results for 1974. Sales increased nearly 20 per cent to $605.9 million and profits about 14 per cent to $49.8 million. Per-share earnings rose to $3.76 from $3.30 the year before. Cosmetic sales were up 22 per cent, health care products and services up 14 per cent.

Michel Bergerac presided at the annual meeting on May 1, 1975. He charmed the stockholders with his relaxed, witty style and his French accent, still as thick as *crème fraiche* despite his having spent all of his working life of nearly twenty years with American companies.

At the meeting it was announced that Bergerac was to be elected chief executive officer, four months ahead of schedule.

THE HOSPITALITY CRUSADE: HOLIDAY INNS

August 1973

A fifty-five-foot-high, star-capped neon sign could pose stiff competition for the stars and spires of Red Square, which may be one reason that Holiday Inn's proposal to build a convention center in Moscow is in dormant status.

But nothing is slowing the relentless spread of American motel culture by the Number One food and lodging chain. "The world's most accommodating people" have had conversations in Peking and negotiations in Cracow, so far, mostly just talk in the Communist bloc.

As of July 31, 1973, however, there were 1,549 Holiday Inns with 237,936 rooms in operation throughout the world from Kyoto, Japan, to Yeehaw Junction, Florida, three times more than its nearest rival, the ITT-Sheraton chain. Fourteen per cent of the motels in the United States are Holiday Inns.

Every three days another one opens somewhere. The African kingdom of Lesotho has a Holiday Inn, and so do the cities of Beirut, Lebanon, and Avignon, France. There are ten in the corporate headquarters city of Memphis, according to the precepts of the founder and chairman, Kemmons Wilson. He believes in staking out all of the arteries leading into a town and planting an inn right in its heart as well.

Since so many American cities have lost their downtowns to urban decay, Holiday Inns have shot up in suburbs and shopping center complexes, near medical centers, in resorts and at every key Interstate highway junction. The international push has just begun.

"We want to be in every major city of the world," the sixty-year-old Wilson said.

In 1951 he took his wife and five children on an automobile trip to Washington, D.C. He was so disgruntled with the fleabag lodging en route that he built his own hostelry on Memphis's eastern fringe. By middle-American standards, it was clean, comfortable, tasteful and affordable ($6.00 a night for husband, wife, and the kids).

His mother, the late Ruby ("Doll") Wilson, a widowed bookkeeper, decorated the motel in chartreuse and white. Her only son kept building motels (and she kept decorating the first fifty) until his franchised network with its "Great Sign" inspired by a movie marquee and corporate name taken from a 1942 Bing Crosby film, made millions for the Wilsons, their associates, and some of their stockholders.

Some of these paper fortunes have eroded recently because Wall Street has become disenchanted with the lodging industry.

Uncertainty about the United States economy, the effect of the energy crisis on domestic travel, and the hot breath of competition from other expanding chains have contributed to investor doubts. The erratic earnings and labor strife in Holiday Inns' transportation acquisitions (Continental Trailways and Delta Steamship Lines) haven't helped. Holiday Inns bought the bus and ocean cargo companies in a $200-million stock transaction in 1969.

But there are no pessimists in the eighty-acre corporate enclave where executives wear "Great Sign" pins in their lapels and expressions on their faces that look like smile buttons.

On their desks are green, loose-leaf "attitudes" books. Published in Dallas, they list 104 personality traits that further positive thinking and, quite possibly, the unswerving corporate goal of 3,000 Holiday Inns by 1980.

"Attitude is the greatest asset you can be possessed of, but you've got to work at it," declared Wallace E. Johnson, the vice chairman. "We don't have problems—just some opportunities. And he that sayeth to himself that the growth of Holiday Inns world-wide has reached its climax is all wrong," said Johnson, one of Memphis's leading Baptist laymen.

"Positive thinking" is the byword and the fuel of Holiday Inns, Incorporated, though its leaders assert they were practicing it long before they met Norman Vincent Peale. Not only as disciples of this business-oriented clergyman but also in keeping with southern capitalism, they have blended Protestant faith and finance with lucrative results.

Holiday Inns, Inc., employs a corporate chaplain. The Reverend W. A. ("Dub") Nance, a Methodist, as is Kemmons Wilson, conducts an executive fellowship breakfast Wednesdays at 7:30 A.M., co-ordinates an interfaith network of 1,326 volunteer chaplains on call at Holiday Inns all over the world, and keeps count of the 500 suicides they are reported to avert each year. He officiates at employee weddings and funerals and provides counseling to those who need it during working hours.

Some of the inns, such as the high-rise Rivermont perched above the Mississippi River at Memphis, have chapels. Rivermont's is paneled in wood, decorated with plastic flowers, and seats fifteen. Roman Catholic, Greek Orthodox, and a variety of Protestant worship services have been held in it.

About 250 inns provide regular Sunday services. Even in one of the Rivermont's black-walled, red-carpeted, $100-a-day suites, the Gideon Bible lies open on a white Parsons table rather than being tucked away in a drawer.

Mr. Nance's staff also supplies the Thought for the Day for the corporate corridors and the paycheck envelopes. (Recent examples: "A little smile adds to your face value" and "An optimist is one who makes the best of it when he gets the worst of it.")

"At our first board meeting we were determined to build a company based on the dignity of man and on Christian principles of the brotherhood of man," said William B. Walton, the fifty-three-year-old president of Holiday Inns and a devout Presbyterian. "If you do really believe in yourself and those you are associated with and do believe that what you are doing is morally right—both business morality and social morality—you can accomplish anything legal you set out to do," he said. Thus he enunciated the creed that filters beyond the Holiday Inns management philosophy into the annual reports and the accounting ledgers.

For example, devaluations of the dollar increased the company's obligations for foreign expansion by $6.5 million in 1973 and $2 million in prior years. Instead of taking a loss through write-offs as incurred, as other multinational companies have done, these amounts were capitalized.

"We think the dollar is coming back," said Frank W. Adams, senior vice president for commercial services. "When it does, we reverse the entries that cause the capitalization of the devaluation. It's a matter of faith in the United States. The dollar will prevail, and when it does these adjustments will be reversed and everybody made honest again."

Faith in the Holiday Inn way extends to the standard eighty-inch-long double beds that were resolutely sent to the Kyoto inn.

"Ultimately the Japanese will get taller," declared John M. Greene, Jr., senior vice president for system standards. "It may take fifty years, but eventually the Japanese will be glad we have oversized mattresses."

Except for minor adjustments, such as four brands of beer instead of several colas in the German inns' vending machines, the motel culture is being exported intact. At first the Germans thought that the two double beds in each room were intended for sexual orgies but now they understand that the jumbo size accommodates two children.

The foreign inns must have air-conditioning and free ice (they'll like it after they try it in northern Europe, goes the corporate rationale), free TV, free lodging for children under twelve sharing parents' rooms, free kennels for pets, three-meal-a-day restaurants, and swimming pools—increasingly placed indoors both at home and abroad.

Most of the European inns return a passport immediately to the registering guest according to the Memphis directive "never separate a guy from his passport."

Precise levels of hygiene and functionalism, published prices, and confirmed reservations by computerized Holidex system prevail on five continents. And, of course, the "Great Sign." Some variations on the neon obtrusion are permitted in deference to local sensibilities. In Japan, the "Great Sign" is a rather small sign atop a pole.

The lack of surprises at a Holiday Inn is a boon to the middle-class traveler, be he businessman or vacationing patriarch. A 1971 guest profile showed how middle-of-the-road he is, with a median income of $17,950, a median age of 39.3, and two or more children (who can stay free in the second of the double beds if they are under twelve).

The system's level of plastic taste, monotonously smack between execrable and excellent, has penetrated beyond its own walls, not at all by accident. The design department receives requests from guests asking to buy the indestructible lamps, the seignorial mural wallpaper, and the mock Bernard Buffet pictures.

In the newest company-owned inns, the decor will be "contemporary," with lots of chrome instead of brass and straight-line, walnut-laminate furniture.

"The public is now ready," said Thomas Thomley, assistant vice president for interior design. In 1973, 53 per cent of Holiday Inns' $885 million corporate revenues and 52 per cent of $75-million pretax earnings came from food and lodging. But 22 per cent of sales and 19 per cent of profits derived from its products division, and almost 72 per cent of that business flows in from non-Holiday Inn customers including the franchises of competitors such as Ramada Inns, Hilton, and Sheraton.

Sixteen per cent of the ten-ounce plastic tumblers used by American motels and airlines are manufactured by the products division's Holiday Press at the rate of 3.5 million a week. The Holiday Press also prints paper placemats, hotel bills, *Holiday* magazine (no connection), and 14 million Holiday Inn directories, in which one can tell immediately that a single in Paducah, Kentucky, will cost $14.50 a night whereas the Holiday Inn near Manhattan's Coliseum will charge $30 (water beds and bridal suites available at higher prices).

The Holiday Press offers an office decorating service for doctors, dentists, and small-business men without a fee. The object is to sell them office machines, baronial desks, plastic orange trees, and copies of Rembrandt's "Night Watch."

The products division's Innkeepers Supply Company exercises an inescapable influence on American taste through its design department and the Institutional Mart of America, "a one-stop supermarket for commercial properties" that has three regional showrooms.

In them are displayed acres of motel front desks and lounges with their fake rustic beams, Olde English fireplaces ("Fireside Human Relationship"), color TV sets with on/off buttons that neither guests nor unskilled repairmen can destroy (and that permit the innkeeper to save $15 a year per room on service contracts), shag and printed nylon carpeting (guaranteed to last five to seven years), and those innerspring and foam rubber mattresses that will endure ten years if turned every sixty days and reversed head to foot.

Pièces de résistance: cocktail lounges to help the innkeeper increase profits through beverage sales such as the Club Escadrille, a "nail 'em up" bar installation complete with murals of World War I aces and airplanes and a ninety-minute sound tape of dawn-patrol dogfights.

It takes 4,000 items to furnish a motel, from swimming pool to ¾-ounce cakes of soap that can be ground up for general cleaning use after the guest departs. The Innkeepers Supply Company sells them all.

The Holiday Inn's decorating philosophy will infiltrate the Far East through the Japanese version of Innkeepers Supply Company recently set up through C. Itoh, a trading company.

"We turn a brick-and-mortar building into a business," said Clyde H. Dixon, the products division president. "As they say about McDonald's, our hamburger's not so hot—it's the system that gets them."

He was alluding to his division's vertical manufacturing and distribution system, but the remark applies just as well to the total Holiday Inn system.

In an inflationary climate, economies are more than ever the order of the day. Holiday Inn restaurants are turning to self-service buffets and room service. Soon the guests may even be stripping their own beds and dropping the sheets into a laundry chute. Future inns may be constructed with prefabricated concrete modular rooms equipped with air-conditioning. Lobbies will be dispensed with, and one cashier will run the front desk and the restaurant.

Nearly one third of the advertising budget has been allotted to promoting the food and beverage operations as a culinary experience. (Such regional variations as catfish in Mississippi and rice dishes in North Carolina are encouraged.)

Innkeepers are being advised to "re-examine your pricing in relation to your markets," which is one way of reacting to the threat of the new budget motels.

The last few years have seen an outcropping of the economy roadside lodgings that charge half the rate of conventional motels.

The accommodations are spartan—none of the niceties of pool or color TV—but just as the ugly, little Volkswagen chewed into an important piece of a market primed for power steering and air-conditioning, so have the budget motels appealed to many travelers who will tolerate the bare minimum in overnight lodgings if the price is right.

The budget chain operators say they can halve their construction costs and that their occupancies ran as high as 80 or 90 per cent compared to the average 69 per cent that the regular motor hotels averaged in 1972.

Among the publicly held budget motel chains are the Scottish Inns of America and Motel 6, a subsidiary of City Investing Company. The more conspicuous of the chains springing up in the southeast are Chalet Suisse International and Days Inns of America. Howard Johnson has started adding its own economy motels, Threepenny Inns.

But the top management of Holiday Inns doubts it is possible to build profitable motels at those discount rates of $6.00-and-up a room.

Holiday Inns were the prototype budget hostelries of the 1950s. In the last decade, the average room rate rose from $8.83 to $16.86 while the occupancy rate declined from 75.4 per cent to 71.7 per cent, still a whit ahead of the motel industry's average.

Holiday Inns, Inc., is essentially a franchise system that has made money for its franchisees as well as its founders. Revenues of Holiday Inns all over the world add up to an estimated total of $1.8 billion a year.

Seven years ago Harold Frankel, an appliance retailer and former mayor of Huntington, West Virginia, paid $700,000 for the franchise of an ailing Holiday Inn one mile off Interstate 64. The road leads to Louisville, Kentucky, and Columbus, Ohio.

"I wouldn't sell the inn for $3 million today," he said. He put his wife in charge of the bar and restaurant and together they lifted the revenues of the 112-room motel from $300,000 a year to $1.5-million. Two thirds of it comes from food and beverage sales, principally the Polynesian Supper Club.

The Frankels' second Holiday Inn franchise will open next fall in downtown Huntington. The twelve-story, $6.5 million property, financed by the First National City Bank of New York, will have

212 rooms, a heliport on the roof, and a Pompeiian supper club with an erupting "volcano."

Holiday Inns, Inc., maintains a ratio of 75 per cent of its inns franchised, with the rest company owned and operated. The franchisees represent a sampling of international financial clout, ranging from real estate developers like Kemmons Wilson and Wallace E. Johnson (officers of Holiday Inns, Inc., who recently sold their six independently held licenses) to foreign governments. The first Holiday Inn in Eastern Europe is being constructed outside Cracow near a Tatra Mountain ski resort as a tourist attraction by Orbis, the Polish Government tourist organization.

Plans for the Czechoslovakian Government to join the franchise network, also as a step to stimulate tourist business, were killed by the Russian invasion of the country in 1968.

In Morocco a joint venture involving the government, Armand Hammer, the chairman of Occidental Oil, and Holiday Inns came apart when the Minister of Tourism was assassinated. The Holiday Inn Marrakech ended up at the World Bank for arbitration of its ownership.

"The peril in Eastern Europe or a Morocco," said W. Jefferies Mann, president of the franchise sales division, "is that the guy you dealt with may not be there anymore. Someone's word doesn't mean a lot over there. If you tried to go in as a U.S. citizen, it would be impossible, though."

ABC-TV owns the Holiday Inn in Weeki Wachee, Florida; the Calloway Foundation operates the Holiday Inn resort of Calloway Gardens in Georgia; United Inns, a big-board company founded by a Memphis dentist, runs thirty-one Holiday Inns in the South. C. Itoh, a billion-dollar Japanese trading company, will spearhead Asian development.

The largest franchisee is American Motor Inns (AMI), which operates fifty-three motels from Maine to North Carolina and in the Caribbean. It reaped an after-tax profit of $3 million on revenues of $57 million in the fiscal year ending July 1973 and is listed on the American Stock Exchange.

AMI sprouted from a pawnbroker's store in Roanoke, Virginia. In 1957 the owners, Adolph and Joel Krisch, their sister, Rosalie, and her husband, Sydney Shaftman, went looking for another business to supplement the pawnbroking unit that wasn't quite enough to support three families.

Pooling their resources into a capital base of $40,000, they started to build a fifty-one-room motel for traveling businessmen, but before it was completed they decided to affiliate with the young Holiday Inn chain. They gave a $3,000 note and agreed to pay 5 cents a day per room for use of the Holiday Inn name and another 5 cents a day per room for national advertising (those were the franchise terms then). They learned the basics of hotel operations from a book borrowed from the public library. Holiday Inns taught them about food and banquet facilities.

Volume the first year reached $150,000 with net income of $15,000. The Krisches and Shaftmans kept building.

In 1969, after the Federal Communications Commission permitted privately owned telephone systems to be connected to public utility lines, AMI started a subsidiary, Universal Communication Systems. The subsidiary offers an interconnection system for hotels and other businesses under a lease-purchase plan. Another subsidiary, American Motel Schools, a correspondence course for prospective motel operators, was sold to one of its employees.

In 1972 AMI brought suit against Holiday Inns alleging unlawful restraint of trade. It had been denied a franchise for a motel near the Newark Airport because another licensee already had one in the area.

[In the fall of 1973 a federal district judge in New Jersey ruled that in such a situation the franchisee is free to enter into a contract with another hotel/motel organization. AMI was awarded $4 million in damages. Holiday Inns appealed the decision.

In December AMI and Holiday Inns announced they were negotiating an acquisition of AMI by the parent licensing company in what was then a $30 million exchange of stock. But in May 1974, after Holiday Inns shares had been drubbed in the market, the merger was called off.]

Prospective Holiday Inn licensees are told that the average cost of building a 120-bedroom Holiday Inn in the United States or Western Europe is about $16,000 per bedroom, that the equity investment should be 25 to 30 per cent of the total project cost, and that the land costs should represent 10 to 20 per cent of the total investment. Feverish urban real estate values and escalating construction costs make those figures look ridiculous in such areas as Japan or New York.

The initial license fee is at least $15,000. Assorted mandatory royalty fees running to 3 per cent of gross sales are levied for use of the "Great Sign," the Holidex reservation equipment lease, advertising, and training for innkeepers and restaurant managers at Holiday Inn University in Olive Branch, Mississippi.

The school, which was started in 1959 in the basement of Founders Hall, the conference building at Holiday Inn headquarters in Memphis, was transplanted to a quiet little town twelve miles southeast of the city at a cost of $5 million.

Holiday Inn University now sits on the edge of a grove of pecan trees, with the Holiday Inn peace-symbol flag symbolizing "World Understanding Through Tourism" fluttering over the driveway. From a campanile donated by Kemmons Wilson in memory of his mother, a carillon peals any one of 125 melodies, among them "I Left My Heart in San Francisco," "White Christmas," and "The Battle Hymn of the Republic."

Three fourths of the students are employees of the franchise holders sent to Olive Branch for training (a three-week innkeeper course, a four-week food and beverage course, an eight-day executive housekeeper course, a five-day sales manager seminar). Knowledge of English is a requisite.

Students check in as though they were guests in the university lobby, which looks like a Holiday Inn. They live in dormitories with standard Holiday Inn guest rooms. The academic environment is intensely efficient but friendly, with closed circuit TV for instruction and background music piped into classrooms for motivation (Beethoven to rouse, banjo music for uplift). There is swimming and tennis for relaxation and a "Gravy Bowl" football competition (innkeepers versus food and beverage) with teams wearing the university colors of red and black to boost class spirit and forge a sense of community.

Holiday Inns, Inc., does not contribute capital to franchises except in Europe, but it does advise on financing. Architectural plans and building contractors must be approved. Since 1962 Holiday Inns, Inc., has bought back about 125 franchises (by issuing new common stock) from licensees who extracted the benefits of accelerated depreciation and wanted to move on to other tax shelters. By the end of 1974 there will be 162 Holiday Inns in forty-three countries outside the United States, and there are vast populations yet to become acquainted with a Holiday Inn.

Some of them will have trouble saying "Holiday" in their own language. The Japanese pronounce it "Horiday." But Lee Berthelsen, the vice president in charge of operations in Europe, the Middle East, and Africa, said, "The wonderful thing about Holiday Inn is that, even when it's mispronounced, it's understandable."

Berthelsen is a thirty-eight-year-old New Yorker by origin, but his mind is as positively upbeat as though he sprung from the soil of Memphis. For an international corporation heading toward billion-dollar revenues, Holiday Inns, Inc., has a management style that is distinctively southern, religious, hard-working, and amiable. Its spirit is contagious. And why shouldn't it be? The company is young. Its founders and their associates have prospered and they are still around to furnish evidence and direction.

The two Memphis builders who begat and nurtured the company twenty years ago have become multimillionaires through their Holiday Inns stock ownership, as well as from independent real estate and construction ventures in which they are partners.

The Walkem Development Company, Inc., which Kemmons Wilson and Wallace E. Johnson control, owns 5.9 per cent of the 29,295,940 shares of Holiday Inns, Inc., common stock.

Wilson personally owns 1,326,262 shares and Johnson owns 813,973 shares. In 1973 Wilson drew $145,150 in salary from Holiday Inns, Johnson $95,150.

Wilson, the chairman, built the first Holiday Inn (it was called a Holiday Inn Hotel Court), conceived the idea of a chain, chose the name and the "Great Sign." He still picks sites for new inns. "Real estate is a sense of feel for some people," he noted. His "feel" is enviable. "It's my great love. With real estate I'm like a kid looking for Easter eggs. Once in a while I find a golden egg. I feel just as at home looking at a piece of ground in France as I do in Tennessee."

Johnson, the vice chairman, has looked after the financing. "I thank God I've always been able to find the money," he said.

Both Johnson and Wilson have been the recipients of the Horatio Alger Award, presented to achievers "in the American free enterprise system" who triumphed through "hard work, thrift, initiative and honesty."

The London *Sunday Times Magazine* named Wilson one of the "thousand makers of the twentieth century." He was born on January 5, 1913, in Osceola, Arkansas, and given "Charles" for a first name and as a middle name—Kemmons—that of the doctor who delivered him. When he was nine months old his father died. His mother, Doll Wilson, an unquenchable optimist just under five feet tall, moved to Memphis and supported herself and her son as a bookkeeper.

At fourteen Kemmons Wilson was working as a delivery boy for a Memphis drugstore. He never got to college. When he was seventeen he bought a second-hand popcorn machine for $50 (he paid it out $1.00 a week), rented space in a movie theater for $2.50 a week, and was soon making $30 a week selling munching fare to the patrons.

"Because I had been in theater business, I realized the importance of a marquee when I was going in the motel business," Wilson says, telling how the "Great Sign" came to be. With his laconic manner of speaking and his open countenance—blue-eyed, sandy-haired, and with a nose that obviously was broken somewhere along the way—he has a certain movie-star quality. Spencer Tracy, perhaps, in better humor and with a southern accent.

Wilson's office is large, cluttered, and hung with photographs of his mother and of himself with world-renowned celebrities such as Norman Vincent Peale, Pope Paul VI, and Princess Grace and Prince Rainier of Monaco (which has a 320-room Holiday Inn on its Avenue Princesse Grace).

"I wanted a sign at least fifty feet tall, with changeable letters like a marquee," Wilson said expounding on the "Great Sign." "I told this fella to make me some sketches. I looked at the one you see now. I had the honor of picking it out. The name came from a Bing Crosby movie I saw on TV. I picked that out too."

At first, the United States Patent Office refused to register the service mark on the grounds that it was based on an intangible, but Wilson persisted and succeeded in obtaining the registration.

That was a considerable while after his popcorn-selling days in the lobby of the Memphian Theatre. The theater manager, seeing what a lively business Wilson was doing, decided to take it over for himself. Wilson sold him the popcorn machine for exactly what he had paid for it, and, with his capital returned, he invested it in second-hand pinball machines that he installed in hotel cafés and drugstores.

At the age of twenty-one he built a house for $1,200 in cash amassed from his pinball ventures, and after he sold it at a profit, he started borrowing to build other houses. He also built and operated seven motion picture theaters.

When the United States entered World War II, Wilson was married and mortgaged to the home-building business. He liquidated his business and signed up for the Air Transport Command, serving from 1943 to 1945 as a flight officer, mostly over the mountainous Asian routes.

Because of Wilson's and other top management interest in aviation (Clyde Dixon is a former World War II pilot and Bill Walton was an instructor of B-17 crews), Holiday Inns has a subsidiary, HI-Air, Inc. It operates the Olive Branch Airport, a fixed-base operation for private and executive jets and also a reliever airstrip for Memphis International Airport. HI-Air also holds one of the largest dealerships for Cessna aircraft. For the first dozen years or so, Wilson doubled as the corporate pilot. "We couldn't afford to hire one," he says, and because he is a man of many parts and tireless energy, he used to dictate letters and memoranda into a recording machine while he flew the plane. Once he made a crash landing without interrupting his dictation.

The airport is part of 3,000 acres of real estate the company stumbled into buying from the city of Olive Branch which was eager to have an airfield. Holiday Inns Industrial Park is being developed on the parcel of land.

While he was serving in World War II Wilson was dabbling in home building back home through his mother, who looked after his interests and followed his instructions. When he returned to civilian life in 1946 he expanded his real estate, home-building, and theater-operating businesses.

In 1951 he took his family to Washington, D.C., on "the most miserable vacation trip of my life." The next year he built his first motel and three more in the following year and a half. After the four were completed, he began to entertain the possibility of a national chain. "I needed a man who could think big with me and the biggest-thinking man I knew was Wallace E. Johnson," he says.

Johnson had been christened "the Henry Ford of the home-building industry" by a national magazine because of his achievements in low-cost housing.

The Mississippi-born Johnson, who was twelve years older than Wilson, had started as a construction worker at fourteen. Like Wilson, he went into business for himself for the first time at eighteen, learned the advantages and pitfalls of debt. In 1940 he tried again. "I was thirty-nine years old and I was making $37.50 a week working for a lumber company. I borrowed $250 and went into business for myself," he said. "Memphis had 20,000 developed lots. I had 5,000 pasteboard signs made that read 'Let Wallace E. Johnson build your home on this lot.' I sowed the signs all over though I didn't own one lot.

"One day I was in the bank making a $5.00 withdrawal and a man in front of me was making a $7,500 deposit and he turned to the president of the bank and I overheard him say, 'Where the heck did this fellow Wallace Johnson come from? He owns more lots in town than any one man I have ever seen.'

"The first year I built 181 houses. Speculative houses, building them for $2,999 each and starting ten houses at one time. People thought we were crazy."

Johnson perfected a production system of standardized parts which resulted in a house being finished every 2½ hours by Wallace E. Johnson Enterprises of Memphis. At the request of General George C. Marshall in 1942, he drew up the plans for the city of Oak Ridge, Tennessee, home of the "Manhattan Project," which developed the first atom bomb.

As the founder of the Memphis chapter of the National Association of Home Builders, Johnson had friends in the business everywhere. Wilson figured that with Johnson's contacts, prominent home builders would be persuaded to construct Holiday Inns all over the country. He explained his plan to Johnson one evening in 1953, and there and then they shook hands on a partnership.

Wilson still says, "I'd rather have the handshake and word of a good man than all of the contracts you can draw. There aren't enough lawyers to keep them."

Johnson invited seventy-five home builders to listen to Wilson's proposals. Sixty-one came, appeared to be enthusiastic, and promised to send in their $500 checks for franchises. But a year later only three had done so. Wilson and Johnson kept plugging away, however, and the franchises began to move slowly.

In 1955 they decided they needed an administrator. They talked William B. Walton, a thirty-five-year-old lawyer and general counsel of the Home Builders Association in Memphis, to give up his practice and become executive vice president. "Kemmons Wilson and Wallace Johnson are two of the greatest entrepreneurs and salesmen this country has ever known," Walton says. "They talked me out of my law practice and promised me $500 a month which neither of them had. Each would contribute $250."

"We were bankrupt," recalls Walton, a man of massive girth and preacher's cadence. "We were $37,500 in the red. Johnson said we could have an old plumbing shop of his for an office. And that's where we started putting together the Holiday Inn system." One of Walton's first acts was the drafting of the constitution for the International Association of Holiday Inns, a trade association and an advisory body which includes all company-owned and licensed Holiday Inns. IAHI makes recommendations for advertising and system-wide rules of operation. Each Holiday Inn pays a per-room assessment into the national advertising fund. Through IAHI, every franchise holder is made to feel he is "part of a team."

At its first meeting on May 25, 1956, Walton reminisced, "we had twenty-one inns and three people on our payroll. Today we have 155,000 on the payroll." Walton owns 112,421 shares of Holiday Inn common stock and in 1973 earned $114,225 in salary.

"I say we have the greatest system in the world. We're the biggest also. Three and a half times larger than our nearest competitor. But you can get big from being greedy and I don't think we've ever been greedy," Walton said.

Walton is one of Memphis' leading Presbyterian laymen, a member of the executive committee of the Mayor's Prayer Breakfast. "We have got to get the country turned around with positive thinking," Walton intoned. "Primarily it's a matter of attitude. There's no secret to building a fifteen-by-twenty-seven-foot room. A fifty-five-foot sign isn't what makes a company great. All we've got is a collection of buildings of steel and concrete and glass. It doesn't have warmth and friendly attitude until the innkeeper gets there."

It was Walton who banished the words "hotel court" and "motel" from the corporate lexicon and christened the motel managers "innkeepers," because it sounded friendlier. He dreamed up the symbol of John Holiday, a jolly host from the days when an inn meant fireside warmth and comfort and shelter from the rigors of travel. Holiday Inns don't use "No Vacancy" signs. If they're sold out, they will help the traveler find another room elsewhere. "That way we make two friends," Walton says.

Walton claims a heritage in innkeeping. During the Revolutionary War, one of his ancestors, Captain William B. Walton was granted a tract of land in Tennessee where he later obtained the right-of-way between Knoxville and Nashville, built a road and constructed inns.

Walton is proudest of the management team he formed at Holiday Inns. "We call it the Holiday Inn family. We've been told it's a bit corny but that's what it is. That was something I believed in, from my four years in the Air Force teaching B-17 crews to work together as a team," he says. "The era of the one-man tycoon, I think that's gone. I think we're living in an era of professionalism. We have a young management team in depth, all those young men in their thirties," he said referring to four senior vice presidents under forty years of age.

Walton is the only one of the corporate troika who intends to retire at sixty-five. There is no mandatory retirement age at Holiday Inns. "There never will be as long as I'm here," Wilson said. Johnson said he wasn't ever going to retire: "I was born in 1901 and my mother is ninety-five and painting." He pointed to a drawing she had recently done from memory of her birthplace in Edinburg, Mississippi.

Walton says he's training one or two men to do his job. Meanwhile, he's so busy ("if anything goes wrong, I'm the guy Mr. Wilson calls") that he doesn't have time to "pack up a bag and drive two hours" to a weekend retreat. So he built a lake house on the ten-acre lake across from his home. He spends Saturdays there, meeting with executives or fishing with his minister.

Walton devised the theme for Holiday Inns of "World Understanding Through Tourism . . . One Road to Peace" that appears in most of its promotions and is printed in six languages in the Holiday Inn directories. It includes a flag in which a global emblem that looks more than vaguely like Pan Am's and a dove of peace are emblazoned on a field of blue.

"We believe we have a chance for two generations of peace," Walton said. "We're country boys and we think that once people sit down and talk together, they get to understand each other. In our case, it's business. When people travel around they understand each other better. We're in every nook and cranny of the United States and soon, the world. Who has a better opportunity to promote the idea than us through our business?"

While Walton occupies himself solely with Holiday Inns and his myriad "people-oriented civic projects" (Kiwanis, retarded children, Vanderbilt and Memphis State universities, the Presbyterian Church), Wilson and Johnson further their separate and partnership deals in real estate, construction, and insurance.

"Yes, we're very much a partnership," said Johnson, a white-haired, gray-eyed man of ample shape. "Kemmons' leadership is in building and drawing plans. I spend my time with the bankers," he added. His secret for borrowing millions and millions of dollars in tight money times as well as easy credit periods is: "If I don't have a way set in my mind how I'm going to pay it back, I don't ask for it. A banker wants to know how you're going to pay the borrowed money back. I also make it a point to know in my mind exactly what the money is for so I can convince the banker I need it. I believed in positive thinking before I met Norman Vincent Peale." One of the Peale books Johnson likes best is *Enthusiasm Makes the Difference*. Says Johnson, "Nothing great was ever accomplished without enthusiasm."

"I've been blessed, too, with one of the greatest wives. Miz Johnson is one of the greatest partners a man could have." Alma Johnson is a partner in his real estate, mortgage, and supply companies and in several investment and development firms.

The Johnsons also founded a nursing-home chain, Medicenters of America, Inc., of which he is chairman, and a cemetery business. (He once told a magazine interviewer that he was investigating means of burying people standing up, in round, form-fitting fiberglas caskets, in order to get eight times as much use out of the same plot of ground.)

Not all of Wilson's and Johnson's ventures have been winners though. Each invested $1,000 in a scheme to raise catfish and bullfrogs on acreage they bought in the Mississippi Delta that had once been used for rice farming. The frogs' legs would spur a market for a culinary delicacy, it was thought. They lost money on the deal after a freight attendant unwittingly killed 1,200 tadpoles by dousing them with ice water and owls destroyed the bug-feeding system for the survivors. But, as Johnson said, "At harvest time, we sold the land to a fella and got a fancy price for it though we never did harvest either catfish or frogs."

Wilson's and Johnson's ventures have tended to be natural outgrowths of their basic businesses—real estate and construction. A similar thread of logic runs through Holiday Inns' diversifications.

In 1969 the company bought TCO Industries, owners of Continental Trailways Inc. and Delta Steamship Lines. The bus company, second largest in the United States, also has a travel agency subsidiary.

The transportation acquisition would have contributed about 30 per cent of revenues and income in normal years but its performance in both these spheres has been erratic because of labor unrest. Besides its vulnerability to longshoremen's strikes at Gulf Coast ports, it was subject to a long-drawn-out strike on its Safeway Trails subsidiary which operates the New York-to-Washington, D.C., route.

Holiday Inns' expertise in franchising was moved outdoors in 1970 with the start-up of a nationwide chain of Trav-L-Parks, aimed at capitalizing on the growth in the camping industry. The recreation areas plugged into the Holiday Inns' computerized reservation system.

At the end of 1973 forty-five parks with 9,284 rental spaces were operating in seventeen states.

Wilson has also built a prototype for a national, franchised tennis center system in Memphis called the Wimbleton Racquet Club. A tennis buff, he often challenges franchise holders and colleagues to postprandial matches, wherever he happens to be. "I tried golf but it was too slow," he said. "It's not nearly as competitive as tennis. You're playing against golf. In tennis, you play against a person."

Yet, despite his competitive streak, he said, "I believe in living and let living." He won't permit his children to work for Holiday Inns because, he says, he doesn't want the employees to "have to fight the competition of my three sons. They all work for me but not in this company. Years ago I told them I want them to have the pleasure of doing for themselves."

Epilogue: January 1975

By the fall of 1974 there were 1,677 Holiday Inns with 263,534 rooms (too many of them vacant) world-wide.

Holiday Inns had opened in Singapore and in Halifax in Nova Scotia; in Caracas and in São Paulo; in Kaohsiung, Taiwan's second largest city; and in Bulawayo, in Rhodesia, a country with which

American businessmen are, by the letter of an Executive Order issued by President Johnson in 1968, advised not to do business because of its white supremacist policies. (But the United States Government was looking the other way as other American businessmen arranged their franchises and their deals there, too.)

Back in Memphis, Holiday Inns, Inc., was contending with a barrelful of challenges, the likes of which had never been envisioned in such deadly combination during the more than two decades of its beanstalk growth.

First, gasoline shortages. Then inflation, which scrapped millions of dollars' worth of Americans' vacation plans. Construction costs, tight money which froze the real estate and building industries, and higher costs for food and foreign development had all narrowed some of the smiles on the faces at the Holiday corporate complex. But the bullish faith and fervor were burbling as always.

In 1974 Holiday Inns, Inc., was almost a billion-dollar company but its profits dropped 29 per cent from the year before. On revenues of $986 million, the company had net income of $32.6 million, compared with the $46.4 million it earned on revenues of $885.7 million in 1973.

Holiday Inns was not alone. The entire lodging industry was suffering, too. Even the budget motels had seen their occupancy levels tumble and the financial bind had caused several mergers and bankruptcies.

Kemmons Wilson was not temperamentally suited to enjoying the company of his competitors' misery. Wilson reacted by reading the temperature of the times. He reorganized Holiday Inns at the top, not disturbing his own role of entrepreneur and free-wheeling idea man.

Bill Walton was relieved of operating responsibility for the whole shebang. He was given the title of vice chairman and the assignment of developing the franchise system world-wide. The two members of the management team just below him were advanced a notch.

L. M. Clymer, a fifty-year-old executive vice president who had come half a dozen years before from the Nashville investment firm which underwrote the first issue of Holiday Inns stock in 1957, took Walton's place as president.

Clyde Dixon, the fifty-three-year-old head of the products division replaced Clymer as executive vice president.

From the outside, Wilson brought in Roy E. Winegardner, a fifty-three-year-old franchisee from Cincinnati, one of the biggest in the system with forty-two Holiday Inns to his credit. He was named first vice chairman and to all intents and purposes, Number Two strategist. Winegardner had started in business as a plumbing contractor in Springfield, Missouri, and had built his first inn in Lexington, Kentucky, in 1958. When he agreed to take the vice chairmanship, Winegardner & Hammons Operations Inc., his franchise company, had Holiday Inns under development in Australia, Fiji, and Brazil. He promised to divest himself of those interests and cancel pending plans for twenty-seven proposed Holiday Inns.

The new first team decided to concentrate hard on marketing. The days of building an inn, plugging into Holidex, lighting up the sign, and watching the guests drive up to the door and register were over. "Now it's marketing, marketing, marketing," Dixon said.

Each division appointed its own marketing director and the food and lodging division, which had accounted for more than half of revenues and pretax profits in 1973, was told to dispense marketing training down to the levels of local innkeepers. A "Kids Eat Free" program was beamed at families with children under twelve.

National sales efforts were stepped up. Holidex was connected with the reservation computers of Eastern Airlines, fly/drive programs co-ordinated with most of the airlines, and bus/drive package programs with Continental Trailways.

In its building plans for the future, Holiday Inns marketers are calculating the long-term possibility that energy problems will alter the highway focus of American life. They will emphasize the construction of downtown Holiday Inns.

On the assumption that there will be more family vacations close to home, they are adding "leisure domes" to new and existing inns. These climate-controlled, overhead structures cover the pool and courtyard areas of an inn, converting it to a year-round recreational area.

The management team in Memphis isn't taking its eyes off the wide world yonder for a minute. Satellite offices for international development are positioned in Beirut, Brussels, Tokyo, Hong Kong, and Rio de Janeiro and one will be opened somewhere in Africa.

The chances of the "Great Sign" looming over Red Square look dim enough for the time being, but then, there's always Mecca.

Wallace Johnson has cut down on his work load but he is still available for attitudinal messages. Holiday Inns may have a few problems but by his sights that means all the more opportunities.

AND THEN THERE'S . . .

THE ENERGY TRAUMA AT
GENERAL MOTORS

March 1974

"For years I thought what was good for our country was good for General Motors, and vice versa."—Charles E. Wilson, otherwise known as "Engine Charlie," former president of GM, at Senate hearings on confirming his nomination as Secretary of Defense, 1953.

Probably no American company has suffered so swift and stunning a blow from the energy crisis as the General Motors Corporation, the quintessence of infallibly managed business enterprise, the Goliath of the world's industrial concerns, which Ralph Nader likens to a nation-state.

In the five months since October 1973, GM has slid into the worst sales slump since the 1958 recession. So far, its car sales are down 35.7 per cent.

GM has been toppled from its pedestal as America's most profitable industrial corporation and replaced, ironically, by the Exxon Corporation. Bewildered security analysts have been predicting first-quarter earnings for GM of anywhere from 35 cents to $1.00 a share, a staggering decline from $2.84 a share in the 1973 first quarter.

The Number One auto maker has closed as many as fifteen of its twenty-two assembly plants and three of its four body plants to reduce the glut of unsold big cars and convert more production to its popular smaller cars. Still, GM will be making fewer small cars next fall than its archrival the Ford Motor Company, Number Two in the industry.

GM has laid off 65,000 workers and has put 57,000 more on temporary furlough. And the troubles of the company, the major influence in the nation's leading industry, have rippled into the economy through GM's 13,000 franchised dealers and 45,000 suppliers.

GM has attracted fresh attacks from its critics. They are charging violations of antitrust laws and accusing the foremost automobile company (which also happens to be the dominant United States manufacturer of buses and locomotives) of thwarting mass transit for selfish corporate gains.

Eighty-four per cent of GM's net income in 1973 came from made-in-America automotive products. The company earned $2.4 billion on world sales of $35.8 billion, a strong increase from the previous year's profit of $2.2 billion on sales of $30.4 billion. But earnings dropped 22 per cent in the fourth quarter of 1973, and the decline has accelerated.

The lifting of the Middle East oil embargo in mid-March of 1974 had been eagerly awaited by GM's executives as a move that would alleviate their company's distress. They had blamed the embargo for sowing "uncertainty and confusion" among car buyers.

Richard C. Gerstenberg, sixty-four-year-old chairman and chief executive officer of General Motors, announced that "business is getting better" and that GM was canceling some of its plans for further temporary plant closings during the last two weeks of March.

"With the prospect that more gasoline will be available soon, we are watching closely for further signs that customer demand for new vehicles will turn up sharply," Gerstenberg said. But he bypassed the question of whether the energy crisis has made an irreversible impact on the auto industry. Many informed observers believe it has.

John Z. DeLorean, forty-nine, GM's maverick vice president and small-car advocate until he resigned a year ago, insists that "the Arab embargo just took a curve and accelerated it. The small-car trend had been growing in momentum for ten years."

But chairman Gerstenberg retorted, "All of us are blessed with almost perfect hindsight and DeLorean's is no exception."

GM's immediate problem seems to be that the shortage of gasoline and its soaring price caused customers to stay away from automobile showrooms, particularly those stocked with standard-size automobiles with thirsty engines. Once the object of a national romance, these all-American land cruisers suddenly were tagged with the epithet "gas-guzzlers."

General Motors has more of these land cruisers than anyone else—4,500-pound Chevrolets, 5,500-pound and nineteen-foot-long Buicks, Oldsmobiles, Pontiacs, and Cadillacs. But it doesn't have enough small cars like its 2,800-pound subcompact Vega.

The late Alfred P. Sloan, Jr., who had built the corporation on the chaos left by its founder, William C. Durant, preached the gospel that bigger is better. The Horatio Alger heroes who have since managed GM faithfully observed his tenets. More add-on equipment brings higher prices and profits.

The first Henry Ford had provided America with a basic black passenger vehicle produced by adapting human labor to an assembly line. The Model T was priced to the lowest possible level. Alfred Sloan converted the public to wider aspirations of affluence and mobility through his merchandising strategy of color, product improvement, and annual model changes.

GM straddled its markets by offering the top quality and price in each consumer category. At the bottom, the Chevrolet division grew to the dimensions of the nation's fifth largest corporation (it sold 3.3 million cars and trucks in 1973). At the top, Cadillac was preeminent in luxury and profit per unit. In the middle, Buick, Oldsmobile, and Pontiac consistently supplied earnings corpuscles to the corporate bloodstream.

In recent months, however, the latterday products of that Sloan strategy have been stalled, undelivered from assembly plants, or gathering dust and 11 per cent finance charges in dealer showrooms.

Such a profit sag would be traumatic for any corporation, but at GM the pain is excruciating. Profits are the machismo of Sloan's heirs in management. He designed the incentive program through which they take home some of the highest salaries in corporate America. The program credits a portion of earnings based on a complicated ratio related to net capital and to a bonus and stock option fund.

It provides that 8 per cent of net earnings which exceed 7 per cent but not 15 per cent of net capital, plus 5 per cent of net earnings which exceed 15 per cent of net capital are credited to a bonus and stock option fund. This is administered by a bonus and salary committee of the board of directors. The committee will also choose Gerstenberg's successor when he retires in November at sixty-five. In September they will find a replacement for Edward N. Cole, GM's president when he reaches the mandatory retirement age.

In 1972 Gerstenberg was the nation's highest paid chief executive. He drew $875,000 in salary and bonus. His 1973 compensation and that of his colleagues was even higher. Gerstenberg was paid $938,000 although he had slipped to second place on the national scale behind Philip B. Hofmann of Johnson & Johnson who received $978,000. Ed Cole was given $846,500, and Thomas A. Murphy, the vice chairman, whom everyone took for granted was being groomed for Gerstenberg's job, was accorded $776,125.

The bonus committee credited $112.8 million, the maximum allowable from 1973 earnings, for awards to some 7,000 salaried employees and executives. Management thus escapes any penalty for the recent earnings decline.

Whether the energy-triggered blow will affect the committee's choices for the top posts is the subject of much speculation by GM-watchers, a breed obliged by the corporation's disciplined secrecy to practice skills like those of Kremlinologists. Radical change, which would be totally out of GM character, would mean reaching outside for leadership.

The torch tends to be passed to loyal insiders. They are an exceedingly homogeneous group of professional managers, who eschew the cults of personality and youth. Except for a few converts to hair coloring, they are grizzled conservatives in dress and philosophy. Only Gerstenberg has permitted sideburns to grow below his ears and his are sparse enough to escape detection except at the range of eyeball-to-eyeball confrontation.

Born and reared in the Middle West, they were educated at local universities or the General Motors Institute, the in-house engineering college whose co-op program enabled many poor boys to work their way through school. President Cole and executive vice president Elliott M. Estes are GMI alumni.

The typical GM executive has spent his entire career of eleven-hour days in the service of one employer. In recent history only

John DeLorean violated that tradition. The son of a Ford foundry worker, DeLorean is an exceptionally creative engineer. Under his aegis GM's stylish and easy-to-handle Firebird, Grand Prix, and Monte Carlo specialty cars were produced.

He is also conspicuous as a six-foot-four-inch hedonist and a connoisseur of racing cars and women.

DeLorean had been hired away from Packard in 1956 by Semon E. ("Bunkie") Knudsen, a GM pioneer's son who quit in 1967 when he didn't win the GM presidency. DeLorean successively revived the Pontiac and Chevrolet divisions at times when they were seriously ailing and was rewarded with a corporate vice presidency. He was subsequently promoted to head the car and truck group, a job that was viewed as the last proving ground for a GM presidency and which yielded him close to $600,000 a year in salary and bonuses. Six months later, in April 1973, he resigned.

In the fall of 1972 he had warned his colleagues at the Greenbrier conference, GM's triennial management powwow for its top 700 executives, that "poor quality threatens to destroy us. Warranty repairs were costing the company $500 million a year," he said. He also spoke of the unspeakable: "Significantly, there has been a serious and disturbing decline in loyalty among the owners of GM products, especially in head-to-head comparisons with Ford. The impact of this declining loyalty will show up in a year or two when the consumer enters the marketplace again." His remarks were prophetic.

He had argued for smaller cars on the grounds that the rising cost of owning and operating a car and the anti-conspicuous-materialism of youth was altering consumer taste. It was "unpatriotic" to permit the rise of the United States trade deficit when that $3.5-billion sum was equal to what the auto industry was losing to foreign competitors, DeLorean said.

He was backed by Cole, at least up into the executive committee meetings where his ideas were throttled. DeLorean's departure leaves open the tantalizing question of whether an independent in flagrant contact with the world beyond Detroit could ever make it to the summit at GM.

These days, DeLorean is driving a BMW around suburban Bloomfield Hills where most GM executives reside. His lifestyle is noticeably less restrained than theirs, however. DeLorean is married to his third wife, a twenty-four-year-old brunette model and actress

named Christina Ferrare. The daughter of a Cleveland butcher, she
has the bones and Vogue-ishly sexy bearing of a Roman contessa.
Mrs. DeLorean earns $100 an hour modeling for fashion magazines
and for *Cosmopolitan* which likes her to pose for its covers display-
ing as much of her breasts as is consonant with chic. These days
that's slightly less than Playboy deems worthwhile. She also has a
two-year contract with Max Factor & Co. to model for its cosmetic
advertisements at $120,000 a year.

The DeLoreans and three-year-old Zachary, the son he adopted
while he was still married to Kelly Harmon, the daughter of Tom
Harmon, the Michigan football hero, apportion themselves among
homes in New York, Los Angeles, and Bloomfield Hills. The consulting offices he opened after he left GM are also in that wealthy
Detroit suburb. They are decorated with the sleekly contemporary
plastic and glass furniture, geometric paintings, and poster-sized
photographs expected in the offices of movie or rock record executives (media which are two of DeLorean's many passions). He
usually reports to work in jeans, turtleneck, and moccasins over
bare feet.

He has partner interests in a Cadillac dealership in Florida, in the
New York Yankees and the San Diego Chargers, and in avocado
and cattle ranches in the West. He is working on producing a small
"ultimate" sports car and a "commuter" minicar that would yield
eighty miles per gallon.

The men who do succeed at GM accept compromise by committee. They govern from the southeastern wing of the fourteenth floor
of corporate headquarters, a gray edifice on Detroit's West Grand
Boulevard furnished in faint-hearted modern uniformity. (Their
offices on the twenty-fifth floor of the GM building in New York,
where they come for monthly board meetings, are decidedly
grander.)

In Detroit the executives are paired in suites with pale blue car-
peting and identical leather-topped desks equipped with push-
button controls for closing and locking doors. On the wood-
paneled walls are color photographs of their peers, of GM cars,
and mass-copy oil seascapes and autumn scenes.

Always within reach is Alfred Sloan's manual, *My Years with
General Motors,* to be conferred on important guests like Nikolai S.
Patolichev, Soviet Minister of Foreign Trade, whose copy was au-
tographed by Richard Gerstenberg.

Some of the insularity of the fourteenth floor may be perceived by outsiders at public events like the annual meetings or the Conference on Areas of Public Concern held in February for 250 institutional investors and opinion molders at the GM Technical Center in nearby Warren, Michigan. In three previous years the conferences were staged to blunt the growing movement for corporate responsibility on social issues such as safety, the environment, and doing business in South Africa.

This year, as the pension fund manager for a major insurance company analyzed it, the chief concern of the guests was "how GM was going to anticipate change over the next few years based on major change in the energy supply."

After six hours of lectures, slides, an unrevealing technical peepshow, and a luncheon at which Gerstenberg preached his favorite sermon on profits for progress, the fund manager confessed he was "disappointed . . . I had the impression of an extraordinarily defensive, almost one-dimensional attitude," he said. Subsequently, he "lightened up" on the holdings of GM stock in the pension funds his company manages.

To outsiders, General Motors presents unwavering and self-justifying positions on energy-related issues of production, safety, pollution, and public transportation. Sometimes its stands are overruled by the pressure of events, such as the halting of production of motor homes, a venture embarked on last year well within sight of the energy crisis. Until early in March management argued that the homes could be used as medical units and mobile offices. Usually, though, not a single crack appears in the management team's line of defense—that GM had correctly anticipated the social and economic change that had rocked the automobile market.

When asked why GM, with its vast intelligence network and alliances with the oil companies, didn't foresee the energy crisis, Gerstenberg replied that no one "visualized the effect of the embargo." However he recalled that an energy task force was set up in June 1972 and that he ordered a system-wide energy conservation program.

Cheap gasoline since the early 1900s helped determine the American way of life—suburbs, big cars, atrophied mass transit. What does GM forecast as the settling point for gas prices and its effect on buyer preferences, the institutional investors asked.

Henry Duncombe, GM's chief economist, hesitated and came up with a 50-cent guess. Others declined to guess.

But then, GM executives seldom buy gas themselves. They never queue up for it. They drive or are chauffeur-driven from their homes in suburban Bloomfield Hills and Birmingham into the executive garages from which they ascend by elevator to their offices. While they are upstairs running the company, the cars are refueled, washed, and cured of creaks and blemishes. After an odometer registers 3,000 miles, the executive is given another Cadillac Eldorado, Oldsmobile Toronado, or Pontiac Grand Ville to "test drive."

The chairman, who once evaded a senator's query on safety costs by referring to himself as "old Gerstenberg the bookkeeper," commented, "I keep asking our economists about a rule of thumb [on the price of gasoline at which purchasers would be discouraged] and they don't give me very good answers. Some people think the freedom the automobile gives is worth a lot. I don't know."

GM is 100 per cent in favor of freedom, as in free enterprise and free markets and freedom from government control although it approved President Nixon's lifting of the automobile excise tax and imposition of an import surcharge in 1971 to retard the growth of foreign automobile sales, mostly small cars, which had grown to 15 per cent. Imports now have 16 per cent of the United States market.

"We've been proponents of no controls on the price of gas," Gerstenberg went on. "There's been a hue and cry that the fellow who needs gas the most [to go to work] will be hurt, but this fellow can do a lot by sharing rides with people."

The question persists: Why didn't GM foresee the trend to small cars if it knew an energy squeeze was coming. Ford plans to have 2.1 million small cars in production in 1975 including two new designs. GM is stretching toward a 2 million capacity. GM's answer this time comes from president Edward Cole. Often alluded to as the father of the Corvair, he is a small-car advocate and a nuts-and-bolts man who knew how to play the profit game: "One of the real problems is what is the definition of a small car. Now we have cars with a 112-inch wheel base that sell a lot, the Chevelle, the Cutlass, the Century, that we think should be classified as small, though others don't define them that way."

Even GM brochures define them as intermediates. The Cutlass weighs 4,500 pounds.

Government and industry standards identify "small" as 3,000

pounds or less, a criterion GM can meet only with the Vega, its German-made Opel, and an 1,800-pound minicar made by its Brazilian subsidiary that it refuses to confirm it will be producing here for 1976.

"What is small today may be big tomorrow," Cole added. Indeed, the Chevrolet sedan grew seven inches in length and 502 pounds in weight since 1968 from design changes mainly to meet government emission and safety standards. In the process, it lost 16 per cent in fuel economy. Now GM has a research program to reduce vehicular weight through the use of plastics, lighter steel, and aluminum.

DeLorean has said he waged a campaign for two projects four years ago that would have scaled down all of the GM cars. The full-size vehicle would have been reduced to the size of today's intermediate and the present compact would have been 600 pounds lighter. The plans were killed in committee. "A lot of people hide behind a committee, you know," DeLorean said. If he were ever to return to industry, he said, "I wouldn't want another one of those committee deals where you sit around all day in meetings."

The men who run General Motors do not tell tales out of committee. Nor do they confess error, with one publicized exception which some still regret. That was in March 1966 when James M. Roche, then GM's president, apologized before a Senate subcommittee for GM's harassment and investigation of Ralph Nader, the consumer advocate whose book *Unsafe at Any Speed* had attacked the Corvair. Frederick G. Donner, the aloof and hard-nosed financial man who was GM chairman at the time, was thousands of miles away on a trip—many suspect, of convenience.

Later, GM settled out of court, for $425,000, Nader's million-dollar suit for invasion of his privacy. Nader used the proceeds to subsidize his consumer activism.

"My wife says Nader wouldn't have gotten off the ground if we hadn't bought all of his books," said Elliott M. Estes, fifty-eight, executive vice president for operations and one of the jollier denizens of the fourteenth floor. Everyone calls him "Pete." He is considered a candidate for the presidency.

"But sure," he added, turning serious, "we have a new respect for our critics. Any time we can't put criticism to good advantage we better look in the mirror. Or make sure we're not looking down a pipe and seeing that nice, shiny Chevy," he said, alluding to the tunnel vision sometimes attributed to the auto industry.

His remarks could be interpreted as a smoke signal of change. Yet some critics assert that GM only seems to change, and then at a glacial pace. They believe that GM's response to the energy punch follows its usual pattern of defensive reaction rather than fore-sighted initiative, which in the last decade has resulted in its worst fears coming true.

Had GM not bucked environmentalists and safety crusaders so stubbornly, it would not have the government interfering in the design of the automobile as has happened with the passage of the Clean Air Act and the National Highway Safety Act.

"If they'd only made minor changes in auto emissions, we wouldn't have such a strong law," said Clarence Ditlow, one of the auto experts in Nader's Public Interest Research Group. The 1975 standards of the Clean Air Act, deemed unreasonable by the oil and auto companies, led GM to make its controversial multimillion-dollar commitment for installing catalytic converters in all but one of its 1975 models.

Peter F. Drucker, the management expert, theorizes that perhaps GM's size "impairs its freedom of action." In his book *Management* Drucker, a long-time professor at the New York University Graduate School of Business Administration and who now teaches at Claremont (California) Graduate School, asks whether "it is forced into doing the wrong things, the things that management itself knows will damage the business."

He asserts that GM "decided not to compete against the small foreign imported automobile" in the 1950s and 1960s because it feared it would incur antitrust problems if it increased its domestic market share, then slightly more than 50 per cent. (Since 1968 that share has dropped to less than 45 per cent and in the last two months to 37.5 per cent.)

Drucker says that GM left the lower end of the market to the imports and concentrated on the more profitable middle and upper ends as Sloan had prescribed. Because GM called the tune for Detroit on prices and technology, there was "no leadership to keep the American-made automobile truly competitive even in its own domestic market," he writes. By the 1970s, when imports were eating into the United States balance of payments, a counteroffensive against the German Volkswagens and Japanese Toyotas and Datsuns had become "a formidable undertaking."

Although the 1973 devaluation of the dollar took the price advantage away from the cheaper imports (the Volkswagen became more expensive than the Vega), the foreigners are now intruding with quality and fuel economy as in the $4,000 Mazdas and $5,000 Audis.

And the American auto industry is undergoing the biggest industrial conversion in peacetime history. The commitment to the small car—however hesitant—will have cost General Motors $2 billion in capital investment since 1970.

Arvid Jouppi, senior vice president of Delafield Childs Inc., a brokerage firm, and a veteran auto analyst, blames the profit-obsession of GM management for the corporation's current plight. "The big error they made was in the 1959–64 period when they should have done all the engineering research work for ten years out," he said. "They tried so hard to get higher prices for the cars and return on capital. They could have cranked that $25 to $40 per car into R&D on engines and car size."

Richard Gerstenberg bemoans the erosion of profit margins. Net income was 10 per cent of sales in the early 1960s, 6.7 per cent in 1973.

But a more significant figure, return on equity, has ranged between 17.5 per cent and 27.7 per cent over the decade except for 1970 when there was a three-month strike.

The average return on equity for all manufacturing industries, as well as for the oil companies (who explain their recent profit increases as catch-ups), has been about 10 per cent during the last five years.

The exact profit margin for each of GM's five automobile divisions "is a secret as well guarded as the ingredients of Coca-Cola," says Bradford Snell, counsel to Senator Philip Hart's subcommittee on antitrust and monopoly and author of a proposal for breaking up the auto companies. However, industry sources estimate that the labor-cost difference between an intermediate-size Chevrolet Chevelle and a Cadillac Coupe de Ville may be $300 while the difference in the retail price can be $3,000.

There are slight engine and transmission differences between the two cars. Interchangeability of components—most of which are manufactured within the GM empire—has been one of the titan's strengths. But increased profit-oriented standardization has erased product distinctions. The same basic bodies are used in several divisions—Body A, for example, for the Chevrolet Chevelle, the

Oldsmobile Cutlass, the Pontiac Le Mans, and the Buick Century, with about a $130 retail price difference between the Chevrolet and the Buick.

"GM is caught in an inversion," Arvid Jouppi said. "Its profitability is declining fast because the big cars on which it always realized its profits are not selling. It has investment lying idle in the big-car plants it has shut down.

"The profound devotion to return on invested capital and on net worth meant they were always there to meet the market if it didn't change too fast. The critical thing now is that the market changed faster than the GM fourteenth floor."

Now the men on the fourteenth floor are hoping they can find ways to extract profits from smaller vehicles. "I can't say we will make as many dollars on the Vega as on the Cadillac," Gerstenberg said, avoiding confirmation of GM's plan to sell a $10,000 Cadillac compact in 1976. Across the board the Sloan strategy of add-on will be applied to small cars with luxury and options. "We're looking for people to upgrade," he said.

However, the conviction rests that the large car will not disappear from American affections, although, Mr. Gerstenberg says, "people may be satisfied with a more fuel-economical engine with less acceleration and performance."

Along with the furious product development for petite luxury models, it seems, will go strenuous efforts toward an average of fifteen-mile-per-gallon efficiency on all cars. This should bring them back to where they were a decade ago and still below what the Vega and many small imported cars can deliver on a highway.

The reason given for confidence in the behemoths is not only profits but encouragement from sales in Canada where fuel remains plentiful. The GM vision of the American family and its needs remains intact.

"The man with a wife and four kids and a shaggy dog can't get into a Vega," said Mack Worden, vice president for marketing and father of seven. Asked about market research and reports of approaching zero-population growth, he responded, "Perhaps the size of the family will come down but this is looking down the road. Probably ten years down."

GM is fed market research from its advertising agencies, its own product clinics, and—"the most influential piece of information," in Worden's view—the annual surveys of GM car owners of the vehicles they are currently driving. "The other one and it is not very scientific," he confided about his research sources, "is that when you're in this business and have oil in your arteries rather than blood, you grasp a feel."

So it is that the men on the fourteenth floor felt the small car was coming but not that fast—not really until "the late seventies"—and that they were keeping up with it at a 7 per cent a year increase in production.

They say they had tried small cars several times since 1959 starting with the Corvair but had been rebuffed in the marketplace. (Even their harshest critics bow toward GM's technological capability and believe that somewhere in the Eero Saarinen-designed Technical Center at Warren, overlooking the ducks on the pond, GM scientists and engineers can find the answers to any technical problem.)

In the bubbling sixties, customers wanted bigger cars and high-performance engines, the defenders of the fourteenth floor maintain. GM spent $50 million to build six-cylinder engines and then customers begged for V-8s. Now, GM can't produce enough sixes for its compacts.

Then GM poured untold millions into the Vega, the weapon to fight the foreign invader. After its debut in 1970, the Vega was plagued with engine troubles, consumer assaults on its safety, and labor unrest at Lordstown, where it was made. "It was a bad child for a while," Cole said. A year ago, there was a seventy-four-day inventory of unsold Vegas. Production cutbacks were contemplated. Now GM can't make Vegas fast enough.

While conceding that small cars may soon account for 65 per cent of the market, Gerstenberg also says, "I don't know that we have a good fix on where the market is going. Soundings are pretty confused now."

GM AND PUBLIC TRANSPORTATION

Amid the confusion, the energy crisis has heightened public pressure for mass transit. In January 1974 GM acknowledged it—characteristically—by adding a division.

To head the new Transportation Systems Division it appointed Donald J. Atwood, a forty-nine-year-old engineer who had previously directed part of GM's government contract work, supplying guidance systems for the Apollo space missions.

"The same command and control capability that GM provided for the space program can be applied to public transportation," Atwood said. He explained that if municipalities obtain the requisite state and federal financing, GM would be ready to act as management contractor as well as vehicle manufacturer for the transit systems. "Through the 1980s, it could be a $150-billion total market," he said, adding that its profitability could not be determined yet.

Though sales of railway and bus equipment account for less than 1 per cent of GM's sales, the auto giant is the major presence in the public transportation market.

Through its Electro-Motive Division it sells 73 per cent of the nation's railroad diesel locomotives. Though Electro-Motive is producing to capacity—four and a half locomotives a day—it resists the gathering impetus toward coal-based electrification of the railroads. Harold J. Smith, Jr., manager of Electro-Motive said, "Prior to the petroleum shortage I would have said electrification would never happen, but since a number of our customers are studying it, we're preparing to be manufacturers of the straight electric locomotive."

Bradford Snell, of Senator Hart's subcommittee, has charged that GM undermined mass transit by such means as steering the railroads away from electrification toward dieselization, using its influence as their largest freight customer.

A suit pending in federal court by the City of New York against GM alleges that the auto company monopolizes city bus manufacture as well as the intercity bus market by its own production and the dependence of its competitors on GM for diesel systems and components.

Donald E. Weeden, a New York investment banker, told the Hart subcommittee that splitting up the Big Three auto manufacturers would help attract new capital for mass transportation and that the spun-off subsidiaries would see a rise in their market value. "Investing in General Motors—the leading producer of locomotives and buses—is like investing in a mutual fund for auto stocks," he said.

For half a century GM has repelled antitrust and monopoly attacks, with one significant exception that did not impinge on its manufacturing capability. In 1962 the United States Supreme Court ordered E. I. du Pont de Nemours & Co. to divest itself of its 23 per cent interest in GM.

The United States Justice Department is weighing whether to reopen a consent decree negotiated in 1965 with GM after a decade of investigating its bus business.

Clearly, GM is not about to be transformed into a mass transportation company. The annual report sets out this statement of purpose: "Cars and trucks are the backbone of American transportation and will continue to be in the foreseeable future."

OVERSEAS: BIG BUT NOT GARGANTUAN

GM casts a large shadow on the international scene, though not large enough to satisfy its management or some of its critics. In 1973 sales of all its products overseas (including sales to its own North American operations) amounted to a record $5.8 billion, or 14 per cent of revenues. Net income was $216 million, or 9 per cent of total earnings.

GM has manufacturing and assembly plants in thirty-one countries from Argentina to Zaire, employing 193,000 persons of whom only 360 are American citizens. In the United States, 590,000 men and women worked for GM last year.

Yet Peter Drucker, the management sage, noting that the most rapid growth in recent years has been in the multinational sector, calls GM "still primarily a United States company." It does not dominate any foreign market except Australia through its Holden subsidiary. In Europe, it holds fifth place. There and in Latin America it has been outstripped by Ford.

GM is striving for an international image these days. "We're pursuing those markets more aggressively. We see the growth potential of the market to be much greater outside the country," Gerstenberg said. Indeed, many believe that the United States auto market, with one car for every 2.5 families, may have approached saturation. The developing nations have 70 per cent of the world's population and only 11 per cent of the automobiles, vice chairman Thomas Murphy pointed out. "We fit the product to the market," he said, alluding to the "basic terrain vehicle" being produced in Malaysia and five other developing countries.

But his remark could also be taken to mean that GM has had the small car technology all along but chosen to keep it overseas. A version of its minicar, sold in Germany as the Opel Kadett and in Brazil as the Chevette, is now being "federalized" to meet United States safety, emission, and damageability rules so that it can be manufactured here for 1976.

The Soviet Union is seeking GM's technological expertise in setting up a vast, new heavy-truck project in Siberia. But in the lengthy negotiations thus far, GM has made clear its distaste for "turnkey" ventures, in which the company simply performs a plant-building assignment. GM wants participation or a good old, capitalistic share of the profits.

The energy crunch has been nicking GM's profits in Europe through labor stoppages and curtailed work weeks in its long troubled Vauxhall subsidiary in Britain and in doubled fuel costs for its prosperous Adam Opel plants in Germany. Opel is second only to the Volkswagen companies in German car owners' affections.

So far, GM has not stepped up imports of the small, quality Opels into the United States through the Buick division. The United Auto Workers have called for temporary import quotas to protect auto workers' jobs, a point of view that the GM free traders reject.

SMALLER SHARE OF MARKET

Under the impact of the energy crisis, new-car sales of the General Motors Corporation have dropped more sharply than those of its competitors.

GM's sales fell 35.7 per cent during the January 1–March 10, 1974, period, compared with declines of 20.5 per cent for the Ford Motor Company and 18.5 per cent for the Chrysler Corporation. At the same time, there was an 18.1 per cent sales increase at the American Motors Corporation, which specializes in small cars.

GM's share of the domestic market has fallen to 45.3 per cent. Its competitors attribute GM's shrinking share of the market to the fact that it did not switch fast enough to the production of smaller cars.

GM's share of the auto industry's total sales, including imports, peaked at 52 per cent in 1962, dropped to 47 per cent in 1969, and fell below 45 per cent in 1973. For the first two months of 1974 GM's share of the industry total was only 38 per cent.

General Motors has cut production by 45.1 per cent through

mid-March. Ford's output is off 28.2 per cent, and Chrysler's is down 23 per cent.

Despite the production cutbacks, GM is still hurting more than its rivals in terms of inventory. While the industry as a whole has a seventy-four-day supply of cars on hand, GM's backlog of unsold cars is 888,000 or 51.1 per cent of the total inventory, enough to last eighty-one days at current sales rates.

Ford's backlog, constituting 27 per cent of the total, is equal to a sixty-nine-day supply. Chrysler's share of the backlog is 18.9 per cent, a seventy-five-day supply. American Motors' unsold inventory is only 51,400 or 3 per cent of the industry's backlog.

The nub of GM's plight is too many big cars on hand. Its Buick, Oldsmobile, Pontiac, and Cadillac models have not been selling well. Its medium-priced cars are experiencing greater sales declines than those of the competition. Nevertheless, General Motors is still the sales leader. Its Chevrolet division has topped the industry except for some strike years like 1970.

In pricing, the manufacturers stay close. The standard-size Chevrolet and Ford four-door sedans both have base list prices of $3,695, while the Plymouth Fury is $3,692. GM's subcompact Vega, however, is only $2,380, compared with Ford Pinto's base price of $2,442.

Auto industry analysts consider shares of the sales market significant. They note that in four months of the energy crisis—November 1973 through February 1974—small cars accounted for 50 per cent of the over-all market. Ford had 51 per cent of its sales in the small-car sector, and Chrysler had 50 per cent. However, GM could muster only 30 per cent of its sales in the small-car field.

The auto industry's ten best sellers so far this year are:

	CAR	SIZE	MAKER
1.	Chevrolet	Full size	GM
2.	Vega	Subcompact	GM
3.	Pinto	Subcompact	Ford
4.	Ford	Full size	Ford
5.	Valiant	Compact	Chrysler
6.	Torino	Intermediate	Ford
7.	Mustang II	Subcompact	Ford
8.	Chevelle	Intermediate	GM
9.	Nova	Compact	GM
10.	Dart	Compact	Chrysler

THE ANGUISH OF THE DEALERS

The last three years were fat years for GM's 13,000 franchised dealers, but that doesn't alleviate much the pain of the recent lean months when sales have fallen 35.7 per cent.

The crux of the dealers' anguish: big cars mean big profits when they sell quickly. When they don't, they incur big interest charges. Small cars mean smaller profits. They've been hot sellers but the dealers don't have enough of them. Besides, complains Howard Wigder, owner of Todd Chevrolet in Perth Amboy, New Jersey, "No one knew that GM made small cars."

GM's advertising has been switched to stress the variety of its compact and subcompacts, all of which are defined as small. However, only two of its 1974 models—the Chevrolet Vega and the Opel Manta (manufactured in its German subsidiary and sold here through Buick dealers) weigh less than 3,000 pounds and can deliver twenty miles or more per gallon of gasoline by Environmental Protection Agency standards. The Vega sells from $2,380 up and the Opel from $3,298 up ("hardly what you might expect to pay for a European touring car of such Aryan qualifications," one ad proclaims).

There are no Vegas or compact Chevrolet Novas in Wigder's showroom. They are in his parking lot already sold and waiting to be driven away. Prospective customers are steered to the hapless, full-size Impalas and Caprice station wagons.

By the custom of the automobile business, the dealer normally paid the manufacturer 77 per cent of the list price of a full size car, 81 per cent of an intermediate, and 85 per cent of a compact or subcompact. But these profit margins have been thrown out of whack by the big-car glut. On one hand, dealers are offering incentive bonuses to their salesmen to push the big cars. On the other, they are saddled with high carrying charges for the stagnant inventory.

Wigder finances his inventory through General Motors Acceptance Corporation, the finance subsidiary, at rates competitive with local banks, currently between 10 and 12 per cent. GM gives the dealer twenty "free days," or grace period, before interest charges are applied. Often as not, the car is in transit from factory to dealer for five days out of that grace period. Dealer profits come from fast turnover. But recently Wigder's inventory of 132 cars and 11 trucks has been costing him an average of $50 a car in monthly interest.

(Vegas don't stay in the showroom long enough to accrue their $30 interest charges.)

"I'd like to know when GM is going to start doing something for me," Wigder said. He and other dealers want GM to extend the grace period from twenty days to ninety. Instead, GM has offered bonuses and rebates, from $150 to $500 on big cars but these apply only after last year's boom-sales quota has been passed.

"You do not help any merchant by relieving him of responsibility to sell what is profit making to him," Mack Worden, vice president for marketing, said in Detroit. He was explaining why GM preferred a carrot and stick to a tourniquet. "Inventory keeps gathering dust. The incentive motivates him to move it," he said. He pointed out that the bonus might be used "at the dealer's discretion" to pay inventory interest charges.

"Everything's run from the corporation," Wigder complained. "The marketing group makes all the decisions but the dealers can't get through to them."

THE LABOR FRONT

GM's energy-induced vulnerability would not be used as an advantage by either the company or the union in local bargaining. That was the unwritten understanding between George B. Morris, Jr., GM's vice president for industrial relations and Irving Bluestone, vice president of the United Auto Workers and head of the union's GM department. The informal agreement followed ratification of a three-year contract last December.

That contract provided for an hourly wage rate of $5.56. Including fringe benefits, GM's labor cost is now $8 an hour.

Some local contracts were signed almost immediately, as in the Chevrolet assembly plant at North Tarrytown, New York, which is being converted from B-body (or big car) to X-body (or compact) assembly lines.

"We settled our local agreement in December," said Raymond Calore, the silver-haired president of UAW Local 664 for the last nineteen years. "We didn't have 3,000 to 5,000 unsettled grievances backlogged like some locals. When GM has one cookie to give out, the bad boys don't get it." The cookie is the production of the smaller car.

Calore sat in his closet-size office in local headquarters a hundred yards or so from the Tarrytown plant, cutting a figure of sporty elegance with his highly polished copper-leather ankle boots, checked trousers, and a yellow turtleneck worn underneath a blue shirt that has "Raymond Calore, President" embroidered in yellow over the pocket.

"We're most fortunate we have understanding people," he said inclining his head in the direction of the factory. "Rather than fight us, we work together. Kuyper got $10 million two years ago for a new building. He convinced Detroit that when the B-body Chevy goes down the drain, we'll still have jobs to build the Nova."

Kuyper is John Kuyper, the plant superintendent for the last seven years. A tall, straight-shouldered man with a direct and amiable manner, he started with GM thirty-six years ago on the assembly line for the 1938 Chevy. "It was about the size of today's compact," he noted.

Kuyper remembers the assembly line with a certain nostalgia. "The days went awfully fast. You had a chance to talk with your fellow people about what you were doing yesterday or tomorrow. You discussed the state of the nation. It was very sociable work like a quilting bee and soon the quilt was completed. We have a wonderful work force here. They're real energetic," he said.

The blueprints for the changeover from the manufacture of the big Chevrolet Impala to the compact Chevrolet Nova and Pontiac Ventura were spread out on a sixteen-foot table in a conference room. "The biggest complication is the training," Kuyper said. "Every man will be shown by his foreman on a preproduction vehicle. We are starting the training with the supervisory people. Then they talk to their relief people and then close to down time we pull in the operating individuals."

The planning for the conversion was being done while the plant continued to turn out 1974-model Impalas at the rate of fifty-five cars an hour. It was hoped that it could proceed at that pace, without laying anyone off, until the normal six-to-eight-week closing in the summertime to get ready for the next model year production on August 1. On that date the Tarrytown plant was to switch to the Nova.

Thus far, its regular labor force of 4,300 had escaped layoffs.

"We're combating a fear, the fear that the situation can get worse," Kuyper acknowledged. "I'm optimistic as far as Tarrytown is concerned though. I'm hoping the compact is what the public is demanding. I like to say we're going to build the Cadillac of the compacts."

The co-operative spirit and mutual trust in effect at Tarrytown are not reflected everywhere in General Motorland. Local negotiations have dragged on in other locations such as Lordstown, Ohio, a name that became synonymous with the "blue-collar blues" of young, rebellious workers after a strike two years ago.

Actually, the residue of discontent that still exists there is mostly attributable to the merger of the Fisher Body plant with a Chevrolet assembly plant. The GM assembly division had ordered such fusions throughout the industrial empire with the object of achieving cost efficiencies and they had usually provoked trouble between competing factions. At Lordstown political maneuvering within union Local 1112 provided the incendiary spark as younger workers challenged the entrenched union leadership.

The Lordstown complex, which looks like a robot city rising out of the cornfields of northeastern Ohio, was shut down again early in March 1974 by a three-day ministrike in the fabricating plant that manufactures the body parts for the Vega. They are assembled in the adjacent plant at the rate of a hundred cars an hour, 1,600 a day, and, at a plant at Sainte Thérèse, Quebec, at the rate of 1,200 a day. A third plant is being converted for Vega production at Southgate, California.

In the Lordstown fabricating plant the 2,000-ton presses stamp out seat and door frames, roof and side panels, and other structural metal parts. The workers are stationed at solitary posts, too far apart to talk to each other. Even if they were closer they could not hear over the pounding roar of the machines. To a first-time visitor it seems like a quarter of hell compared to the quieter, brighter, more sociable (if still deadly monotonous) environment of the assembly plant.

But the spirit is in fact better in the fabricating plant, in part because its union local, number 1714, resolved its leadership differences. Youth is now in command.

In 1972 a group of younger workers contacted Lowell Dodge, director of the Center for Auto Safety in Washington, D.C., one of Ralph Nader's affiliate organizations. They were concerned about the sloppiness of procedures in the Lordstown plants and the quality and safety of the parts and assembled cars they were turning out.

They charged that inspectors were being told by foremen to "buy it." In the language of the auto factory, this means that the inspectors were being ordered to ignore parts with missing or weak welds. Rather than send the parts or the cars in which they were installed back for repairs, the inspectors were told to sign the forms stating that government standards had been met. If the inspector refused to "buy it" he might be disciplined.

Dodge passed the complaints on to the United States Department of Transportation and his letter was published in Local 1714's newspaper with the names of those who had alerted the consumer watchdog agency. The government sent inspectors to Lordstown. Meanwhile the UAW in Detroit backed the men by encouraging them to register their complaints as grievances. During the negotiations for the last contract, the union demanded and won the right to have a health and safety representative in each plant with more than 1,000 employees.

"The matter has long since been resolved," said John B. Sutherland, the manager of the fabricating plant. "We had no idea who were the employees involved," he added, sounding uninterested.

"The company knew who we were," said Larry Crotty, the thirty-year-old, long-haired president of Local 1714. A welder, he currently holds the safety representative job. "The fact they say they didn't know is a tactful retreat on their part. Let's say it was a little misunderstanding on both sides. We will always be concerned about safety. It's good that people care enough about their jobs to stand up and improve things.

"It's a younger generation way of thinking," Crotty went on. "We don't put up with things that the older generation used to put up with. When I first hired into another GM plant I came upon an old timer. He had scars on his neck. He was a welder who had spent years with the company and he was bragging about his scars. It was part of the job and he accepted it. I said, 'When I leave I'm not going scarred and cut up. Like I can see and hear and if I can make things better, I will. If you got a problem you don't have to accept it.' By doing this, we get labeled radicals. If that's what it takes to improve things here, I'm a radical 100 per cent."

Now, despite the understanding in Detroit, energy has intruded upon local bargaining. Union representatives say local management has been exceptionally resistant to relatively minor cost items—such as the installation of additional showers. "They say, 'We can't do that, we aren't making any money,'" a union negotiator reported.

The labor side is fully aware of the importance of uninterrupted Vega production to the corporation, both sides declare.

Absenteeism in the assembly plant at Lordstown has diminished to a rate of 7 per cent which is higher than the GM average. Thomas Del Bello, the six-foot-seven-inch personnel director, asserts that "absenteeism and overtime are correlated. If a guy can work a forty-hour week in four days (drawing $225 gross pay), he takes off." And Lordstown has been scheduling overtime.

As John DeLorean had said during a discussion of Lordstown and what it implied for the American industrial future, "Our society is considerably less materialistic than it used to be. A lot of guys who have earned enough in three days to satisfy their fundamental needs have no interest in a gross accumulation of money. They aren't interested in working more. And the pay rate at Lordstown is higher than for other companies in the area. This poses a problem for labor and management.

"A lot of work has to be done to put the worker back on the team. It doesn't matter that the work is dehumanizing. The worker is part of the machinery today. I think some of the executive jobs are fifty times more boring than the assembly line, though. I worked a line two summers when I was going to college, once at night and once on the day shift. It was not an unpleasant experience. We talked and joked around. I enjoyed the association with the working guy and I've always tried to maintain the mechanism of association with him.

"Why is it that in Japan, there's this gigantic enthusiasm? By our standards, we can't visualize how anyone can be motivated that highly. That's because we've had this clear division between labor and management instead of realizing that we are all part of X Company trying to survive in the market place."

In the Lordstown assembly plant, Boston Williams, a twenty-seven-year-old black foreman, who was given human relations training for his job as part of GM's system-wide effort to improve its labor climate, said that "people fear for their jobs. They figure they can take the Vega away from us. Now everybody is fighting like crazy to get the hundred jobs done an hour."

In the third week of March 1974 one of every four of GM's factory workers has been laid off. Some 65,000, or 15.1 per cent, have been furloughed indefinitely. Irving Bluestone warns that "these are depression layoffs." He and Leonard Woodcock, the UAW president, have not refrained from recalling that the late Walter Reuther told the auto manufacturers to produce a small car "named desire" back in 1948.

Bluestone, a gray-haired, scholarly man who majored in German at New York's City College in the 1930s and planned to become a teacher, looks at economic indicators and sees what the chieftains on the fourteenth floor of the GM building at the other end of Detroit from UAW headquarters either do not see or refuse to discuss.

In his plain, impersonal office in Solidarity House, the UAW seat at 8000 East Jefferson Avenue, once the estate of the late Edsel Ford, overlooking Lake Michigan, Bluestone talks of the approach of zero-population growth.

"Fewer new families being formed, fewer homes being created. This must have an impact on future sales. They say we haven't surfeited the two-car family." Bluestone is referring to the GM decisionmakers. "Now they are talking about expanding into the three-car family.

"I would suspect there are limits to that kind of growth, particularly if we have an oil shortage. If we think of growth on a fairly sustained basis as there was after World War II, we may be making a serious blunder.

"Rather than continuous growth, we should look at what ZPG means to the future growth of the economy and the exhaustion of resources and track those and then look at the future of selling cars. That would be facing reality."

Bluestone wonders about the auto industry's market research. "I can't imagine any industry making so many blunders. In the late forties, when obviously the small car was on the horizon, they decided to do nothing. In the fifties, the imports started coming."

Bluestone recalled how, in 1965, a Democratic congressman from New York, Jonathan B. Bingham, wrote to the Big Three companies urging them to get into small-car manufacture. At the time Bingham did not foresee the energy crisis. He was arguing on behalf of less traffic jams and taking competition away from foreign manufacturers.

All three companies turned down his suggestion, citing the larger profits in big cars.

"When Ford brought out the Pinto in 1969, it was twenty years late," Bluestone said. "Even the compact was not a Big Three decision. It was American Motors' decision. It's like dragging them kicking and screaming into the twentieth century."

Meanwhile, about 40 per cent of those laid off have a financial cushion for their fears. Those with twelve months' job seniority can draw supplemental unemployment benefits for one year amounting to 95 per cent of after-tax pay minus $7.50 a week. Part of this is from state unemployment payments.

GM CONSERVES ENERGY

Every other ceiling light has been turned off throughout GM's far flung empire as the mammoth system conserves energy under its historic motto, "Do It Better for Less."

GM's corporate energy czar is Gabriel N. Tiberio, a forty-nine-year-old engineer with industrial pollution expertise. Using computerized controls, he co-ordinates the program under the goal, established early in 1973, of reducing energy usage in GM plants 10 per cent a year.

"In 1972 we produced 6.2 million cars using 234 trillion B.T.U. (British thermal units), or 37.7 million B.T.U. per car. In 1973 we produced 7.1 million cars using 239 trillion B.T.U.," he announced. "That means 33.7 million B.T.U. per car, or a 10.6 per cent reduction."

Those figures—whoppers like all figures applicable to GM—boil down to accomplishments of many dimensions—from the dimmed lighting and the thermostats set at 68 degrees to the car pools with computers helping the employees locate suitable partners. Chairman Gerstenberg even ordered the executive committee to share rides, but the team spirit on the fourteenth floor cracked.

Gerstenberg told executive vice presidents Oscar Lundin and Pete Estes to ride with him, although Estes prefers to take the wheel himself rather than to be driven by a chauffeur. As for Tom Murphy, the vice chairman likes to get to work earlier than anyone else, so he rides alone.

GM Air Transport, the corporate fleet of sixteen jet aircraft achieved a 45 per cent fuel economy in one month by reducing flight speed to that of commercial aircraft and by confining its base of operations to Willow Run Airport. Previously, executives could be picked up as well at Detroit City Airport and at Pontiac Airport nearest their homes in Bloomfield Hills.

But the more significant savings are being effected in GM's 117 plants. GM depends on electricity for 23 per cent of its energy needs, on natural gas for 40 per cent, on oil for 6 per cent, and on coal and coke for 31 per cent. The shortage of natural gas and the zooming price and doubtful supply of coal create quandaries about shifting from one fuel to another as in the coal-and-gas fired boilers which generate 40 per cent of the needed steam. Conversion to coal would save 2,400 barrels of oil a day.

But coal raises environmental questions. GM has invested $3.5 million since 1968 to develop a sulfur dioxide scrubber system, introduced last month at a Chevrolet plant in Parma, Ohio. It is expected to remove 90 per cent of the sulfur oxides from flue gases.

A new steam generating system being installed at the GMC Truck and Coach plant in Pontiac, Michigan, will permit the burning of 55,000 tons of industrial waste as a boiler fuel, equivalent to 5.3 million gallons of oil.

Another $6 million is being invested to drill and develop a natural gas field adjacent to the Vega plant at Lordstown, Ohio. GM has proposed selling the gas at wholesale or field prices to the East Ohio Gas Company and buying it back at retail rates in its Central Foundry at Defiance, Ohio. It has also offered to sell 50 per cent of the gas delivered to the foundry at field prices to the public utility for its customers.

THE POLLUTION-CONTROL BATTLE

It looks like an oversized, stainless steel hot-water bottle. It will add thirty pounds to the weight and $150 to the cost of a 1975 automobile. It's called the "catalytic converter" and it affords a dramatic example of GM's unrivaled ability to make a controversial investment decision entailing hundreds of millions of dollars and thereby impose national standards.

The catalytic converter is also a symbol of the dented romance between GM and the oil industry.

That enduring affair goes back to 1924 when GM and Standard Oil of New Jersey (now the Exxon Corporation) became equal partners in the Ethyl Gasoline Corporation to market the antiknock leaded gasoline necessary for high-compression engines. (In 1962, the partners sold their interests.) Later, GM spurred the oil industry to develop premium gasoline, up to 100 octane for big, high-performance engines, a major cause of air pollution.

The oil companies and the auto manufacturers were united in their opposition to the Clean Air Act of 1970, and what they asserted were its unreasonable standards for reducing engine-exhaust pollution by 1975.

Later they divided on tactics. Since 1970 GM has spent $800 million for emissions control research, including close to $100 million related to the development of power plants other than the internal combustion engine.

The first indication of a lovers' spat came in 1970 when GM announced all of its cars would be able to operate on 91-octane low-lead or unleaded gas. The oil industry has expressed resentment at the extra refining costs required.

GM was preparing the way for its catalytic converter, an add-on device which oxidizes the offending hydrocarbons and carbon monoxide from engine exhaust. With pollutants thus cleaned from the exhaust, the engine can then be tuned to give the better mileage that customers are now demanding.

GM, however, has lowered the promises it made for the converter from 18 per cent fuel economy to about 8 per cent, a figure that Ford and Chrysler consider optimistic.

The oil companies and the other auto manufacturers have denigrated the converter's effectiveness. They preferred the tactic of pressing the Environmental Protection Agency to persuade Congress to extend the 1975 standards and give them time to modify or replace the conventional internal combustion engine.

On April 12, 1973, the EPA agreed to a one-year deferral of the 1975 standard but imposed interim standards, including a rigorous one for California that requires use of the converter.

GM pushed the button for its AC Spark Plug division to proceed with a facility at Oak Creek, Michigan, that will be the world's largest producer of catalytic converters. Starting April 29, 1974, it will turn out 6 million units a year for GM and other customers such as American Motors. GM has contracted to buy $100 million worth of platinum and palladium for the catalyst from South African mines.

The oil companies object to being put to the extra refining costs to produce the unleaded gas that the EPA has ordered in time for the 1975 model cars. They say it will put a strain on crude oil inventories, and Wyatt Walker, vice president of the Continental

Oil Company, predicts "it will lead to a wasteful octane race on unleaded gas."

Moreover, GM's commitment to the conventional internal combustion engine with the add-on converter is being called into question. Chase Econometric Associates, Inc., a subsidiary of the oil-oriented Chase Manhattan Bank recently issued a report forecasting that the stratified charge engine will power two thirds of new automobiles by 1985. The Honda Motor Company of Japan already has one in production.

The report forecasts that the internal combustion engine will recede to minor position and that the rotary engine, representing a far more fundamental engine change, will capture one fourth of the passenger vehicle market. GM has secured the rights to the German-developed Wankel rotary engine for $50 million (the licenses are held by Curtiss-Wright Corporation and Audi-NSU and Wankel Gm.b.H. of West Germany), but has had to postpone its introduction in the 1975 Vega until its mileage performance can be improved.

Meanwhile GM president Edward Cole, mentor of both the Wankel engine and the catalytic converter, denies research reports that the converter throws off potentially dangerous chemical byproducts. "Everyone likes to make me the bad actor for the catalytic converter," he said. Then he went on, stoutly, "Barring inventions, the internal combustion engine will be the engine for the 1980s."

FRIGIDAIRE IS GM, TOO

Dayton, Ohio, suffers from energy backlash. GM is the city's largest industrial employer. Since December 1973 the toll of curtailed production of auto components in four of its divisions—Delco Moraine, Delco Products, Inland, and Frigidaire—has mounted to 4,500 layoffs. About half are in the Frigidaire division, the nation's third largest manufacturer of home appliances (behind the General Electric Corporation and the Whirlpool Corporation). Frigidaire is also the largest manufacturer of compressors and controls for automobile air conditioners for GM's big cars as well as for Ford, Mercedes-Benz, and Jaguar.

A new lightweight aluminum compressor will be produced for the air-conditioning units of 1975 compact and subcompact cars. It was developed by Frigidaire engineers in 1971. "We saw the advent of the small car then," John Weibel, Jr., the forty-nine-year-old chief engineer, said matter-of-factly. His remark underscored the technical capability and flexibility of GM's divisional entities as well as the restraints placed on them by the centralized committee system.

One out of four American homes have Frigidaire appliances—so Frigidaire production is affected indirectly by energy through the state of the economy and the turns in consumer spending.

"Appliances only use 5.3 per cent of the total energy consumed in the United States," Frigidaire engineers and marketing men repeat hopefully.

Nevertheless, they are redesigning home air conditioners—oddly enough—from small to big. Larger condensers and evaporators are more efficient they say.

Frigidaire stole the lead on rival manufacturers in July 1973 when it introduced the Touch-N-Cook range, a first step in bringing the computer to the kitchen. The control system, which permits the range or wall oven to be programmed for cooking in the owner's absence, operates on computer circuitry with 12,000 infinitesimal transistors mounted on four small chips behind the control panel. Frigidaire's engineers envision it as leading to an energy-saving system for the entire home, with all appliances, the furnace, and the hot-water heater operated from a single panel.

"That's ten years away," said Weibel, accustomed to the "evolutionary rather than revolutionary" thinking of the corporation. "Maybe we need some crisis like this to jog us," he added.

COMMITTEES WITH CLOUT

GM runs by Alfred Sloan's prescription of "decentralization with co-ordinated control," otherwise known as rule by committee. Perhaps the most important, certainly from a long range point of view, is the bonus and salary committee. Next fall it will meet in a room just off the rosewood-paneled board room in New York, to pick the new chairman and the new president.

In the organization, GM's seventy-eight subsidiary companies here and abroad are grouped into ten divisions. The autonomy of the division heads is restrained by the advice of one or more of nine specialized policy groups and by a twenty-four-member administration committee.

Operational authority is vested in the executive committee consisting of the six top corporate officers—at present, chairman Gerstenberg, president Cole, vice chairman Murphy, and three executive vice presidents, Elliott M. Estes, Richard L. Terrell, and Oscar A. Lundin. Property acquisitions and appropriations over $150,000 must win their blessing. All appropriations over $250,000 must be approved by the finance committee of twelve. It consists of Messrs. Gerstenberg, Cole, Murphy, Lundin, former chairmen James M. Roche and Frederick G. Donner, former vice chairman George Russell, and five outside directors.

Since money is the oxygen of manufacturing, power resides in the finance committee. But the five members of the bonus and salary committee may have the ultimate clout. They all serve on the finance committee as well. By fixing all salaries above $75,000, they effectively act on all top appointments. All promotions above general manager or staff department head pass before them. And when Cole and Gerstenberg "hang up their cleats" next fall, as Gerstenberg puts it, the committee will recommend the successors to the full board of directors.

The present members of the bonus and salary committee are Eugene N. Beesley, sixty-five, former chairman of Eli Lilly & Company; Stephen D. Bechtel, Jr., forty-eight, chairman of the Bechtel Group; Howard J. Morgens, sixty-three, chairman of Procter & Gamble, on whose board Beesley serves; and the two former GM chairmen, Donner, seventy-one, and his successor, Roche, sixty-seven.

Donner is considered the archetype of the financial man, chilly in manner and hostile to outside pressures. He was the sponsor of Gerstenberg "the bookkeeper."

Gerstenberg had begun his preparation to become the eighth chairman of the board of directors of the General Motors Corporation by signing on as a timekeeper with the Frigidaire division in 1934. A native of Little Falls, New York, he had graduated from the University of Michigan the year before.

For the next thirty-six years, he held successively better bookkeeping jobs until in 1970 he was lifted from the post of executive vice president for finance to the summit as vice chairman. From there he had only two years to wait, before becoming, at the age of sixty-two, the chairman and chief executive officer.

Despite the narrowness of his lifetime career experience and his modest appearance—there was nothing to put him head and shoulders above any other short, gray-haired, bespectacled businessman—Gerstenberg bloomed in the spotlight role of chairman. Critics neither frightened nor antagonized him, and his crisp, peppery responses won a grudging admiration for the assurance and steely nerve they revealed. His vision of the company and the country remained unswervingly eighteenth century motorized.

GM tradition has tended toward a financial man as chairman and chief executive officer and an operating man as president (though GM's army of public relations men lay stress on former chairman Roche's marketing experience). Since 1967, when Cole became president, that post has been filled by a highly inventive engineer who's simply crazy about cars.

The man and his career bore complex and conflicting streaks uncharacteristic of latterday GM leaders. Cole was at once an independent and a team player. He indulged in the passions—both professional and personal—that his peers disapproved of. But he never went as far as John DeLorean.

"We're running a team operation, not a bunch of prima donnas," he said, giving his version of the small car debate. "Looking back, I feel that maybe John was right in putting a little more emphasis on the smaller car, but it was a general decision and I went along with it. And I did go back and push the Vega," he said.

A short, pear-shaped man with a well-lined face, youthful brown hair, and smiling eyes, Cole had been divorced and remarried to Dollie Ann Fechner McVey, an outspoken divorcee who cultivated the attention of the press. Cole's own openness with reporters incurred corporate displeasure on several occasions. He once told them that GM was going to install glass-belted tires on its cars, a fact later shown to be true although James Roche, the chairman, at the time promptly denied it.

In 1971 Cole pooh-poohed motor-mount failure in GM cars, saying that the condition was no more serious than a flat tire or a blowout. Within weeks, however, GM recalled 6.7 million cars because of motor-mount failure. It was the largest recall the auto industry ever had.

Cole was one of the villains of the Nader movement because of his identification with the Corvair, a paternity he was not eager to accept completely. The small, rear-engine car that was GM's answer to Volkswagen and that Nader called "unsafe at any speed" was developed while Cole was chief engineer and general manager at Chevrolet.

He maintained that the car held the road while taking turns at high speed. Ralph Nader said it rolled over and was a safety menace. His book damaged sales and production on the car was stopped in 1969. "No man in the last twenty years had the authority and the knowledge to make safe cars, and didn't use it, like Ed Cole," was Nader's far-from-last words on the subject.

Even critics like Nader bowed to Cole's engineering ability, though.

Cole came to GM at the age of twenty-one as a co-op student at General Motors Institute under the sponsorship of the Cadillac division. His talents so impressed his superiors that he was taken out of school and assigned to a special engineering project before graduation.

Cadillac was a small company and "everyone did everything," he recalled. "We didn't have a union to tell me I couldn't touch a lathe. I don't think any young person today could have the exposure and the opportunities I did."

By 1946 he was chief engineer and in 1950, works manager of Cadillac. The Korean War gave him his decisive chance: he was assigned the project of building the Walker Bulldog tank and got it into production three months ahead of schedule. In 1952 he was promoted to chief engineer of the Chevrolet division, where he redesigned the V-8 engine and a Chevrolet car to accommodate it in record time. In 1956 he became head of Chevrolet.

His account of how he was tapped is just like every other top GM executive's tale of promotion. "I was called in to see Mr. Curtice [Harlow Curtice, then president and the last operating man to preside at the summit] and we sat there a good hour talking the time of day," Cole remembered. "Finally he got around to asking me, 'Would you run Chevrolet?' and I said, 'I don't know anything about running Chevrolet.' I thought of the complexity of this thing and if I failed it would be catastrophic. I took three days to think it over and then I decided that if I didn't take it, I might not have a job, that this was as far as I would go in GM."

Cole said he didn't know he was going to be president, either, when he was dubbed in 1967. "I thought Knudsen had the inside track," he said. "Roche called me in. Donner was sitting there. He

said, 'We've got a new organization chart we'd like you to look at.' "
Cole's name was inked in as president.

Cole went as far as he did by being more than an engineer. He was also a high-pressure salesman—of cars and of his ideas. Even when he was president of GM he drove a car with a Wankel engine at over a hundred miles an hour to demonstrate to his associates his faith in the rotary engine. He always clinched his demonstrations with cost arguments.

In recent months there have been hints that his colleagues were glad to see him go. Gerstenberg complimented Cole in an interview in the *Wall Street Journal.* "I guess you would describe Ed as the kind of a guy to whom you might say, 'Ed, I'd like to move the General Motors Building across the road,' and he'd say, 'Do you want it facing Second Avenue or the boulevard?' " Then Gerstenberg whittled Cole down to size: "Ed wants to go faster than anybody goes anytime on anything. He's very impatient with anything else."

Just such a restless temperament is what outsiders believe GM needs at the top. The prospect is not in sight unless the committee breaks with the practice of elevating carefully groomed candidates.

THE SUCCESSION SWEEPSTAKES

With both Edward Cole and Richard Gerstenberg due to retire in the fall of 1974, speculation abounds as to their successors. If the energy crisis does not jolt the company from its habit of selecting well-coached insiders, the prospects are fairly predictable. There are three leading candidates.

Thomas Aquinas Murphy, the vice chairman, is considered the likely choice for chairman because of his financial background. Besides, the tall, gray-haired Murphy looks and acts as though he were the chairman. Black-rimmed bifocal spectacles afford his one note of individuality. (The rest of the GM leadership seems to have swung to metal frames with slightly tinted lenses.)

Murphy likes to be at his desk at 7 A.M., before anyone else, a habit that excused him from Gerstenberg's energy-conservation directive of executive car pooling. "I like to get into the office and set the pace for the first half of the day, but there are guys who find out about this habit and try to get in to see me early. They think, 'I can get at that guy for a clear shot,' " he explained to a visitor, in a display of what the Detroit auto newsmen insistently describe as Murphy's Irish wit and charm.

On the moderately cluttered desk in his Detroit office are a plaque inscribed with two crosses and the legend BLESS THIS MESS and a framed cartoon that says, "I don't do anything but I do it very efficiently."

On the blond oak-paneled walls hang one turbulent seascape and one tranquil autumn scene. The color photograph of the trium-virate—Cole, Gerstenberg, and himself—is the only distinguishing clue to his status. The lower the rank of the top GM executive, the more companions he has in his official group photograph.

Murphy was born at Hornell, New York, in December 1915, moved to Chicago as a boy, and received a B.S. in accounting from the University of Illinois in 1938. He promptly joined the GM comptroller's staff in Detroit and was transferred fifteen days later to the financial staff offices in New York, where he spent the next twenty-nine years working his way up. "The one thing I miss in Detroit," he said, "is walking to work. I always lived within walking distance of the office in New York."

Murphy lives in Bloomfield Hills now but keeps a New York *pied-à-terre,* a co-operative apartment on Sutton Place, a ten-minute stroll from the GM building. His neighbors have commented on the humility he has retained even at a salary of close to $800,000 a year. Murphy has been seen taking the family garbage to the apartment incinerator.

In 1967 Murphy was transferred back to Detroit as a comptroller and was named treasurer the following year. Suddenly and significantly, he was given operating experience as vice president in charge of the car and truck group in 1970.

"Mr. Roche sent for me to come into his office and there were the members of the executive committee. Here I was the treasurer of the corporation and I had no inkling of what was to happen," he said. "Mr. Roche told me of some organizational changes that were to take place. Mr. Roche is a fine leader and here he is taking time to tell me about executive changes, I thought to myself. Finally, he got around to telling me. 'Estes will be in charge of overseas and we have in mind you taking charge of this spot,' he said.

" 'For once in my life,' I said, 'I have to question your decision; I'm a bookkeeper. I've been in the financial end all my life. I can count the plants I've been in. I don't know the first damn thing about running a plant.' He said, 'Don't worry about that, this is the job we think you can do.' And so I said, 'If this is what you want me to do, all right.'"

In 1971 GM "Kremlinologists" said, "Ah ha!" when Murphy was named vice chairman, leapfrogging over president Cole into the spot Gerstenberg vacated to become chairman. The vice chairman has responsibility for financial and overseas operations. "My ambition is not to travel," Murphy said. "When my wife wanted to vacation in Europe, I said, 'Why do we have to go there, I like it so much here.'"

Of the three executive vice presidents, normally considered candidates for the presidency, Oscar A. Lundin, sixty-four, is disqualified by age. That leaves two.

Elliott M. Estes, the fifty-eight-year-old executive vice president for operations, is conspicuous by his jet black hair and mustache and his affability. He likes to leave home in Bloomfield Hills at 7:15 A.M., a bit later than most of his peers and at the wheel of his own car, rather than being driven by a chauffeur, "to see if the darn bells don't work." Nevertheless, he complied with Gerstenberg's car-pool command. "Terrell's always saying, 'I was born on a farm, I get up at five.' And I say, for chrissake, it's too damn early. I was on a farm, too, but you don't have to keep doing it all your life," Estes complained.

Born in 1916 in Mendon, Michigan, Estes joined GM in 1934 as a co-operative student at General Motors Institute where the tool-crib supervisor gave him the nickname "Pete." "He asked me my name and I said, 'Elliott Marantette Estes. Marantette is my mother's maiden name. She was French.' And he said, 'I never heard any of the three of them. You look like a Greek or a Wop. I'm gonna call you "Pete."' I never lost the name." Estes guffawed at the memory.

Estes eventually received a degree in mechanical engineering from the University of Cincinnati. He worked under the late Charles F. ("Boss") Kettering, GM's revered engineer-inventor and proceeded upward through the Oldsmobile and Pontiac divisions. He was named general manager of Pontiac in 1961, of Chevrolet in 1965. John DeLorean followed in his footsteps, making his mark in territories just previously held by Estes.

When he was appointed head of the car and truck group in 1969, Estes jokingly compared himself to DeLorean. At a press conference, he turned up the collar of his navy pinstripe suit jacket and said, "I didn't wear my turtleneck."

A year later, he was put in charge of overseas operations, a job that placed him in New York for nearly three years. Late in 1972 he was brought back to Detroit to his present post. Some handicappers think his "nuts-and-bolts" background gives him an edge for the presidency.

But Estes said, "I don't even think about it. Why, I have so much better a job than I ever thought I would have. I started out throwing butter out of a churn when I got out of high school. I wasn't even going to college.

"In this company, if you do the job you're given to do and do it the best you can, all of these things take care of themselves. In our organization, people just automatically rise to the top and over the years we've ended up with the best people."

Richard L. Terrell, the fifty-five-year-old executive vice president in charge of car, truck body and assembly divisions, is tall, gray-haired, and congenial. He describes himself as "an engineering, operations, marketing man but also trained in financial disciplines." Asked about GM's future product mix and the possible shrinking down of car size, he replied, "I don't see any difference in the size of people walking around."

Terrell was born in Dayton and raised on a tobacco and dairy farm. He is the only one in top management who has no college degree. He went to work in GM's photographic department as a $65-a-month messenger in 1937 and was shortly thereafter laid off in what he calls "Roosevelt's recession." But he was taken back and made a career on the nonautomotive side of GM. Terrell was to become manager, successively, of the Electro-Motive and Frigidaire divisions until he was given his present post in 1972. "They picked a guy who had never worked in the auto industry," he said.

He disclaimed ambitions for the presidency. "My age is against me," he said. Besides, he added, under the GM system, "people become accustomed to the fact there's always more than one man available for each job. It doesn't make it easy for the one passed over but the new fellow always seems better."

Energy Plus Recession at GM: April 1975

The Watergate crisis in Washington had driven Richard M. Nixon from the presidency in August 1974. The nation had a chief executive who, one year before, hadn't even been considered a dark horse. Gerald R. Ford, it was observed, when the former congressman from Grand Rapids, Michigan, took the oath of office, was bringing the spirit of Detroit to the White House.

Then on Monday, September 30, the directors of the General Motors Corporation convened to perform their duty of ratifying the succession for the nation's mightiest industrial enterprise. They filed into the rosewood-paneled board room on the twenty-fifth floor of the GM Building at 767 Fifth Avenue in New York and took chairs that had their names engraved in brass plaques on the backs. Former chairmen gazed down at them from their portraits on the walls as the directors made their choice.

For chairman, it was—as everyone assumed it would be—Thomas Aquinas Murphy. Like his two immediate predecessors, Richard Gerstenberg and James Roche, he was an arch conservative in political, economic, and management theory and a Roman Catholic.

Though Frederick Donner, the essentially finance-oriented leader of GM had retired from the board the previous spring (he was the last chief executive who would be allowed to linger until seventytwo) and was not present to cast his vote, the new chairman would always be known as a "Donner man." Murphy was the epitome of the bookkeeper.

For president, the board didn't deviate from expectations either. The only one reportedly surprised at the election of Elliott M. Estes, the good-natured engineer, was his wife. Typically, Estes was not notified of the honor that was to befall him until the Friday before the board meeting. He telephoned his wife immediately. Mrs. Estes' response: "Are you kidding? Is this for real?"

The Estes appointment, though undistinguished, would not be criticized within the GM frame of reference. What did astonish everyone was the other two appointments.

Richard Terrell, the executive vice president who had been paired with Estes in an office suite in Detroit, was named vice chairman. Oscar Lundin, the third executive vice president, was also given the title of vice chairman. It was the first time GM had two vice chairmen at the same time.

Robert Irvin, automotive news reporter for the Detroit *News* and the most respected of the industry scribes, noted further that "in fifteen years, GM has gone from an organization table with one man at the top, to two, then three, and now four men."

Just as the company was crying poverty and getting ready to announce huge worker layoffs and a shaved dividend, the nests at the top had been given an extra layer of feathering.

Gerstenberg had his explanation ready. "Our business is more complicated, our worldwide problems are much more complex and we thought it would be good to expand the top management a bit."

There were two likelier possibilities. Each additional member curtailed the power and responsibility of the others. And each member of the team was rewarded for not rocking the boat. The team took care of its own and perpetuated itself.

So the GM Kremlinologists noted that Lundin, a month short of his sixty-fourth birthday and due to retire in little over a year, was being given a promotion. In the distribution of titles, this loyal financial man who had started out as a 60-cent-an-hour payroll clerk in the Chevrolet gear and axle plant in 1933, was designated as the one who would act for the chairman if he were absent or incapacitated.

Terrell, on the other hand, was fifty-five, three years younger than Murphy and Estes. After Lundin retired, would there be anyone or anything between him and the chairmanship?

The next tier had been broadened, too. Instead of three executive vice presidents, now there were four, all of whom had worked for no other employer except General Motors. F. James McDonald, fifty-two, the general manager of the Chevrolet division, would head the automotive components group which meant he would oversee the domestic auto business. Howard H. Kehrl, fifty-one, who had been in charge of the car and truck group, John DeLorean's old job, was to take over design, engineering, environmental, manufacturing, and research. Reuben R. Jensen, fifty-three, in charge of overseas divisions, would have the nonautomotive portion of the business. The former steward of that territory, forty-nine-year-old Roger B. Smith, was given the financial, public relations, and government relations responsibility and would report to Lundin. Straining his credibility somewhat, the redoubtable newsman Irvin pronounced the group "a youth movement at GM."

At last, the GM handicappers had a new favorite to egg on. It was Smith, a short, reddish-haired, adolescent-looking man who would only be fifty-six when Murphy would retire from the chairmanship. Smith clearly had the financial men's hands upon his slight shoulders.

Before being seasoned with nonautomotive experience, Smith had climbed the rungs of the financial staff, starting with a job in the comptroller's office in Detroit after leaving the University of Michigan with bachelor's and master's degrees in business administration. He had been promoted regularly through the accounting sections and the treasurer's staff (with an important transfer to New York as director of the financial analysis section) until in 1970, he was named treasurer and one year later vice president in charge of the financial staff. The moving finger had written—Smith.

The four members of the second team were also appointed to the board of directors. Gerstenberg explained that too. "With the addition of these four younger men to the board, we have broadened our representation and we think this is good." In fact, they intensified the ingrown character of the corporation.

Furthermore, though Gerstenberg would stay on as a director for another five years, exercising the retired GM chairman's right of gray eminence, Cole was leaving the board as he left the presidency. He was going to start a new air freight company.

His last months as president had not been tinged with the treacly sentiment that usually marks the farewell of an elder who had given his entire adult life to a corporation and performed a number of engineering and production feats at crucial times. Perhaps the *Wall Street Journal* had speculated correctly in February of 1974 when it wrote that "Edward Cole may be last of a dying breed in the automotive world . . . an engineer in an industry dominated by finance men."

That month as the New York *Times* embarked on a six-week series of interviews and visits throughout the GM empire, Cole's name was not on the list prepared by the public relations department of those to be interviewed. An appointment was arranged after the oversight was questioned. Cole was unusually tense, touchy and defensive.

At the annual meeting in May, Jerry Flint of the New York *Times,* a veteran GM watcher, noticed that Cole sat at the end of the rostrum wearing sunglasses and that Dollie Cole did not put in her usual wifely appearance. "Guess who's not coming to dinner," Flint quipped.

The most telling blow was delivered on the eve of Cole's official retirement. In the last week in September GM announced it was postponing indefinitely the introduction of the Wankel rotary engine in its cars because it couldn't meet pollution standards without sacrificing fuel economy. The sporty new subcompacts, the Chevrolet Monza, the Buick Skylark, and the Oldsmobile Starfire, would make their 1975 debuts with conventional piston engines instead of the Wankels they had been promised.

Just days before, McDonald of the Chevrolet division had said the Wankel was being postponed until late in the 1975 model year. Cole, who had been the Wankel's godfather at GM, had been talking optimistically about its economy and emissions performance right up until the end.

But his enthusiasm had been undercut on the financial side. While Cole was whistling bravely, Murphy had told an interviewer that he "just can't see it sweeping the board" unless there was "a breakthrough," which he quickly added, seemed doubtful.

On September 24 Gerstenberg sealed the Wankel's fate, citing cost as well as emissions and fuel economy. GM had invested over $100 million in development work on the engine and had paid $45 million in royalties by the end of 1974 to the European patent holders.

The mothballing of the Wankel not only added a sour note to Cole's departure. It dashed the hopes of a bonanza for Curtiss-Wright Corporation, which no longer could expect to license the engine to other auto manufacturers if GM had lost interest in it. Curtiss-Wright's shareholders were disappointed since the price of their stock would continue to languish in the doldrums as a result of the decision.

But then the shareholders of GM were no more consolable in the realization that their investment was worth about one fifth of what it had been ten years ago, in current dollars, which did not take into account the dollar's erosion by inflation. In 1965 GM had traded as high as $113 a share; in the fall of 1974 it fluttered down to 30. So much for buying a share of America when one bought GM.

It was also in September that Richard Gerstenberg and the other elders of the corporation began to step up their attacks on environmental and safety standards imposed by the government as a result of the public interest reformers' movement of the sixties.

Their opposition was not new. It had merely subsided to grumbling in recent years. Now they sighted a fresh sales tack in the public anger over inflation. From 1972 to 1975 "regulations for emission controls, occupant protection, and bumpers have added about $270 to the cost of every vehicle we produce in the United States," Gerstenberg said. Assuming a yearly sale of 13 million cars and trucks by the auto industry, he estimated that the auto makers would be spending $3.5 billion a year for these additions. "It is an unproductive use of capital," Gerstenberg asserted.

Since it was unlikely that Congress would repeal the environmental and safety legislation, Gerstenberg and Henry Ford, who echoed the same inflation theme, proposed a three- to five-year moratorium on pollution standards.

Gerstenberg asked that some of the safety equipment such as head rests and side-door protection beams be removed. Estes warmed to his presidential role by charging that the seat-belt interlock system had contributed to inflation by adding a cost without adding equal value to the customer.

It was one tactic—an unconvincing one—for diverting the public disgust and disbelief over car prices. The 1975 model was already an average $500 more expensive than the model of the year before, and there was no assurance that further increases were not forthcoming. The average model still weighed more than 4,000 pounds and went thirteen miles on a gallon of gasoline.

Students of economics and just plain unwilling car buyers were asking how could it be that as demand for cars was declining, prices of cars were rising? It was as though the apple had fallen upward. Was the law of supply and demand suspended by GM and the industry it led?

In October, while the administration in Washington was still debating whether the United States was in a recession, new car sales hit a ten-year low. GM's third quarter earnings fell 94 per cent, to $16 million compared to $267 million in the same quarter the year before. It was the lowest level for any quarter in which there had not been a strike since World War II.

Unrecovered cost increases for materials and wage increases during the last three model years that the company had absorbed to the cumulative tune of $500 per vehicle ($200 of that sum was in the 1975 model) were blamed for the earnings drop this time.

As industry sales for 1974 ended at 8.9 million cars, 23 per cent lower than the 1973 record of 11.4 million cars, GM revised its forecast. The 1975 model year would score sales of from 10 million to 9.5 million or perhaps 9 million passenger cars, Murphy was saying. Lynn Townsend, chairman of the Chrysler Corporation, had a darker estimate—6 million cars.

Even small cars were selling poorly in the fall of 1974. One reason might have been that a gussied-up Nova compact cost $150 more than a Chevelle Malibu Classic intermediate, one size larger.

On Monday, November 4, the GM board met and voted to cut the year-end dividend 64 per cent to 85 cents a share.

Two weeks before Gerstenberg's official retirement, Thomas Murphy made his first television appearance as a GM chairman-designate. That week, President Ford let the word recession drop from his lips and Alan Greenspan, chairman of the President's Council of Economic Advisers, said that there was no question that the auto industry slump was having an impact on the entire economy.

Smiling hesitantly, Murphy said that the sales lag was caused by "just a little lack of consumer confidence at the moment." He expressed confidence that the car industry "is a growth industry, the backbone of our economy, the backbone of our transportation system."

Meanwhile, Mack Worden, the irrepressible marketing man, urged salesmen to get out and sell, as his prescription for the economy. And newspapers carried advertisements with Gerstenberg's signature over this message:

"Buying a new car now is a good investment. For you and for our economy. . . . When you buy a new car, you help America's economy. Your purchase can contribute to growth for the nation. It can pay off in more jobs, more revenue for government. More strength for businesses—large and small. This helps everyone.

"Right now is the time to buy a new car. It's a common sense investment for you and for our country."

Not only Alfred Sloan haunted the corridors of the fourteenth floor. Engine Charlie lived on there, too.

At the end of January 1975, nearly one quarter of a million workers in the auto industry were laid off, 91,000 of them by GM. Tens of thousands despaired at the prospect of their supplemental unemployment benefits being exhausted by the spring.

GM released its sales and earnings figures for 1974. As expected, they were the worst since 1970, the year of the sixty-seven-day strike and the second worst since 1961.

Sales had fallen 12 per cent to $31.5 billion, profits 60 per cent to $950 million.

The quarterly dividend was cut from 85 cents to 60 cents. The top officers said they would not participate in the bonus plan in order that the relatively modest amount available for that fund ($5.9 million compared with $112.8 million in 1973) could be spread among the lower-level managers.

GM had been the last of the auto manufacturers to succumb to some form of price cutting to budge the stalled inventory of 1975 cars. A system of rebates in the range of several hundred dollars for each new model purchase had been put into effect. In late February, a week before the rebate program was due to expire, the prices of GM's smaller cars were reduced from $100 to $300 each by making some standard equipment optional.

When Thomas A. Murphy was asked why GM had been so slow to recognize customer price resistance, he answered, "It takes a little while for some of us to read the market."

On March 5 the auto manufacturers at last received some encouraging news from the federal government. Russell Train, head of the Environmental Protection Agency, recommended to Congress that current emission standards be extended through 1979 models. He was granting the delay that Detroit had asked for. He said his decision was based on the discovery that catalytic converters installed on 85 per cent of 1975 model cars produce a sulfuric-acid pollutant that poses a health risk for asthmatic persons. If the more stringent emission standards were not postponed and the catalysts used to meet them, the sulfur emissions might rise to intolerably high levels.

"At some point, the catalysts may begin to do more harm by creating sulfuric acid than good through additional control of hydrocarbons and carbon monoxide," Train warned.

Also in March GM looked for capital for a major revamping of its lines. For the first time in twenty-one years, it went to outside markets to finance capital spending with a $600-million offering of thirty-year debentures and ten-year notes. The GM borrowing was the largest fixed-income financing by an industrial company ever recorded.

The proceeds of the issue were to be used for working capital, retooling, real estate, plant, and equipment. Over the next five years GM would be spending about $2.1 billion for its new product program.

By 1977 its standard and luxury cars—like those of the other auto manufacturers—will be slimmed down to the size and weight of the 1950s. The weight losses of as much as 700 pounds on some models of cars will not mean a sacrifice of interior room, the auto executives promised. Nor will prices be reduced. "Car buyers can in effect look forward to paying more for less car," noted Agis Salpukas, Detroit bureau chief of the New York *Times*.

By 1978 GM will have a new series of compact-size cars on the market delivering twenty to twenty-five miles per gallon of fuel. The present intermediate size cars will have been phased out.

But GM will be thinking and producing small well before 1978. By the fall of 1975 the new subcompact Chevette—smaller than the Vega—will go on sale. The new, small Cadillac made its debut in April. Looking suspiciously as though it were bred from the genes of the Mercedes-Benz, the "Seville" baby Cadillac has a list price of $12,479, near the very top of the existing line of mammoth Cadillacs.

In its registration statement for the $600 million offering, GM had noted the uncertainties facing the industry. Doubts about the eventual decline of fuel prices, shortages of materials and of energy to run the automobile plants. Doubts about the size of the auto market if the economy continued to be depressed or stagnant. "It is not possible to forecast the net near-term or long-term effects of all those factors on a corporation's results," it said.

Looking on the bright side, as is his wont, Pete Estes was saying that the smaller GM cars become, the more salable they will be in overseas markets. It was a Panglossian idea.

In February 1975 the foreign auto manufacturers' share of the U.S. market was tabulated at 21.3 per cent, an increase of more than 5 per cent in one year.

STRICTLY PRIVATE

ESTÉE LAUDER: A FAMILY AFFAIR

Spring 1973

In January 1973 at age thirty-nine, Leonard A. Lauder replaced his mother as president of Estée Lauder, Inc., the $100-million cosmetics company bearing her name. She took the title of chairman formerly held by her husband, Joseph, who became executive chairman. Their younger son, Ronald, twenty-nine, had been recently appointed executive vice president of Clinique Laboratories, Inc., the company's newest and fastest-growing division for allergy-tested cosmetic products.

"The key fact is," the new president declared in an interview in his office in the General Motors Building, "that it doesn't mean anybody has retired. It does not change the power structure."

Such open acknowledgment is not always forthcoming from someone who refers to his mother as "my boss." But Leonard Lauder generally behaves in a straightforward, self-assured manner, almost as a counterpoise to the fanciful dynamism of his mother. She has been America's reigning beauty queen since the deaths of Elizabeth Arden and Helena Rubinstein and is the surviving foe of their rival, Charles Revson, chairman of Revlon, Inc.

The feud between Revson and Mrs. Lauder provides gossip, drama, and a bit of comic relief to the beauty world, which has lost some of its excitement since the deaths of those earlier enemies, Miss Arden and Madame Rubinstein.

Revlon, Lauder, and Rubinstein all moved their corporate headquarters to the General Motors Building at 767 Fifth Avenue when the white skyscraper was completed in 1969. Charles Revson contracted for the four top floors, the forty-seventh through the fiftieth, while the Lauders settled on the thirty-seventh and parts of the thirty-eighth and thirty-ninth. Fortunately, the two territories are approached by different banks of elevators. "Can you imagine my mother meeting Charles Revson every morning?" Leonard Lauder asked in a tone of mock horror that anticipated the fur flying. Once when Mrs. Lauder did encounter Revson at a promotional gala at Bergdorf Goodman, she did not hesitate to give him a piece of her mind.

The Revson-Lauder battles have been waged in the social arena both have so passionately sought to conquer. Revson's yacht, *Ultima II,* and his Park Avenue triplex (once inhabited by Madame Rubinstein) are scored against the Lauder houses in Manhattan, Palm Beach, and the French Riviera and a London flat. The honey-blonde, hazel-eyed Mrs. Lauder seemed to have pulled ahead when she won the late Duke of Windsor and his Duchess as regular dinner guests.

Much more important in the business scheme, however, is the product competition. Estée Lauder swept into men's cosmetics with Aramis in 1965 and Revlon's Braggi arrived in 1966. "He even stole our tortoise paper from Aramis," Mrs. Lauder said irately, alluding to the noticeably similar Braggi packaging. "Everybody copies somebody but everybody can change it. Even if I copy, nobody knows I copy. There had been bath oils before but I made my bath oil into a fragrance."

She called it Youth-Dew and it made the entire industry dance to the tune of long-lasting scent. Today it is the world's best-selling fragrance in dollar sales, pouring $50 million a year into the Lauder income account.

Lauder's Clinique made health-oriented cosmetics chic for the first time, beating Revlon's Etherea to the market in 1968.

Revson has increasingly insinuated himself into advertising for Revlon's Ultima II products, as a man telling women how to be desirable, while the Lauder fragrance ads emphasize that a woman created the scent. "There's no one who has her nose," her son the president said.

Lauder also has an enviable hold on prestige department and

specialty stores. In the United States Lauder products can be bought only through 2,000 such stores and branches. The greater number of Revlon products are distributed through drugstores as well.

Although selling through department store counters is less profitable than other means—because the manufacturer shares advertising, promotion, and sales salaries with the stores, and these costs may run as high as 50 per cent of retail sales—fashion cachet comes through those outlets.

"Sure, I could pick up another million in earnings by breaking our traditional distribution pattern, but we are the keystone of department store cosmetics and if we weaken that, we will undo ourselves," Leonard Lauder said.

Though he declined to disclose profitability, he tantalizingly said, "We're not as good as Avon but as good as, if not better than, most of our competitors." In recent years, Avon's profits have run to 12 or 13 per cent of sales, while Revlon's beauty earnings have hovered around 7 per cent.

Revlon, with $500 million a year in sales, is now the second largest company in the $5-billion beauty industry (after door-to-door Avon Products, Inc., with $1 billion). However, Revson seems determined to turn Revlon into a diversified company with a strong pharmaceutical base.

Revlon went public in 1955. Its stock has often been a favorite of Wall Street, which is now paying court to family-owned Estée Lauder, Inc. The Lauders still hold all of the company's stock, never having rewarded any outsider with a single share, although they compensate their executives well and offer them responsibility and respect (benefits not always prevalent in the ego-ridden beauty business).

"We," said Leonard Lauder, referring to the Lauder triumvirate of father, mother, and himself, the older son, "look upon ourselves as winders of the clock or directors of the symphony orchestra who try to stimulate our group of talented and brilliant people to do the best they can."

Although an executive operating committee of four senior officers was created to relieve the son of daily administrative detail just before he was promoted from executive vice president, all executives still report to Leonard or his parents. The change of titles at the top doesn't mean, he indicated, that any of the Lauders are relaxing the ethic of hard work that shaped them as a family and a company. (The fruits of their single-mindedness are manifested in a family manner, the chief Lauder philanthropy being a series of adventure playgrounds in Central Park in New York.)

Even Lauder daughters-in-law have been periodically pressed into public relations and product planning service, giving make-up demonstrations in stores and on television, offering opinions on new lines. Neither Leonard's wife, Evelyn, nor Ronald's wife, Jo Carole, has had a corporate title; their remuneration is one of the secrets a private company can keep.

But the reins of control are divided into the same areas of expertise as they were from the start, Queen Estée in charge of product and promotion, the men in the family seeing to it that the products get delivered and make money.

The Lauder legend is the newest in an industry that builds on hyperbole and dreams and it is still being written. The Lauders seem very sure of where they are going, but Mrs. Lauder, at least, is still creating her past. The true story is woven of the warp and woof of American success, with plenty of hard work, sheer gall, triumphs over adversity, clean living, and modest antecedents. With similar scenarios, men have been elected to the White House and to the presidency of billion-dollar corporations, but Mrs. Lauder may be pardoned in doubting its effectiveness in selling beauty products. There is, after all, a tradition of cardboard royalty in the cosmetic business. Both Arden and Rubinstein had married emigré Russian princes and achieved crested monograms.

In 1946 Joseph Lauder, a New Yorker who had had his ups and downs in several small businesses from textiles to luncheonettes, formed a partnership with his wife to market a few preparations developed by her uncle, John Michael Schatz, a cosmetics chemist. Schatz had come to New York from Vienna in the 1930s, and his niece, Estée Mentzer Lauder, had peddled his preparations among a widening circle of her friends and acquaintances.

Then as now, selling cosmetics to women in their homes was a proper occupation for a middle-class housewife with no capital except her free time, her pushiness, and an instinct for every other woman's vanity.

Avon's billion-dollar empire is constructed on a sales organization of hundreds of thousands of such housewife entrepreneurs. Few of them ever make more than pin money, though. Mrs. Lauder and her husband realized that and as soon as they were able, set about establishing a wholesale organization with distribution through retail stores.

But Estée Lauder's sales pitch has remained essentially the same. First there was the Danube strain. True or not, there exists in the beauty business a conviction that Hungarians hold the secrets of flawless complexions. Estée Lauder's mother came from Budapest and, of course, she was a great beauty who met Estée's father in Vienna (to which he had come by way of Bratislava). "My mother was so beautiful that a man fifteen years younger married her," she has said, as usual raising more questions than she answers. The sound of violins echo still in the releases issued by the public relations department of Estée Lauder, Inc. Not only is there an allusion to her "beauty-conscious Viennese family," but the press biography of her daughter-in-law, Leonard's wife, states that "the former Evelyn Hausner comes from a family noted for generations of Viennese beauties."

Then there is the medical theme. Estée Lauder used to brag about three uncles who were dermatologists in Vienna. Her press release said that as a young girl she "dreamed of becoming a skin doctor . . . but fate stepped in with marriage—to handsome Joseph Lauder, and the subsequent birth of two sons, Leonard and Ronald. So a next-best career for Estée was developing beauty treatments for women."

One of the first products Mrs. Lauder sold (it's still on the Lauder line) was Schatz's herbal Creme Pack. In the old days when everyone in the cosmetics business was less cautious about the claims they made for their products, she boasted that her uncle put the Creme Pack on Vicki Baum's scar and that she advised a buyer from Saks Fifth Avenue, who had been in an automobile accident, to apply it. Vicki Baum, a writer whose play *Grand Hotel* had been a Broadway hit in 1930 was the only celebrity link Estée Lauder could muster at the outset.

Mrs. Lauder seldom finishes a sentence or a train of thought. She hurtles on to other topics, so no one ever knew what the Creme Pack did for the writer and the buyer. One was just left with the assumption that near magic was involved or, at the very least, something very beneficial.

Certainly if Mrs. Lauder uses the product it must be good since she has that so-called Hungarian complexion. A half dozen years ago a stranger accosted her at the hairdresser and, as Mrs. Lauder related the incident, the woman pulled her hair back looking for tell-tale signs of cosmetic surgery and shouting, "I've known Estée Lauder for years, she must have had her face lifted!" Mrs. Lauder says she rejoined, "I know women who look the same today as they did twenty to twenty-five years ago because they use our products."

Nor was Mrs. Lauder ever shy about sharing her make-up secrets with others. "Elizabeth Arden can't make up her own face," she once said and proceeded to show her skill by giving her three-minute make-up application to a stunned visitor, briskly tucking Kleenex in the neckline of the captive's dress as she went about it.

A woman who remembers Estée Lauder mesmerizing the neighborhood matrons of West End Avenue in the years preceding the outbreak of World War II recalled how she would go up to someone she had never met before, criticize her make-up, and proceed to tell her how to correct it. "She would end up selling her $40 worth of cosmetics," the woman said.

"Beauty is my life," Mrs. Lauder once said. "I used to stop women on the street and on trains and give them tips." She even helped a startled Salvation Army sister. "There's no excuse for looking untidy," she maintained.

The technique may sound abrasive and insulting, but it doesn't come across that way with Estée Lauder's good-natured, motherly execution. For there are very few women, at least among those born before the Flower Generation, who do not believe their fortunes might improve with a new hair-do or a touch of lipstick or some new facial treatment. No older woman is immune to the blandishment, even one for whom a king gave up a throne.

Some of those who watched Estée Lauder's ascent on the wobbly social ladder of Palm Beach reported with gleeful malice that she had bought her friendship with the Duchess of Windsor with a supply of lipsticks. The reputation of the aging royal celebrities for exacting tribute from the socially ambitious had been well documented by then and so had Mrs. Lauder's spontaneous gifts of her products. But a proper rejoinder might have been that, to paraphrase George Bernard Shaw, duchesses are no different from flower girls when it comes to lipsticks.

Mrs. Lauder says she met the Windsors on an Atlantic crossing of the S.S. *United States*. According to her version, the Duchess said she wanted to meet her because she had been using Estée Lauder products for ages. The Duke said that Youth-Dew was the only fragrance he liked. They had cocktails together and the friendship ripened in Palm Beach, Paris, and other points distant from West End Avenue.

The Lauders went into business in 1946 with a basic line of half a dozen products: her uncle's wondrous Creme Pack, a "Super-Rich, All-Purpose Creme" ("It's all-purpose because I don't believe in night cream. How does a cream know it's dark outside," she once explained), a cleansing oil, a face powder, one shade of lipstick called "Just Red," and one shade of eye shadow (turquoise).

The products were sold privately, through the mail, and in a few beauty salons. It wasn't until two years later that Mrs. Lauder landed the crucial specialty store account. Saks Fifth Avenue agreed to give her counter space. The products sold well and Saks's buyer provided an introduction to Bonwit Teller's cosmetics buyer. New York became Estée Lauder's first market. For the next dozen years or so, Mrs. Lauder spent a major part of her time and energy making personal appearances and signing up other specialty stores and department stores throughout the United States. In 1958 she ventured to Canada and the following year across the seas to Harrod's, the London department store.

"One year my mother was away twenty-five weeks," said Leonard Lauder, describing his adolescence. While his mother traveled, his father worked from 8 A.M. to 7 P.M. seven days a week, and Leonard made deliveries in the afternoon and on weekends when he wasn't attending high school classes.

The tom-toms of publicity accompanied Mrs. Lauder's journeys. She cultivated the beauty press, one of the least critical in the journalistic craft. Most beauty editors consider themselves an adjunct of the advertising department of their magazines or newspapers, as well as heralds of new products and services for their readers. Most of them acquire a taste for luxury that their modest salaries would rule out were it not for the luncheons in fine restaurants, the exquisite gifts at Christmas and after the publication of sizable stories, and the shower of products tendered by the cosmetic manufacturers usually through their publicity representatives.

Mrs. Lauder's taste for luxury is insatiable—it has been quiet Joe Lauder's lot to figure out how to pay for it—and she shared it with key members of the press. In the early days she took them to lunch at New York's Number One celebrity hangout, Sherman Billingsley's Stork Club. Later on, she wooed them at one of the arrogant French restaurants where fashionables herded to be noticed or invited them to parties at one of the Lauder mansions. An interview in her office brought forth champagne and cookies; a pleasing story might result in antique silver candelabra being sent to the writer's home.

The press was appreciative, too, for Mrs. Lauder's reliability in generating copy to fill their columns and hold the interest of their readers. Her products were good and her personality an odd mixture of mama and medicine woman. If her autobiography changed with the seasons, all the more entertaining albeit confusing.

Tales of childhood in Milwaukee interchanged with anecdotes about Scranton, giving rise to reports that she was a coal miner's daughter which she denied. A member of her family once divulged that her formative years were passed on the frontier where the borough of Queens meets Nassau County on Long Island. A beauty editor who recounted her own Sicilian background to Estée Lauder at lunch one day came away convinced that Estée Lauder was half Italian and convent-bred. Mrs. Lauder was mistress of the throwaway diversionary remark. "They're old Tiffany and belonged to my mother in Vienna," she announced, within earshot of a *Women's Wear Daily* reporter who was attending a dinner in the Lauder Manhattan chateau. Mother's alleged possessions were silver soup plates and matching service plates displayed at one of Estée's little dinners for twenty-two. For those who enjoy watching social climbers maneuver up the rocky slopes to acceptance, Estée's act was no less entrancing than that of a marine scaling a crag during an exhibition of guerrilla survival training.

First, she took Palm Beach, disarming that playground of aging parvenus through their Achilles' heel, charity. The Lauders bought a white, oceanside villa of twenty-seven rooms and furnished it with Chippendale furniture, Meissen china and jewel-studded silver appointments. They went there for the Christmas holidays, in February, and part of March.

"This is my English home. This is not a beach home," she instructed a visitor. "I want to live here as formally as in New York. I love houses. That comes from Milwaukee. I never could see having to take children's bicycles up in the elevator," she said.

No matter how grand her pretensions, Mrs. Lauder never fails to be maternal and down-to-earth. She once hopped out of her pale blue Cadillac on Palm Beach's Worth Avenue, dressed in a white and navy blue suit, accessorized with pearl, diamond, and sapphire jewelry, to invite a reporter to come "for tea and some Sara Lee."

The dowagers with older money and the middle-aged brides of the newer tycoons who were Palm Beach's social arbiters may have ignored the Lauders in the beginning and even cruelly disparaged them. But the same arbiters justify their excessive lifestyle by a ceaseless round of balls and parties that raise money for respectable diseases and hospitals.

The Lauders bought the high-priced tickets to the balls which they always attended. Aglitter with nuggets of jewels and a French designer's dress, Mrs. Lauder usually caught the attention of photographers and society chroniclers. She also made generous contributions of Lauder products as favors to the charity balls, which rivaled each other in dispensing take-home loot for the wealthy guests.

When the Duke and Duchess of Windsor dined at the Lauders' and the event was recorded in the New York *Times,* Estée Lauder's social position was never again to be demeaned.

Palm Beach and the Windsor coup only whetted Estée Lauder's gargantuan social and palatial appetites, which by then she was beginning to be able to afford. For in the late 1960s her company had begun its phenomenal growth spurt. In 1966 the Lauders bought a Renaissance mansion of twenty-five rooms and eight baths in Manhattan from the estate of Arthur Lehman, the investment banker, for $500,000. She proceeded to decorate it in a style that would have suited the Doges of Venice. Portraits of Spanish kings glowered from the stone walls beside enormous Flemish tapestries. Damask upholstery had been woven in Venice to look antique.

"Everyone who sees the place tells me, 'This is not just a home, it's a castle,' " she told Virginia Lee Warren of the New York *Times* and then went on to intimate that she was no stranger to wealth. "In Milwaukee a woman used to come to our house every day just to brush my mother's hair," she said.

To drive that point home further, she instituted a rule of having only black-tie dinners in her Manhattan and Palm Beach homes. After several of them had been reported and photographed in detail, from the handmade Alençon lace over gold lamé tablecloths to the headlight diamonds worn by the hostess, Mrs. Lauder developed a crime phobia. Her publicity representatives pleaded with the press not to mention her jewels or the addresses of her dwellings.

Meanwhile Estée Lauder moved to greater triumphs on the European continent lunching and dining with the bereaved Duchess of Windsor in Paris after the Duke's death and entertaining another widowed friend, the Begum Aga Khan, on the French Riviera. Having outgrown their house in Cannes, the Lauders bought Villa Abri in the hills at Saint-Jean-Cap-Ferrat, that incomparable sliver of multimillion-dollar real estate already staked out by big spenders like Mary Wells Lawrence, the self-made advertising woman, and assorted titled and cinema celebrities. "All my friends are here or close by," Mrs. Lauder said loftily and then reverted to her essential modesty. "I think any villa in Cap Ferrat is a good investment. Buying here is like buying a diamond. You can always get your money back."

If, as some construe it, Estée Lauder bought her way into the social milieu she craved with gifts and hospitality her guests could not resist, she was only using a technique that had served her well in business. The lure of the giveaway—inducing customers to try her product because she was certain they would like it and come back for more—was one of those historical business decisions, dictated solely by the need to compete against the Goliaths.

When the Lauders went into business in 1946, they earmarked what was to them the staggering sum of $50,000 for the advertising that everyone knows is essential for the building of a brand-name product. They called on the panjandrums of advertising like Grey Advertising, Young & Rubicam, and Batten Barton Durstine & Osborn, offering their precious stake, and were rebuffed. One million dollars was the minimum for an advertising campaign, they were told.

After they realized that no one would take their advertising account, the Lauders gambled on an alternative marketing scheme. They would allocate the $50,000 for samples of their products to give away at fashion shows and through mailers ("Take this coupon to store X and get a free box of face powder").

"People trooped in to get the free sample, liked it, and bought it again," Leonard Lauder said, reconstructing the miracle. "If someone had given them the name of a small agency that would have run with the $50,000, we might not be in business today." A C & R Advertising, Inc., now handles the Lauder billings which run into seven figures.

Estée Lauder's version is slightly different from her son's. "I gave my stock out to charity, and God has been good to me because of that," she said. She referred to a benefit luncheon at the Starlight Roof of the Waldorf-Astoria. "I gave them a $3.00 lipstick. It was a time during the war when you couldn't get metal cases. They said, 'Why don't you give plastic?' When I give anything, I give something. I had forty calls after that asking couldn't I do the same for them and I said yes. I feel God has repaid me for when I started I couldn't afford it. May God help me," she said, raising her right hand, "if you give, you get."

Regardless of who was responsible—divine intervention, as Mrs. Lauder would have it, or the "luck of our own imaginative way of handling things," as Leonard sees it—the giveaway sampling technique that the Lauders pioneered won the imitation of an entire industry. Today it's called gift-with-purchase and it has the cosmetics and fragrance manufacturers boxed into costlier and unhappier competition. Recently, Charles Revson's son, John, devised the variation of purchase-with-purchase, which permits a customer who places a minimum order to buy certain additional merchandise at a discount.

Similarly the Lauders broke into the fragrance field in 1953 "backwards," not with a perfume but with a bath oil "that doubles as a perfume." The son said, "It was that intuitive sense of two people trying to take on the Establishment and knowing that if you meet them head on, you won't make out."

The double-purpose bath oil was named Youth-Dew. It now comes in several dozen versions, including a skin perfume at $25 an ounce. Like subsequent Lauder scents (Estée Super Perfume, Azurée, and Aliage), it had what Lauder publicists term "impact." Nonenthusiasts find its staying power can be erased only by intensive scrubbing.

Some stores discontinued the scented Youth-Dew mailers inserted with monthly bills because of complaints from husbands who received the statements at their offices, tucked them into their pockets, and later met accusations from their wives.

Suzanne Grayson, a product and marketing consultant for the cosmetics and fragrance industry, tells of the time she gave her driver's license to a clerk at a rent-a-car office. The clerk was wearing Youth-Dew. When she returned the license, the scent was transferred to Mrs. Grayson's pocketbook and nothing she could do would banish it. "That's why Estée Lauder is so successful," Mrs. Grayson explained. "She sold that fragrance all by product development and by sampling. No advertising, no psychology. Essentially, she was saying, if you like my fragrance, I'll give you more of it."

The Lauder cosmetics tend to be higher priced than those of competitors—the lipsticks sell for $3.50 and $4.00, compared with $2.00 for Rubinstein's, $3.00 for Arden's, and $2.85 for Revlon's Ultima II—but Lauder fragrances are priced lower. Although the essential oils come from France and are said to be used in the same concentration as $50-an-ounce French perfumes, there is less packaging and the customer is told to use Lauder fragrances more lavishly since she's paying less for them. Two and a half ounces of Youth-Dew Eau de Parfum Spray sells for only $7.00, a third of what an equally aggressive French scent would be priced at (if, indeed, any scent can lay claim to being so dominating), and one million bottles of the spray are sold a year.

The year that Leonard joined the company 80 per cent of its promotional budget was thrown toward Youth-Dew. "We realized we had a sleeper," Leonard Lauder said. But the sampling or giveaway program was like "planting an acorn. It didn't bear fruit for another year, but then it started to hit."

By 1960, the year that the million-dollar mark was passed, the company was incorporated, the international market was tapped (Lauder products are now sold in 70 countries), and Youth-Dew was becoming a major part of the business.

Until then—despite Estée's grand public gestures—the company had been strictly a mom-and-pop business, aided and abetted by older son Leonard. Even baby brother, Ronald, was pressed into service after classes at the Bronx High School of Science, one of New York's public schools for the brainy. Leonard had attended it, too. "I helped father make the creams," Ronald said with some distaste, harking back to 1958 or 1959. "And frankly I hated it. Some thirty or forty ingredients go into a face cream and I always had this phobia that I was forgetting something. You can't taste a face cream to see if it's right as you can when you're cooking," said Ronald. As a teen-ager he preferred to exercise his scientific knowledge in a culinary vein.

It was Leonard, then, the serious, steady first-born, upon whose shoulders the responsibility for running the business was deposited early. "My parents always had confidence in me," he says. When he was sixteen and just graduating from high school, they planned to take a vacation and leave him in charge of the factory "which was about five times as big as this office," he said, looking around his presidential lair, a spacious but not vast retreat, furnished as a study-living room in sturdy contemporary furniture and art. "But I came down with chicken pox so they couldn't go."

He went on, as if anxious to dispel any connotation of nepotism, "What people don't realize is that I—to borrow Dean Acheson's phrase—was present at the creation. There isn't a single job in this company, with the exception of the IBM jobs, that I hadn't done. But it wasn't part of a training program. I would hire my own replacement."

Leonard went off to college at the Wharton School of the University of Pennsylvania, then into the United States Navy for three and a half years. There he acquired valuable experience as a supply officer under a number of different senior officers. In retrospect, it was important to win approval for performance from non-family executives. After military service he returned to his parents' business and to evening classes at the Columbia Graduate School of Business where he fell asleep more often than not.

"The only thing business school taught me was the simple matter of how to recognize you have a problem and how to solve it," he said. In business school, as in the Navy, the only adult years spent away from his family, he also learned from observing "a number of brilliant, able people" not to believe in his own infallibility.

"If you have a problem, find someone better than you to solve it. There are people here who are better at twenty different things than I. The best education for me was the knowledge that you can always get someone better than you to solve it. The question is how do you stimulate them?" The Lauders apparently decided that the best way to do that was with respect, consideration, high salaries, but not one share of stock in their company.

No one in the outside world ever impressed Leonard as much as his own parents, though. "Mrs. Lauder is enormously ambitious for her company," he said, using the impersonal reference to his mother for business discussions. "She has the ability to keep everyone on their toes. My father has an enormous ability to direct and organize vast logistical movements."

Of his own abilities, Leonard said, "Mine fall in between. When I think of their accomplishments," he said in an idolizing tone, "nothing will ever replace the hours they worked. Every dollar was weighed. That's what made us good. We look for the most effective means of promoting the products. They never believed in salesmen, for example. And we have a very few of them, even today. All the money the competitor put into salesmen, we put into the product. We gave a better product and promoted it better. We'd send the stores charts to fill in after they'd count stock once a month. The buyers would send the charts back to me and after dinner I'd sit with my coffee writing out the order for them. It's amazing how much can be done with a few people.

"Today we're more sophisticated. We know all about IBM and marketing, all those wonderful business tools. But we're probably not running the business any better and probably making less money than we would have fifteen years ago when we were less sophisticated. We're on a big antisophistication kick. Less IBM reports, less copies to everybody that they have to answer. We keep ourselves hungry for office space. If a job is not getting done, instead of getting a second person plus a secretary to do it we get someone else to do it. We believe in a hungry organization, hungry for sales, hungry for income, hungry for the amenities of life."

When Leonard officially joined Estée Lauder, Inc., in February 1958, its sales were $850,000 and its employees numbered five. In fifteen years, sales were multiplied one hundred fold and there were more than 1,000 employees.

"The first million is the hardest," he said. Estée Lauder, Inc., attained that golden number in 1960, after fourteen years "with hard work, having a good product, and generally making the right decisions," he said.

But even as the company stretches for the $200-million mark, the Lauders still observe the same boundaries of authority of their humble beginnings. Originally, Estée and Joe "split authority down the middle," as Leonard described it. Joe took finance and operations as he still does in his vigorous sixties, basing himself at the plant in Melville, Long Island. Estée reserved command over sales and marketing until Leonard staked out his claim in marketing and advertising in 1959.

Except for the dimension, nothing much has changed. When it comes to choice of products, "we will defer to Mrs. Lauder's ultimate decision," Leonard said. "I can blithely spend millions on a certain investment without asking anyone, but I wouldn't launch a body lotion that contains fragrance without her signed approval," he said.

Mrs. Lauder, who has never lost her touch as a make-up artist, disapproves of false eyelashes. They do not appear in the Estée Lauder line. However, hypoallergenic lashes (which are far more difficult to test and develop) are in the Clinique line, which is marketed not only to the allergic but to younger women who like "pure," fragrance-free cosmetics.

Mrs. Lauder likes blue (as Elizabeth Arden saw the world in pink). So Lauder packaging tends to be blue or green, as is the period French décor of the corporate offices (with the exception of Leonard's, which is in contemporary coppers and golds, and Ronald's, which is a stark white cell).

The company projects the image she has cultivated. It combines quality and scientific research, expensive fashion and unsnobbish but insistent social tone. Despite her poses, Mrs. Lauder remains friendly and maternal, a sixtyish grandmother of four with the dreams and energy of a woman half her age.

"To the public, Mrs. Lauder is the great creator, and indeed she is," said Leonard, attempting to draw the table of organization of a multimillion-dollar family company that grew, efficiently and expediently, but seemingly quite naturally.

"But one of the things that brought the company from here to here"—he raised the flat of his palm as an imaginary marker—"was the harnessing of her creative ability with the creative ability of some other people and wrapping it all up in a package that works. The areas that my parents knew other people were good at, they let other people do."

For instance, the Private Collection line of Lauder fragrance was introduced in 1973 at $70 an ounce. In price, at least, it represented a radical departure from the Lauder mold. "The fragrance is all hers but before she gave it the final O.K., she consulted with Evelyn [Leonard's wife], who wore it and liked it. The package was designed by Ira Levy, corporate art director, under my direction and Mrs. Lauder's approval."

Her son, Leonard, explained the informal rules and relationships that are understood without being written down. "She'll open an ad and say, 'This looks terrible' and we'll say, 'O.K., we'll know next time' or she'll say 'It's great' and we'll say, 'We'll do more of it next time.'"

"People [at Lauder] get promoted and she'll read it in *Women's Wear Daily,* but there are hirings we won't do without her and Joe's approval because they will be working with those people."

There is no corporate pecking order. Yet Becky McGreevy, the vice president for public relations, a serene southern belle who won her diplomatic spurs in the service of Elizabeth Arden, knows that publicity matters concerning *Vogue* and the New York *Times* are taken to Mrs. Lauder, whereas those to do with *Glamour* or the Chicago *Tribune* go to Leonard. If it concerns a new office in Paris, it will involve Mrs. Lauder. If it's in Germany, it will not. Details from the English office are routed to Estée or Leonard Lauder, those from the Japanese office to neither. "You can't put this on an organization chart," Leonard said. "For a highly structured business, which we are, this is highly unstructured. I suppose you'd have to say the business is run the way all of us interpret it, ten hours a day."

Just as his mother will not let her history be pinned down to factual roots, so her son Leonard, for all his business school training, is reluctant to disclose the authority lines in his family's business.

"I never understand what is the difference between chief executive officer and chief operating officer," he said, with a shade of irritability in his voice. "Either you are or you aren't the boss. I'm running the company," he said firmly, and then he added, "but I refer to Mrs. Lauder and Mr. Lauder as my bosses. Maybe I'm the chief operating officer."

Then there's his baby brother, Ronald, an inch or two taller, a decade younger, and appreciably different if for no other reason than, as Leonard points out, "I hired everyone here and he came after most people were here."

The brothers bear an almost carbon-copy resemblance to each other and to their father, with their wavy brown hair and dark almond-shaped eyes. Both sons have almost but not quite completely mastered stammers.

But where Leonard is Joe's counterpart, feet on the ground, eye on the figures, level-headed, and not carried away by anyone's flight of imagination, Ronald is his mother's son. "He's very much like Estée in his instincts and tastes. He's got a lot of class," says his brother, Leonard.

"I'm very much a hedonist," Ronald says. "I'm not for sitting here until 3 A.M. going over my figures. Leonard eats, sleeps, and drinks this business as my parents do. I less so. I'm interested, but it's a different type of feeling. I'd be lying if I said from the time I was six I wanted to run Estée Lauder.

"I'm a different type of person than Leonard is. Besides, when I came in, it was already a major company. It was very small when Leonard started and he was part of the building. I can't get a feeling I'm starting anything," Ronald said, and then he amended, "I get a bit of that feeling with Clinique. I can talk all day about the greatness of Clinique. I'm anxious to create something myself," he confided. "I want a totally separate identity. I don't want to get a pat on the head and that attitude 'Are you helping your mother?' I stay away from all the people who knew me when I was in the cosmetic business when I was twelve and fourteen. The minute someone calls me 'Ronnie,' I know they knew me a long time ago."

Ronald Lauder hints that he might find happiness elsewhere if only he were as sure of maintaining the Lauder lifestyle. "I consider cosmetics my hobby. Art is my business," he declared and then lapsed eloquently into the subject of how he buys and sells "drop-dead art." He meant the drawings and watercolors of Picasso, Matisse, Rembrandt, and other gilt-edge artists the price of whose oil paintings bolted into the stratosphere before the Lauders arrived at the marketplace.

"My taste and my mother's are similar," he said. "If not for my wife stopping me, I'd like to install myself in a palace."

Ronald sits in a chaste white office, smaller than any of his mother's clothes closets, behind a Saarinen pedestal table and chairs. On the wall is a French museum poster of an Ingres exhibition. He bought the poster at Bloomingdale's because he has the original drawing of the painting by the nineteenth-century artist that it reproduces. Ronald admits that his father, "who is my treasurer," doesn't understand his art acquisitions at all. He describes himself as "a sensational businessman," but he dreams of a Lauder museum named, of course, after Ronald Lauder. He and his wife are ascending through the committee system at the Museum of Modern Art (the museum of the Rockefellers and the Paleys). Jo Carole Lauder is a member of the junior council, the training farm for the board of trustees. He is on the committee on drawings. The Lauder Foundation has made contributions to the architectural design fund. Jo Carole, whom Ronald calls "my early American bride because she comes from Bloomington, Delaware," collects early American furniture.

"I'm an accumulator. I'm 50 per cent interested in cosmetics, 50 per cent in art," says Ronald, who always manages to fit a museum visit into his business trips. On a recent mission to the J. L. Hudson department store in Detroit, he coaxed six cosmetic buyers to a Géricault exhibition at the Detroit Institute of Arts. He describes their reluctance as though he were Samson among the Philistines.

Shortly after Ronald put in his disagreeable time in the cold-cream factory, his family's fortunes soared and his own higher education for a gentleman's life began. He followed Leonard's footsteps to the Wharton School of the University of Pennsylvania but took his junior year in Paris. Then he went on to the University of Brussels for a masters degree in international business, acquiring fluency in French, German, and Flemish. In 1966 he took a short apprenticeship in humility at the Lauder plant then being constructed in Antwerp. His next assignment was in the Paris office as marketing manager to launch Estée Lauder in France. "I adored it. I looked upon myself as a young playboy, I had a fantastic apartment on the Left Bank in the Seventh Arrondissement and lived the life of Aly Khan for six months," he remembers fondly.

Alas, he was called home to military service. He reported for duty in the U. S. Coast Guard, "the only guy reporting in suit and tie," he recounts. "I was told, 'See the commander.' I thought my mother had telephoned," Ronald continued, extracting the last drop of humor from the tale. "But when I finally got to see the commander he said, 'You know, my mother loves your products.' And I said, 'You know, my mother does too.' I was very popular after that."

Ronald spent a minimally uncomfortable career in the Coast Guard at Governors Island, typing and putting his speedwriting skill to use as a secretary. In 1968 he was free to resume his destiny at Estée Lauder, Inc. He moved from various sales and sales promotion jobs to Clinique and a year after arriving in that new and star-touched division he became its executive vice president.

"In each job he's had he was exactly the right person at the time," brother Leonard says. "In my estimation he's probably one of the most capable, rounded cosmetic executives in the business. He's the most well-balanced, broad-thinking twenty-nine-year-old executive I've had the pleasure to meet."

At another time and in another office, Ronald says of Leonard, "He's the most knowledgeable person I've ever met in the cosmetic business. He knows how to market better than anyone."

As for Estée Lauder, Ronald says, "My mother is brilliant. Intuitive. You will not meet anyone smarter than her."

Of his father, Joseph Lauder: "He's super with money, a very great balance to myself and my mother. Without him, we'd be in the poor house with the things we want to buy."

Ronald continues: "Am I as brilliant as my mother or my brother? No. Can I control money the way my father can? No. Am I a child of this environment? Yes. Am I a typical twenty-nine-year-old boy? No. I'm a businessman in my own way. When I come to a store, I won't negotiate. I have the finest product and you should have it, I tell them. It works. When I have a sales meeting in Los Angeles, I have it at dinner at the Bistro. It's very important to me that Clinique be run as sophisticatedly and elegantly, as top notch as possible.

"My strength is I really enjoy what I'm doing. I run the thing the way it should be done. I'm also the most happy person I know. I'm extraordinarily content. I'm the sweetest guy I know. I love people."

Ronald runs Clinique with what he calls a "low profile" and the able assistance of Carol Phillips, an astute merchandiser with a fanciful flair for product promotion. Miss Phillips was hired away from a job as beauty editor of *Vogue* to act as midwife for Clinique and stayed on as baby nurse and governess.

The Clinique line is promoted and sold independently, almost as though it were disavowing Estée Lauder, a clever marketing strategy inasmuch as the customer it is drawing—young, natural, and very much on the qui vive—is likely to be put off by the Junior League airs of the Lauder image that succeed with another audience.

Clinique and Estée Lauder counters are likely to be found at opposite ends of a department store floor. At Bloomingdale's, the New York department store that has become a cult with moneyed, youth-worshiping sophisticates, there are two Clinique counters, one on the main floor half a block away from Estée Lauder, the other nestled upstairs in a young sportswear department.

The maintenance of separate and in some ways rival product lines is a strategy developed by General Motors with its Chevrolet, Pontiac, Buick, Oldsmobile, and Cadillac divisions. The cosmetic industry has been imitating it zealously in recent years.

Concerned about one-product dominance, the Lauders broadened the make-up and treatment lines throughout the 1960s, continually adding new products that compete with one another as well as bringing them new customers.

Early in 1972 "we started to sense a splitting in the market, in that older people," Leonard said and then he corrected himself, "our regular customers," he went on, "still demanded products for specific purposes like 'You must do something for my dark shadows under the eyes.' But the young kids were turned off by the hocuspocus. So we uncomplicated."

Primary Four, a new group of multipurpose products, was introduced, bringing the Lauders back to where they began twenty-six years before with one all-purpose cream and one shade each of powder, lipstick, and eye shadow.

New lines and new market forays cost money and may take four or five years to turn into the black—as Clinique did late in 1972 although it was introduced in 1968. A private company need not apologize if its ventures progress slowly.

"If we had been public, I would never have launched Clinique," Leonard said. "We took a bath before it started paying off. The same with Aramis. We're just starting in the Japanese market, and that will take an enormous drain. We don't feel we're ready to go public because we have too much investment spending to do." The Lauders have always financed their expansion through earnings and normal credit, he said.

Wall Street drools at the prospect of a Lauder stock offering, not only because of the company's growth and leadership but also because it is the only sizable cosmetic prize still in private hands. In recent years, pharmaceutical companies and conglomerates have snapped up many of the noted beauty companies—not always with dazzling results.

Elizabeth Arden was left in turmoil when its octogenarian founder died without having set her affairs in order, and it was acquired by Eli Lilly & Company. The Squibb Corporation took over Lanvin-Charles of the Ritz. British-American Tobacco has Germaine Monteil and Yardley tucked among its cigarette and herring properties. Max Factor merged with Norton Simon Inc., the food processing, beverage, and publishing giant. [In the fall of

1973 Helena Rubinstein went into an alliance with Colgate-Palmolive.]

For the last five years Estée Lauder, Inc., has been managed as though it were a public corporation, with statements by outside auditors, quarterly reports, and separate corporate profit centers. Growth is planned at a compound rate of 15 to 25 per cent a year for the next five years. Everything is in order for a public offering of the stock except the family decision.

"We still have a few things left to do before we can look and say should we or shouldn't we," Leonard Lauder said. "The advantages would be money and diversification of family assets. The disadvantage is that for the first time we'd have partners."

BEINECKE'S TREASURE ISLAND

Summer 1973

The misty island of Nantucket, thirty miles off the Massachusetts mainland, has long been a summer hideaway for the rich.

Its seasonal wealth derived from pedigreed names like the Yankee Lodges and Coffins, the Long Island Roosevelts, and the Beineckes, whose fortune was made in trading stamps.

During the last few summers, however, a different kind of money has been flowing into Nantucket. It comes from corporate summits, recent financial coups, and lucrative professions.

Some of the newcomers arrive by corporate and private jets. Many come by sea, in yachts and power cruisers that tie up at the Nantucket Boat Basin, one of the best serviced and most luxurious basins on the eastern seaboard. On a typical August day $15-million worth of seaworthy craft is moored there, mostly registered in the names of corporations or charter companies.

The newcomers' presence has added a slick coat of modern varnish to the Nantucket brand of economics. Like the cobblestoned streets and gray-shingle cottages, it had been a mixture of eighteenth- and nineteenth-century—laissez faire and straightforward monopoly.

The boat basin, which some old Nantucket residents criticize as being too Palm Beachy, has lured the kind of visitor who will buy a

$3,000 painting in ten minutes, exactly the sort Walter Beinecke, Jr., had in mind.

This fifty-five-year-old New York venture capitalist, who gets what he wants with the vim and enthusiasm of a door-to-door Bible salesman, is Nantucket's biggest summertime employer and its most controversial landlord.

In the summer of 1968, as his master plan for "trading up" the island's economy within the context of historical preservation was moving into high gear, "Ban the B" and "No Man Is an Island" buttons appeared on sports shirts and linen dresses. They are out of circulation now and the bitter personal abuse to which Beinecke was subjected has been muted.

"I used to be like a puppy dog, wagging my tail whenever anybody said anything nice to me about what I was doing here and becoming sad and sulky whenever anybody criticized me," Beinecke told a reporter for *Life* magazine at the height of the protest movement. "But now I've developed very tough skin and nothing anybody says about this project, good or bad, affects me much emotionally."

A tall, gray-haired, bespectacled man, he roams the heart of the island town, clipboard in hand and attired in unmemorable sports shirt and trousers. With his old-shoe appearance and superficially mild manner, Beinecke might easily be mistaken for an absent-minded ornithologist or a local master carpenter. But after a brief conversation, the iron will and the confidence of divine right are revealed.

The combination of lots of old money and the Puritan ethic tend to make an ambitious economic royalist like Beinecke an awesome opponent. The sovereign knows best, after all, and acts from purest motives.

Similarly, Beinecke's cousin William S. Beinecke, chairman and chief executive officer of the Sperry & Hutchinson Company, once told stockholders at the annual meeting who were demanding answers to the losses sustained by the S&H trading stamp and promotional services division, "I don't answer leading questions."

The Beinecke cousins are forever being confused with each other. It annoys Walter, Jr., to be referred to as the Green Stamp heir. He invariably is. Sometimes Yale men have to be restrained from making reverent remarks in his presence. But it's cousin William S., the

S&H chairman, who is a 1936 Yale graduate and a trustee of the Yale Corporation.

Walter Beinecke, Jr.—he has no middle name—did not attend Yale or any college at all, although he is an active trustee of Hamilton and Kirkland Colleges. He has contributed, however, to the extensive Beinecke family gifts to Yale. "It's a tribal endeavor," Walter said, alluding to the fact that thirty-four Beineckes participated in the philanthropy. The most renowned of gifts is the Beinecke Rare Book and Manuscript Library.

Walter, Jr., is a director of Sperry & Hutchinson, the trading stamp company founded in 1896 by Thomas Sperry and Shelly Hutchinson. In 1903 Hutchinson sold his interest to William Sperry, Thomas's brother.

In the 1920s three Beinecke brothers—Edwin J., Frederick W., and Walter—joined the company. Frederick and Walter married daughters of William and Thomas Sperry. William S. Beinecke is the son of Carrie Sperry and Frederick Beinecke, Walter, Jr., the offspring of Katherine Sperry and Walter Beinecke. The Beinecke family owns 5.7 million shares or 58 per cent of the common stock of Sperry & Hutchinson. Walter's holding is down to 5,550 shares of the common stock and 9,000 shares, or 17.7 per cent, of the cumulative preferred.

He once worked for S&H as a sales vice president. Since only one Beinecke could be at the top and in the mid-1960s there were six Beineckes at work in the company, Walter, Jr., left to set up his own diversified investment company, the Osceola Operating Corporation. Its offices are in the S&H building on Madison Avenue in New York City.

Osceola's principal business is Christmas Club A Corporation, organizer of bank saving clubs. Founded in 1910, Christmas Club was acquired by Osceola a dozen years ago.

Osceola Graphics of Easton, Pennsylvania, another entity, is a specialized printing concern that prints bank documents, magazines, and trade journals. Osceola Broadcasting owns three radio stations in Florida (Osceola was a Seminole Indian leader who waged guerrilla warfare in the Everglades). Osceola's major real estate property is Rainbow Springs, a Florida tourist attraction. At one time, Osceola was in a joint venture with the King Ranch, raising cattle on 95,000 acres in the Everglades.

Walter Beinecke is also an investor and former officer of Executive Airlines, a financially troubled New England commuter airline. He divides his time mostly between New York and Nantucket. In winter, he commutes to his Manhattan office from Williamstown, Massachusetts, where he and his wife, Mary Ann, recently moved because they liked the educational environment of the college town for their youngest child, Walter Beinecke 3d, who is nine. The Beineckes were both previously married and share eight children from past and present marriages.

An off-islander, or summer visitor, Beinecke has been coming to Nantucket since he was four and he knows and loves every cobblestone, heath, bog, and coatue cactus in its star-crossed history.

Nantucket is one of the last outposts of the United States on the Atlantic. The next stop east is Portugal, the natives like to claim. First settled three hundred years ago by dissident Puritans, it became the greatest whaling port in the world during a hundred-year span from the mid-eighteenth to the mid-nineteenth centuries.

Herman Melville's Captain Ahab sailed out of Nantucket on the *Pequod* in search of Moby Dick. Evidence of the great fortunes amassed from whale oil by families like the Coffins, Folgers, Starbucks, Macys, and Husseys survives in the fine wooden houses still standing in the center of the town within strolling distance of the harbor.

A fire in 1846 wiped out the waterfront and business area. And when, in 1859, Colonel Edwin L. Drake struck the first oil well in the United States near Titusville, Pennsylvania, whale oil was superseded as a source of light. In less than a decade Nantucket was a ghost town, its chief industry erased. Most of its citizens fled to the mainland to make a living. The population dropped from 15,000 to 2,500.

Nantucket stagnated for nearly fifty years until, at the turn of the twentieth century, wealthy families discovered it as an unspoiled summer resort. Its eighty miles of beaches attracted a tourist trade that by the early 1950s had swelled the summer population to about 25,000.

Small businesses such as an ice plant, a lumber yard, a gas manufacturing plant, and several tank farms for fueling boats sprang up at the waterfront.

"What should have been the town's front yard, if you wanted to have a historic place or a modern resort, had become the backyard,"

Beinecke said. "But the messy hunk of waterfront was economically no longer viable in a modern resort business."

In the meantime, while Cape Cod across Nantucket Sound had fallen prey to the developers, seven acres of dunes on Nantucket were selling for $1,500 in 1957. But a study of tourism made by the State of Massachusetts and the federal government around that time warned of the threat that megalopolis growth and the leisure society would produce.

As a writer for *Boston Magazine* put it, "Enter Walter Beinecke, Jr., an island visitor since boyhood, who decided to show his gratitude by preserving the island—or by making it his fief, depending on your point of view."

In 1957 Beinecke and his father founded the Nantucket Historical Trust, through which many of the island's Greek Revival mansions and other landmark buildings have been restored. One of the churches had lost its steeple in a hurricane a century ago; Beinecke had a replica constructed in Boston, flown over to the island, and installed by helicopter. Rent from commercial tenants of properties like the Jared Coffin House, an 1845 jewel now operated as an inn, is used by the charitable trust for further restorations.

"I'm a trustee of the National Trust for Historical Preservation which is chartered by Congress. It's a voluntary business," Beinecke said. "Historic preservation has to have a low priority as to federal funds, and if you're interested in preservation, you have to do it within the American economic system. I'm trying to show that you can run a commercial part in a form that, if not beneficial, at least isn't damaging to the historic quality.

"All the evidence indicated that we'd be exposed to greater mass tourism. In Nantucket you're dealing with a finite quantity of land. Everything of value, commercially and philosophically, is related to a small scale. We had to find a way to relate a modern economy to prepare for this onslaught and do it in a way to preserve the town.

"Nantucket should face the water," Beinecke believed. "Fifteen years ago, I went to a management consultant who is the best marina expert in the country. He said build a marina in the creeks [the wetlands in the far southern corner of the harbor]. I said, 'I know that's too far out of town.' I'm a leftover sort of merchant. Everyone will be mad at us. I waited two years and I went to the second best marina builder. I bought another study. It was bound in plastic instead of leather but it said the same thing.

"My father once said, 'Only a fool makes the same mistake twice.' I said I know they're wrong. Obviously we asked the wrong thing. We said marina which means superyachts. So this time we asked, 'Now how do we reactivate the waterfront'."

In the early 1960s Beinecke and three colleagues, a banker, an architect, and an accountant, set up Sherburne Associates, a realty company in which he is managing partner. Sherburne acquired key parcels in Nantucket's business district and along the deteriorating waterfront.

Sherburne is reputed to control 80 per cent of the business district. Beinecke says 50 per cent is closer to the truth. However, in economic as in military warfare, strategic location means more than total area.

Through the Island Service Corporation, a Sherburne subsidiary, Beinecke constructed the Nantucket Boat Basin with an investment one qualified local source estimates at $15 million. Beinecke, whose zeal for privacy in all his operations tends to inflate gossip about his wealth, scoffs at the figure.

"We have not poured in millions," he insisted. "We put it together with commercial financing from a life insurance company that gave us a medium seven-digit figure long-term mortgage.

"Why, that $15-million figure reminds me of the time my wife sneezed as we landed in Nantucket. When we reached home we received a telephone call lamenting the fact that she had been taken to the hospital with pneumonia."

Beinecke's grand plan for Nantucket invites comparison with what the Rockefellers have done at Williamsburg, Virginia, a parallel he doesn't discourage. He has said, though, "I cannot afford to do what Mr. Rockefeller did and make a museum out of a town. I wouldn't want to do it anyway. It's much better to keep Nantucket a living town."

He describes his motivation in terms of Nantucket's architectural and historical treasures—buildings to be at the core of the commercial district. In the pre-Beinecke era, the adjacent waterfront area had decayed into a gateway for steamers that brought tourists of the post-card-hot-dog-souvenir ilk. The specter of mass tourism and sharpshooting real estate developers hovered over a town that had no zoning restrictions.

Efforts to impose the latter crashed against the community's rock-ribbed Yankee independence and aversion to joint action.

"I'm afraid they carry individual freedom too far," Beinecke has said.

"I'm an opportunist," he declared. "To me there were two opportunities. Improperly used real estate is an economic opportunity to someone. Also there was the movement necessary to protect the historical part of town from unregulated commercial development."

Sherburne not only bought properties but also persuaded tenants like the A&P to eschew concrete barrack construction and acres of parking area and to harmonize their quarters with the landmark character of the town.

"We don't say they should reproduce or restore the commercial area. There were no 10,000-square-foot stores in colonial days," Beinecke said.

"Until the 1950s, the two chains, A&P and First National, were in two, twenty-four-foot Momma and Poppa stores. Then came the pressure to buy cheaper and bigger. First National moved out of the town and built a shopping center alongside the highway.

"Four-sided concrete and not a blade of grass. It was very successful. It had parking and good prices. A&P wanted to do the same. It would have ruined us. The value of downtown real estate is based on traffic. If two year-round traffic producers had been removed, Main Street would have degenerated to small business. We tried to keep them downtown and combined that with the opportunity to clean up the industrial backyard.

"We tore down the lumber yards, the ice plant, and two tank farms. We made Main Street a block longer. We built a shopping center at the foot of Main Street. A&P has space and parking as part of a vibrant downtown. The local Five & Ten, the laundromat, and the liquor store relocated with them."

Beinecke reasoned that the "romance of the island and its small size and scale" dictated fewer bodies, so he would have to attract fewer but wealthier tourists to "a quality resort with quality merchandise."

He went on: "The most controversy has been about restricting the number of tourists. It's not racial or social but economic. You can't tell people who live here, 'You live in a historical landmark so you can't buy color TV or send your kids to college.'

"But you can tell them that if they're selling hot dogs, they can't make money unless they sell them to 4,000 instead of 2,000. And we say, 'That way you'll destroy the asset.'" The alternative Beinecke presented was to rent a hotel room and sell a couple of sports coats to the fewer, better-heeled tourists.

That meant finding co-operative tenants.

"The romance of an island is hard to come by. It dictates the quality approach," Beinecke went on. "But we didn't have quality stores. Which do you get first—quality customers or quality merchandise? We took the long way—building up the real estate structure that can support that marketing policy, then bit by bit feeding in the merchandise. Up to now we've been opportunistic. We'd grab a tenant who would be cooperative. But we found we could live with some of the local merchants too.

"We give short-term leases, one year, to those who won't be part of our future. We work closely with tenants who allow us to trade up," said Beinecke. The tenants are granted long-term leases with 5 to 10 per cent of sales for the landlord.

"This was very controversial," he admitted. "The Yankee philosophy is, 'My business is mine.' We had to sell the idea that 'this is a partnership and you won't prosper unless we do.' It has been hard to sell. We've raised rents in some cases. Next summer we'll be more arbitrary on leases. They'll have to agree to stay open certain evenings or keep their lights on. That's not the old Yankee way. They stand or fall by themselves. This is enlightened self-interest."

He "declined to renew" the leases of unco-operative tenants, such as the private steamship company that was bringing 1,500 tourists at a time to the island.

Its lease went to a new operator "who saw it our way—decent, clean, frequent service but landing no more than 450 passengers at a time." A bus operator who agreed to use smaller buses received the prized right of access to the dock.

"It's using economic clout," Beinecke acknowledged. "We've been charged with snobbism. I guess we are discriminating economically and I don't know how to find a political or social justification for it. But if we're to survive as a town, we have to pick our market. To make a living, we have to keep the essential character of the island."

Sherburne Associates owns and operates the two leading hotels, the family-style Harbor House and the White Elephant, where the rates run from $47 to $151 a day, and a 20-cent newspaper can be bought for 30 cents at the reception desk. Sherburne also runs two of the better restaurants and the Sweet Shop, which sells $1,000 worth of 35-cent ice cream cones a day.

"We spent eight years putting together a real estate picture that allows us an important amount of local scope," said Beinecke, indicating that he has finished his buying phase and will concentrate on finding other tenants of distinguished national reputation.

"We don't have legal authority, but we do have an opportunity to influence the character of trade in a form that is favorable to the town," he said.

The Beinecke vision has won national architectural awards as well as the respect of many of the Nantucket businessmen who share his long-term objectives. But many are leery of monopoly, even when it wears an enlightened face. Those who feel victimized in the new Nantucket blame Beinecke for every facet of their plight. The Thomas Devines own the Overlook Hotel, a rambling rooming house on a side street a few minutes' walk from Main Street.

Mrs. Devine complains that "the selectmen wouldn't give us a license unless we put emergency lights in the hall. It cost us $3,000 and it wasn't necessary for the few times the lights go out for about twenty minutes. Jared Coffin and the White Elephant didn't have emergency lights. Beinecke isn't fighting us personally. It's political.

"When the Nantucket Electric Company phased out gas, we couldn't store pyrofax in our hotel, so after twenty years we had to buy all new electric equipment. It cost us $10,000 easily. When the gas company became electric, the electricity rate increased. We're walking with knives in our back. Beinecke controls the company," Mrs. Devine asserted.

The century-old Nantucket Gas and Electric Company had been a division of an off-island utility holding company. Many Nantucket businessmen say it had been badly mismanaged and insufficiently equipped until a group of local investors, including Walter Beinecke, took control and recapitalized the company in order to pave the way for an expansion program. Beinecke has about 20 per cent interest in the company.

Public hearings were held and the dwindling number of gas customers were offered favored rates if they would convert to electricity. But the impact on the old rooming houses was severe because of the expense required to make any alterations on their rickety properties. Since the conversion occurred simultaneously with the residential building boom, plumbers took advantage of it by raising the prices of their services.

Painful as it has been for the small businessmen, many of the repairs to their antique buildings were necessary. One local anecdote concerns a waterfront restaurant that was discovered to have a leaky pipe from an upstairs bathroom poised over the kitchen stove on which its famous quahog clam chowder was cooked. A boatload of day tourists lunched one day at the restaurant and departed with an epidemic of what is usually called "Montezuma's revenge" or "Delhi belly" when it is contracted in more exotic regions.

Mrs. Devine still feels threatened. "We have a colored family who want to buy our hotel," she said. "We don't want to sell but we may have to."

But there are beneficiaries of Walter Beinecke's Nantucket strategy, too. Since he prefers tenants who co-operate in preserving the "romance of the island," often they find that such co-operation can prove lucrative. James H. Cromartie, an artist, sells his acrylic paintings of Nantucket sea and farm views from a narrow, three-story gallery and studio on Old South Wharf. He is paying $6,500 rent this season, about ten times what similar space along the wharf would have brought four years ago. But he is not vexed with his landlord.

"He brings in the right people," Cromartie explained. "Why, yesterday, a man walked in and in ten minutes he bought a $3,000 painting. He was a CPA."

The twenty-nine-year-old artist paints his realistic scenes from memory during the winter months, which he spends near Tampa, Florida. This summer his paintings start at $3,000. Five years ago a Cromartie fetched $150.

A couple of summers ago New York's Governor Rockefeller strolled off his brother Laurance's yacht, which was tied up at the Nantucket Boat Basin, and into the Cromartie gallery. He bought several paintings, and this encouraged purchases by the late Roger Firestone and other business titans.

"I'm a proven commodity now," Cromartie said. "When the stock market goes down, it's good for me. People know my painting is more sure than stocks."

Another of Beinecke's co-operative tenants who seems to be doing well is Kevin Shore. Three years ago this Dartmouth graduate, now thirty-one, left Arthur Andersen & Company, a public accounting firm, to set up a lobster fishing business in Nantucket. His Off Shore Enterprises, Inc., is expected to gross $500,000 this year.

Shore has over $200,000 invested in a boat and fishing gear and another $60,000 in a refrigerated facility on the wharf. His crew, all of them college graduates like himself who didn't want to spend their lives behind desks, go fishing for lobster from the middle of June to just before Christmas, and for cod and haddock during the winter months.

They bring in 7,000 pounds of lobster at a time which they sell at $1.80 a pound to wholesalers on the mainland. Shore has also leased the Sail Loft restaurant from Beinecke as "an experiment" in the retail trade in addition to his wharfside fish store, the Nantucket Lobster & Seafood Company.

"I'm going in an integrated direction," he said. "It all depends on attracting qualified people, but I plan to grow to a larger handling capacity here and to have an outlet near the Midwest, say Pennsylvania, to which I can ship by air. I'd like to expand to five boats and five outlets. My idea is to get people not connected with the fish business," said Shore, who was raised in Gloucester, Massachusetts. "We're rethinking the rules. One of my people was in the insurance business and the rest have different types of business backgrounds."

Another entrant into the offshore fishing business is Harold Berger, retired president of Marionette Mills Inc. of Coatesville, Pennsylvania. "As a hobby," he charters his forty-six-foot Sport Fisherman at $350 a day, usually to groups of four or six. His wife, Carolyn, runs an art gallery from their home on Nantucket from June to October. In the winter Berger sails the boat out of the Bahamas.

In their summer gallery on Straight Wharf, New Yorkers Malcolm and Annette Parle specialize in producing portraits of captains of industry. Parle was a stockbroker who turned full time to his hobby of photography during the Wall Street slump of 1970. His wife was a fashion designer who had always liked to paint. Now they work together in a New York studio in winter and during the summer in their Nantucket quarters rented from Beinecke.

A business leader like R. D. Hubbard, president of Safelite Industries, Inc., of Wichita, Kansas, comes to the Parles to be photographed for his corporation's annual report. A color photo is taken for an $85 fee. The photograph is taken in the Parles's hundred-year-old Old Barn Gallery on Lily Street. The subject sits in a converted horse stall, having combed his hair and straightened his tie in an adjacent grain room. Their gallery on Straight Wharf, a few yards from where the tourists disembark, serves as their sales and exhibition hall.

If the executive is pleased, he may order the picture in an imposing oil-on-canvas version, baronially framed at $550 or more, for his boardroom or living room. Sometimes he commissions portraits of his wife and children, too. Only the Parles and their subjects need know that they didn't sit for the long hours that oil portraiture traditionally requires.

Melva Chesrown and Floyd Smith formed a partnership and opened The Gift Box on South Water Street in 1967. He was a former vice president for marketing for Bigelow Sanford Inc., "looking for a transition from flying 75,000 miles a year." He found it, staying put on Nantucket. Miss Chesrown commuted between Nantucket and her New York public relations firm for several years until she decided to settle down on the island. She has also handled public relations for Beinecke.

"When we first started, we were the only quality gift shop here," she said. "Since then, two or three have come along but they haven't affected us because we keep growing. That has to mean the business is here and that there has been a trading-up process.

"Eventually, there will be steps to eliminate the day-tripper boats by not letting them have space on the wharf," she said, divulging the next step in Beinecke's master plan. "Some of the most vicious opposition to him has come from those who benefited most from what he has done," she said.

Chesrown and Smith have developed a needlepoint business to give themselves a year-round base. Designs by local artists are translated into kits containing design and yarn that sell at retail for $35 to $125 (up to $500 and $600 for rugs). There is also a wholesale business selling to needlework shops, and a mail-order business with a catalog list of 25,000.

"The mail order tapers off in the summer, thank God, and is big in the winter. It keeps the help busy then," Smith said. "Depending on what happens to the wool market, we could be doing a quarter of a million dollars in a year or two with needlework."

A couple of years ago, at the age of thirty-nine, Robert Tonkin left a job that required him to be constantly on the road for Sears, Roebuck & Company. He had been manager of advance store planning. "I was traveling six days a week, living in an apartment in Chicago, vacationing in Nantucket, and commuting weekly to New York," he said, shuddering at the memory. Tonkin, now forty-one, operates a store that sells off-the-beaten-path gifts and antiques. He specializes in English antiques ("there's a dearth of American antiques," he said) and local gift items like the apple gargoyles, carved from fruit and shellacked, that sell for $57 to $135.

"It's a big item for Europeans and we're getting more and more Europeans," he said. A French tourist had just given him $1,495 for an English drop-leaf table.

A year ago, the owner of Four Winds, a small gift shop on Straight Wharf, asked Tonkin if he'd like to buy him out. "I didn't have any money and he didn't need any for a year and a half so I did," Tonkin said. Four Winds caters to what he calls "the $3.00 and $5.00 trade," meaning mostly the day-trip visitors.

Like all the artists and merchants along Nantucket's three central wharves and most of the shopkeepers in the best locations in town, Tonkin has as a landlord the ubiquitous Walter Beinecke. Nantucket is, undeniably, in the throes of a boom that Beinecke helped fuel, although informed observers are not sure that it has yet provided a handsome return on his investment.

The Pacific National Bank, the island's commercial bank, has had an average increase of 15 per cent a year in demand deposits during the last three years. "Mr. Beinecke has been an important economic force," says Henry G. Kehlenbeck, vice president of the bank. "It bothers some people, though, to have it all in one man."

There are other symptoms of growth for which Mr. Beinecke cannot be blamed or praised. Residential real estate values have been rising 15 per cent a year. In 1972 new mortgage volume came close to $10 million. A condominium complex with $45,000 units, advertised as a tax shelter, has disrupted sewage facilities of the Madeket section of the island. The Nantucket Conservation Foundation, headed by Roy E. Larsen, vice chairman of Time Inc., has acquired 14 per cent of the island for permanent preservation.

Meanwhile, lines are being drawn between foes and proponents of a federal bill proposed by Senator Edward M. Kennedy to set up a national island trust to restrict further real estate development.

"I came here to retreat from America," said the Pacific National Bank's Hank Kehlenbeck, who fled the hectic pace of banking in Syracuse in 1967 for Nantucket's alleged tranquillity. "I'm working twelve hours a day. I came too late."

THE KOHLERS OF WISCONSIN

May 1973

Some of America's leading citizens bathe in Kohler bathtubs. Kohler engines power the garden tractors of suburbia and the sampans of southeast Asia. Kohler stand-by electric plants purr in motor homes and yachts. Kohler precision controls in the Saturn and Atlas rockets helped send astronauts to the moon.

Yet invariably when the name of Kohler is mentioned beyond the periphery of this model Wisconsin village, four miles west of Sheboygan, the listener nods and asks about the strike. It was one of the longest and bitterest strikes in labor annals. It started on April 5, 1954, and whimpered to a halt on September 1, 1960. And it was finally settled only after litigation that took five more years.

In December 1965 the United States Supreme Court upheld a ruling of the National Labor Relations Board, which had found the Kohler Company guilty of unfair labor practices and ordered it to pay $4.5 million in back pay and benefits and to reinstate most of the fired strikers.

"Rightly or wrongly, everyone knew the name Kohler because of the strike," said Herbert Vollrath Kohler, Jr., the thirty-four-year-old chairman of the privately held company. "Many of our customers became customers because of the position we took." In 1973 he was trying to change the corporate image under the handy umbrella of the company's centennial fete.

With his dark beard, pearly smile, and debutante-stagline good looks, the chairman bears an uncanny resemblance to his grandfather, John Michael Kohler, an Austrian-born agricultural equipment manufacturer who came to the United States in 1854. The grandfather added enamel coating to one of his products, a combination horse trough and hog scalder, and sold it to farmers as a bathtub.

From that discovery on, the Kohler Company has been in the forefront of spreading America's undisputed contribution to modern civilization: the efficient bathroom. With sales in 1972 of $159 million, more than half of this derived from plumbing fixtures, the Kohler Company is the second largest in its industry, after American Standard, Inc.

"I feel we would not have the relationship we have today with the union if not for that strike," Kohler said. He was voicing a refrain heard from both partners in this now seemingly contented marriage between labor and business.

As the Kohler Company whirled through its hundredth anniversary like a dowager who has imbibed at the fountain of youth, Local 833 of the United Auto Workers was simultaneously celebrating its twentieth anniversary of the signing of its first one-year contract with the company. A year after the signing, in March 1953, the union called that strike.

As with couples who remarry after nearly murdering each other, the relationship is confusing to all but the bride and groom. Here it can be explained by the perversities of human nature, by the lack of alternatives to remarriage, and by the passage of time. The principal figures in the strike have died, retired, or moved away.

The present alliance must also be viewed against the background of an almost incestuously homogeneous community of a state like Wisconsin where nineteenth-century German socialist ideas flourished. Wisconsin's Republican party produced both the La Follette family and Senator Joseph R. McCarthy.

Few strikes have been as painfully divisive as the one at Kohler. It pitted Local 833 against the company that had been the only employer many of the strikers and their families had ever known. It tore some of these families apart even at graveside. It severed the Teutonic calm of the community. Fear reigned after mass picketing, vandalism, and company-instigated eavesdropping.

The company did not lose money during the strike because, two months after it began, it reopened the plant and hired other workers. The United Auto Workers spent $12 million in strike benefits, a sum that could never be recouped. "It was written off, charged to experience," said Egbert Kohlhagen, the sixty-seven-year-old recording secretary of Local 833. "The money was well spent because the union won the battle. It would have been a bad thing for unionism if the company had won."

Labor and management still disagree, though amicably, about who won the strike and what caused it. As part of its centennial panegyrics, the Kohler Company commissioned a film, *May Your Sky Always Be Yellow,* depicting the company and its young leader as defenders of individual choice. In the film, a child is allowed his preference for coloring the sky with yellow crayon.

By standing fast in the strike, the company thwarted the union's demand for a union shop and secured for its workers "the right to join or not to join a union," Herbert Kohler, Jr.'s resonant baritone voice proclaims during the film commentary. Union leaders invited to view the film demurred but ever so mildly. They insist that the union shop was never a serious demand and that it was taken off the table in 1955.

Raymond Majerus, regional director of the UAW (who, with his father and brothers, was a Kohler striker), declared: "I've said to the company that they've learned their lesson and we've learned ours. They learned we can't be pushed around.

"But we found out there is a different way of doing business with them, a good deal different than most companies. We accommodate their hang-ups. They don't ever want to be confronted, so we let them color their sky yellow."

Majerus described the wage-bargaining tactics since the strike ended: "You can't say to them, 'That rate is too low.' We say: 'That casting is too rough, the powder is too hard in the enamel shop, there's dust blowing around from somewhere, so we can't make the rate.'" Until recent years there was a high incidence of lung disease.

"It's not the worst way to do business, and it's proven successful," Majerus said. "Now we have among the highest wage rates in the industry where once it was the lowest."

Kohler wages, averaging $4.54 an hour, are among the highest in the Sheboygan area, where thirteen locals have organized other businesses since the Kohler strike.

The hard-fought provision for arbitration of grievances has never been used, so harmonious has the poststrike climate been.

The union's contract with the Kohler Company contains a clause providing for reopening of wages every three months. In practice, this happens only once a year as a concession to the company's dislike of cost-of-living escalator clauses.

"We always get something so decent we have no need to go in the next quarter," Kohlhagen said.

"Ours is an arm's-length relationship and one of respect," Majerus asserted. "We never say we'll never have trouble again, but we hope not."

The controversial union-shop issue has been left dormant. However, the UAW says it will be the Number One issue next year when the present contract expires. If so, Herbert Kohler observed coolly, "then we'll have an interesting contest."

Meanwhile, the union was conducting a membership drive as part of its anniversary rites. It claims that 65 per cent of the 4,000 industrial workers at Kohler already belong.

So, as both company and union choose to interpret it, an industrial tragedy served the happy purpose of harmony. But that's not how one qualified observer sees it.

"This is learning the lesson the hard way," said Walter J. Kohler, Jr., who was governor of Wisconsin from 1951 to 1957. "I think the strike could have been avoided. Both sides were at fault."

He sold his Kohler Company stock in 1953 "because I didn't want to be in the position of calling out the National Guard to protect my own investment." He added: "It was as clear as the palm of your hand that there was going to be a strike." When it came, he said, he was prepared to call out the militia "if necessary, but it wasn't."

The former governor, a lean patrician of sixty-nine, is chairman of the Vollrath Company of Sheboygan, a manufacturer of stainless steel equipment. In 1947 he bought control of the company which had been founded by Jacob Vollrath, his and Herbert Kohler, Jr.'s great-grandfather.

After graduation from Yale in 1925 Walter, Jr., started out "to learn the business" at the Kohler Company, which his grandfather had founded and which his father, Walter Kohler, Sr., had dominated from 1905 to 1940, first as president and then as chairman.

Walter, Jr., attained the position of secretary of the company in which he was frequently in dispute with his father's younger half-brother, Herbert V. Kohler, Sr., who became president in 1937 and then chairman in May 1940 following Walter, Sr.'s death. Herbert, Sr., resolved to wriggle out of his elder brother's shadow at last and to wrest absolute control of the company. It became apparent that there would be nothing but frustration and token roles for Herbert, Sr.'s nephews and so after Walter, Jr., returned from service in World War II as a lieutenant commander in the Navy, he looked for a show of his own to run and took over the Vollrath Company. He continued to run it during his three terms as governor as his father, who had been governor from 1929 to 1931, had run the Kohler Company during his administration.

Although there were no written conflict of interest laws at the time, Walter, Jr., acknowledged that "I was criticized for running Wisconsin on a four-day week. But so were the legislators. They went home every Thursday afternoon and returned Tuesday morning. So I went to Sheboygan Thursday evening and was in my office Friday through Saturday noon and back to Madison Monday evening."

Independence of mind and action had been Walter, Jr.'s trademark. He once affronted fellow Republican politicians in his dairy state by refusing to pose for a campaign photograph milking a cow. "I don't know how to milk a cow and I won't pretend that I do," he said.

Walter Kohler, Jr., came to be known as "the education governor" because of the expansion of the university and state college system during his tenure. A fiercely loyal supporter of President Eisenhower, his brand of Republicanism was much too liberal for many of the state's industrialists (among them his Uncle Herbert), as well as for adherents to the cause of Senator Joseph R. McCarthy.

After the senator died suddenly in May 1957, Walter Kohler, Jr., entered the race to fill the unexpired Senate term over the objections of the McCarthyites and was easily defeated by the Democratic candidate, William E. Proxmire.

Since then, the affairs of the Vollrath Company have been his main occupation, although these days, his son, Terry, operates Vollrath from the post of executive vice president.

Two of the governor's three brothers also made provisions for their families outside the Kohler Company. Robert Kohler acquired a plastics company in Sheboygan and Carl Kohler started a machinery company, Kohler General, for his sons. "Carl foresaw there were just too damn many Kohlers for one company and his children would have a rough time," the former governor said.

His late brother John's son, John Michael Kohler, Jr., is the only living Kohler besides Herbert, Jr., who is still employed by the Kohler Company. He is director of distribution relations and pricing and also serves on the board of directors.

The history of the Kohler Company is a regional saga of complex genealogy and emotion. The Kohlers are a clan of strong-minded businessmen, with opinionated wives and spinster sisters who are given to culture and philanthropy.

The founder, John M. Kohler, produced two separate branches of the prolific family tree. After his first wife died, he married her sister. Control of the company is now vested in the second branch through Herbert, Jr.

By Lillie Vollrath, the first wife, the founding father had three sons, Robert, Carl, and Walter, Sr., and three daughters, Marie, Evangeline and Lillie Babette.

The sisters never married. They are remembered as large-featured women who dressed in black in the winter and white in the summer and gave out baskets of food to the employees on Christmas Eve. Sister Marie was the dominant female, a civic and cultural leader and social reformer of a mild sort. She served briefly as secretary of the Kohler Company, and while her brother, Walter, Sr., was governor, she helped to draft a new State Children's Code. She also hired a sculptor and architect from Munich to design the Waelderhaus, a replica of the Kohler family home in the Austrian Alpine province of Vorarlberg; it became the meeting place for the Kohler Village Girl Scouts and the Women's Club.

By his second marriage to his wife's sister, Wilhelmina, John Michael Kohler had one child, Herbert Vollrath Kohler, Sr., who was destined to lead the family and the company into strife and dissension. Herbert married a would-be social leader from Chicago, Ruth DeYoung. Her mission was to bring culture to the boondocks and she did so with a vengeance, importing a wide range of notables from the rasp-voiced senator from Illinois, Everett Dirksen, to Fritz Kreisler, the Austrian violinist, to inform and uplift her family and fellow citizens in the model village of Kohler.

Since her death in 1953, her daughter, Ruth DeYoung Kohler II, has carried on the distaff tradition of arts and letters and philanthropy. Ruth Kohler, a shy and massive woman of thirty-two, directs the John Michael Kohler Arts Center established in the Victorian mansion in Sheboygan that was the home of her grandfather, the company founder.

Herbert Vollrath Kohler, Sr., chafed in the orbit of his older half-brother (or, as some reason, his three-fourths brother inasmuch as their mothers were sisters and the degree of consanguinity therefore especially intense). Even if there had not been a sixteen-year age difference making them more like uncle and nephew rather than siblings, the relationship would have been difficult. Walter Kohler, Sr., was a man not easily outperformed in his lifetime.

All of the founder's sons had a crack at running the company, but it was Walter, Sr., who shaped its character during his thirty-five-year reign. A man of unbounded creative energy and multiple interests, he led it into its small engine and electric plant diversifications. He also left a social imprint on the company and its community.

Walter Kohler, Sr., refined the custom of paternalism. He, of course, wouldn't have called it paternalism, his son, Walter, Jr., remarked. "But it was enlightened paternalism," Herbert, Jr., explained in the centennial film, *May Your Sky Always Be Yellow*. (In the celebration of the seventy-fifth anniversary of the company over which Herbert, Sr., presided, the contributions of his dead but to him still larger than life brother Walter, Sr. were given only token mention.)

Walter Kohler, Sr., shortened the work week at the factory from sixty to forty-eight hours. He established the American Club, an inn intended as a halfway house for immigrant male workers from Central Europe, who were housed there until they could send for their families. At its dedication in 1918 he explained the choice of its name. "It was thought that with high standards of living and clean, healthful recreation, it would be a factor in inculcating in the men of foreign antecedents a love for their adopted country," he said.

The American Club has continued to function as a hostelry and recreation center for nonswinging singles. The rate these days is $3.50 a room, on which the company does not lose money. Among the present boarders are a handful of blacks whom the company has coaxed to the all-white Sheboygan area to alleviate the tight labor supply.

Although a couple of thousand Spanish-American agricultural

workers migrated to the lush farmlands of southern Wisconsin during the last decade, Sheboygan and its environs fifty-five miles north of the city of Milwaukee are still smotheringly Central European. This is Lawrence Welk country.

At one time, a public ordinance prohibited lodging for blacks in Sheboygan, and when ball players and other black celebrities came to town, they were covertly put up at the home of a clergyman. At the last count, the only black that Sheboygan could call its own was one postman. There was a black co-ed who had been crowned Miss Sheboygan, but she, in fact, was a Chicagoan attending a nearby college.

Walter Kohler, Sr., didn't stop at temporary housing in his goal of planting the American dream in his workers' souls. He brought John Philip Sousa and his band to town for the dedication of a community park. (Every August the company still sponsors beer-and-bratwurst picnics for 18,000 employees and their families there.) Under Walter, Sr., the company organized classes in civics, English language, and American history for the new immigrants. Then he provided them with a wholesome environment in Kohler Village, which was incorporated in 1912. In 1923, after a decade of planning, he started building a garden-industrial community there.

He had gone to Europe in 1913 with a Milwaukee architect to study the garden cities of England and the industrial housing developments in Germany, such as those of the Krupp Steel Works. Back in the United States he retained the Olmsted Brothers, the Boston firm of landscape architects and city planners, to lay out the plan for the village.

One of the Olmsteds' fundamental precepts was the green belt of 3,000 acres which still protects the village from encroaching developers. Tidy houses are set back from immaculate lawns on curved streets with $20,000 neo-Tudor workers' homes next to $100,000 neo-Georgian houses belonging to the senior executives.

Kohler Village is economically if not socially integrated. Its only bona fide mansion is Riverbend, the house that Walter Kohler, Sr., built along the Sheboygan River. It is occupied now by his daughter-in-law, Julilly Kohler, a writer of children's books and widow of his son John.

Sometimes called "a garden at a factory gate," Kohler Village, which has a population of 1,738, respects the prairie and the woodland glens. The tree-shaded streets, the tennis courts and the nine-hole golf course open to employees and residents, and the high school with its indoor-outdoor swimming pool look like a suburban Eden.

Only the black smoke, belching from the iron foundry smoke-stack and emitting the acrid odor of a metal furnace, which is carried on days when the wind prevails from the west mars the man-made paradise. The company is spending $6.6 million to refurbish the foundry with smoke-free electric furnaces.

The sole business enterprise in the village is a gas station.

On no subject except the strike is Kohler's management more defensive than the suggestion that the village might be a company town. Compared with old Kentucky coal mining company towns, it surely never was. In those models of the worst kind of industrial feudalism, the company usually owned everything in town, from the houses to the stores and even the jail. The workers overpaid for their foodstuffs with company-printed scrip money, had their rent deducted from their pay, and were evicted from their homes if they displayed too much loyalty to trade unionism.

The Kohler connection was always benevolent. In the early years, the company built many of the homes and sold them at cost to the employees. It organized the Kohler Building and Loan Association to help them finance the purchase, usually at rates below those prevailing in the area. Walter Kohler, Sr., encouraged home ownership for his workers because he believed it was "the American Way."

In bad times, terms were eased still further. Wilmer Weinhold, incumbent president of the Kohler Village board of trustees, is a maintenance electrical supervisor at the plant and a second-generation Kohler employee. "During the Depression my father couldn't pay the principal, just the interest," he reminisced. "So they ended up extending his original ten-year contract. There were only three or four foreclosures in those years and they were for people who showed no interest in keeping their homes. The company was as benevolent as you could get."

Today benevolence is out of fashion, if not pretty near illegal. Through its home improvement division, the company sells parcels of land in newer areas still to be developed. Purchasers' architectural plans must conform to master standards. There is a repurchase option in many of the deeds, giving the company right of first refusal to the highest offer. But the company owns no more than half a dozen houses. And early in 1973 the Kohler Building and

Loan Association was acquired by a savings and loan association headquartered in Sheboygan.

The presence of the company, with its industrial tax base, insured an incredibly low tax rate for residents of the village through the years, but inflation and mushrooming educational needs throughout the county have sent the rate climbing to the point where many believe the advantage over nearby Sheboygan will soon be erased.

Today about 75 per cent of the 600 households in the village are headed by employees of the company. Four of the six members of the village's board of trustees work for Kohler, two of them in blue-collar ranks, two in lower management. A Kohler vice president is president of the school board and Herbert, Jr.'s wife, Linda, is an active member.

"I'm sure the residents don't want me to tell them what to do," said the company chairman, who prefers the word "participation" to "paternalism" these days. "We aren't always going to get our way."

The company now pays only 25 to 50 per cent of the cost of recreational activities, such as the Kohler baseball league; once it footed the whole bill.

The Kohler stables, which owed their origin to the fondness for English riding of the Kohler family and the company officers (who used to appear in the saddle every Sunday afternoon), have been transformed into a breeding and training operation for Morgan horses which are Herbert, Jr.'s favorites.

However, the stables are being run as a business rather than a benevolence by the home improvement division of the company. The American Club, the thousands of acres of green belt real estate, and the beef cattle farm which somehow just grew out of that grazing land are also listed as profit centers.

Walter Kohler, Sr.'s benign stance of great wise father to his employees went much deeper than his concern for the way they lived and played after working hours. The conditions under which they labored were far more agreeable than those in other heavy manufacturing industries of the era. Early in the century, through the Kohler Benefit Association, employees had life, health, and accident insurance, safety training and death benefits. Only slightly did these mitigate the high rate of lung disease, which is one of the side effects of plumbing-supply manufacturing with its iron furnaces and enamel bake-ovens.

Kohler employees felt more secure than many other working men and women elsewhere in the country during economic slumps because Walter Kohler, Sr., declared it a point of pride to keep them on the job, even if the job was only painting fences and even if, as in the 1930s, it only lasted eight hours a week. "I have always insisted," he said in 1932, "that it is the most important duty of management to provide workmen with as much regular employment as possible."

That year, the bottom fell out of residential building, which was the chief market for Kohler plumbing products. Kohler employees were kept turning out fixtures and fittings. These inventories were then warehoused until, as it happened, World War II came along and they could be sold in a shortage-prone environment at greatly appreciated value.

Walter Kohler, Sr., may have been foresighted in anticipating some of the concerns of working people, but he never brooked trade unionism in his own company.

True, during his one term as governor of Wisconsin from 1928 to 1930 to which he was elected as a conservative Republican after defeating the progressive Philip M. La Follette in the primary, Walter, Sr., had signed almost two dozen bills advanced by organized labor. One of them outlawed the "yellow dog contracts" under which employees gave up union membership as a condition of hire; the governor believed that union membership was a matter of individual choice. But that stated belief in principle didn't alter his opposition to a union within the Kohler Company.

Back in 1897 the first of three strikes that would stain its history was called by twenty-one members of an iron molders' union over a change in pay rates. Union recognition was not at issue and the strike petered out without any record of a formal settlement.

Then in 1934 the American Federation of Labor organized Kohler's production and maintenance employees into one of its federal union units. Walter Kohler, Sr., refused to bargain with them. A picket line went up around the plant that July. The sheriff of Sheboygan County summoned several hundred deputies to protect the plant. In the riot that followed, two strikers were killed and more than forty were injured. Martial law was declared. Walter Kohler, Sr., threatened to close down his model village and relocate the plant.

He never carried out his threat, but during the next and last six years of his life he frequently lashed out at President Franklin D. Roosevelt, accusing the New Deal of inciting labor to a "rule-or-ruin" campaign.

Out of that 1934 clash, however, came the Kohler Workers Association, an independent union which defeated the AFL's federal union in an official election conducted by the National Labor Relations Board in September of that year.

Walter Kohler, Sr., died in April 1940 at sixty-five. "He died of a broken heart and everybody knows it," intoned the governor of Wisconsin, Julius P. Hall. "He was crucified by organized labor in an unjustified strike, when he had done more for labor than any man in Wisconsin . . . He was a great humanitarian. He was crucified by little people, jealous and envious."

Walter Kohler, Sr., had owned 42 per cent of the stock of the company, an amount short of absolute majority but enough for effective control. His half-brother, Herbert Kohler, Sr., then forty-nine and president, seized the company reins by assuring himself voting control beyond his own insufficient lot of 18,000 shares.

Each of Walter Kohler, Sr.'s three unmarried sisters owned 21,000 shares. Evangeline and Lillie were persuaded by their younger half-brother, Herbert, to tender their irrevocable proxies to him. At their deaths, their shares were willed to his children. Marie died in 1943, leaving her stock to the Kohler Foundation, which the sisters and Herbert had organized in 1940 as a vehicle to support their educational and other social impulses. With this new total of shares that he could vote, representing almost 50 per cent of the outstanding stock, Herbert, Sr.'s direction of the company was not easily challenged.

The Kohler Workers Association had flourished and grown strong under the support of the company since 1934. But after World War II a group of younger workers returned from military service and formed an aggressive faction within the KWA, pressing for affiliation with the United Auto Workers.

Discontent with their limited say in working conditions and with the company's authoritarian posture had been mounting even in so staunch a member of the KWA as Egbert Kohlhagen (today the recording secretary of the UAW Local 833).

"If Herb or the Kohler Company could have seen the light and played ball with the KWA and bargained the way they should have, there probably would be no UAW today," said Kohlhagen, calmly looking back over the years from the spartan headquarters of Local 833 in Sheboygan. "But they tried to put us in our places. That was their big mistake. Sure it was Herb's doing. You only have a union when the employer doesn't do what is right."

In 1951 the UAW had failed in a KWA election to win recognition as the bargaining agent for the Kohler employees. But in June 1952, after the leaders of the KWA had voted to affiliate with the automobile union, an NLRB-conducted election was held. This time UAW Local 833 received 53 per cent of the votes cast and was certified as the exclusive representative of the Kohler employees. It took from the following August until February 1953 for a one-year contract to be hammered out.

That agreement had a termination date of March 1, 1954, but as early as three months before then, the company and union negotiators were meeting and exchanging proposals. What became known as "the seven major issues" developed at the outset and lingered unresolved throughout the strike. They were: seniority, noncontributory pensions, a paid lunch period for enamelers, insurance, arbitration on grievances, wages, and union shop security.

The union maintains that the last two were not principal issues, but the impression that the demand for the union shop was the unreconcilable difference lingers in the popular memory and in company propaganda.

Whatever the fact may have been, there is no doubt that Herbert Kohler, Sr., a man of mercurial temperament and fragile ego, saw the union as a threat to his family and his economic creed.

His right hand and chief negotiator during the strike, Lyman C. Conger, is alternately recalled as his gray eminence or his loyal, more flexible servant. Apart from the strike, he was an amiable good citizen, active in the Boy Scouts and other civic affairs.

"Father felt strongly that the company had a right to manage itself and I don't believe his ideas ever changed," his son, Kenneth Conger, asserted. A lawyer like his father, he had resolved he would never work for the Kohler Company, but he relented and now is assistant secretary of the corporation and a member of the management bargaining committee. Labor regards him as tough but fair. "It was inevitable that there would be a bloody battle," he said reflectively. "There was a brand new union that wanted to show their muscle and on the other side, two strong people, Herbert Kohler and Lyman Conger. I don't think the parties agree now what the strike was about."

It began on April 5, 1954, when 2,778 pickets encircled the plant. The union had taken a strike vote two weeks before. The company retaliated by announcing that all employees who reported for work would receive the 3-cent-an-hour wage increase the union had turned down. The union's opening demand had been for a 20-cent-an-hour increase.

But few employees could penetrate the picket barrier even if they had wanted to. The plant was closed for eight weeks and then the company won a court injunction prohibiting the mass picketing. The Kohler gates swung open, and the workers—some new, some ex-strikers—began to trickle back. The fate of the strikers whom the company fired and refused to reinstate remained a sticking point all the way up to the United States Supreme Court.

Kohler and Sheboygan are communities of almost intolerable intimacy, where one is unlikely to go shopping or drop in at a bar for a drink without meeting kin or someone affiliated through the webs of intermarriage. The strike, which lasted a decade and surpassed previous records of labor discord, ripped family ties and friendships. One striker turned his back on his nonstriking brother at their father's bier. Blows were exchanged at church picnics and in taverns. Bridge clubs disbanded.

Repercussions were felt on the national scene. In 1958 the Senate Select Committee on Improper Activities in the Labor and Management Field, headed by John L. McClellan, the Arkansas Democrat, began taking testimony on the strike, which had already consumed three years of hearings by the National Labor Relations Board.

The Senate hearings, which produced evidence damaging to both sides as well as to the standing of politicians and labor leaders, became a showcase for the excesses of political partisanship. Senator Barry Goldwater, who was then building the reputation as a Republican conservative crusader that would make him a presidential candidate in 1964, flailed at Walter P. Reuther, head of the United Auto Workers, accusing him and his union of power madness, lawlessness, and subversion.

Reuther and his aides disavowed almost all of the disruptions except the picketing, though he conceded that the UAW might have done more to discourage them. The union paid the legal bills of two strike leaders who were indicted for violence.

Largely through the efforts of Senator John F. Kennedy and his brother Robert, then counsel for the committee, the hearings brought to light the preparations that Herbert Kohler, Sr., had made for the strike. After the one-year contract was signed in 1953, the village police force was doubled in size and equipped with supplies of tear gas and riot guns. The company hired detectives to spy on strikers and union officials.

The union did not hesitate to use its own weapons. As the strike dragged on, the company was faced with a nationwide boycott of its products by the UAW and its sympathizers. Some large customers avoided Kohler products lest their own employees refuse to install them. But the company maintains that it gained more new customers who admired its resistant stand than it lost to union solidarity or fear.

Herbert Kohler, Sr., had become a hero to some. He had stood fast, spurning all overtures including those from his nephew, Walter, Jr., then the governor of Wisconsin. In 1958 the Old Timers Council of the National Association of Manufacturers named him "Man of the Year." Walter Reuther of the UAW, whom he had dubbed "a Moscow-trained socialist," christened him "the most reactionary, antilabor, immoral employer in America."

Then, in 1960, the NLRB ruled that the Kohler Company was guilty of unfair labor practices under the Taft-Hartley Act. It ordered the company to resume good-faith bargaining and to reinstate most of the strikers, though not seventy-seven of the strike leaders. What had started as an "economic strike" had been converted to an "unfair labor practice" strike prolonged by the company, the board members said. "Spying" on strikers, "investigating" their leaders, and "evicting" some workers from company-owned homes were among the practices cited.

The company, as expected, appealed the decision to a federal court. Though on the whole pleased with the order, the union appealed the failure to reinstate the strike leaders.

When the United States Court of Appeals for the District of Columbia upheld most of the board's decision in January 1962, the company appealed to the United States Supreme Court, which declined to hear the case.

Herbert Kohler, Sr., resigned the presidency of the company in July 1962, though he continued as chairman. His successor, James

L. Kuplic, was the first nonfamily president the company had ever had.

It was Lyman Conger who induced the company to sit down again with the union. Having run out of courts, it had no other choice. Suddenly Conger seemed to have changed his mind about many of the original strike issues.

A contract was signed on October 8, 1962. It gave the workers improved fringe benefits worth about 14 cents an hour and some concessions on seniority and arbitration. But there was no direct wage increase beyond the five raises the company had granted to workers on the job during the strike. The farthest the company went on a union shop was an agreement to deduct dues from workers who requested it in writing. The contract disappointed many of the rank-and-file union members. "It is workable and fair to the company and the employees," Lyman Conger said.

But though the contract was signed and was to be renegotiated smoothly in succeeding years, the company still resisted a final peace treaty. The Kohler Company kept appealing the reinstatement and back-pay provisions. It was cited for contempt by the NLRB in May 1963 for "piecemeal" compliance with the 1960 order. In September 1965 the United States Court of Appeals found Kohler guilty of contempt for failing to reinstate all of the 1,400 strikers that had been deemed entitled to resume their jobs and ordered the company to pay them $4.5 million in back wages and pension benefits. Fifty-seven of the seventy-seven strike leaders were to be taken back as well.

A few weeks later, the Supreme Court upheld the Court of Appeals ruling. Now Kohler had no choice but to agree, and at last an inglorious chapter in labor and human relations history was closed.

At the signing of the final settlement just before Christmas 1965, Emil Mazey, the secretary-treasurer of the UAW prophesied "a new day in labor relations with Kohler."

Lyman Conger's statement was somewhat more restrained. "Now we look forward to going on with more constructive things," he said. Even his former foes acknowledge that he carried out the mandate of the Supreme Court gracefully and assured the transition into the new era of good feeling with the union.

"We feel we shouldn't hold anything against him," Eggie Kohlhagen said recently. "Conger was between two fires. He was very faithful, a good man for the Kohler Company, especially for Mr.

Herbert Kohler, Sr." Kohlhagen has the perspective of longevity. He came to work in the accounting department at Kohler in 1925. Four years before the strike began, he received his gold watch for twenty-five years of service and his membership in the Quarter Century Club, another of Walter Kohler, Sr.'s legacies. At the end of 1965 the company presented gold watches to other employees who had not been on the job for eleven years; they had racked up their service requirements just before the strike. The resumption of the gifts was a signal that bygones were indeed bygones.

Lyman Conger became chairman and chief executive officer after Herbert, Sr., died in 1968, keeping the seat warm for Herbert, Jr.

Conger retired in the summer of 1972, was succeeded by Herbert, Jr., and died suddenly in the fall. His death was another landmark on the road to concord. With the disappearance of many of the chief contenders and the healing lapse of the months and years, bitterness was ebbing on both sides.

"We had to try to forget, in order to rebuild the union," Eggie Kohlhagen said. "We had to swallow a lot of things. The people who took our jobs during the strike are on the elective body of our union today. We have chief stewards who once were strike breakers. And they do a better job than some of us older ones, such a good job you forget they were strike breakers."

His friend Arthur Fox retired two years ago. He had been a bathtub enameler for thirty-seven years and a captain on the union side during the strike. "Sometimes you run across a certain person like at a retirement party and it reminds you. But why carry on? Life is too short. My granddaughter is going with the grandson of one of the real so-and-sos. What am I supposed to do?"

And in the upper reaches of Kohler Village, the Herbert Kohler, Jr.s, exchange dinner visits with their cousins, former Governor and Mrs. Walter Kohler, Jr.

Herbert V. Kohler, Jr., a Yale graduate like his father and cousin, Walter Kohler, Jr., came slowly to his role as dynastic and corporate leader, but he seized it with gusto and some of the wooden swagger of an apprentice in a summer stock company. He tends to pose for photographers with his pipe clenched between his teeth, bearded jaw jutting towards the horizon, and his chunky body straining against the impeccable herringbone tweed of his vested suit.

In his boyhood memories of the strike there loom the bodyguards hired by his father, as well as the beatings from his peers. "Children developed great animosities toward children whose parents were doing something different than theirs," he said tactfully.

But most of these parents are gone and the children are grown and determined to shape their own world. In the case of Herbert, Jr., it entails giving the Kohler Company "a whole new look," for which he has devoted a centennial year of public relations.

That effort was to win the Silver Anvil Award of the Public Relations Society of America as a program that advanced a favorable corporate image to ninety million Americans at a cost of $2 million.

By contrast, as the centennial mark caught up with Vollrath Company, its chairman, Walter Kohler, Jr., tried to ignore it. He finally succumbed to the entreaties of his salesmen and sanctioned the sending of commemorative plates that cost about $5.00 each to 1,800 of the company's best customers. The former governor also conceded that an open house in the factory and a picnic for employees and their families might be appropriate for a company that had been in business one hundred years.

"I've learned things and I'm sure the union has," Herbert Kohler, Jr., says. "We've learned to respect each other and the power each of us holds. We've learned not to get locked in certain philosophical positions from which we have no alternatives. I personally believe in most of the positions the company took during the strike and the union believes in most of its positions. But I doubt we'd ever have a clash again."

Though the company has no compulsory retirement rule, deaths and circumstances have enabled Herbert, Jr., to build a management team whose average age is in the mid-forties.

His ambitions for the company are large but not grandiose. His minimum goal is 10 per cent sales growth compounded annually. Sales were $159 million in 1972, up from $132 million the year before. Net income of $6.9 million, up from 1971's $4.4 million, was the highest in Kohler history.

The Kohler Company had slumped in the 1970 recession, and in 1969, it had been found guilty of price fixing in a federal antitrust suit against major plumbing manufacturers. But the future of plumbing today looks like pink champagne, one of the bold accent colors for bathroom fixtures introduced in 1964, that has invigorated sales.

"We want to give the American public the kind of bathroom

products to make their life in the bathroom as exciting and stimulating as possible," Herbert Kohler, Jr., declared.

In 1972 the engine and electric plant division of the Kohler Company, which accounts for 35 per cent of sales, turned profitable for the first time and provided 23 per cent of the company's earnings, vindicating a stubborn faith of half a century.

Like everything Kohler makes, these products had a rural beginning. In the 1880s a primitive machine called a "horsepower" was made in its foundry. It consisted of a series of iron gears turned by four to six horses hitched to a revolving shaft. The mechanical energy it developed was transmitted through a universal joint and drive shaft to a hay baler, pump, or milling machine.

In the 1920s this simple power machine was developed into an engine for the Kohler electric plant, or "automatic power and light," as it was christened. This Kohler generator did away with the need for storage batteries. Operated by the turn of a switch, it offered farmers their first fully automatic source of power.

Today, standby power systems like the Kohler units are considered indispensable for hospitals, commercial buildings, yachts, and motor homes; they operate Mexican coffee-bean shredders, Philippine and Thai fishing boats, and half of the lawn and garden tractors built in the United States.

Kohler got into the manufacture of precision controls during World War II as a government contractor, and although its contribution to the military machine ceased when the war ended, Herbert Kohler, Sr., insisted on continuing the division.

He considered it a source of distinction for the company and its employees, more so than plumbing, and maintained that the pride of craftsmanship in meeting the exacting tolerances of precision controls would be reflected in the parts of the factory that were satisfying more mundane needs of society.

Today Kohler produces a number of hydraulic, pneumatic, and control valves for aircraft landing gear, fuel and hydraulic systems, and various controls for the aircraft, aerospace, and jet-engine industries.

The whoop-de-do of the centennial, which had Herbert, Jr., and his troops flying all over the country in the company's Lear Jet, occasioned conjecture about the possibility of a public stock offering.

The chairman denied such plans were imminent. "We'll do it if it's necessary to attain certain growth objectives," he said. "I'm not particularly eager for it nor am I reluctant. I just don't need it to finance my ambitions or the family's right now."

As far as its stock ownership goes, the Kohler Company is still mostly a family affair, controlled largely by one member of the family, Herbert V. Kohler, Jr.

He and his thirty-two-year-old sister, Ruth, and his thirty-year-old brother, Frederic Cornell Kohler, a student, have 35.4 per cent of the 165,000 shares of common stock.

An additional 38.4 per cent of the shares are in the hands of thirty-four other Kohlers. Of these, only one, John M. Kohler, Jr., a great-grandson of the founder by his first wife, is still employed by the company.

The Kohler Foundation owns 14.7 per cent of the company's stock Herbert Kohler, Jr., is its president; his wife, Linda, is vice president. She steers the $200,000 annual income from its $6 million of assets into educational channels, such as scholarships to high school students, support of the John Michael Kohler Arts Center, and an arts center at the University of Wisconsin.

Employees of the Kohler Company own 6.7 per cent of the shares. Outside interests have the remaining 4.8 per cent. The trickle of stock into nonfamily hands came about when two grandsons of Walter J. Kohler, Sr., sold or forfeited their stock.

One grandson, Conrad Kohler, pledged his 2.5 per cent interest as collateral with the Commercial Discount Company, a subsidiary of the Canteen Corporation which was acquired by the International Telephone and Telegraph Corporation. Under an anti-trust settlement, ITT has taken steps to sell its Canteen holding to Trans World Airlines.

Conrad's brother, Carl J. Kohler, Jr., sold his stock to the Marshall Company, Incorporated, of Milwaukee which placed 3,850 shares on the market in July 1969. The price was then $215 a share. It has since advanced to $240 bid, making the interest of Kohler's chairman, his sister, and his brother currently worth $13 million.

Postscript: Spring 1975

A new contract between the company and the union was negotiated over the summer of 1974 and signed on October 1. It provided for an election in which the union gained the shop security it had so long sought.

The company insisted that employees hired before January 1, 1965 would become union members only if they so elected. Those who were already members had to remain in the union.

"It kept the senior Kohler's promise never to force anyone to join the union," Eggie Kohlhagen said. According to the final tally, some 275 of the 3,800 hourly employees elected not to join.

"The company was willing to co-operate and we did our share of compromising," he added.

THE WHEELER-DEALERS

FROM CASKETS TO CABLE:
WARNER COMMUNICATIONS

Summer 1972

Almost as naturally as snakes shedding their skins, the conglomerates of the sixties have been transforming themselves into the seventies companies "with direction."

One of the most dramatic corporate metamorphoses is that of Warner Communications, Inc. (WCI). In one decade it has gone from coffins and car rentals to the rainbow frontier of cable television. In that same period it has become the twenty-fourth fastest growing company on the *Fortune*-500 list where its 1971 revenues of $373,840,000 give it 294th place.

Despite his preference for sharing credit, the architect of this feat (by his colleagues' consensus) is Steven J. Ross, a forty-four-year-old, silver-haired, ex-football player, who married the daughter of a leading mortician and became an instinctive financial conglomerateur. Since the death on July 1 of William V. Frankel, the sixty-eight-year-old chairman and co-chief executive officer of Warner Communications, Ross has become undisputed captain of one of the nation's luckiest and nattiest management teams.

Unlike many other companies that have grown by acquisition, Warner Communications (which some investors still forgetfully call by its former name, Kinney Services) not only survived the stock market wring-out that closed the swinging sixties but also it has a shiny, new glamour attributable in part to the human properties it now possesses.

Dr. Peter C. Goldmark, inventor of workable color TV, the long-playing record, and the video cassette, belongs to Warner. So does a fraction of Gloria Steinem, in whose new feminist magazine *MS* Warner invested $1 million for a 25 per cent interest (its only minority position).

Mick Jagger and the Rolling Stones, the idolized rock performers, have been signed up by Ahmet Ertegun, the pop music sultan and president of Warner's Atlantic Records.

Three of this year's top ten box-office movie hits, by *Variety*'s reckoning, are *The Clockwork Orange, Dirty Harry,* and *What's Up, Doc?* made under astute budget controls instituted by Ted Ashley, the former superagent and talent packager who is chairman of Warner Brothers, Inc., the film subsidiary.

Then there is Alfred R. Stern, grandson of the late Julius Rosenwald, the Sears, Roebuck financier. A cable TV pioneer, Stern swam into the Warner net last December when his TeleVision Communications Corporation, with $6-million revenues, was bought for $32 million in a characteristic exchange of stock.

Cable TV (CATV) companies are considered hot in Wall Street these days as were electronics companies, data processing companies, and natural gas companies in days gone by.

The limited proof of profitability shown thus far by most cable companies is of little matter. Those who have the faith believe that cable TV is on the verge of a communications revolution that will make magic on the tube and money for developers and stockholders.

In July 1972 Warner bought another cable company, Cypress Communications, for $65 million in stock. Alan N. Cohen, executive vice president, conceded, "We're paying a very high price but not relative to what we think these companies will be worth five to ten years out."

But Dennis McAlpine, a CATV analyst for Tucker, Anthony & R. L. Day, asserted: "Excluding Ross's desire to be Number One in cable, there is no justification for the price paid for Cypress. But he's doing it on paper, so that makes it somewhat easier. He'll give away as much paper as he thinks is necessary, because the more cable he buys, the higher his multiple goes."

"Multiple" is Wall Street lingo for the relation of the price of a stock to its earnings. The hotter the stock becomes in the affections of investors, the higher its multiple soars, and investors speculate on the future potential of the company or its industry, not on its immediate earning power. The stock of American Television & Communications, a company with revenues of $13 million, for example, has been selling for 140 times earnings.

McAlpine is one of several analysts who evaluate a cable company's stock price either by the number of connected subscribers or by cash flow. The Cypress acquisition will give Warner 360,000 subscribers, which would have put it second only to Teleprompter if two other competitors, Cox Cable and American Television & Communications, had not just announced their intention to merge. Warner now falls back to third place.

But, according to McAlpine, "Ross has been extremely successful in conveying the impression to the financial community that CATV will be a meaningful portion of WCI even though it is less than 10 per cent of sales. To me, WCI is still a record company and a movie company."

For WCI in 1971, records and music publishing accounted for 44 per cent of revenues and 66 per cent of income, while movies were 33 per cent of sales and 14 per cent of income.

Ross said in August of 1972: "Our main thrust in acquisitions will be in cable, but if something allied came along, we'd look at it. We have gone through the name change. We put communication up there."

And he has shown that Wall Street loves a conglomerate by any other name. "Before, it was truly a conglomerate. It's still a conglomerate, but now a directed one," said Harold Vogel, a leisuretime analyst for the brokerage house of Paine, Webber, Jackson & Curtis. He has been recommending the stock as a long-term investment in cable for institutions and as a movie and record company for short-term investors. "People either like it or hate it," Vogel observed. "There's a little reluctance on the part of those who have been burned before, particularly on movie stocks. But some have more faith in cable." Vogel said he was "sold across the board on CATV. There's no question it will qualify as one of the five fastest growing industries in the next five or ten years."

Vogel is not one of those who are distressed by such conglomerate characteristics of Warner as its complicated capital structure, the seventeen dense footnotes to its annual balance sheet, and the four and a half pages describing lawsuits (mostly involving the record division) in its last prospectus.

"The footnotes put some people off and the capitalization is very complex. They wonder what's going on," Vogel conceded. "Some people fault the management for being wheeler-dealer, but they came through '70 and '71 in fine shape, earnings-wise, and haven't impaired the company. Now you can see a direction. They're not like Gulf & Western, in zinc and auto parts and movies. Sure, the management is very slick, but it's done the right things at the right time."

Fade in, as they say in the film biz, on Steven Ross, a six-foot New Yorker who has a metal plate in his left arm to prove his honorable discharge from a short-lived career as an end for the Cleveland Browns. "It was a lucky break," he now says. "I had to go out and work for a living."

Ross has the tall, broad-shouldered, broken-nosed charm, which can be as good a passport to success in business as a wealthy father or old-boy network ties. His father was a builder who had lost everything in the stock market crash of 1929 and went to work for a plumbing supply concern. Son Steve played football at the Naval Training Station where he was assigned after enlisting from high school and later at Paul Smiths College on Saranac Lake, New York, where he caught the attention of the pro football scouts. Ross will carry the football creed with him wherever he goes, even into the temples of the money-changers. "When you're hit, you get up. In another minute or so, there is another play. You'll have the opportunity to rectify your mistake in a minute and hit back," he was to say twenty or so years later when he was playing with paper instead of a football on the fields of conglomerate finance.

Ross would also be grateful then, or so he would stress, for the ability, acquired from football, to "work with a team."

Now the year is 1954 and, having tried selling men's slacks and children's clothes, he is marrying Carol Rosenthal, whose father, Edward, and uncle, Morton Rosenthal, own the Riverside Chapel in New York City, hub of an eclectic chain of funeral parlors.

The Riverside on Manhattan's West Side, said to be the nation's most successful funeral chapel, handles the remains of New York's bourgeois Jewry. Universal, midtown on the East Side, offers a nonsectarian ambiance while Frank E. Campbell, in the East Eighties caters to the chic, the celebrated, and, more often than not, Christian.

On his honeymoon in the Virgin Islands, Steven Ross investigates a deal to buy a laundry there, but he is put off by lack of an abundant water supply. He has already lost out on a deal to buy a children's camp in Maine.

So he lets his father-in-law coax him into the funeral business. "I don't know anything about it and it's not exactly the business I would have chosen for myself," he demurs.

But the Rosenthals are having problems in the limousine and monument sides of their business. "We could use young blood," they tell Ross.

They put him into a three month funeral director's training program which requires him to work twelve hours a day, six days a week.

That regimen violates a piece of wisdom Ross's father had given him. "There are three categories of people. One individual sits with his feet on the desk and dreams all day long. When the day is over, he has done nothing. The second person gets up at the crack of dawn, works eighteen hours a day with never a moment to put his feet up and dream. The third sits in his office with his feet on the desk and dreams a little. Then he takes them down and does something. Go into that category," the elder Ross advised his son, "because there's no competition there."

The Rosenthals have an anti-nepotism rule which says that no relative can start out making more than $75 a week. Ross had been earning up to $20,000 a year selling kiddie sportswear.

Ross never reaches the embalming room, a requisite training area for a licensed funeral director, which he has no intention of becoming. He concentrates on administration and the opportunities for making deals to acquire other funeral businesses. He inquires why the company's hundred limousines sit idly in the garage from 4:30 P.M. to 8:30 A.M. doing nothing. How about making a deal with a limousine company that needs cars in the evening?

Nothing comes of that idea. But someone asks Ross why, since each limousine costs $10,000, they don't lease them instead of tying up all that money owning them?

Someone else suggests that since the business is such a large user of limousines, it can buy them for less than it would cost to lease them. Ross becomes intrigued with the idea of car rental.

Fade out and in again on a $250,000 bank loan that he has secured for Abbey Rent-a-Car and Abbey Limousine, which he and five partners, the Rosenthals and their relatives, have started with $10,000 capital.

In April 1959 they rent a store attached to a garage at Sixty-fourth Street and Third Avenue for $100 a month. Abbey has a fleet of a hundred cars. "It's a real gamble," Ross admits.

In a year, Abbey Rent-a-Car is going nowhere and Ross hits on the idea of offering an extra service: free parking for rental customers. "The funeral business is a great training ground because it teaches you service," he said. He had also developed a tenet: "It takes as much time to talk a small deal as a big deal."

So Ross stepped into a telephone booth on Third Avenue one spring day in 1960 and called the headquarters of Kinney, then the largest local parking-lot operator according to the listings in the yellow pages of the telephone directory, which Ross scanned before deciding whom to call. He asked to speak to the president because he had an interesting idea for a merger.

What he proposed to Caesar Kimmel was that Kinney give free parking to Abbey car renters and the use of its name in exchange for 25 per cent of Abbey "at true value, which is next to nothing, but it may be something, and if not, you won't be parking many cars."

The deal was signed two weeks later. "Changing our name gave us stability," Ross realizes, now that he has done it again.

The arrangement was too successful. The jump in the number of rentals and cars to be parked was costing the Kimmel side dearly. So Ross proposed a merger with an exchange of stock between the two companies. (Kimmel is now an executive vice president of Warner Communications.) Ross then expanded the merger to a four-way deal, bringing in his father-in-law's funeral business and an office cleaning business owned by a brother-in-law of Ross, Albert Sarnoff, and his brother, William. The Sarnoffs, nephews of General David Sarnoff, the creator of RCA Corporation, were also private label razor-blade manufacturers.

The various businesses provided the cash flow for the Rent-a-Car business, he recalls, while the parking business was a means of "sitting on real estate."

That was in December 1961. The Kinney Service Corporation was born. "They chose me president because I wasn't running anything. I was running in between," Ross said. "I did have the idea of going public, not to be a conglomerate but because if Rent-a-Car was to grow, it would need enormous amounts of money."

"One leading banker said, 'It won't go,'" Ross was later to repeat with satisfaction. Someone introduced him to Salim L. Lewis, an investment banker with Bear, Stearns & Company. Lewis thought it would go. Kinney Service, with revenues of $17 million, went public in April 1962, with an initial offering of 1.45 million shares at $9.00 a share.

The company, which had net earnings of $700,000, suddenly had a market value of $13 million. Though it made its debut at an unauspicious time—the Black Monday or bear market drop of 1962 had occurred the week before—Kinney stock was unscathed.

Kinney kept growing in sales and stock price for the next five years through the persistent acquisition of funeral, car rental, and cleaning companies, most often by exchanges of stock.

In 1966 a $25-million stock deal produced a merger with National Cleaning Contractors, Inc., whose head, William V. Frankel, took the chairmanship of Kinney with responsibility for real estate services, while Ross, as president, honed his specialty, acquisitions. (Last year, his presidential salary was $240,000.)

As a sop to the ego of Frankel, who was sixty-two, the title of chief executive officer was shared by him and Ross. "It was a little strange," Ross acknowledged. "Say, strange is a good name for our company."

Frankel was another father figure for Ross who claims he has had three—his own father, his father-in-law, and Frankel. "We've had disagreements but never arguments. Bill and I never made an operating decision. Our responsibility was making sure we had the right presidents for the operating companies and that we made the right long-range planning and the right financial decisions.

"But I sort of felt we lacked total direction," said Ross, who never seemed to have mustered much enthusiasm for the essential services in which his corporation was engaged.

He appointed a long-range planning committee to make a study of American business. It pinpointed five growth industries: real estate services, leisure and entertainment, business machines, money management, and airlines.

Ross noted that airlines reminded him of the Rent-a-Car business in possible revenue explosion and also in profit squeeze. So in 1968 a $30-million stock swap with National Periodicals Publications, Inc., a distributing company, enabled Kinney "to play the airline game without investing," because the growth of airline travel would increase newsstand magazine and paperback book sales. Or so he reasoned.

It provided a foothold in distribution and publishing, which is currently not Warner's strongest suit. Comics are drooping and efforts to build a paperback publishing company have been costly. (A deal to acquire Simon & Schuster with its Pocket Books division, a paperback pioneer, fell through.)

However, *Mad* magazine which Warner owns and the distribution business (*Playboy* being one account) are thriving.

Just before the NPP deal, Kinney drove significantly into the entertainment field with a $12-million purchase of the Ashley Famous Agency (whose client list included Tennessee Williams and Arthur Miller) through the issuance of a Series B convertible preferred stock.

Ross met Ted Ashley at breakfast one Saturday morning, and by the end of the afternoon, they had shaken hands on a deal. "After meeting Ted, I realized what a tremendous plus he would be. Management. If we wanted to go into the leisure business, the first thing we wanted was management. I didn't want to operate any business we acquired," Ross said.

Ashley was a forty-five-year-old self-made promoter of other people's artistic talents, a poor runt from the Brownsville section of Brooklyn who started in the mailroom of the William Morris Agency at the age of fifteen and before he was old enough to vote had himself become an agent and powerful manager for actors and writers. Later he put together television productions for his clients, on which he collected the usual 10 per cent agent's fee.

"I had built a talent agency business from one man," said Ashley, a bearded bantam who looks like a professor of philosophy in Gucci loafers and custom-made blazer. "The business was profitable but it was like a good restaurant. It had a ceiling. After you filled every table and raised your prices, how much further can you go? With an agent, 10 per cent is 10 per cent.

"I made the deal with Steve on the same day for two reasons. It was so homogenized from a business point of view. A company that aspired to do things in leisure and had the resources. Second, one of my principal skills had been in relating to people.

"Now I wanted to move aggressively. This deal had the ring not of blue sky but a forward look plus a business look which I liked because I would end up with stock. Within six to nine months, the Kinney people deepened their commitment to leisure."

In 1968 Kinney Rent-a-Car "was shucked off because it was creating havoc on the balance sheet with that horrendous-looking debt. If we ever wanted to do a large acquisition, who would finance us? I thought we should move out of Rent-a-Car," Ross said.

The Sandgate Corporation bought the rent-a-car business for $11 million in long-term notes. Meanwhile, Kinney had acquired subcontracting companies in the painting, flooring, and acoustics fields. "To fulfill our real estate services," Ross said. "I said to Bill Frankel's son, Andrew—everyone calls him Pete—'You keep an eye on this.'

"But Ashley was the key acquisition. After six months, we had an embarrassment of riches in executive talent. And how far can a talent agency business go? Maybe there's something in the entertainment business we should buy. Since we have the management, maybe we need a vehicle to put management to work in. So we went back to the long-range planning committee."

In due course, the committee culled information on forty companies. Twelve of Kinney's top management then repaired to Florida for a three-day powwow.

At the head of the list of companies was Warner Brothers-Seven Arts Limited. It consisted of two unequal parts, an enfeebled movie company that might or might not be susceptible to being turned around and what Ted Ashley called "a pot of gold called records." Its two recording companies, Warner/Reprise and Atlantic Recording were superbly managed and had an enviable hold on the lucrative pop music industry.

The planners decided that they could sell off the movie company's real estate and film library if need be, and even if they didn't make out in the movie business, they would still have an excellent leisure acquisition through the record companies. The price of the deal was predicated on what they thought the record business was worth. "We wouldn't have gone into the movie business without the record business," Ross said.

So in the spring of 1969, with the Ashley management talent at his elbow, Ross negotiated his biggest coup, a $400-million tender offer for Warner Brothers-Seven Arts.

He engineered the deal with a new Series C convertible preferred stock, callable in ten years. Ross figured out what to trade with, after badgering his accountants for a security that would give him a tax-free deal. "I just kept asking the pros, 'Why can't you?' Accounting and putting deals together and spin-offs seem much more scary than they really are," he said. "I just use good common logic."

Not that it was all smooth sailing. "The market didn't understand what we were trying to do," said Ross, using the conglomerateur's standard explanation for a slide in the price of its stock upon reports of an attempted acquisition. Warner stock "headed south, it fell out of bed."

Then Commonwealth United Corporation made a rival tender offer for Warner.

But in July 1969 the board of Warner Brothers elected in favor of the Kinney offer and the deal was consummated. As part of the agreement, Kinney sold the Ashley Famous Agency to Marvin Josephson Associates to avoid a conflict of interest with its new entertainment holdings. Ted Ashley stayed with Kinney.

Ross dispatched him to Burbank, California, where the Warner studio was located, with the mandate of chairman and chief executive officer of Warner Brothers, Inc. Ashley had never run a movie company before but he didn't hesitate to move in forthrightly.

Within six weeks he replaced seventeen of twenty-one top executives. "We selected with an unusual eye on being competent, being super high on a level of tune-in, taste, and adaptability," said Ashley, who sometimes lapses into murky speech patterns he would never accept in a movie or TV script. "This is not the old Hollywood where all the writers and actors were under contract to Louis B. Mayer. We're in the business of developing material that would be interesting to creative people. The rest is persuading them, in establishing intimate strong relations with talent so that their impulse is to go over to Warner Brothers. Our executives don't compete egowise with the talent.

"But we're very budget-conscious. Before you get past that crosswalk, we say, 'Now what will it cost you?' "

Desperate deals with independent producers who collected exorbitant fees for pictures that wildly overran budget projections had made Hollywood a financial disaster area in recent years.

"Every line in a script is translated into a dollar sign," Ashley said. "One line can cost you $3,000 or $300,000. If the producer comes back with a number that has little relation to the market for the film, we won't make it. If the budget makes sense, we negotiate with the principal components, the actors, writers, and producers."

Ashley brought in John Calley, who had started as an NBC messenger boy and worked up to being an independent producer, to be chief of film production. Frank Wells, a lawyer and former Rhodes scholar, was named president of Warner Brothers, Inc.

"The trick in running the company," Ashley said, "is to go like an orchestra and for everybody, when they go home, to feel like a soloist. But at the opening of every meeting we hear from the numbers guy." The movie business scored a remarkable recovery with the Ashley team, after an initial write down at the end of 1969 of $59 million in the asset value of films in the Warner inventory. Massive write-offs were just what Wall Street had come to expect from movie companies, and so in the last few months of that year, the price of Kinney stock sank from 39 to 23.

But with careful cost pruning, a number of winners, starting with films such as *Woodstock* and *Summer of '42,* were unleashed. At an average production cost of $2.5 million per film, Warner's has put behind it the boom-and-bust cycles that hurt many movie companies in recent years.

Woodstock was a lucky bolt out of the blue that struck two weeks—at first obscurely—after Warner Brothers was locked into the Kinney stable.

Ted Ashley had told Ross, "A funny thing is happening in a small town in upstate New York. Our record people, especially Ahmet Ertegun, say their vibrations from young people are coming from a place called Woodstock."

Propelled by "the funny feeling," the Warner executives went to Woodstock expecting some 100,000 young fans to turn out for a routine rock music festival on August 15, 1969. Instead 200,000 braved rain, mud, and bad drug trips to join in the spontaneous pop cultural combustion of the era.

The movie and record rights were secured for $100,000, a nominal enough risk. The film earned $13 million and, as Ross said, "helped us live in the movie business for a while."

The script for a little nothing of a film, *Summer of '42,* was handed to Calley one morning at 10 A.M. He bought it at 12:05

P.M. and that $1.3 million investment yielded $20 million in domestic film rentals.

"Our movie company is very profitable," Ashley said, "because we haven't had to take a lot of money from hits and put them in a vacuum caused by gaping losses. With careful control, this is a damn good business. It's part a commercial business and part an art form. If the art form is accompanied by good taste and the business by real discipline, there is no reason to go broke.

"From the first day, we decided we weren't going into the business of the $25-million movie. The Wall Street theory about movie companies goes back to *Cleopatra* and those epic pictures. If they don't work, they bury the corporation," Ashley said.

Ashley and Ross had been steered to Woodstock by Ahmet M. Ertegun, the forty-six-year-old founder and president of Atlantic Recording, a musical phenomenon in his own right.

The son of a Turkish minister to the United States, Ertegun and his brother, Nesuhi were jazz aficionados who, in 1948, started pressing their own records and challenging the established labels (RCA, Columbia, and Decca). The long-term contracts they negotiated with the soul and country-music artists and English rock groups of the sixties paid off as the record industry grew from $600 million in annual sales to close to $2 billion in that decade.

The Erteguns and their associate, Jerry Wexler, sold Atlantic for about $17 million in 1967 to Warner Brothers–Seven Arts. Within three years their company was raking in almost that much in earnings, as they capitalized on their ties with established performers and discovered new ones. Aretha Franklin, Dizzie Gillespie, and the Rolling Stones recorded under the Atlantic label.

Atlantic continued to operate out of its "very funky office" over a drugstore on Broadway at Sixtieth Street even after its Warner parent was sold to Kinney "against my better judgment," Ertegun said. "I'm not used to working for anyone, or to associating with people I don't know," said Ertegun, speaking in the hybrid inflection of the international swinger.

With his compact form encased in conservative, expensive tailoring, the goateed Ertegun carries the aura of a Middle Eastern financier. Through the efforts of his wife, Mica, a Romanian-born brunette who used to announce she had lived on a chicken farm in Canada, the Erteguns' parties are regularly reported in *Women's Wear Daily* and other fashion journals.

Ertegun said he had been pleasantly surprised to find his worst fears evaporating as Ross and Company left him pretty much alone: "They never call me. I call them. I don't think they've ever questioned anything I've ever done. I never thought we'd find this sort of harmony.

"In the music business, it's very hard to find professional executive talent. There's no training ground like the one we had in the forties when people started their own independent companies, to teach how one presses a record, how you can tell by listening to a singer on a street corner whether he's someone the world is waiting for. We're blessed with that.

"We're very good in our business. Artists are drawn to the companies which have done well with people they have known. We're able to take a group like the Rolling Stones—they were with a good company, a good label. But many people thought they'd reached the apex. We started with them anew. We were able to beat all the previous sales figures and get more involved with them in a personal way [their first album for Atlantic, *Sticky Fingers,* rang up $1-million sales almost overnight]. We really are musical people. Money is one thing, love is another. Love with understanding. It's a regenerative process."

Ertegun was explaining why the Warner record companies hold such an enviable place in the pop music industry. During the last five years annual sales of recorded disks and tapes in the United States have doubled. The industry's barometer of success is the gold record, awarded by the Record Industry Association of America whenever a 45-rpm "single" record sells more than one million units and whenever a 33⅓ long-playing record achieves more than $1 million at the manufacturer's price. Warner's record companies have culled about one fourth of the gold record awards.

The other golden goose acquired with Warner Brothers-Seven Arts was the Warner/Reprise operation. It is run by its founder, Mo Ostin, who had sold it to Warner Brothers-Seven Arts in 1963, and by Joseph Smith, an ex-disk jockey and publicist. Ostin had kept Frank Sinatra's flame burning lucratively under the Reprise label (as part of the deal, Kinney bought out Sinatra's interest in Warner Brothers-Seven Arts for $22.5 million in cash and convertible debentures). But Ostin had also stayed in step with youth by signing soft rock groups and artists like The Grateful Dead, Peter, Paul & Mary, James Taylor, and Jethro Tull.

A year after the Warner acquisition, another folk, rock and classical record company, Electra Corporation was bought by Kinney for $3 million in cash and notes and $7 million in convertible debentures. In 1972 still another wonder boy, thirty-year-old David Geffen (also an alumnus of the William Morris Agency mailroom), who had become an agent for rock singers, took his Asylum record company into the Warner fold for 100,000 shares of stock.

While Ross was leaving the operation of the entertainment companies to their capable managers ("We run an autonomous operation," he said), he goaded the long-range planners to keep their eyes peeled for new frontiers. The Ashley crowd was concerned about the dwindling theater audience for movies. Fifty per cent of the American public was going to the movies only once or less a year. The movies they saw were on their television screens.

"The mountain must go to Mohammed," the Ashley team said, sighting in their crystal ball the risky route of cable television.

"Cable will ultimately be a bonanza for motion pictures, in that every home will become a theater," Ted Ashley said.

In 1971 about 2,500 cable systems were serving about 14 million people in 4.5 million homes, a count that had to be measured against the 70 million TV sets owned in the United States.

A report by a leading think-tank firm had projected a market of 30 million homes for cable television by 1980. The estimate implied an available audience of 90 to 100 million for movies. The film industry hadn't seen anything like that for more than thirty years. "The cable business will pick up a large part of the audience we lost. It caters to the essential lethargy that made TV work. Movie-going may be limited to the young people who are the current audiences," Ashley said.

Again, Ross was intrigued. "But how will cable be built?" he asked. "There are no major companies in the field and it needs enormous sums of money."

A cable television system delivers high-clarity TV signals and increased channel capacity into the home through a coaxial cable. The industry began in 1949 with the laying of the first system in Astoria, Oregon. Since then it has had a roller-coaster history, fueled by vistas of futuristic technological marvels and gold rush returns to investors. But a series of roadblocks have kept it mostly in smaller markets where subscribers long for better reception and programming than they can receive on their ordinary sets.

The roadblocks had been thrown up by the federal government, instigated initially by opposition from established television stations and movie theater owners who feared the threat to their audiences from pay television. Since 1966 the federal government had prohibited importation of distant signals into the top hundred markets (the big cities) by the cable systems. But by mid-1971 it looked as though the Federal Communications Commission would lift the ban, which in effect it did in March of 1972. This predictably discharged a new wave of speculative fever on Wall Street for cable television.

But the horrendous costs of building cable systems remained. These were running at $5,000 a mile for overhead wires, $10,000 a mile for underground systems. A typical rural system of 25,000 subscribers might cost $10 million to build and return annual earnings of $125,000. In New York City the cost of laying the cable alone was about $115,000 a mile.

Even the most optimistic cable promoter conceded it would take five years to generate cash flow and ten years to get a payoff on investment. What then was the incentive for financial backing of a cable company? The analogy of a toll road on a tunnel, for one. Though capital cost was high, operating cost was modest once the system was in place. And of course, the backer could gamble on vast appreciation in value for systems built now with the potential of stunning profits from future sale or operation.

"Maybe we should be in cable," Ross concluded.

The decision would mean tremendous infusions of capital—Alfred Stern has said $250 million to $500 million would be needed in the next five years—and radical corporate change.

"Cable will tie up a lot of money. How will we posture ourselves? Maybe we should make our company very simple," Ross mused. "The funeral business doesn't belong any more. It's muddying the water. The last acquisition was in 1964. Funeral has no charisma. It just doesn't fit," he declared.

In September 1971 the funeral business was sold to Service Corporation International for $30 million in cash and notes. Real estate services, as Ross was calling the rest of Kinney, was spun off for $43.5 million with a listing on the American Stock Exchange as the National Kinney Corporation; William Frankel's son, Andrew, was given the presidency. A 50 per cent interest in the common stock and 3 million more shares of the convertible preferred of the

new company were retained by the old Kinney, which, after soundings of Wall Street sentiments, changed its name to Warner Communications, Inc.

"They're very Wall Street-conscious," said Harold Vogel, the
Paine, Webber analyst, uttering one of the greatest understatements
of all time. In the bosom of the Kinney/Warner family, the wooing
of Wall Street was a concern second only to breathing.

Vogel had been one of the analysts invited to give their opinions
of what the name should be. "From a Wall Street standpoint, we
said, we recognize Kinney. Warner didn't go over too well," Vogel
recalled. The recent downbeat fortunes of the old Warner Brothers
movie company was fresh in analysts' minds. "But if you go to the
ordinary man on the street and tell him you like a company named
Kinney in the entertainment field, he says, 'Who?' If I say, 'Warner,'
he knows," Vogel ended up saying.

Late in 1971, 600,000 shares of Warner common stock, then
valued at $17.9 million, were exchanged for another cable TV busi-
ness, that of the Continental Telephone Corporation.

Lazard Frères arranged the major deal for TeleVision Communications with Alfred Stern, whom Ross saw as a manager for the
CATV empire. Stern had realized that his small, independent company would have trouble raising big chunks of capital.

The fifty-year-old Stern fitted into the Warner Communications
management picture like a thoroughbred in a Central Park riding
stable. Scion of a family whose fortune permitted patronage of
the arts and such philanthropies as black education, health, and
some left-wing causes, he is lean and understated in dress and dry
humor. Stern has a driving need to be a statesmanlike entrepreneur.

After ten years as a vice president at the National Broadcasting
Company, he had organized a cable television company in 1962.
About $1 million had come from the Rosenwald family invest-
ment company, Starwood Corporation, and from Stern's friends.
John Bristol, an investment manager for educational institutions,
had put in $3 million in exchange for debentures, while the Chase
Manhattan Bank had granted a $6-million loan, the largest it had
ever made to cable television.

The cable TV company operated at a loss until mid-1968 when it
managed to show earnings of $206,000 on revenues of $3.7 million,
just in time to make a public offering of its stock. Going public was

necessary if TeleVision Communications Corporation was to make the acquisitions of other systems essential for it to become the major force in cable that Stern wanted it to be.

When Ross came along, TVC had 180,000 subscribers and was running in fourth or fifth place in a race led by Teleprompter Corporation, the Number One cable company that had been put together by a promoter named Irving Kahn [who was to go to prison in 1973 for attempting to bribe officials in Johnstown, Pennsylvania, to obtain exclusive CATV franchises].

TVC had had a misadventure when building a cable system in Akron, Ohio. It was the first major market to have two-way capability. But it carried an $18-million price tag with a question mark of whether it could be recouped: a strike of installers and an increase in monthly rates in the midst of a selling campaign caused a drop in subscribers to nearly half of what had been counted on.

Stern needed lots more money for TVC and had been shopping around, unsuccessfully, among the Wall Street investment bankers for help. He had wanted to "go it alone" but, even given the exaggerated multiple of cable stocks, in order for the price of his stock to reach the point where he could buy and build cable systems on the scale he wanted, the company would have had to be producing earnings of at least $5 million a year. TVC's gross sales were only $6 million.

When Ross let it be known he was looking for a way into cable TV, Robert Ellsworth of Lazard Frères introduced him to Stern.

As he recollects Ross's persuasive wooing technique in arriving at a sale price for his company, Stern says: "He told me, 'How Wall Street looks at the deal is very important for you, as the company to be acquired, as it is for us. If it looks like we [Warner] made a great deal, then it will be reflected in the increase of the stock price and it will turn out well for you and all of your stockholders.'

"I realized it was part of salesmanship. He's used it before," Stern said. "But the stock was selling at 30 then and look where it is now." At 48⅝ in mid-August of 1972. On paper, Alfred Stern and his wife and children with 250,000 shares are more than $4.5-million richer.

The enthusiasm of Ross and his associates for cable TV has instilled some "worry" in Stern, who keeps stressing the numerous question marks strewn across the road to profitability. How will cable television be operated in big cities? What services will subscribers demand and be willing to pay for? "We won't turn around and be profitable just on television signals in major markets," Stern said. Then there is what he sees as "the riskiest part"—programming. "Everybody talks a good game about programming but who is going to undertake the cost?"

Dennis McAlpine, the analyst, commented, "Prior to being acquired, Al Stern was vociferous about the future of cable TV. He's becoming more conservative now. If I had to live up to all the things Ross is saying, I'd be scared, too."

Stern had told someone who asked if he were frightened, "I'm pleased to let Steve and his people let us grow by leaps and bounds. My worry is if they get enthusiastic and then someday tell me to run it all. I tell them, 'You don't overstep my ability to run what you've acquired.'

"But we're calling the shots. If we say we can't absorb this fast, they're not telling us to. I'm a member of the board of Warner Communications and a member of the executive committee. They really don't run anything, though they know what's going on. They have left us alone."

Ross ebulliently scratches figures on a yellow pad. "Let's attack the risk. Let's even say we're 1,000 per cent wrong about cable. Say we need $300 million to build a systems network. We have $50 million in cash," he said, projecting 1972 after-tax earnings of $50 million on revenues of $510 million.

"We don't have to re-employ it," Ross continued. "Though we're in records and magazines, we don't manufacture or print them. [The Warner record companies subcontracted the pressing of their records.] We have $90 million in cash and marketable securities we don't want to touch for cable. It will sit there, so we'll be in a position to make some deals if the economy turns down.

"We have those National Kinney shares, with a market value of $130 million. We have no intention of touching that. But, if five years down the road, cable needs it . . . we have this preferred C stock. In 1979 someone has to give me $175 million for that," he said, assuming the price of Warner common will not drop. "So $175 million plus $130 million, that's $300 million. Suppose cable is a total disaster. I haven't affected my balance sheet. I haven't used cash or present earnings. We take big gambles, but if we're wrong we won't be wiped out," he concluded confidently.

"In this company, we make mistakes, but they're small mistakes because they're covered by other things," he added. "Would we have gone into the movie business without the record business? No. The movie business is easy to close down if you have to. You sell off real estate. You let people go. And we didn't rush into making expensive pictures.

"With Rent-a-Car, we had the advantage over Hertz because we made our mistakes on a nickel and dime basis. We don't risk too much."

Warner has started negotiating for the raising of $125 million in debt for cable. A fundamentalist might ask who pays for the loan on a disaster.

Meanwhile, Warner is optimistically bent toward cable TV and that vast market for motion pictures Ted Ashley sees it yielding. Next fall Stern's new Gridtronics plan (which would deliver special material to a subscriber for an extra fee) is scheduled to start offering first-run movies on a trial basis.

Stern has maintained that the profit turn-around for cable TV can come only through extra services and fees in major markets. Pay TV entertainment is one such source. With the eloquence and research support of Dr. Goldmark, Stern is emphasizing to the local communities where he is seeking franchises his company's potential for alleviating urban problems through health care and educational and municipal services.

Peter Goldmark emanates the aura revered in Wall Street of the scientist who knows how to make a buck. He was president of CBS Laboratories for thirty-five years. At sixty-five, he has the energy of a hyperactive Boy Scout.

He weaves a spell of the future few would care to reject. "Cable can perform services which could improve the quality of life for the people of the community," he says. "Telecommunications can make possible early diagnosis and preventive techniques in health care. It can go after the youngest people in school. Examine them. Feed the data into a data bank in the health center.

"There are not enough physicians. You can start massive training for assistants—in nursing homes, schools, prisons. Cable TV can be the link from the institutions to the center of health, the hospital. There can be diagnostic consultations by two-way cable. The data can be collected and the symptom dealt with by the doctor on duty coming on television and looking at the patient. The assistant feels the patient. The doctor watches on the screen while talking to the patient. Then he can say whether to bring him to the hospital or not. Meanwhile, the vital data is collected in the bank.

"This is our contribution to the town's well being."

(In other words, just give Warner the cable franchise for your community.)

"In the schools, programs can be generated to one or more schools," Goldmark goes on. "It makes possible sharing teachers. And parents can switch it on at home and see what's going on. This idea will dispel the notion that cable is just entertainment. It's a superior, vital communication artery."

Dr. Goldmark was set up in business by Warner last January with a $1.5-million research guarantee and a 20 per cent stock incentive.

He had been dreaming of going into retirement from CBS to his own company, but in association with a "large, solid, well managed company that would grow." He didn't want to have to worry about financing.

In the fall of 1971 he had run into Spencer Harrison, an executive vice president of Warner Brothers Inc. whom he had known when Harrison was at CBS. Goldmark confided his dream to Harrison.

"Ever heard of Kinney?" Harrison asked. It was just before the name change. "Yes, parking," Goldmark replied.

Harrison told him that Kinney (about to be Warner and into cable TV) wanted a technical development arm to offer guidance for its new activities. Goldmark got the impression that Harrison was ready to lead him to a dotted line, but he held out and a few days later flew to Los Angeles to make a presentation to Harrison who had rounded up Ashley, Ross, and Alan Cohen, a tax lawyer who acts as Ross's right hand.

They met at Harrison's home. "I talked from 9:30 A.M. to 4 P.M.," Goldmark recounted. "Then Steve Ross took over. Rarely have I met a person with such quick understanding who hadn't been in communications all his life. It was fantastic chemistry. At 4 P.M. I could transfer my dreams to them.

"They had the same dreams as I but much vaguer. The vague architecture suddenly became solid. Instead of being owned by people who couldn't care less about you, our company will be your company, they told me. Here was every important facet I was looking for."

The deal was signed in New York a few weeks later, and in

January 1972 Goldmark Communications Corporation set up its laboratories in Stamford, Connecticut.

It immediately undertook studies in electronic publishing, the use of an entertainment satellite system, and those two-way cable television applications for community services. It obtained a grant from the federal government to develop an electronic audiocommunications system to bring urban amenities to rural communities.

Who can tell what Warner Communications will get into next? It already has a bank (a 61 per cent interest in the Garden State National Bank of New Jersey), which it acquired back in 1969 when the long-range planning committee was pointing to money management as one of the promising fields.

One of Warner's directors, Charles A. Agemian, formerly an outspoken vice president of the Chase Manhattan Bank, pointed out the growth possibilities in northern New Jersey. He retired from the Chase to become chairman of Garden State. Because of a change in federal banking law in 1970, Warner will have to divest itself of control of the bank by 1980.

Warner has its Disneyland—the Warner Brothers Jungle Habitat, a wildlife amusement park in West Milford, New Jersey. The $5-million preserve which just opened is expected to make money on its own, as well as bring "carry-over value to children's movies on TV."

Ross has indicated he'd like to soft-pedal his football past, though he and friends once tried and failed to buy the New York Jets in a personal deal. "If Warner ever did acquire a ball club, I can see what would happen to the stock," he said, smiling and simulating dread. "They'd all say, 'Ross has to have his football team.'"

It could, he acknowledged thinking once, "relate to cable TV."

The Winter of Discontent: 1974–75

There's good news and bad news at Warner Communications, Inc., to use last year's outworn cliché. But more bad than good, so let's have the good news first.

Ross and Company had guessed wrong. The great big gusher in the Warner Brothers-Seven Arts acquisition had turned out to be the movies, not the records. At the end of 1974 they contributed 44 per cent of Warner Communications' gross revenues of $720.1 million and 61 per cent of its operating income before taxes. Profits from movies and to a lesser extent records absorbed losses of $21.3 million in cable and foreign publishing.

The Ashley team at Warner Brothers in Hollywood had produced one winner after another. *Deliverance* and *What's Up, Doc?* released in 1972, had been made according to the well-enunciated, modest budget theory. They had grossed $20 million each in the North American market. *Billy Jack,* a home-made-looking film about a half-breed, originally released in 1971 and then reissued and merchandised with saturation booking and heavy TV advertising, touched the anti-Establishment chord in American audiences numbed by Watergate. It made box-office music, grossing $13 million as a 1974 reissue. *Day for Night* by the French director François Truffaut satisfied the art-film goers. *Blazing Saddles,* a comedy Western that cost $2.6 million to produce and was thought to appeal only to sophisticated urbanites, earned $16.5 million in rentals in 1974.

Americans, it seemed, were going out to the movies again. Movie theater attendance was up to one billion customers in 1974, the best admissions record in a decade, though still nowhere near the four billion of 1946.

The Exorcist, a monster shocker of a movie, released by Warner almost as a corporate Christmas gift for '73 raced to become one of the biggest moneymakers in Hollywood history. Originally budgeted at $5 million, it overran into double digit millions. Grossing $66.3 million in rentals in 1974 *The Exorcist* streaked respectably behind *The Godfather,* a predecessor blockbuster that once had kept Paramount's conglomerate Gulf & Western looking robust. *The Godfather* grossed $85.7 million in U.S. and Canadian rentals, still the all-time winner.

The Ashley team no longer had to apologize, though, as they had in the summer of 1972: "We don't have a *Godfather* but . . ."

In the summer of 1974, however, Ted Ashley announced he was withdrawing into part-time activity. The usual semantic obfuscation accompanied the announcement. He wanted to be free of day-to-day operational and executive responsibilities, but he was tied by an employment contract guaranteeing his exclusive services to Warner until 1980. "He can't sell popcorn for another movie company," said a member of the corporate staff in charge of massaging Wall Street.

The Warner spokesman let it be known that Ashley had a kidney ailment and a new romance and was suffering the blues of a man who had climbed to the top of the mountain by the age of fifty-two. The operation of the film subsidiary was entrusted to Frank Wells, who succeeded Ashley as chairman and chief executive officer, and John Calley, who took Wells's presidential chair.

The investor relations man also had an explanation for the departure of Alan Cohen, the former tax lawyer who had been Steve Ross's second in command as executive vice president. Cohen had left to become president of Madison Square Garden, disappointed, it was said, because Ross never let him be president of Warner Communications. Ever since the death of William Frankel, his co-chief executive, in 1972, Ross had kept both titles, president and chairman, to himself.

Ross had plenty to do these days, though not hardly at all that which he liked to do best, deal-making. He was switching around the players on his team. He had taken Spencer Harrison from the film production company and assigned him to be executive vice president for corporate development of Warner Cable Corporation (as TeleVision Communications had been rebaptized). An electronics expert, Gustave Hauser, had been brought in to be president and operating officer of Warner Cable. That left Alfred Stern free to worry about the Washington scene and problems of regulation of the cable industry, in short, to fill the statesman's role he preferred.

Ross tried to insert himself in operations of the record companies, but the star managers' temperaments were more easily ruffled.

Ross invited Emanuel Gerard, of Roth, Gerard & Company, a financial consultant on the entertainment industry, to serve as a corporate minister without portfolio or internal gadfly.

In February of 1973, when Warner stock had started fading from its 1972 peak of 50 to around 27, Gerard told the *Wall Street Journal,* "At these prices, the stock is a raging buy." By the end of 1974 it had reached 7.

After he arrived in September of 1974, Gerard's mission was to demolish the dozens of bright ideas that Ross usually brought into the office after a weekend of letting his restless imagination roam. Gerard's presence was calculated to reassure Wall Street, a corporate function also known as "developing interest in the stock." [In March 1975, Gerard was named executive vice president.]

The bloom was off the Warner rose in the depressed stock market. Though Warner revenues were galloping ahead, earnings were barely more than the year before. In 1974 the company had net income of $48.5 million on revenues of $720.1 million compared with earnings of $47.3 million on revenues of $549.6 million in 1973. Earnings per share (a favorite analysts' measure of the go-go years) had been boosted by a periodic buying in of company shares. A number of companies had used that tactic during the prolonged recessionary bear market in an effort to improve their position.

Warner had borrowed in 1973 to buy 3.4 million of its outstanding shares at an average price of $15.50. Interest on the loans combined with a paper loss of about $20 million on the value of the repurchased stock made for an uncomfortable squeeze. In 1974 another 1,364,556 shares were bought in at an average cost of $10.12 per share. Early in 1975 an additional 640,972 shares were acquired. In two years more than one fourth of its previously outstanding common stock had been repossessed. Warner's total interest expense had climbed $9.7 million to $30 million in one year.

At the end of 1974, Warner had a paper loss of $68 million on its corporate portfolio of stocks, $197-million worth that Ross had invested in better days as a reservoir for future acquisitions. The size of the portfolio made Ross the object of courtship by brokers who wanted his trades. Its character was conservative enough, almost the antithesis of what Warner Communications represented, rather like Elvis Presley in a Brooks Brothers suit. The largest commitment was to utility stocks, with dollops of General Motors, Ford Motor, and IBM. All of these had shriveled in stock market value.

Furthermore, as if trying too late to do penance for their sins, Wall Street analysts were looking carefully at balance sheets. In Warner Communications they saw a bloat of $272 million in long-term debt lying on a shareholders' equity of $347 million.

One of the things that bothered Wall Street most was the Uris deal. In the summer of 1973 National Kinney Corporation made an agreement to buy Uris Building Corporation, the company that had defaced the island of Manhattan with acres of second-rate office space. Kinney was obligated to make a tender offer to minority shareholders at $15 a share by June 30, 1974, for which it would have to raise $60 million.

The glut of New York office space, aggravated by a downturn in the general economy, was already apparent in 1973 when the deal was signed. In the spring of 1974 banks began foreclosure proceedings on one of the new Uris office towers, which had required a $62-million construction loan to build. Uris also disposed of an interest in a suburban office complex "in lieu of foreclosure."

As things went from bad to worse, Ross took the unconvincing stance of citing the bad deal as the result of operating autonomy. Andrew Frankel, chairman of Kinney, and his people had made the deal even though Ross knew it was bad for its Warner parent (which still owned 47 per cent of Kinney), Ross let it be known. It seemed as though Ross was going to be able to wriggle out of that tight spot by selling 5 million of Warner's 6 million shares of National Kinney to a French real estate developer who had backing from European institutional investors. But the agreement was terminated in June of 1974.

The Uris merger was completed that month after Kinney obtained a $50 million bank loan, half of it guaranteed by Warner. Kinney's attempts to sell some of the Uris office buildings to Prudential Insurance Company of America failed, too, and by the end of the year it was reporting a sharp drop in earnings which it blamed on higher interest rates and increased borrowing because of Uris. Kinney's troubles were reflected back to Warner. Interest expense was eating into its profits, too.

Ross and his financial boys were looking closely at profits. "They're more important now than when everyone was buying our future," his publicist said.

The budgets and capital expenditures of the operating subsidiaries were being picked over by the corporate financial men. Cost control had even caught up with the golden record companies. Though their coups continued—Dave Geffen had signed Bob Dylan when the modern music idol came out of retirement and into a six week concert tour, Ertegun's Atlantic had found a "superstar of tomorrow" in Bette Midler, and Frank Sinatra had returned to the Warner label—the record industry was hit with a shortage and then a price rise in the vinyl for its disks as a result of the petroleum crisis late in 1973. Artists' egos had to be assuaged when fold-over jackets (that cost 15 cents more than an ordinary sleeve) were canceled as an economy measure.

There still were lapses into the big splashes of yesteryear. In September, after Richard Nixon had retreated to San Clemente, a sick and broken man, William Sarnoff secured the publishing rights to the former President's memoirs for $2 million. Warner Paperback

Library had already paid $1 million for the rights to *All the President's Men,* the book by the two reporters who broke the Watergate scandal.

In 1974, Warner Communications disposed of its foreign publishing operations, taking a pretax loss of $15.3 million.

A major area of concern was cable television. Though it constituted 4 per cent of sales, its contribution to the profit columns of the balance sheet were written in red ink. In 1974 the cable division posted a pretax loss of $7.3 million on gross revenues of $30.8 million. Of that loss, $6 million was from a write-down of some of the smaller cable TV systems.

Warner Cable had 500,000 subscribers in thirty-one states and was operating 130 cable systems which made it Number Two. "But we stand ready to be Number One," Alfred Stern said, noting the myriad woes of the largest cable operator, Teleprompter, whose stock had practically slid off the Big Board at about $1 a share. Teleprompter stock had been suspended from trading at one period while the SEC looked into its business operations. Investors had chilled considerably in their rapture for cable stocks. The backlash had been felt not only by cable companies but by conglomerates like Warner, which had once benefited from the impression that it was more of a cable company than it actually was.

Warner had invested $30 million to build new cable systems in 1973 before the decision was made to "revaluate," as Ross said. An agreement in principle to buy Sterling Communications, 70 per cent owned by Time Inc. and which shared the franchise to operate cable in Manhattan with Teleprompter, was broken off. The price would have been $20 million. Warner also gave up franchises it had been promised in Dayton and Birmingham because the return on capital looked too dim.

The entire cable industry was pulling back. The national rate of growth in subscribers had dropped from the 16 per cent that had stimulated those investor expectations in the first two years of the seventies to 10 per cent.

Rural communities seemed saturated, and as one cable operator said with depressing candor, "Cable bombed in the cities and we will be a long time recovering from it." The operators had underestimated the cost of laying urban cable as well as the services that the big-town customers would demand. Fewer city dwellers subscribed than had been assumed. They also canceled at a higher rate.

Warner's Gridtronics, the plan for delivering eight first-run movies a month on pay TV for an extra $5.00 to $6.00 fee had ended up as another expensive learning experience for the company. In part, it was the reverse side of the movie theater attendance trend that was exalting Warner's movie company. And it seemed to dash—at least, until another trend appeared—the high hopes of Ted Ashley and others for movies in cable television.

"We're now convinced that movies alone won't do it for the pay-TV entrepreneur," Stern said. "Even with movies, distant signals will have to develop other fare for the urban consumer. We know now it will have to be layered—some movies, some sports, some educational."

As for the human services that Stern and Dr. Goldmark had so persuasively described, "the well-designed system to put the services into the home—what must be the cornerstone of urban cable—just doesn't exist yet," said Stern. (Early in 1975 Dr. Goldmark bought back for $1,000 the shares of his company owned by Warner and phased out of the relationship by drawing down as a consultant his $100,000-a-year salary still due on his contract which had two years to run.)

Experiments with selling merchandise on cable TV had shown that customers found it too much trouble to pick up the telephone to place their orders. "Until we have a system where a home owner can push a few buttons and order up the shows he wants, we can't look to the goodies," Stern said. "Clearly it will happen, and when it does, the software people will come forth with the programming. I'm willing to wait."

He sounded relaxed, but then he could afford to be. On paper he was $6 million poorer than the day his TVC married Warner Communications. He had sold off only 50,000 shares of the Warner stock he had received. Stern and his family still held 220,000 shares which made them only slightly less interested in Warner Communications than Steve Ross and his wife and children, who had 251,000 shares. Ross's father-in-law and uncle-in-law, who were still vice chairman and vice president as well as directors of the company, controlled another 269,000 shares.

But Stern was realistic. "Had I not made this merger, there would be a real question for my company as there has been for the others, will they survive? How do they exist in the meantime?

"Clearly, I'm better off for myself and the stockholders of my company than if Steve hadn't come to see me one day.

"I still have confidence in the company. Steve used to say the stock was going to 70. Everybody's view has changed. They don't think of companies moving with that multiplication of current sales price. I can see Warner Communications selling at 20, which is better than 7. If we can get the Uris problem solved and if we can get a different awareness of the company.

"We make a lot of money. We have a tremendous amount of cash. We're a solid, profitable company. Warner Communications will come back and when it does, it's clearly Number One to take advantage of cable. And they may be in other businesses."

Ross was not available to elaborate on what those businesses might be. Or how he felt about himself and the company. Stung by a hatchet job on him and the company in the November 15, 1974, issue of *Forbes Magazine,* he was avoiding interviews. Maybe he was following the advice his father had given him when he was twenty-one: "To avoid criticism, say nothing, do nothing."

His consultants may have suggested that too much Ross was hard for Wall Street to swallow in its new mood of somber caution. The full-page color photograph in the 1972 annual report of Ross against the background of the Rockefeller Center skyscraper, in which he had rented office space for corporate headquarters at $4 million a year (even Ertegun had been uprooted from Atlantic's Broadway digs) had diminished to passport size.

Ross was a shadow of the wealthy man he had been on paper. He couldn't buy anything—in the way of companies, that is, because his Chinese money (as Wall Street called the inflated securities conglomerateurs used for their purchases) was devalued, for the time being at least. He seemed to have difficulty selling, too, as in the case of his Uris-plagued National Kinney interest.

But he still had the wages and perquisites of chief executive office. His $240,000-a-year salary in 1973 had been raised to $385,008 in 1974. The sum earmarked for his retirement was still $113,388 a year. Uncle-in-law Morton Rosenthal was drawing $75,000 a year as a vice president, with $40,617 a year for his pension.

Then there was the FI Fund, in which Ross, Morton Rosenthal, and ten other executives had interests. The corporation had contributed $3.4 million to this investing partnership which had been set up for five years. The limited partners, such as Ross, had put in a total of $345,000. As was not intended, stock market losses wiped out their investment. Three stockholders challenged the fund in court as a waste and spoliation of company assets and a diversion of corporate opportunities.

It certainly appeared to be another example of how a favored few in a corporate setting stand to make money without risking much of their own. Only in hard times, such as these, do they stand to lose. And even then, less of their own than the corporation's. In February 1975 the stockholder suits were settled with an agreement that the FI Fund would be terminated and its assets would belong exclusively to the company. The partners surrendered their right to recoup their investment losses.

Ross still enjoys the lifestyle of the corporate grandee—the constant flying back and forth to the Coast and abroad to confer and survey the properties; all the interesting, attractive, funky, kinky, marvelous people one meets if one is a concurrent magnate in film, music, and television. Everyman's dream come true. Hadn't his father instructed him in the uses of dreaming?

He had the power and the fun of playing with other people's money as though it were his own. One day the climate would change for cable television, and then posterity might record Steve Ross as a pioneer.

All in all, he'd gone a long, long way from those uncharismatic caskets.

THE VERY PRIVATE PRITZKERS

October 1973

The Pritzkers? Who are they? That's what New York's inbred publishing world was suddenly asking in the fall of 1973. Late in the afternoon of Sunday, September 23, and just in time to make the headlines of the Monday morning newspapers, David J. Mahoney, chairman of Norton Simon, Inc., and an adept publicist of himself and his corporation, announced that he had sold *McCall's,* the women's magazine, to Refco Enterprises Inc. for an undisclosed amount of cash and notes.

Publishing industry gossip quickly established that the sum was about $8 million and that behind the corporate shell of Refco stood Jay A. Pritzker of Chicago and his family.

Everyone knew why Dave Mahoney wanted to sell. *McCall's* had been a bone in his throat. He never shared the fleeting impulse of his mentor and one-time boss Norton Simon to be an arts-and-letters personage. And his publicly listed, billion-dollar consumer goods company needed something more than what a nicely convalesced magazine like *McCall's* could offer to stimulate its growth image in Wall Street. Besides, his own tastes lay more in the direction of the Beautiful People.

A week after the *McCall's* sale was consummated, he bought one of the Beautiful People's favorite dressmakers, Halston, for pretty much what Jay Pritzker had given him for *McCall's*. Except that the Pritzkers paid in cash and Mahoney's deal with Halston was done with Norton Simon stock, which subsequently came tumbling down in the bear market.

Mahoney insisted there was no connection between the two deals beyond the fact that he wanted to get out of publishing and on with his strategy of building a consumer goods, brand-name products company.

He thought that Halston could lend instant superchic to Max Factor & Company, Mahoney's healthiest acquisition to date. But Factor carried a Hollywoodish aura of old pancake make-up. On Halston's tony name, the introduction of an expensive fragrance could be hung.

Jay Pritzker had come along and helped Mahoney out. No one in the New York publishing crowd could really figure out why he had bought *McCall's*. Or for that matter, who Jay Pritzker was. For the provincial Manhattan circle whose landmarks are "21", The Four Seasons, and the Greenbrier Hotel in White Sulphur Springs, West Virginia, Pritzker was the new mystery boy in town.

Actually, the name Pritzker (usually expressed in the plural) had been fairly well known to the sophisticates of the financial community. "There is a network in this country that people come to with deals," observed one such insider, "and the Pritzkers are in the deal network. They're just someone else to sell something to."

Unlike some in the network (such as Charles Bluhdorn of Gulf & Western Industries, Inc., and Meshulam Riklis of Rapid-American Corporation) but very much like others (such as Charles Allen, the Wall Street investment banker), the Pritzkers abhorred reading about themselves and their deals in the newspapers.

Airline people have known about the Pritzkers since Jay became a director of Continental Air Lines a dozen years ago. David Mahoney is a member of that board, too, although the *McCall's* deal did not come out of that relationship. Mahoney's troubleshooter, E. Garrett Bewkes, Jr., had mentioned to Ira Harris of Salomon Brothers, one of Norton Simon Inc.'s Wall Street investment bankers, that he wanted to sell. Harris played matchmaker with the Pritzkers.

Jay has continually flirted with the airlines ever since he emerged from World War II, in which he served as a Navy pilot, and tried unsuccessfully to run a Mexican airline. Through him, the Pritzkers held a large stock position in Western Airlines.

Hotelmen know the Pritzkers through the Hyatt Corporation, America's fastest growing luxury hotel chain, which they built practically from nothing during the last fifteen years. Jay is chairman and his brother-in-law Hugo M. ("Skip") Friend, Jr., son of a longtime Illinois appellate judge, runs the company as president.

Chicagoans associate the Pritzkers with philanthropy. They are annual six-figure contributors to Jewish charities. The Nicholas J. Pritzker Center on the city's South Side treats emotionally disturbed children. Since 1968, when they gave the University of Chicago $12 million, its medical school has borne their name. Jay is a trustee of the university.

During the last year, their name has also popped up in local newspaper exposés documenting the relationships between Mayor Richard Daley's political comrades—Alderman Thomas Keane, for instance—and the city's mightier real estate developers, among whom the Pritzkers must be counted. Keane is presently under indictment on conflict-of-interest and conspiracy charges.

As a result of the Keane revelations and the *McCall's* acquisition, the Pritzkers have had to deal for the first time with the surrender of their cherished privacy. Jay's brother, Robert, the shyest Pritzker, wondered aloud if the family ought to retain a public relations consultant—to keep its name out of the newspapers.

For three generations they had managed to do so without professional assistance, simply by shunning contact with the press and sidestepping proxy fights and contested tender offers. "It cost us $20 million to avoid take-overs," Jay's father, A. N. Pritzker, said. "People come to us with deals because they want to avoid publicity."

In pre-Hyatt days the Pritzkers seldom did business with the public, and until the *McCall's* deal, they refrained from buying companies in the chatty, communications industry.

None of this means that the Pritzkers are antisocial. They are, in fact, a gregarious clan, much given to banter and verbal horseplay and disinclined to take themselves too seriously. Theirs is a trim, informal management style. Pritzkers dial their own business telephone calls.

They are a family that practices exceptional "togetherness," a term coined by one of *McCall's* earlier management regimes as a promotional slogan, though the Pritzkers were unaware of that coincidence when they made the deal to acquire it. Invariably they are asked whether they think of themselves as modern American Rothschilds. Jay laughed when the question was put to him and retorted, "Of course not. We're Litvaks."

He was making an in-group, Jewish joke in keeping with the family modesty. It was as if, when compared with the Rockefellers, a millionaire might assert that he is merely a farmboy from Wisconsin or Texas. The Rothschilds are the Sun Kings of Jewish wealth, and their family cradle, Frankfurt-am-Main, Germany, was traditionally regarded by Jews as an area considerably more distinguished than any in Eastern Europe. "Litvaks" is the term for Jews from Lithuania or northern Poland. Even funnier, though, is the fact that the Pritzker origins were in the Ukraine, which makes them, by strict construction, not Litvaks but "Russians."

Nevertheless, A. N. Pritzker once told a Chicago newspaper reporter that his father "taught us the principle of all for one and one for all." He did not credit the proper source for the principle, the Rothschilds.

The founding father, Nicholas J. Pritzker, migrated to Chicago from Kiev in 1880 at the age of nine. He became a pharmacist, then studied law and established a general practice in 1902. He sent his three sons to law school and they eventually came into his firm although Harry, the eldest, first served as an assistant state's attorney, earning the nickname of "the lightning prosecutor."

Arthur J. Goldberg trained as a young lawyer in the Pritzker firm before going on to renown as a labor lawyer, a Cabinet member, and an Associate Justice in the United States Supreme Court.

For the last thirty years Pritzker & Pritzker hasn't accepted outside clients because of potential conflicts of interest with the Pritzker enterprises, which are too numerous for any one member of the family to recall at a given moment. "I have a poor memory," Nicholas' second son, A. N. (A for Abram) Pritzker, the Papa Bear of the clan, told a reporter who was attempting almost futilely to interview him during a flight from Chicago to Newark. His tone was jocular.

Jay Pritzker tried to explain why he couldn't say for sure whether the family, as often reported, controlled hundreds of companies. "You see, Marmon has twenty-one profit centers," he said, running his finger down columns of figures in a report of that family-owned conglomerate. "And Keystone has eight or nine warehousing locations each doing $10 million or so," he said in a reference to one of Marmon's component companies. "So how many businesses is Marmon? One or many?" he asked.

Furthermore, the Pritzkers are financial beachcombers, always collecting or creating shell companies. Refco, the purchaser of *McCall's,* was a shell lying around from one of their real estate enterprises, Jay said.

In one three-week period in the fall of 1973, the Pritzkers are known to have bought *McCall's,* the rights to the Coot (a problem-beset all-terrain vehicle) from Cummins Engine Company, and a 12 per cent block of stock in Altamil, a truck equipment concern. Those are merely the deals that required public notice by Securities and Exchange Commission regulations.

Pritzker & Pritzker, which recently moved from its LaSalle Street offices to one of the skyscrapers housing the First National Bank of Chicago (the family's banker) currently has three partners. They are A.N. ("seventy-seven going on thirty-three," an employee says), his brother, Jack, sixty-nine, and A.N.'s oldest son, Jay, fifty-one. "I just always wanted to come into my father's office," Jay said. "When I was five years old, he put my name on the door of one of the offices, and when one of his friends came to work for him and needed my office, he bought it back from me with a flower."

Harry Pritzker, A.N.'s and Jack's brother, died in 1956. Another partner, A.N.'s youngest son, Donald, then thirty-nine and president of Hyatt, died suddenly of a heart attack in 1972. Only one of the founder's direct descendants, all male, wandered afield professionally. A.N.'s middle son, Robert, forty-seven, is an engineer and the family operations man.

A fourth generation of partners is in the making now that Jack's son, Nicholas, and Jay's son, Thomas, are attending the University of Chicago Law School and have declared their intention of joining the firm.

Though they don't practice law in a staid, conventional sense, the Pritzkers would rather be considered lawyers than financial operators (or wheeler-dealers, as they are often called).

Although they retain outside counsel when they need specialized knowledge such as in SEC or trademark matters, Jay Pritzker said he couldn't imagine doing what they do without legal background. "We move quickly and assess risks without waiting for someone else to advise us. Lawyers can give you such useless advice. If you're not a lawyer, you're afraid there's something you ought to know," he said. He bought the first Hyatt hotel near the Los Angeles airport for $2.1 million in 1957 and the Marmon-Herrington Company in 1960 by scribbling his offer and terms on scraps of paper.

"Dad is probably the most brilliant lawyer you ever met," he said of his Harvard-trained father, in one of the rare deviations from the family cult of nonpersonality. Reluctantly posing for a newspaper photograph after the *McCall's* deal, the Pritzkers were adamant about being photographed as a group standing in a straight line so that no one would look dominant.

"We're a family unit," Jay emphasized.

Indeed, in those relatively few public transactions where the Pritzker name appears rather than being hidden behind the blind identity of a trustee or a corporate shell like Refco, it is usually as the Pritzker family. They almost always act through numerous family trusts set up in the 1930s. Individual family members don't deal for their own accounts, Jay said, "because if the deal is significant, you would feel an obligation to the others."

Through these trusts, the Pritzker family owns 34 per cent of the common stock of Hyatt Corporation (which is traded over the counter and had revenues of $242 million in 1973) and 50 per cent of Hyatt International Corporation, which was spun off in a rights offering to shareholders in 1969.

The 1971 proxy of the Marmon Group Inc., the last before the company merged itself into privacy, showed that the Pritzker family owned 91.3 per cent of the stock. Marmon grosses about $265 million a year from nonglamorous, nonconsumer activities such as automotive parts and building equipment.

"The things we do are so intertwined," Jay said, again stressing the team spirit. However, despite the family likenesses (Pritzkers tend to medium size, joviality, gentlemanly comportment, and unostentatious generosities), there are distinctions.

A. N. Pritzker, who looks like a benign Aristotle Onassis, drafts many of the contracts, forges the links to the giants such as the Prudential Insurance Company, the David Rockefeller interests, Tenneco, Inc., and the Ford Motor Land Company, which are Hyatt's partners these days. It was he who steered the family out of law practice into deal making, often as not in a corner of the Standard Club, Chicago's exclusive Jewish city club. The family chuckles over the fortune he made and lost in Florida real estate speculation in the 1920s.

He has outlasted many of his cronies such as Walter Heymann, the ailing former vice chairman of the First National Bank of Chicago (whose son Robert, a senior vice president of the bank, is on the Hyatt board), and the late Arthur Greene, a finance company investor.

A.N. and another associate, James Alsdorf, bought the Cory Corporation in 1941 for less than $50,000. They took it public in 1947 and sold it in 1967 to the Hershey Foods Corporation for $23 million.

Dealing with outside partners is a family characteristic. Each member establishes his own relationships and then commits the family to them.

A.N. carries his business in a makeshift notebook covered in clear plastic that his secretary reconstitutes every month or so. It contains his credit card numbers, telephone area codes, airline phone numbers, half a dozen closely typed pages of individuals' names and phone numbers, and a mortgage rate table.

"Math is my forte," he said. A.N. is forever thrashing out the mathematics of a deal with the aid of the rate table and an electronic pocket calculator. He will interrupt his sons or even a grandson on the telephone at dinnertime to announce the solution to a particularly difficult problem.

In his wallet is tucked a 1934 passport photo of his father and Jay, then a precocious grammar school graduate. It was taken when the two embarked on a six-month visit to the Soviet Union and Palestine.

A.N.'s younger brother, Jack, is the real estate specialist and "the world's nicest guy," according to his nephew Jay. "Jack can buy 3,000 acres in Florida and no one hears about it and it's better that way," he said. "My business isn't the best publicized part of our business and I've tried very hard to keep it that way," Jack said affably.

On the other hand, Jack recalled, "the first time I knew we had acquired *McCall's* was when some of our people in Florida called asking me for jobs there and I said, 'We did?'"

The Pritzkers are casual about keeping each other informed, a fortunate attitude since they are constantly flying off in different geographic directions. "We should but we don't confer. Once a year we say, 'Now we gotta get organized.' Our last weekly get-together was six months ago," Jay said.

In 1959 the Pritzkers bought acreage in the Chicago suburb of Rosemont at about 75 cents a square foot from associates of Alderman Keane whom Jack describes as "an acquaintance." The sellers made money on the deal and so have the Pritzkers. The land, which is near O'Hare Airport, has appreciated tenfold as has real estate near most major jetports. The Pritzkers held it for a decade before deciding to build the dazzling pink Regency Hyatt O'Hare Hotel.

In the spring of 1973, the Better Government Association of Chicago and the Chicago *Sun-Times* revealed that the hotel had received a $2.7-million assessment cut in 1972 from the Cook County Board of Tax Appeals, whose chairman was then Alderman Keane's brother, George. The reduction was based on a statement for the seven months in 1971 when the hotel opened and started operating at an expected loss, rather than for 1972 when it turned a sizzling success.

The Pritzkers maintain that assessments are usually based on figures of the previous year. "Next year it will surely be more," Jay said. "I don't think we get unusual tax breaks."

Nor does Jack consider it out of the ordinary that he has extended a secured loan to Mayor Donald Stephen of Rosemont ("he's kept it paid up to date," Jack said), or that he and Mayor Robert Atcher of suburban Schaumburg Township are real estate partners there.

The Pritzkers have extensive properties in various stages of development in the swiftly growing area northwest of Chicago. Among them is the 3,750-acre Centex Industrial Park (Centex Corporation of Dallas is the partner in that venture), as well as thousands of acres recently annexed to Waukegan.

Another real estate deal figures in taxpayers' suits which allege giveaways of leases of public land. Jack obtained a ninety-nine-year lease to a 2.5-acre parcel of land in 1955 (one of many held by municipal trustees), at annual rentals from $750 to $1,300 a year, or a total of about $109,000 for the life of the lease.

The lease was assigned to a Pritzker Foundation and an Alsdorf Foundation (established by A.N.'s partner in the Cory deal). It was then subleased to the Cory Corporation at rentals of close to $100,000 a year for office space in a building the foundations had

constructed on the land. Those rentals can be renegotiated every
ten years.

In this one of many instances, the Pritzkers had the foresight and
the contacts to secure undervalued property in which they saw and
realized the potential for improvement and appreciation.

A superficial glance at the real estate record would indicate that
Jack's relations with the Democratic Daley machine have been cor-
dial and profitable. But the family has contributed to political campaigns of both parties. Jay formed the Chicago committee of Concerned Citizens for the Re-election of Richard Nixon in 1972.

Since the death of Donald, the most ebullient Pritzker and a dead
ringer for Buddy Hackett, Jay has been the most visible member of
the clan. The handsomest Pritzker and the one with the most dash-
ing lifestyle—he is an intrepid skier and balloonist—Jay is the chief
deal architect. His voice is chronically hoarse from talking on the
telephone.

His brother Robert, the quiet engineer and operations man, has
the management flair. He flies economy class to set an example for
the cadres while A.N. and Jay go first class all the way.

When the family took a little leap into the heady world of film
financing (through one of its minor subsidiaries, Movie Service
Functions Inc.), it was Robert who decided not to be involved
with anything X-rated. "It's not that Bob's a prude but as a matter
of principle he doesn't want to be involved in a *Deep Throat,*" Jay
said. "I don't mind sex movies so much, but I'm opposed to
violence in movies and TV."

Bob runs Marmon Group Inc., the family's diversified manufacturing umbrella under which *McCall's* will probably be sheltered.

Marmon's evolution over the last twenty years provides an example for the Pritzker technique. In 1953 Jay and Robert acquired the
assets of Colson Company, a caster-manufacturing concern whose
president was eager to retire and willing to sell to a bargain hunter.
As Jay elaborated, "GM doesn't need us. Opportunities occur either
when there's conflict that can only be resolved by a sale or when
people are getting on in years and want to sell. You cannot buy
when a seller is not anxious to sell."

Jay and Bob sold off Colson's unprofitable bicycle division and
used the recuperating caster remainder as a vehicle for other acquisitions. Among them: L. A. Darling Company, a store-fixture con-

cern bought from an estate; Marmon-Herrington Company, acquired from an elderly pioneer auto racing manufacturer. The Pritzkers disposed of Marmon's money-losing military vehicle division and expanded the profitable segment in coal mining machinery.

They changed the corporate name to Marmon Group Inc. and continued buying and "straightening out" troubled companies such as American Steel and Pump Company, Detroit Steel Products, Keystone Pipe Company, and Fenestra Inc. The latter was bought from the Gulf American Land Corporation, which had been fighting a three-year battle for control of the building equipment company.

"We buy where we can improve management and reduce the amount of assets necessary to run the business. The financial maneuvering is prologue. The management is everything," Jay said. He went on, "If the initial venture is only moderately successful, that can be good enough for us because it can be used as a keystone to build another company. The entity itself must pay off what we borrow to acquire it though."

His explanation may illuminate the mystery of the *McCall's* purchase which one magazine publisher likened to "buying a restaurant on a street with ten restaurants." In 1972 *McCall's,* which had been losing money for almost two decades, earned $2.5 million on revenues of $48 million.

Sensitive about being tagged as financial manipulators, Jay Pritzker asserted his intention of keeping *McCall's* alive and publishing. He denied he bought it for a tax loss, as was the case surely in some of the Pritzker deals.

The possibility was there, however, and it limited his downside risk. In magazine accounting, the cost of obtaining subscriptions is written off as an expense when occurred, while the income from the subscriber is spread over the life of the subscription. And if a magazine falls apart, it still has the liability of fulfilling its subscriptions.

In the 1950s, he bought Rockwood & Company, an unprofitable chocolate company in Brooklyn. After trying in vain to run the company, he sold its candy business to Tootsie Roll Industries Inc. and kept Rockwood's corporate shell. Among Rockwood's assets was an inventory of cocoa beans carried on the books at a fraction of current market values. This accounting valuation enabled Rockwood to acquire such properties as the first Hyatt Hotel and the Selby Shoe Company. The latter was picked up after a Selby family fight and a proxy contest, whittled down, and sold to the United States Shoe Company.

Jay Pritzker acquired the plywood company E. L. Bruce in 1962 by flipping a coin with the Crown family, a Chicago tribe with whom the Pritzkers are often compared. The flip took place in the offices of First National Bank of Chicago, which wanted to dispose of a 15 per cent interest in Bruce, which it held as collateral for loans to Edward M. Gilbert, a bankrupt conglomerateur.

Jay called heads, and heads it was. The Pritzkers unsnarled Bruce's affairs, built up the company over the next six years, and sold it at a profit to Cook Industries Inc. But the profit "wasn't commensurate with the effort," Jay said, "except for one thing. It convinced the bank that we knew how to run a business. The notion had been around that we were just financial maneuverers."

Over the same period of time, moreover, Jay had been increasing the substantial positions he had been taking in the lumber and plywood business. He bought three companies, for about $20 million each, at what were essentially distress sales. The Michigan-California Lumber Company was bought at an auction, and Timber Products Company, acquired from Cypress Mines.

Chicago Mill and Lumber Company, the most important of the lumber acquisitions, was an eighty-three-year-old company that manufactured wooden shipping containers. During 1964 it was the battleground for a proxy fight between its management and a group of insurgent stockholders led by John F. Maher, a Houston industrialist. The battle landed in the courts where the incumbents won a narrow victory. A compromise slate of directors was elected.

As Jay recalled, "I was sitting in the offices of Eastman Dillon in New York when somebody mentioned that this stock was available. I said, sure I'd be interested at such and such a price, and three days later, the stock arrived."

The stock consisted of some 200,000 shares, of which 150,000 were owned by the thwarted dissident John Maher. The price was $40 a share, which Maher later said yielded him a capital gain of $1.5 million.

The Pritzkers thus owned 41 per cent of Chicago Mill and Lumber. Two months later they bought the assets of the company and changed it from a publicly held corporation to a privately operated one.

In all of the lumber and plywood deals including E. L. Bruce, the Pritzker family acted in partnership with another family, the Gonyeas of Springfield, Oregon. Jay Pritzker and Will Gonyea are the principal agents for their respective families. "I make the deals and leave the problems to Will. He runs the companies," Jay said.

He indicated, somewhat elliptically, that there wasn't much fun left for him in lumber since the field had become concentrated during the last decade, with little opportunity for independent operators like the Pritzkers and their partners. The lumber businesses continue to be operated and developed, but by the Gonyeas.

With Hyatt Corporation the Pritzker family has done both. The Pritzkers have provided both financial and operational strategy. In creating a luxury lodging chain, they have maximized their profit potential and minimized their personal risk.

Hyatt is the notable exception to the Pritzkers' rule, in that they created it practically from scratch and then invited the public into the business through a stock offering. The family owns 2.77 million or 34 per cent of Hyatt's common shares, which are traded over the counter [in the fall of 1973 at about $12, a year later about $3]. Travelers associate Hyatt with adventurous architecture and luxury hotelkeeping.

Hotelmen credit Hyatt with helping to reverse a business exodus from central cities. It chose its sites chiefly in two areas calculated to draw the free-spending businessman—near airports and in urban downtown hubs that could be a magnet for trade conventions. No less imaginative daring has been used to finance the hotel chain.

Hyatt also provides the only shred of glamour in the Pritzker empire. "We get a kick out of Hyatt," Jay said. "It's a fun business. You meet interesting people and go to interesting places. And we started it."

Despite Hyatt, the Pritzkers have slight contact with the Beautiful People. Dave Mahoney of Norton Simon recounts the phone conversation he had with Jay about an invitation to the opening of Las Hadas, a Mexican resort developed by the Patiños of Bolivian tin fame and fortune. Socialites and their hairdressers and fashion designers were brought from across continents and oceans to produce a bonfire of publicity.

Jay told Dave Mahoney that his wife, Cindy, wanted to go and

that he had heard that men would be expected to dress in white
suits. Was it true and where would one find a white suit in mid-
winter, Mahoney says Jay asked him. After letting him know he
himself disdained such gatherings, Mahoney directed Jay to an unfamiliar address in Chicago. Jay leaped at the conversational bait,
but the address turned out to be the headquarters of Good Humor,
the ice cream business Mahoney had once headed, before selling it
to Thomas Lipton. The anecdote reveals as much about Mahoney,
a self-made boy from the Bronx who has gone far on rugged charm
and friendships with important people but who once admitted he
wasn't always sure of his manners when in the company of social
birds of paradise, as it does about the business benefactor he was
putting down.

Hyatt Corporation is the product of Jay's whim in 1957 to buy
the Hyatt House near Los Angeles for $2.1 million because he
thought it was the only comfortable airport hotel he had ever been
in.

It had been built in 1953 by Hyatt von Dehn, a financial operator
and real estate developer who had bought up land near military
bases. So it was that he built the first major airport hotel, at Los Angeles International Airport, on property he had acquired there.

The hotel was usually booked to capacity. It ran at a 98 per cent
occupancy rate which, in the lodging business is tantamount to a
gushing oil well. But the owner needed cash and that day in 1957
Jay Pritzker wrote out his offer and telephone number on a piece of
paper. A day or two later he received the call that put the family in
the innkeeping trade.

Through its real estate activities, the family had some hotel interests but no conscious plan to build a chain. The following year,
Hugo ("Skip") Friend, the brother of Jay's wife, Cindy, was dispatched to California to tend to the building of other airport
hotels, in Burlingame, California, and Seattle, Washington. The
Burlingame hotel, five minutes away from the San Francisco airport and now the Hyatt corporate headquarters, was built with
floating construction that permits the tidal movements from the
bay to ebb and flow underneath.

Skip Friend was then thirty-two and an experienced dabbler in
the mortgage and apparel businesses. "I was very new to hotels. I
slept in one once," he said.

Early in 1960 the youngest son of A. N. Pritzker, Donald, then twenty-seven and recently graduated from the University of Chicago Law School, went out to see what was happening.

"He never went home. He was the moving force in developing the expansion of the hotels," Friend said. Despite a five-year difference in ages, the two had been close since they were children growing up in Chicago and vacationing in northern Wisconsin.

Moreover, Donald, the roly-poly extrovert of the family and the equal of his brothers Jay and Robert in ambition and mental agility, had a need to establish his own orbit, rather than being a satellite of Jay, who was ten years his senior.

Jay, who terms Donald's death in 1972 "a devastating loss" recalled with a mixture of sadness and mirth how his youngest brother achieved his independence. "Don had me in a vacuum. He was in California and I was in Chicago and he wouldn't send me any information. Then he wanted to be president and I said to him, 'Lose thirty pounds and you can be president.' He didn't quite lose thirty pounds. I wish he had. But I let him become president," said Jay, who is the chairman of Hyatt Corporation.

Don suffered a fatal heart attack while playing tennis in Honolulu at the age of thirty-nine and a half.

"We have this kind of relationship," Jay said, using the memory of Donald to illustrate why the Pritzker family functions so well and seemingly free of natural rivalries, fraternal and intergenerational, and soon with the advent of a fourth generation, cousinly.

"The only reason it works is because of the multiplicity of activities. Otherwise, we'd be all over each other, given our natures. We work to make it work," he said.

From 1962 to 1966, under Don's direction, Hyatt built and acquired half a dozen motor hotels near West Coast airports and terminals.

The first Los Angeles hotel and the Burlingame hotel which opened in 1959 had been tucked into the shell of Rockwood & Company. The Pritzkers would get the first mortgage on the hotel properties and their various partners would put up the equity.

In 1962 the Pritzkers organized the Hyatt Corporation of America which owned the land and operated the hotels. Stock was issued to the public, 350,000 shares at $10 a share. The funds so obtained were to be used in acquiring other hotels. The price of the stock soon drifted down to $4 a share.

The rapid depreciation that real estate affords makes it highly desirable as a tax shelter for a private investor, but depreciation and start-up building costs drag down earnings which in turn tends to depress the price of the stock of a public company. So in 1967 the Pritzkers reorganized. Like an amoeba, Hyatt divided in two, a real estate holding company and a hotel operating company. The original company kept the ownership of the existing hotels and was renamed Hotel Equities Corporation. It returned to the status of a private company. A second company was spun off to operate the hotels. It became the publicly listed Hyatt Corporation.

The gathering momentum of earnings and fast-paced growth under a new formula for hotel construction and style considerably improved Wall Street's regard for the Hyatt stock.

In the meantime, the decisive moment in Hyatt's destiny had arrived in February 1966 when Skip Friend and Don Pritzker were persuaded by a Chicago broker to look at the concrete shell of a hotel in downtown Atlanta, Georgia. The 800-room Regency Hotel was being built as a convention center, but its revolutionary design had intimidated the major hotel chains whom the developers had tried to entice to lease or buy it.

The architect, John Portman, had endowed the hotel with a twenty-three-story lobby. Around the skylit courtyard planted with lush greenery, balconies of rooms were layered. A glass-caged elevator soared like a capsule through a shaft in the center. From a conventional hotelman's point of view, the design wasted space and its luxurious appointments seemed needlessly extravagant.

"Donald and I stood in the lobby, we saw the atrium," Skip Friend remembered. "We said to each other, 'If we don't get into this, we ought to be out of the hotel business.' We were just a small motor hotel chain on the West Coast, but we went ahead. It took the Pritzker family twenty-four to thirty-six hours to get the $18.9 million we paid." The family put together a package of roughly a $13 million first mortgage and $5 million in cash.

At the time, it seemed to be a gamble that could have wiped the family out of the hotel business if it failed. But it succeeded, and in retrospect it was a bargain since the purchase price came to $25,000 a room. A decade later, the cost of constructing such a hotel had mounted 70 per cent.

The building which set the blueprint for the renascent American "grand hotel" attracted so many spectators that guests had to push their way through gaping crowds to their rooms. But as a consequence of being talked about and of its meticulous comfort and service, the hotel won solid bookings from conventions and business travelers to the hub city of the industrial Southeast. The hotel has since been earning $2.5 million in pretax profits on revenues of $18 million.

From the Hyatt Regency Atlanta, the thrust of the company was toward the operation of new hotels built along the same principles of innovative architecture and deluxe style to cater to the middle- to upper-crust traveling executives.

Some forty such hotels of large and medium sizes are to be in operation by late 1974. Among the more spectacular are the 750-room Hyatt Regency O'Hare, its atrium sheathed by what appears to be pink stainless steel walls rising out of the flatlands near Chicago's vast airport; the 1,000-room Hyatt Regency Houston, with its futuristic look of a space center; and the 840-room Hyatt Regency San Francisco in Embarcadero Center, with its revolving roof-top restaurant surveying the bays and bridges. Not all are vast Regencies. There are the 300-to-500-room Hyatt Houses in smaller cities like Richmond and Winston-Salem, with appropriately scaled down room rentals.

The Hyatt hotels in downtown sites are frequently conceived as part of larger, integrated real estate developments, which include office buildings, apartment houses, and shopping centers and are sponsored by powerful interests such as the Ford Motor Land Company, Tenneco, Inc., the Prudential Insurance Company of America, Massachusetts Mutual Life Insurance Company, and the Ogden Corporation.

Hyatt operates the hotels on long-term leases from these developers or from their private holding company, Hotel Equities Corporation, which still owns some of the older hotels. Hyatt receives a percentage of sales and gross operating profits (something like 20 to 27 per cent of the latter). The Pritzkers are thus assured of steady rentals from Hyatt to Hotel Equities. They also stand to gain from appreciation of their Hyatt stock.

The Pritzker family isn't putting any of its own cash into building hotels in the United States, although they are overseas. Hyatt gets a lease-management contract from an owner such as Ford or Tenneco on condition that Hyatt will raise working capital in the range of $800 to $1,000 a room. Hyatt borrows the money from the banks at a bit over the prime rate and is reimbursed for the interest from the owner. Hyatt's investment and risk thereby boil down to zero.

In 1974 Hyatt took over the management of three hotels in California from PSA, an intrastate airline. One hotel is the *Queen Mary,* the former luxury liner, berthed in Long Beach.

In 1969 a rights offering was made to stockholders of Hyatt Corporation to buy shares in a new company, Hyatt International. The Pritzker family owns about half of that stock, which is also traded in the over-the-counter market. Hyatt International operates hotels overseas—mostly in remoter areas like Manila, Bangkok, Hong Kong, Bali, and Singapore. In a hotel being built in Iran, the shah is a partner. Hyatt Corporation and Hyatt International are totally separate financial entities—despite the commonality of their major stockholders—and maintain only marketing and promotional relationships, similar to that between Hilton Corporation and Hilton International.

Early in 1973 Hyatt Corporation bought the 300-room Four Queens Hotel and Casino in downtown Las Vegas, Nevada. The hotel rents its rooms at $14 a night to a Greyhound Bus clientele, hardly kin to the Regency patrons. The acquisition, according to Skip Friend, "lets us drop our toe into the gambling business," a whirlpool with different currents from those in innkeeping.

Through acquisitions back in 1968, of Northridge Industries Inc. and DuPar's Restaurants Inc., Hyatt Corporation operates lodges and motels and coffee shops. These are being sold off because "we're committed to the quality end of the business," Friend said.

Another acquisition of the same year, Elster's, has become a growing subsidiary that provides interior design and furnishing services for hotels. Most of its clients are non-Hyatt hostelries.

Hyatt has demonstrated to the hotel industry that it can operate first-class hotels and can build an organization to do it. A major emphasis has been on marketing, particularly to the national organizations that hold conventions.

Another stress has been on youth in management. "We have the most aggressive, young, hungry fighters in the field. We've gambled with young hustling guys," the forty-seven-year-old Friend said. Men barely into their thirties are assigned to manage brand new 800-room hotels. William Hartauer, senior vice president-finance is thirty-six. "We think you make up in motivation what you lack in experience," Friend said.

Hyatt keeps its people motivated both with crack training programs and profit-sharing plans. "We don't view people as employees but as partners. Personal relationships are vital to what we do," Jay Pritzker has said.

In 1972 Hyatt branched into the health care field with the acquisition of Setco, Inc., a small chain of acute care general hospitals. "We felt the deal making of a hospital was very similar to the expertise of the hotel business," Friend said. "In a hospital, you're feeding them, bedding them down, and building a facility." Hyatt Medical Enterprises Inc., the subsidiary that Setco became, develops hospital properties with doctors as limited partners. The doctors end up with tax-shelter benefits and Hyatt Medical receives contracts to run the hospitals.

Hyatt also was the first to borrow an idea from European developers for the recreational condominium sector of real estate. Through Innisfree Corporation, a subsidiary, apartments in resort areas of California were sold on a time-sharing ownership basis. Purchasers bought one month possession of a unit so that instead of paying $75,000 for a chalet at Lake Tahoe, a water-skiing family might buy the August ownership for $10,000, with $2,000 down and mortgage payments for the balance at $125 a month. Snow skiers would buy January and February slots, and so on.

It sounded like a developer's dream since in theory he would be selling the same unit eleven or twelve times and making more money. In practice, Innisfree ran smack into the economic downturn, and with the collapse of the housing market Innisfree was stopped in its tracks.

The Pritzkers don't like to lose money, but they do so gracefully and with their sense of humor intact. "When you go to bed knowing you're going to lose $250,000 tomorrow, at least there is certainty," said Jay, recalling a squeeze when President Getulio Vargas of Brazil committed suicide as Jay was hedging Rockwood's cocoa beans.

The Pritzkers lost impressively in the 1970 demise of the brokerage house Blair & Company, in which they had been stockholders. "But no more than we put in," Jay said as lightly as though he were a fruit-stand operator contemplating a rotten apple.

There have been so many Pritzker deals over the years—those that worked out and those that never came to pass, such as a Bernie

Cornfeld deal in Palm Springs, the proposed purchases of Loews' Hotels, REA Express, and nibbling around the edges of Armour & Company. The Pritzkers have dabbled in retailing and cement, and in 1973 they bought an interest in the battered Chicago Bank of Commerce. Reports of their financial clout range from $400 million to just short of nearly $1 billion, but the guesstimators often confuse assets with revenues.

"We really don't know ourselves," said Jay. "I know what I'm worth," A.N. countered with a mirthful roar. "The whole thing is a game," Jay said earnestly. "If you're not having fun, you shouldn't play. We're competitive type guys, though, and we're out to win."

Epilogue: May 1975

The Pritzkers galloped into 1974, wheeling and dealing, buying and selling, and efficiently operating the many companies in their mostly private conglomerate.

But the deals grew bigger and increasingly more public. In retrospect, 1974 may have been the year when the Pritzkers learned to appreciate the wisdom of their old ways, from which they had slightly strayed. They also realized, if they had ever doubted it, how sweet and advantageous privacy could be.

One of their smaller deals was flipped in record time. In May 1974 they bought *The Chicagoan,* a sickly infant of a magazine that had been born the previous October to Jon and Abra Anderson, a Chicago Gold Coast couple who had journalistic aspirations. Mrs. Anderson is the great-granddaughter of John D. Rockefeller, Sr.

"Bob and I didn't want in, we didn't in the worst way," Jay said in October 1974 a month after the magazine had been resold. "But Bill Pattis wanted to be a publisher. It was a lark for him."

S. William Pattis, who was to enjoy his publishing urge for five months, was another of the Pritzkers' numerous partners. He is an advertising sales representative (*The Chicagoan* was one of his clients), as well as president and an investor in the National Textbook Company, "a little tiny company," as Jay called it, that Bob Pritzker had picked up somewhere. Pressed to be more precise, Jay indicated that "tiny" means sales of less than $200,000 a year.

The Pritzkers deferred to their partner's wish in their amiable way, until, as Jay said, "we saw the numbers coming in." In September 1974 *The Chicagoan* was sold to a rival monthly, *Chicago Guide*. The Pritzkers took a loss, shrugging it off lightly. They can always find a use for a modest loss.

The short-lived transaction rekindled the speculation of the previous year at the time of the *McCall's* acquisition, that Jay Pritzker had a secret desire to be a communications czar.

He was forced to deny the report all over again, and in the process avow that there wasn't a bit of romance in his soul as far as business was concerned. "After the first week or two, businesses are all the same, whether a prosaic foundry or something glamorous like making movies or publishing. The fun is to create something. We get a big kick out of creating successful companies but not in any one line of business." Unlike other conspicuous deal makers, the Pritzkers did not go into movie financing in order to meet actresses. "I met a tax accountant once," Jay said laughing.

Sure, he went so far as to admit, "you would like to buy a New York *Times* or a Washington *Post,* if you really would have an influence on your times.

"But," he quickly added, "opportunities like that never present themselves to us and are not likely to. I think we're realists."

The Pritzkers are also, above all else, bargain hunters. Those who have brought to them sound, well-run companies whose owners wished to sell at the prevailing price in the marketplace or more, are politely and candidly turned down. No prize has seemed worth the top dollar to them, at least at the time they initiated a deal.

Even as he disclaimed an interest in publishing, Jay Pritzker was acknowledging the happy irony of the success *McCall's* had had since he bought it.

Despite all the pressures of soaring costs and economic downturn on the publishing business, *McCall's* had managed to raise its cover price and increase its newsstand sales. It had also increased its advertising pages. Robert Stein, the editor, and Raymond Eyes, the publisher, laid much of the amazing vigor of the women's magazine at the door of the Pritzkers who had given them full autonomy.

Jay Pritzker made one memorable visit to *McCall's* shortly after he bought it. David Mahoney of Norton Simon, from whom *McCall's* was purchased, had suggested he hire John Mack Carter, the editor of *McCall's* direct competitor, *The Ladies Home Journal*. Rumors of a management upheaval at *McCall's* were circulating in

the trade, sparked by a *Gallagher Report,* a newsletter that is seldom caught without an ax to grind.

Jay appeared in *McCall's* offices on a Friday morning in 1973
and was confronted by Stein and Eyes demanding their day in court.
They produced figures to show how they had brought the magazine
from a decade or more of losses to steadily increasing profitability
over the last three years. They told him of their plans to improve
earnings still further by cultivating an audience of suburban women
and adding other enterprises for the magazine like mail-order recipe
cards and a cooking school.

Jay listened throughout the morning and early afternoon. Then
he called a meeting of the staff and told them not to worry about the
John Mack Carter rumors. He had confidence in Stein and Eyes and
wanted everyone to keep doing what they had planned to do. After a
celebration drink, he left.

A year later Jay Pritzker commented, "They're doing just fine.
The numbers are outstanding." He wasn't sure why, he mused, but
then he wasn't in the habit of reading the magazine nor did he identify with its supposed constituency.

"If *McCall's* had been unsuccessful, we could have used the tax
loss," he said. "But it is turning out to be a successful venture so we
have a good business and the satisfaction of knowing we made the
right decision in letting Bob Stein and Ray Eyes alone."

But this didn't mean that he was going to take Norton Simon
Inc.'s other publishing units, such as the healthy *Redbook* and
the McCall Printing Company, which always teetered between
red ink and marginal profitability, off Dave Mahoney's hands. He
had advised Mahoney to take his bath now while the price of his
stock was down so low as to make other acquisitions unlikely anyhow and write off the printing company for which no one in his right
mind, least of all a Pritzker, would have paid a fair price. So far,
Mahoney hasn't dared. The chief executive of a public company is
understandably more timid about taking his medicine in write-offs
or omitted dividends than a businessman who has to answer only to
himself and his associates with no one else looking.

So much for publishing. Pritzker didn't spend much time worrying about that business in 1974. He had newer, bigger deals to
juggle.

Jay had dusted off one of his shells, the GL Corporation. "It's a
holding company, something we had on a shelf from when we

needed a parent company a couple of years ago," he explained to a perplexed questioner. He didn't remember what the initials stood for, though.

The Marmon Group Inc., the holding company for the Pritzkers' publishing, movie financing, machinery, and building equipment companies had been folded into GL.

Then, in April of 1974, GL made a tender offer for 500,000 shares of the common stock of Hammond Corporation at $10 a share. The closing price of the shares on the New York Stock Exchange the day before the offer was made, was 7⅞. Bob Pritzker had been buying 501,100 Hammond shares during the past months and had asked for a seat on the board of directors in February.

As the leading manufacturer of electronic organs, Hammond was a consumer-goods company, something the Pritzkers usually stayed away from, and its stock was traded on the Big Board. It also manufactured several lines of work and dress gloves. Its Gibbs Manufacturing & Research subsidiary produced electronic controls and precision instruments. With sales of $135 million in 1973 and net income of $5 million, it presented a picture of fairly good health and reasonable prospects. It had assets of $61 million and what Jay Pritzker called "reasonable liquidity and a good earnings history." It was to be a friendly take-over on invitation of the management of the company.

The Pritzkers borrowed the $9.5 million required to buy the one million or so shares, from the First National Bank of Chicago, the family banker, with an unsecured loan at an interest rate of ½ per cent above the prime rate.

The Pritzkers ended up with 47 per cent of the stock, or undisputed control of Hammond. Robert Pritzker became chairman but did not disturb the incumbent president and chief executive officer. Though the Pritzkers had served notice during the tender that they might merge it with one of their properties and turn it private, they did not immediately do so.

During the summer and fall of 1974, however, the price of Hammond stock receded several points, incurring paper losses of a couple of million dollars on the investment. In October Hammond omitted its quarterly dividend.

Meanwhile, early in 1974 Jay Pritzker had started accumulating over 800,000 shares of Cerro Corporation, paying $17 to $18.75 a share on the New York Stock Exchange for the stock of a once-rich copper mining company that had seen its properties in Peru and Chile expropriated. Cerro was now just another so-so conglomerate with sales of $636 million from activities in metal manufacturing, trucking, and real estate development.

Cerro had loyal stockholders with memories of the good old days when South American copper mines were continuously disgorging wealth for the benefit of Yankee investors and when its stock was selling in the 40s as it last did in 1969. Early in 1970 Robert P. Koenig, who had been president and chief executive for a golden era of 20 years, looked for a successor. He would become chairman.

Ward Howell, the headhunter he hired to conduct the search, advertised the job in *Fortune* magazine. The ad drew seventy-five replies, from which C. Gordon Murphy emerged as first choice. The copper industry then asked, "Who is Gordon Murphy?" just as the publishing industry was to ask in 1973 who the Pritzkers were.

For Murphy was a stranger to the metals business. He was of that breed highly esteemed in the conglomerate climate of the fifties and early sixties, an engineer with a graduate degree from the Harvard Business School and experience with diversification at several companies including Litton Industries, one of the prototypical conglomerates.

Murphy was also very skilled in drawing remuneration contracts. He exacted from Cerro a five-year contract with a starting salary of $180,000, that was to jump to a base of $200,000 after one year. Incentive compensation and other benefits brought it to $357,391 in 1973. If he were to be disabled, he would draw one half of his base compensation. He also received options on 50,000 shares of Cerro common stock at $26.50 a share with loans to exercise them at 4 per cent interest. A year after he took over, Koenig was gone. "Murphy fired me," he said.

Murphy's mettle was tested from the outset with a variety of problems that sharply cut into profits. Some of them were not of his making, namely, government expropriation of the Chilean and Peruvian copper mines. Other problems were definitely traceable to his diversification program. A stereo-tape club was sold off at a loss of $4.5 million. An interest in a cement company was divested at a gain of $2 million.

Through Murphy, Cerro had also become a partner of the Pritzkers in one of Jack's Florida real estate ventures. Cerro's residential real estate development subsidiary, Leadership Housing Incorporated had sold a large tract of property to the Pritzkers for $22.5 million in cash and notes. LHI and the Pritzkers split the costs and profits on the development and sale of housing and golf courses on the property. Other joint ventures in Florida were added later, with the Pritzkers providing the financing and LHI performing the developing and managing functions.

By late 1973 Murphy was concerned about Cerro being raided by bear-market bargain hunters. Like many companies whose stock had declined in price under the weight of its own troubles, as well as those of the economy at large, he had decided that Cerro should buy up some of its own stock. In September a tender offer was made by Cerro at $15 a share for 419,000 of its shares in addition to 112,400 shares that were purchased in the open market. This action served to boost earnings, as well as to serve notice on potential raiders. Several had been sniffing near the campfire.

Cerro contained several appetizing morsels. It had a $135-million tax loss from the government of Peru's expropriation of the Cerro de Pasco mining operations, a tax credit that could be applied for up to ten years beginning in 1974. The government of Chile had paid for its expropriation with $3.2 million in cash and $38.6 million in seventeen-year notes guaranteed by the Central Bank of Chile at 9 per cent interest; there was a likelihood that the notes would be prepaid in less than two years.

Cerro also had $70 million in cash on its balance sheet and, as the Pritzkers were to point out in the prospectus of their forthcoming tender offer, a material part of Cerro's per-share book value of $44 a share was "represented by liquid assets." During the first six months of 1974 Cerro stock was trading at between $13 and $19 a share, considerably below book value. "Cerro has a lot of valuable assets if properly managed. It presents both an opportunity and problems," Jay said.

Murphy invited the Pritzkers in. Several other members of Cerro's board tendered their shares willingly.

In June, the Pritzkers' GL Corporation made a tender offer for 1.5 million shares of Cerro at $19 a share. The formula was the same as with Hammond. The $43 million needed to buy the tendered shares as well as those already bought by Jay early in 1974 was lent without security by the First National Bank of Chicago at one half of one per cent above the prime interest rate for two years (the prime rate was then 11.8 per cent). Citicorp, the New York bank, then shared the loan with the Chicago bank.

Again, the Pritzkers were borrowing the money to take over a company—albeit with the consent of management—and the acquired company would repay the loan. GL had a net asset value of $62 million. Cerro's shareholders' equity was $350 million. And once more, they had served notice that the company might be merged into another Pritzker company and turned private.

Cerro was the biggest fish the Pritzkers had ever attempted to swallow and it also had more irate stockholders, at least one of whom was employed by a major newspaper. This friendly take-over therefore did not go unnoticed. It was given ample airing in the press.

The stockholders were posed with the classic dilemma: to tender to the Pritzkers or wait for better days. Or to protest that, if the company went private or were otherwise stripped of its assets, they would have been deprived of the fair worth of their investment.

In theory, their indignation was justified. They did not, however, consider a reality that the Pritzkers saw. Cerro was a has-been company, at least as it was then composed. Shorn of its mining operations, its chances of bonanza profits were remote. The assets that looked so alluring to the Pritzkers or other would-be raiders were not likely to be rewarded in the stock market. There, exciting prospects and sparkling performance prompted a rise in stock prices; seldom did a hoard of cash or other liquid assets stir the market. Actually, as David Mahoney of Norton Simon Inc. was learning, Wall Street was made uncomfortable by uncommitted cash reserves.

There was therefore a rationale for a Cerro stockholder to put aside his vexation with the Pritzkers for buying his company out from under him and instead grab the tender money in a sinking stock market and invest it elsewhere. So many Cerro stockholders came to that conclusion that the Pritzkers had an awkward twenty-four hours after the tender offer expired, at 5 P.M. on July 16, 1974, as they figured out how many tendered shares they could accept. They had offered to purchase 1.5 million shares which would have given them working control of the company and they received tenders of 3.2 million shares.

But according to Section 382 of the Internal Revenue Code, they would have lost the benefit of carrying forward the company's pre-

vious tax losses if they had exceeded a certain percentage of ownership. That provision withdraws the privilege from a company that
substantially changes both the nature of its business and the number
of owners of its stock from the previous year. The loss of the copper
mines had altered Cerro's business, and so to be on the safe side the
Pritzkers settled on taking 2.8 million shares, or about 45 per cent
of the common stock.

In September 1974 Cerro and GL announced they had agreed in
principle to a merger between Cerro and GL's Marmon Group, subject to the approval of holders of two thirds of Cerro's outstanding
shares. The Cerro shares owned by Marmon would be voted in
favor of the merger only if a majority of other shares voted for it.
Whether the new Cerro-Marmon shares would be listed on a stock
exchange was not stated.

Then abruptly, on September 20, plans for the merger were suspended "until early in 1975." The excuse given was "the need to
give further consideration to various complex business accounting
and legal matters which are attendant upon a transaction of this
size."

The disgruntled shareholders who had not tendered their shares
and the press critics patted themselves on the back for having halted
a take-over. Had they consulted a securities law expert they would
have learned that a short-term swing in stock ownership by insiders,
such as the contemplated merger could have been construed, was
prohibited by Section 16B. of the Securities Exchange Act. The law
makes the insiders vulnerable to stockholder suits, something the
press had never mentioned.

In the meantime, however, the price of Cerro stock had dropped
seven points, piling up a paper loss for the Pritzkers of $25 million
on the Cerro stock while they were paying over 12 per cent interest
on money borrowed to acquire it. Furthermore, because of the
greater number of shares tendered than they had anticipated, the
size of the loan had increased from $43 million to $68 million.

With the shrinkage in the stock market value of Cerro and the
bulge in the size of the loan, the Pritzkers found themselves in the
unaccustomed position of having overpaid for something. Under
the swift change of circumstances, Cerro was no bargain.

Its price "was no longer reasonable," Jay admitted. Nor was
Hammond's. "We never leveraged like this before," he also conceded. "Leverage" was the financial maneuver with which countless

fortunes like the Pritzkers' had been made. The formula is "borrow to buy." As long as the property acquired yields enough income to cover the interest on the loan and the expenses of operating the property, the formula works. It is a glorious success when the prices of everything except the cost of the loan are rising. When the value of the property declines and the loan interest stays up, the leverage is reversed and the squeeze is on. The Pritzkers were in a squeeze considerably larger than when Jay was hedging cocoa beans back in the Rockwood days.

He talked about it calmly. Even if a merger with Cerro never came to pass, he said, "we can afford to pay the loan." The loan had been made to GL. Marmon, GL's biggest holding, was debt-free and throwing off earnings of $10 to $15 million a year on revenues of about $260 million. And with uncontested control of Cerro, they could run it as a subsidiary.

The graver problem with Cerro was its management. Jay had always said, "Management is the crux of anything. We're on the record of being management conscious."

Yet there was nothing in Cerro's management during Murphy's nearly five years of administration to inspire great hope. He was a man of the go-go sixties who could draw imaginative blueprints for conglomerate building. So far, the seventies seemed to call for a different kind of imagination and leadership. Yet the Pritzkers acted as though they were impotent to replace him. Angry stockholders to the contrary, they had a reputation among businessmen and bankers who dealt with them for being fair to the point of generosity. Once, in confessing that he was not an effective outside member of the board of directors of a company (such as Continental Air Lines) because he would not openly challenge management, Jay had said, half jestingly, "I believe you go with the guy who brought you." If you're unhappy, he added, you can resign from the board. Quietly, he meant. Not like Arthur Goldberg who had left the board of TWA making public statements about the faults of the director system.

And Gordon Murphy had brought the Pritzkers to Cerro. As a member of the Cerro board, which he had joined before the tender but after his first purchases of the stock, Jay did not demur when Murphy started renegotiating his already ample contract with terms that gave him the economic standing of an auto magnate rather than the head of an undistinguished company with revenues well below

$1 billion a year. A new five-year agreement signed on June 12, 1974, raised his annual compensation to $638,260.

So it seemed that the Pritzkers had bitten off a tough chunk of steer instead of the usual succulent tidbits. And they had strained some of the cardinal family principles. They had acted quickly and decisively—the preferred speed for wheeler-dealers—but perhaps this time haste had left undetected a few serious blemishes. Jay knew very little about the history of Cerro or of Gordon Murphy before the marriage banns were posted. "I'm not interested in the history of a company unless it impinges on the present," he had once said. He had looked only at balance sheets.

Without a conscious intention of aggrandizement, Jay had gone for big game where the family had usually hunted small to medium-size quarry, which is why, Jay said, "nobody paid attention to us before." He contemplated the future with surface equanimity. There was the pride of "grace under pressure," which another wealthy family named Kennedy had exerted in politics. It was the same for the Pritzkers in business deals. Win some, lose some.

There was no danger of any members of the family being chastised by the others. "If it works out, it's my deal. If it doesn't, it was yours anyhow," Jay said reciting one of the family mottoes with a smile.

Besides, he said with an air of resignation, "What else are we going to do?"

Except make deals.

A week before Christmas 1974 Cerro Corporation announced a management realignment. Robert Pritzker had been elected to the board and had been appointed chairman of a newly formed three-member executive committee, to serve with his brother Jay and C. Gordon Murphy.

Effective May 13, 1975, following the annual meeting of shareholders, Robert Pritzker would replace Murphy as president of Cerro. Murphy would continue as a consultant.

Apprised of the news by the *Wall Street Journal,* Robert Koenig, who had brought Murphy to Cerro in 1970 commented, "He ousted me. They ousted him. That's retribution for you."

But that was not the last of it. In mid-February 1975 the Pritzkers indicated their impatience. Without waiting until May, they sent Murphy packing. His resignation was announced with that of Charles B. Harding, the chairman. Robert Pritzker succeeded

Murphy as president, Jay replaced Harding as chairman. They did not spell out who was to be chief executive officer.

A spokesman explained the changes. "There's nothing going on that needs Mr. Murphy's personal attention. The Pritzkers can do the job just as well."

Murphy was reached at home by a reporter for the *Wall Street Journal*. "They paid out my contract and I'm at home," he said.

Once, when elaborating on the importance of management and his belief that it was less expensive to pay off and get rid of an unsatisfactory manager than suffer through the end of his contract, Jay Pritzker had said, "I'd rather send him around the world once." With his finger, he traced a voyage clockwise. "And then I can send him around twice." His finger moved counterclockwise.

When stockholders saw the proxy statement for the annual meeting, they learned that Murphy would be traveling de luxe. In exchange for his resignation, he received $1.95 million plus office space and secretarial assistance for six months at a cost to the corporation of $16,000.

Six stockholders filed suits challenging the take-over of Cerro and the payout to Murphy.

MINORITY REPORT

BLACK EXECUTIVES IN
NEW ROLE AT CUMMINS ENGINE

October 1973

A nearly all-white town of 27,000 famed mostly for its modern architecture and the Ku Klux Klan tradition of its environs seems an unlikely mecca for black executives hoping to rise in the corporate world.

Yet during the last eight years, some hundred black managers and executive trainees have moved to Columbus, Indiana, precisely for such professional achievement, and they have come despite their apprehensions about the setting. A black corporate middle class thus has been grafted onto a community whose nonwhite population previously consisted of about 400 unskilled, low-income people.

The newcomers were imported mostly by the town's dominant industrial employer, the Cummins Engine Company. The results have been mixed, and not always as expected.

"It's been really smooth, and the main reason is that they brought in a large number of the Harvard variety," observed a local newspaper editor.

From mid-1972 through the spring of 1973, blacks with highly regarded credentials were named to three of Cummins' corporate-officer slots—a minority representation thought to be one of the highest in American industry.

Delmar Barnes, forty-five years old, an accountant with tax expertise, was promoted to corporate comptroller. Ulric St. Clair Haynes, Jr., forty-two, a New York management consultant, bank director, and a member of various corporate and cultural boards, was appointed vice president for management development. James A. Joseph, thirty-eight, a Yale-educated clergyman and foundation director, was named vice president for corporate action. Also, in that period, a popular black candidate for corporation directorships, Franklin A. Thomas, thirty-nine, president of the Bedford-Stuyvesant Corporation, New York City, was elected to the Cummins board. William Norman, thirty-five, a retired Navy commander, was hired as director of corporate responsibility and William Mays, twenty-eight, as assistant to the president. Irma Seiferth, thirty-two, became college relations manager and the highest ranking black female in the company. She started at Cummins eight years ago as a clerk and has no college degree.

Cummins made these appointments in a disappointing year for earnings. In 1972 the diversified engine manufacturer had a scant profit of $8.2 million on sales of $521 million. Cummins blamed a two-month strike, price controls, and start-up expenses for its international expansion program. However, the company's sales and earnings in the first half of 1973 made new highs.

Cummins has avoided broadcasting its social performance for some of the same reasons as those expressed by other corporations in similar situations.

Employee relations at Cummins are already strained by rumors that the new minority members were lured by inflated salaries. Though few salaries are disclosed at Cummins, their pattern seems in line with current levels for sought-after candidates. For example, a state university M.B.A. with business experience is paid $17,000 a year. Ulric Haynes termed the rumors of bonanza pay "a national myth."

Furthermore, many companies believe publicity tends to generate lawsuits; most of the government's equal employment opportunity cases have been instituted against companies of some size and visibility, such as the American Telephone & Telegraph Company and Sears, Roebuck & Company.

Then too, J. Irwin Miller, Cummins' sixty-four-year-old chairman, major stockholder (40 per cent of the common stock is owned by his family), and the town's most influential citizen, is one of the nation's more unassuming multimillionaires.

Yet, without his deeply felt and insistently conveyed belief in social justice, the Cummins Engine Company would not have been able to attract blacks of such caliber.

"The chairman of the board is very much a humanitarian," said Bill Norman explaining why he had left the stimulating crucible of Washington, D.C. (where he was a special assistant to Admiral Elmo R. Zumwalt, Jr., Chief of Naval Operations) a few months ago, for this placid and ingrown Indiana community. At most parties in Columbus, a guest isn't asked where he works but rather in which department.

J. Irwin Miller is someone to be reckoned with in American business, and he has put his imprint on political, cultural, and religious zones as well. But he prefers to operate from the background. A dignified six-footer, with a Hoosier twang and a folksy air of diffidence, he tends to coerce by example rather than by barking directives.

A Republican party contributor who exercises independent voting habits and regularly vexes its conservative wing, he backed New York City Mayor John V. Lindsay's abortive bid for the presidency in 1972 and that of New York State Governor Nelson A. Rockefeller in 1968. *Esquire* magazine ran a cover story proposing J. Irwin Miller as the Republican candidate, entitled "Is It Too Late for a Man of Honesty, High Purpose and Intelligence to Be Elected President of the United States in 1968?" The party must have believed it was; Miller later appeared on President Nixon's so-called "Enemies List."

In the early 1960s the National Council of Churches of Christ in the United States elected a layman as its president for the first time. He was J. Irwin Miller and even after his term of office expired, he continued to wield significant influence. In the early 1970s lay activists on the council's staff provoked an inquiry into the social behavior of corporations whose common stocks were held in church investment portfolios. This research offensive led to shareholder resolutions that publicized such corporate activities and policies as operations in South Africa, where the government enforces racist policies, and job discrimination against minorities and women in plants and offices in the United States.

Miller displayed ambivalence toward these activists. Though he occasionally singled them out for praise, he let it be known that he did not want to be associated with outside advocates who were stirring up trouble for business. Miller indicated that the force of example from himself and his philanthropic foundations would be a more effective lever against his corporate peers. Both his foundations and the Ford Foundation, on which he served as a trustee, turned down applications for funding from the church groups mounting the corporate attacks.

In 1963 Miller had helped to organize the first civil rights march on Washington. He has channeled his family's philanthropies into support for racial equality and minority development.

As an architecture buff, he has put his home town on the map as the American city with the highest per-capita distinction in public building design. It started in 1935 after he had returned from taking a bachelor's degree at Yale and a master's at Oxford. Miller prodded his father to have the building committee of the First Christian Church hire an architect of courage and note. They chose the late Eliel Saarinen, who designed for them a house of worship with a rectangular nave and a brick campanile eighteen stories high. Its geometric purity appalled the citizens of Columbus, who since then, however, have had to grow accustomed to even more astonishing architecture. Later on, Saarinen's son, Eero, a Yale classmate of Miller's, designed the North Christian Church in the shape of the hexagonal Star of David and capped it with a soaring, cross-topped spire to denote the Judaic origin of Christianity. Columbus dubbed it the "holy oil can," but by that time not without a certain pride.

Other architects of international repute such as I. M. Pei, John Carl Warnecke, and Kevin Roche have designed schools, libraries, and civic edifices for Columbus, while some of the town's nineteenth-century commercial structures have been painstakingly renovated.

The Cummins Engine Foundation, a corporate trust, guarantees the architectural fees for any public building in Columbus. Over the last twenty years, the foundation has paid out more than $2 million for this purpose.

Though he is chairman and chief executive officer of Cummins Engine Company, J. Irwin Miller has his office in a restored building belonging to the Irwin-Union Bank & Trust Company of which he is also chairman. His personal wealth, which has been estimated in the low hundreds of millions, derives from the prescience of several of his ancestors on the frontiers of railroading, real estate, corn refining, banking, and industrial machinery.

In 1919 William G. Irwin, Miller's Uncle Will, staked Clessie L. Cummins, an inventor with an idea for building a better oil engine. Cummins perfected Rudolf Diesel's engine which had been patented in 1892 and used for pumps and agricultural equipment so that it could be applied to transportation. The company established a niche for itself supplying power for yachts until the stock market crash of 1929 wiped out that market.

After Irwin Miller came home from being educated in the East and abroad and settled down to tending this sickly member of his family's numerous business interests, the Cummins Engine Company penetrated the highway truck market. World War II gave the engine a chance to show its performance on the international supply routes. Today Cummins Engine is the world's largest independent producer of diesel engines for highway trucks, locomotives, and mining and many industrial applications.

Because of its size (in 1973, it was 234th on *Fortune*'s list of the nation's 500 largest industrial corporations), its profitability, its ingenuity in manufacturing, and its treatment of people, Cummins has been a magnet for ambitious, young men on the corporate make.

It was Irwin Miller's credibility, though, "and the very bright people at the top" that caused black men like Bill Norman to think "the location was a secondary factor."

"It's the people, the company, and its philosophy that take priority," he said.

Like the other black supertalents at Cummins, Norman makes it clear that this is an interlude in his life. He hopes it will be a valuable and instructive one and that he will return to Washington one day in a political appointment in government. "For most of us who came here, Cummins Engine represented something different from the norm as an experience in business environment. I want to take this experience and use it for other things," he said.

The top management of Cummins is believed to share Irwin Miller's convictions about racial equality and social justice. The company's commitment to achieving "population parity in the work force" is spelled out in the annual report. But no one pretends that the message has thoroughly seeped down to middle management.

"I'm disturbed about the placing of minorities," one white manager said. "They may not all be qualified."

Everyone at Cummins knows that Del Barnes's sole rival for

comptroller was Adrienne Savage, a white woman. Mrs. Savage came to Cummins twenty-two years ago straight out of college and with a degree in accounting. She advanced fairly rapidly up to her present job as director of corporate financial accounting and reporting, which she now feels is "probably the end of the line."

Openly disappointed at losing out at the comptroller's spot for which she considers herself qualified, she discussed the decision with top management. "I asked the vice president for finance why, and we had a candid, blunt conversation. Part of the management group thought it was more important to have a black at this time, I was told. Although in some other areas it was felt his strengths may have outweighed mine." Barnes's tax experience and analytic ability were mentioned.

"Del called me before he accepted, to ask how I would feel about it," she said. "I appreciated the fact he was concerned enough to do that. He said, 'I couldn't do the job without you,' and I said, 'Never fear.'"

Acceptance of the blacks was encouraged somewhat by the corporate policy of at least surface egalitarianism in other areas. Cummins has done away with reserved parking for executives. There are no executive washrooms. And executive offices are no more than open recesses along distant walls. A former warehouse contains the corporate headquarters.

Everyone is on a first name basis. "Except Mr. Miller. There's something about Mr. Miller," a very junior executive said.

For most of the black professionals, their apprehension about living in a small, southern-minded community (the nearest cosmopolitan center, an hour's drive away, is Louisville, Kentucky) proved unfounded. In Columbus, they discovered, monotony is a more serious problem than racial adjustments.

The tenor of the boredom is uneven. Both *Last Tango in Paris* and *Deep Throat*, the two films that made pornography chic and expensive in New York in 1973, played in Columbus, and *Last Tango* came back for a second run.

One of the top black executives noted with some irony that he was unable to hire a black for domestic work. He believes the low-income resident blacks of Columbus resent the presence of the newcomers. He was able to engage a white cleaning woman easily.

The activism of some of the earlier black arrivals at Cummins erased some of the expected problems, such as finding housing.

Columbus now has an open-housing ordinance, and almost all of the new black families live tranquilly in prosperous, mostly white sections of town and countryside. The excellence of the company-donated 350-acre recreation site, Ceraland, and other public facilities has made the question of membership in this area's two country clubs not worth bothering about.

DELMAR BARNES

Delmar Barnes, the comptroller, came to Cummins in February 1967 as manager of tax planning.

"My coming was fortuitous," he said.

Barnes grew up in Washington, D.C., received a bachelor's degree in business administration from Virginia State College in 1950 and after serving in the U. S. Army Ordnance Department in the Cleveland district, became an agent for the Internal Revenue Service there. He did graduate work at Western Reserve University and became a certified public accountant.

Barnes was also a football buff. One Sunday evening in the winter of 1965 he found himself on a plane bound from Cleveland to Indianapolis seated between two other football aficionados. They were John T. Hackett and James A. Henderson, executive vice presidents of Cummins Engine. The three started talking football, and before the plane landed, the two Cummins executives also knew the professional credentials of their fellow passenger.

The airplane encounter slipped out of Barnes's mind until the following May when he received a letter from the pair stating that Cummins was expanding its internal audit and tax department and that there might be a place for him in it. It took eight months to persuade him to accept.

"I had reservations about moving to Columbus, you better believe it," Barnes said. "I had great apprehensions about the effect it would have on my family. My wife was less apprehensive than I, though. Pauline was from Cleveland but she had lived in small towns. My kids didn't care." Mike and Cynthia Barnes were then eleven and eight, respectively.

"We talked candidly with the Cummins people. I inquired in the community. I asked several ministers. It was all positive but still I had concern. Yet, it was a challenge professionally. I was comfortable where I was but I had gone as far as I could in federal service.

Could I do the job here and would I like it, I kept asking myself. Job-wise, it's been a positive experience. I proved I could do it," he said.

From manager of tax planning, he was promoted to tax counsel, then to corporate comptroller. He is responsible for the development and audit of accounting systems, financial reporting, taxes, and corporate auditing. He reports to the vice president for finance which, logically, is the next rung of the ladder and a post no black man has ever held in a major industrial corporation.

"I've had great rapport from the top down, and—knock wood—I've never had a people problem here," he said. "I was told before I came here, 'You will be with people who are sympathetic,' and I have been. I don't feel there has been resentment. In the tax department I could create relationships within the company. When I was promoted to this job, there were all sorts of phone calls, telegrams, and handshakes from well-wishers. I'm sure I enjoy their support," he said.

Nor does Barnes think he has reached a dead end as comptroller. "I harbor hope that something will open up," he said. "This company is very dynamic." Then he added, "I wish we were ten miles outside San Francisco, though."

As soon as he said that, Barnes regretted the statement lest it sound ungracious. And so he expounded on what he tells other blacks who are weighing whether to accept job offers from Cummins in Columbus:

"I tell them they must compare Cummins with other companies in the community as well as on a national basis and that if they do, Cummins would give a good account of itself.

"I tell them the job satisfaction will be there. But there's an after-five problem. If a small town lifestyle will be difficult for them and they know that, then I tell them they'd better look closely."

Barnes still has "some reservations about the small community. Things happen here that get noticed where in other areas there would be anonymity."

He was alluding to a minor but still disagreeable episode. Pauline Barnes had been stopped by a policeman and given a traffic ticket for going through a red light at 4:30 A.M. She was chauffeuring their son, Mike (a teen-ager who was still below the legal age for night driving) to a job that started at 5 A.M. Mrs. Barnes's receipt of a traffic ticket was published in the local newspaper in what Barnes felt was an unwarranted play of an unimportant event.

When the Barneses first moved to Columbus there were a few unpleasant incidents. Barnes found he had to go to Louisville to get a haircut. Local barbers said they "weren't trained to cut Negro hair." Several of the black professionals got together and had that problem resolved through the town's Human Rights Commission.

Before the same sort of collective effort had succeeded in getting an open-housing law passed, the search for a home in what was then a tight market proved to be tedious. "It took six months of looking. We viewed fifty houses," he said.

On the other hand, Barnes was invited to join the country club, but he declined. "I didn't need the prestige," he said.

The dimensions of small-town life gave him great pause and still do. "By and large, your friends are Cummins people," he said. "In Cleveland I knew people from all walks of life. There were revitalizing forces, different areas of concern. It gave you new enthusiasm. There were people on the sidewalks, people knocking on your door. Here you have to drive to see someone or to get somewhere.

"In the city we always had choices. We don't have them here. When we came, there was only one and a half movies in town. Or we could go to Cincinnati and add three hours' traveling time to our evening. Three times a year I go to the pro football games there. Here, there is a high school program or I can go to the pro basketball games in Indianapolis.

"I find I have an impulse to leave, less and less," he admitted. "I'm forty-five. I guess I'm adjusting to slowing down to the point of taking it in stride," he added with a faintly rueful smile.

In Cleveland, most of Barnes's friends were black. Here, "fiftyfifty or more are white," he said. "I suppose that's a plus about Columbus. It confirms the fact that it's the person, rather than the complexion, that counts. My children have tipped to an even greater scale because, after all, the black population in town is one per cent or less."

He is a past president of the William R. Laws Foundation, through which many of the black executives at Cummins have tried to upgrade the education and motivation of Columbus blacks.

Barnes reflected before going on. "I suppose I wish there was a greater balance for my children. I can see changes in their mode of life. They don't identify with things black. Take music style. My son

is interested in music. But more in the ballads of Simon and Gar-
funkel. In an urban setting, he'd have more allegiance to black
artists like Aretha Franklin. It's not a great tragedy. But when I was
growing up in Washington, I could go to theaters and stage shows
that were predominantly black. As well as to white ones.

"My kids have gotten away from looking at the numbers or ranking people. They're moving toward something new and yet I lament
they are moving away from something that should be part of them.

"Columbus is a difficult place to create a unified black experience. Though there is a small number of blacks who might like to do
so, there is no concentration so if they could do something, it
wouldn't be spontaneous. The smallness prevents a black focal
point.

"That wasn't what it was supposedly all about—people living
where they want to—was it?" he mused.

ULRIC ST. CLAIR HAYNES, JR.

"Yolande, you're too pretty for Columbus," a neighbor told the
Haitian-born wife of Ulric St. Clair Haynes, Jr. In New York Yolande Haynes had been a fashion model and actress. In Columbus
she blooms as an exotic flower.

If Yolande Haynes's beauty and temperament have been un-
settling for Columbus, her husband's looks and comportment have
stirred more sophisticated circles. Well over six feet tall, even featured, and trimly bearded in Vandyke style, Rick Haynes's movie-
star handsomeness would be disturbing enough in most social and
corporate contexts. As he once acknowledged, "Everyone knows
Negroes are supposed to be oversexed, superathletes." Most blacks
have had to fight that stereotype in the business arena. But then,
Haynes's self-assured outspokenness, backed by intelligence and
impeccable professional credentials, make it impossible to ignore
what he is saying.

For example, he scored as "absurd and ill-conceived" the well-
publicized attempt of the Episcopal Church to put shareholder pressure on General Motors Corporation to withdraw its operations in
South Africa.

"Alas, it is all too typical of the white liberal establishment to em-
bark on a course of action for the benefit of the 'oppressed' without
ever consulting the oppressed," he wrote, stating his point of view in

the New York *Times* in the spring of 1971. Citing the case of Pola-
roid Corporation, he argued that an American company could deal
the most effective blow to South Africa's policies of racial separa-
tion by improving the pay scales, technical qualifications, and status
of its nonwhite employees in that country. Because of its shortage
of skilled labor, the white government would be forced, from economic necessity, to tolerate such breaches in the wall of apartheid,
he maintained.

Haynes was born in Brooklyn, New York, in 1931 of British
West Indian parents. He grew up in what was to become the all-too-
famous ghetto of Bedford-Stuyvesant.

He never forgets his origins though most people who meet him
assume he must come from the narrow sliver of the black aristocracy. He once recalled his feelings of outrage when he was invited to
a meeting at the exclusive Metropolitan Club in New York and
found himself being served by a waiter who was one of his father's
old friends. The double awareness that he was one of the few black
men invited as a guest within the club's restricted portals and that
his father's friend was overcome with pride at seeing him there
depressed him profoundly.

In order to get an education of better quality than his home district afforded, he fibbed about his address so that he could be admitted to Midwood High School, then one of the borough's best public
secondary schools, situated in a middle-class Jewish section.

He went from there to higher levels of New England's academic
elite, first to Amherst College, where he was one of two blacks in his
entering class, and then to the Yale Law School. With his LL.B. in
hand in 1956, he submitted to seventy-eight interviews at white law
firms from which he received not one job offer. The only opportunity worth taking was as an executive assistant with the New York
State Department of Commerce in the administration of liberal
Democratic Governor Averell Harriman. During the next ten
years Haynes moved to a series of jobs with the United Nations, the
Ford Foundation, the United States Department of State, and the
White House National Security Council Staff, building an expertise
in African affairs and acquiring the finishing touch of travel and residence abroad.

A cocktail party conversation with a tax lawyer for an international oil company about developing local managerial talent in
Third World countries led to an introduction to Spencer Stuart, a

management consultant. In 1966, just as big business was starting its frantic search for black professionals and managers, Stuart's firm gave Haynes financial backing as a minority executive recruiter. "Please don't refer to me as a black headhunter," he quipped. Haynes left government for private enterprise, setting up his Management Formation Inc., a Madison Avenue-based subsidiary of Spencer Stuart and Associates.

He convinced black professionals to quit the safer shelters of government, university, and nonprofit institutions for managerial jobs with white companies. He tried to persuade the companies to make the jobs more than window dressing.

In the process, he became an authority on minority recruitment and development and equal job opportunity and a visiting lecturer at the Harvard Graduate School of Business Administration. He also gained visibility with the Establishment and was invited to join the boards of Marine Midland Bank of New York, Unionmutual Stock Life Insurance Company of New York, and several nonprofit organizations such as Lincoln Center. He and Franklin Thomas were the first blacks to take directors' seats on that summit of social and cultural power in New York. But Haynes also donated his time and energies to black causes as a trustee of Hampton Institute and treasurer of the Dance Theatre of Harlem.

Having become what he called "everybody's black director" did not keep Haynes from recognizing the shallow effectiveness of minority representation on boards. "Board membership has not been as powerful a push to effect change as one might have thought," he said in 1972. He suggested that some of the appointments to boards of public figures, such as civil rights leaders (or widows of civil rights leaders) were "cosmetic." "I feel it is more important that blacks who serve on boards, in addition to serving for their blackness, also serve a disciplinary function, such as being a marketing expert or a textile expert," he said.

He went on to say that the addition of blacks to boards must be "carefully orchestrated in one symphonic piece," with an effort to get them into middle management and above.

Privately, Haynes was discouraged by big business' showing in the latter regard. Later, he was to reveal that he was emotionally drained by the two-faced performance that consisted of grand declarations of corporate purpose and resolve and next-to-nothing delivery of responsible positions.

After he had left the "headhunting" game, he recalled his dismay at clients' unwillingness to put their money where their mouths were. Unlike employment agencies, executive recruiters are paid by employers, usually 25 to 30 per cent of the first year's compensation of the candidate they find for the job. So Haynes was in a position to contradict the widely held belief that blacks were being paid extravagant sums to integrate white companies.

The Cummins Engine Company had been a client from the beginning of his association with Stuart, and when it made him an offer, in the fall of 1972, of a job that he was assured was not the usual minority job, he decided he could not refuse it.

"I always wanted to merge my interest in business with my international experience," he told those who assumed that he had been sitting near the top of the power structure in New York and couldn't imagine why he would climb down to go to a hick town in the Midwest.

"I was overextended," he said after he was settled in Columbus, referring to his crowded calendar of chic associations and activities in the East. "I was being useful for symbolic reasons but not having fun."

Besides, he had been divorced from his first wife for various reasons of incompatibility, including his desire to have children, and now married to Yolande. She wanted a family and wasn't terribly scared of tackling Columbus.

Yolande Haynes had gone from her native Haiti to Miami in 1962 to work as a department store buyer, then on to New York where she swam with the growing tide of interest in black and Oriental fashion models. She had been a mannequin for Emilio Pucci in his salon in Florence and had acted in the movie, *For Love of Ivy,* with Sidney Poitier.

Having seen and conquered several large ponds, she saw little terror in a few years' sojourn in a small one in Indiana—even if signs calling GET US OUT OF THE U.N. embellished the cornfields and if every once in a while the Ku Klux Klan burned a cross in a town forty miles away from Columbus.

Besides, her husband said, "It will be refreshing not to be presented with ambiguity in race relations. In New York you never knew whether a taxi driver won't give you a ride because he's a racist or for some other reason.

"The South is much better than the North in race relations. The

North is unregenerate," he said. He had analyzed the terrain and had decided that whereas Indianapolis is midwestern, Columbus, just forty-five minutes' drive to the south, was really southern.

So the Hayneses rented out their brownstone house in the Clinton Hills section of Brooklyn, where they didn't dare permit their two-and-a-half-year-old, French-speaking daughter Alexandra to stray from the yard, and moved to Columbus where she and the family dog could nonchalantly walk a half a mile in the countryside to a friend's house.

For $57,000 they bought a three-bedroom, contemporary-style brick house one and a half miles from Rick's office and furnished it with their Museum of Modern Art-caliber modern furniture and African sculpture. Yolande planted a vegetable garden in the spring. A gifted cook of international leanings, she wonders sometimes whether Columbus would support a first-class restaurant if she opened one "to keep busy." So far, she fills her days chauffeuring Alexandra to and from her Montessori nursery school, antique hunting, and looking for bargains in the supermarket. "For wives who are not self-sufficient, it could be stifling here. You have to make your own stimulation," she said.

She and Alexandra have accompanied Rick on several of his trips across the country and abroad.

The Hayneses probably spend more time together here and in a less frenzied environment than they did in New York. They don't have to struggle to secure time on a tennis court or to run the social and philanthropic superachiever's course. Rick gave up his New York cultural board memberships except for the Dance Theatre of Harlem and became involved with a local arts council. "I'd like to bring dance here," he said and added slyly, "just as long as it includes square dancing."

He sometimes misses the exhilaration of New York, "the thrill of survival." But then, he remembers, "In New York, I was twice stopped by cops for jogging. In New York, a black man running is a criminal."

Perhaps there have been a slight or two here. Last summer the Hayneses invited a hundred friends, neighbors, and Cummins colleagues for a buffet dinner. Yolande ordered a rib roast of beef at the supermarket and when she offered to pay for it with a $17-check drawn on a local bank, the butcher wouldn't accept it. "I don't know you," he said.

"Was it because I'm black?" she wondered and then concluded, "No, it was because he was stupid."

Haynes won't speculate about his long-range potential with Cummins. "I'm of that generation of young executives who don't feel committed to one corporation for life," he said. "Those days are gone forever."

JAMES A. JOSEPH

James A. Joseph, vice president for corporate action, also prefers not to predict his future in the company. "I'm still adjusting to being a businessman," he said.

His title embraces responsibilities in corporate philanthropy, governmental relations and public affairs, community relations, human resources development, and affirmative action programs. Most of these are areas traditionally assigned to blacks in corporate showcases, but because of Cummins' exceptionally strong social commitment and multinational character, the title carries more influence and dollar power than it might seem. Besides, Joseph is also executive director of the Cummins Engine Foundation which disburses over $1 million a year in grants and contributions to educational, religious, and civil rights organizations.

In 1954 the directors of the Cummins Engine Company decided to contribute up to 5 per cent of pretax profits to the foundation "to affirm and promote humane living" and have since maintained this rare level of corporate philanthropy. The national average in annual charitable giving by corporations is less than 1 per cent, a figure deemed excessive by some stockholders, such as Evelyn Y. Davis, the sensation-seeking New York gadfly who never fails to offer a few proxy resolutions against charitable contributions during the annual corporate shareholder meeting season.

Joseph transferred to the corporate roster of Cummins from the foundation side. He had been associate director and later president of the Association of Foundations, which comprises the company foundation and two Miller family foundations in Columbus. Between those two terms of office, he was chaplain of the Claremont Colleges in California. "Just because I'm an ordained minister, no one should get the idea I'm a corporate chaplain," he said.

He was born in Opelousas, Louisiana, in 1935, was a big man on campus at Southern University in Baton Rouge, served as an officer in the U. S. Army for two years, then collected fellowships at the Yale University Divinity School from which he graduated in 1963.

During the next four years, he taught at Stillman College in Alabama and the Claremont Colleges and also led groups of students and local citizens in protest and demonstration efforts to desegregate public facilities in the South.

While he was working with church-related civil rights groups in Tuscaloosa, Alabama, in 1963 and in the Mississippi Delta in 1965, he was threatened and harassed by the Ku Klux Klan.

In 1967 he was coaxed to Columbus by Philip C. Sorensen, the idealistic lawyer and one-time lieutenant governor of Nebraska whose brother, Theodore, had been counsel to President John F. Kennedy. Philip Sorensen was taking the executive directorship of the Association of Foundations and wanted Joseph to be his associate.

"Some of my friends thought I was out of my mind to come to southern Indiana, the birthplace of the Klan," he said. "And the John Birch Society was founded in Indianapolis," he added. "But I've never had an encounter here with the Klan. When they had a parade here in town last year, no one paid much attention."

Joseph stayed in Columbus for two years as associate director of the foundation, then went back to the campus as chaplain at Claremont. In 1970, when Sorensen resigned the foundation post to become chairman of Campaign GM, the spearhead of the stockholder movement for corporate social responsibility, Joseph was asked back to Columbus to succeed him, thereby becoming the first black to head a major foundation.

He was enticed by the foundations' triple thrust in religion, minority, and community development affairs, but he also had foreboding about their small-town setting.

"My wife and I were used to an urban or a campus lifestyle," he said. Doris Joseph is a Vassar graduate whom he had met in New Haven when he was at Yale and she was a social worker there.

"And I had all kinds of apprehension that first time in '67," he said. "But I was surprised and delighted to find a number of people like me who had the same apprehensions and a number of natives who were pretty open.

"I came because of the challenge. It was the kind I wanted to accept at this moment in history," he said. Furthermore, the schools were good. The Josephs have two children, Jeffrey, now ten, and Denise, four.

In 1967 the Josephs had some problems in buying a house. "The usual things," he said with a smile. And from 1967 to 1969 he had worked to get the open housing ordinance passed in Columbus, to change the educational curriculum, and to bring an infusion of black teaching talent to the schools, "to more accurately depict our heritage."

So when the Josephs returned in 1970 after the Southern California interlude, Columbus had become somewhat more open and diverse. "The second time we came, we made the decision on the basis of knowing the community," he said. "But we still had some apprehension," he recalled. "The first day we arrived, our son went to play with kids on the block and one called him 'nigger.' He was seven. It made us a little more apprehensive. But he since became close friends with them."

Joseph and his family are in Columbus because, he says, "Basically, I'm interested in the use of power for social change.

"In 1960 the arena for social change was the church and civil rights. Then the focus became the university. Now it's clear that the center of power and the source of influencing change is the multinational corporation."

The post of vice president for corporate action is a new one. He is supposed to set a style of operation for corporate social accounting on an international scale. Internally, questions of corporate responsibility will be assessed in regard to acquisitions and mergers as well as within the company's existing divisions. Externally, the policies of foreign governments will have to be considered. One of the projects under his aegis is a reappraisal of Cummins' operations in South Africa.

Although Columbus "has always been rather unique, an oasis in the desert," he said, referring again to the historical role of the Klan in southern Indiana, Jim Joseph does not claim that racism has vanished among the 12,000 employees of the Cummins Engine Company. "All I ask is that it not be part of official policy," he said. "With the very progressive top management attitude here, though, I think you can bank on that.

"But there's another kind of problem for me. I go to outside meetings as vice president of this company. Inside, I'm also on the policy committee and function on the decision making level. But at a meeting of my peers from other corporations, I'm usually the youngest as well as the only black. And I have a different background from the others. I consider myself a social scientist working with business to determine by what means it can be socially responsible.

"The people I encounter at these meetings don't have that background. I'm also pretty outspoken and I raise resentment, whether because I'm black or because I'm young, I'm not always sure. Sometimes it's overtly because I'm black.

"But I'm always the guy that brings them the challenging word. I don't emphasize the positive," he said.

Jim Joseph doesn't speculate where this will lead. "I can't predict where society is going," he said. "I'm committed to influencing the use of the multinational corporation. For the time being, I'm committed to the corporate life.

"I don't see myself as president of a multinational corporation," he said. "But then I never saw myself as vice president either. I never conceived of the possibility of working from the perspective I am.

"The question some of my friends ask is, have I sold out?" Joseph worries about that and whether a black man in his position is in danger of losing his soul. "I could become satisfied with the status quo and cease to be the internal critic which is the role I'm playing now. Or I could get tired of the frustration."

In a speech to a teachers' conference in Indianapolis, Joseph identified himself as neither an integrationist nor a separatist. "I prefer to think of myself as a militant in the tradition of Du Bois and Douglass, belonging to the same company as the martyred Malcolm, Martin, and Medgar," he said.

On that occasion he was discussing what he called the "misplaced debate on separatism versus integration."

Perhaps prophetically for his tenure in the corporate life, he said, "The problem for any black man, wherever he works or lives, is to maintain his right to be himself. When his self-autonomy is threatened by his involvement in multiracial institutions, he must retain the right to disengage himself rather than compromise his principles as a person or his pride in his heritage."

WILLIAM MAYS

"Architecture doesn't mean anything to me, and even the money wouldn't count if I thought I was going to sit here for the next ten years," declared twenty-eight-year-old William Mays, who weighed the Cummins offer to become assistant to its thirty-nine-year-old president, Henry B. Schacht, against bids from Xerox, Dow Chemical, Eli Lilly, and Procter & Gamble. (Mays had worked at Lilly and P&G before returning to Indiana University to earn his M.B.A. degree.)

"I didn't know a diesel from a gasoline engine," he said. The presence of the three black officers—Barnes, Haynes, and Joseph—tipped the scale in Cummins' favor.

"I don't know of any other corporation where you can touch a black who is in a position to do something," Mays said. "Del Barnes is really the comptroller here. Without his signature certain things don't happen. If I'm going to be an ice breaker, I'd rather break ice from the top down, as I think a black can do here."

Mays described his job as "a training exposure position from which I will move in a year to a line position, probably in marketing or sales. Most blacks have a tendency to move into staff positions, but I prefer to be on the firing line," he said.

Mays is the first black to hold the prized presidential assistant's job. He acknowledges: "If I were a guy with the same ability and not black, I might not have been able to touch these strings. There's nothing particularly outstanding about me.

"In the past, blacks were not able to touch these strings. It was drilled into us that we were going to fail. We didn't have a history of success in business. My family didn't sit around reading the *Wall Street Journal*. Many white people we're competing with have this advantage.

"I overcame this at P&G. I did well and it motivated me to go to business school. I had sales responsibility for a million-dollar territory when I was twenty-three. But I said, I'm still not moving as fast as I should be.

"I wouldn't have come to Cummins Engine if not for the three black vice presidents," he said.

THE SEIFERTHS

"There is no significance to the three black officers, because blacks don't move up in this corporation," asserted Jesse Seiferth, Jr. "I have no great thought that some day I'll be a director," he said. (At Cummins, as in many companies, director is the middle managerial rank just below vice president and officer.) "And you won't find any black in middle management who thinks he's going to be a director."

He came to Cummins in 1965 as an executive trainee in the first wave of black recruits. He had just graduated from Tougaloo College, a black institution in his home state of Mississippi. He was the first graduate of his school to be recruited by a major industrial company. "I wanted to be more than a Mississippi teacher," he said. "I had high expectations because I didn't know anything about business," he said with a bitter edge to his voice.

Irma, his wife and kindergarten sweetheart in Natchez, worked to put him through college. When they moved to Columbus she started at Cummins as a clerk at the bottom of the hourly wage scale while he entered at the bottom of the salaried rung. "She closed the gap," he said.

"I've gone further than any black who came in as a college trainee but I haven't been promoted all along like my white counterparts," he asserted.

His ambitions lie in finance and operations. After the initial six-month training program, he says, he "bounced from one area to another," from computer programming to corporate reporting analysis, never getting enough responsibility and training. "Even the hourly employees were getting promoted. I concluded I had to get out. I had to go back to school to do better."

He took a leave of absence from Cummins to study for his M.B.A. at the University of Indiana while his wife kept working to support him and their two daughters. "I thought I could use my schooling as leverage," he said.

Since returning to Cummins with his master's degree in 1971, he has continued internal job-hopping. "I don't know where it's going to lead," he said. "I feel I've got a well-rounded background and still I wonder where I'm going. I've interviewed other companies, but they offered entry level jobs as though I'd never worked."

Meanwhile Irma Seiferth's career took a startling upward turn. In 1970 she asked to be admitted to a program for training hourly employees for exempt jobs. From there she advanced swiftly in the personnel department. In her current post she supervises a staff of campus recruiters and travels to leading universities to conduct interviews. No one notices her lack of a college degree. Almost everyone is taken by her intelligence, her easy manner, and her wide grasp of issues. Irma Seiferth's dynamism and her manifest destiny for success are all the more striking when encountered alongside her husband's brooding defeatism.

"I'm a woman," she said, jokingly accounting for her achievement.

"She's in personnel," said her husband. "If I had a choice again, I'd be in the nontechnical side."

"The nontechnical people get more promotions. We know where the conservatives are in most companies, on the technical side," Irma Seiferth elaborated. "There is a frustration problem for most blacks in still predominantly white companies," she said with matter-of-fact sadness.

The Seiferths' combined incomes amount to $35,000 a year. It isn't finances that makes them unhappy, they say. It's Jesse Seiferth's job.

Moreover, they find little satisfaction in their after-work social environment. Their first five years in Columbus, they lived in apartments. Then they built a house. "At first the neighbors all came over—out of curiosity," Irma said. "Since then they've stayed away. I don't initiate friendships. I've been hurt too many times."

The Seiferths were instrumental in gaining the passage of the open-housing ordinance and Jesse was the guinea pig in a test case before the Human Rights Commission involving the unwillingness of barbers to cut the blacks' hair. Irma served as a member of the Columbus Human Rights Commission for three years.

By now the Seiferths have spent eight of the fourteen years of their marriage in Columbus and Jesse says, "This is the only place we've been where we had such a situation as this as far as friends. It makes you wonder who you could depend on in an emergency." Even when they were stationed at an army base in Georgia during Jesse's military service, they found the predominantly white community more open-hearted.

As for the blacks in Columbus, "they have their own problems," Irma said. "It's a very status-conscious community. A phoney kind of atmosphere."

She worries most about what it will do to her daughters, Karen, thirteen, and Gina, ten. Especially the older one. "I want her to have a dual exposure to dating black boys as well as white, and this she won't have in Columbus," she said fretfully. "I don't want white boys to exploit my daughters."

THEODORE JONES

Houston-born Theodore Jones asks himself if his lifestyle and training in industrial relations will hamper his upward mobility in the corporation. At twenty-five, he has a degree in sociology from Notre Dame University and two years of personnel experience as a counselor to Cummins' factory and clerical employees. Most of them are white. (Because of its location, Cummins has been far less successful in attracting minorities for its plant work force than for its managerial jobs.)

A number of the employees are troubled, and alcoholism is a problem Jones frequently deals with. But many are disconcerted by having to discuss personal matters with a black man like Jones.

"A lot of people are up-tight about psychology—'Are you a shrink?' they ask me—and about the shoes I wear and the way I comb my hair," he said. His husky form is heightened by a lofty Afro and wine-colored platform boots.

"I've had people who would rather talk with another person than me. It's nitpicking," he said. "People appreciate the old shuffling stereotype. Some of the general foremen say I'm too cocky. Some of the hourly people question my credentials. A doctor who's a GP prescribes barbiturates for an alcoholic and I come along and question the dosage."

Jones has been with Cummins for two years. His first assignment was in its Fleetguard division in Cookeville, Tennessee, which has a population of 14,000 and an academic enclave, Tennessee Technological University. Life for a black in the company, he said, was "like a plantation.

"But I liked it because I had a good supervisor and I wanted a good job opportunity in a new area of the country. And I was able to engage in different things. I took the racism for granted."

The offer to transfer to Columbus included an increase in pay. But for him and his wife, a Purdue University graduate who grew up in Cleveland, it has also presented "more of a hassle in terms of housing and interaction than Tennessee."

"The games people play," he said, recalling their home-hunting experiences, under the auspices of the company's housing service. Exorbitant rentals were asked of them, he said, and when they accepted one, the owner decided he'd rather sell than rent. After five months, the Joneses moved to Indianapolis where he is studying for a master's degree in industrial psychology at Purdue and commuting to work in Columbus.

"Of course, I think in terms of upward mobility here. This company is M.B.A.- and Ivy League-oriented. I don't have Ivy. Is there a possibility for me to get on the fast track, or will I be refrigerated?

"I'm beginning to think you have to buy into the whole ball game—the legitimate area with legitimate friends, the Little League and the North Christian Church [Irwin Miller's congregation]. Or you don't make it."

JAMES C. NICHOLAS

James Nicholas weighed the offer he received from the Cummins Engine Company in the spring of 1972 with the slide-rule precision and objective self-interest that the Harvard Graduate School of Business Administration teaches its students. Ask not only what you can do for the company as what the company can do for you, might well be the B-School motto.

Nicholas was twenty-nine when he took his M.B.A. degree and the Cummins offer. He was married and the father of three children and had no time to waste in getting on with his career.

Raised in Maryland, he had served four years in the Air Force directly after graduating from high school. He had worked for RCA as a data acquisition technician while earning his bachelor's degree in business administration at Morgan State College in Baltimore. Then came the grueling two years at Harvard, with its implied promise of the inside track on the big-business route. Nicholas' major was in marketing management.

Of the jobs offered him on graduating, he chose the job as senior automotive planning analyst at Cummins, partly because of the community. He was convinced that Columbus had a "top-notch educational system" for his children, who range in age from seven to ten. "Then, other things being equal, Cummins Engine gave me the opportunity to advance more quickly than other institutions because it is not as bureaucratic, not as strait-laced. I ascribe this to its being multinational, which also had the advantages of expanding my horizon. The management is young and seems to be enlightened and progressive.

"Intermeshed with the style of living for the children was the fact

I wouldn't be distracted by commuting and urban problems. A man has to spend as much time at work as he can in the early years.

"My master goal is advancing to general management, if not at Cummins Engine then with another company. I decided that Cummins Engine will provide me a better vehicle to advance than Procter & Gamble."

Nicholas' wife is a clerk in the company's research center. "Being black, she doesn't have that many friends to partake of teas and social life," he said dispassionately.

"The social factor is important to the enterprising young businessman, from the time he awakens until night, and most blacks seem to be categorically excluded from that," he declared.

"Specifically at Cummins Engine, there seems to be more obstacles in our way than for the whites, but I was aware that anywhere in business I'd be faced with that. You may be invited to play tennis with the vice president or to the boss's house for a party. You may get one invitation but you never receive the second or third.

"You expect over time the rate of covert prejudice would have slowed and that you would not be subjected to such a high degree of it. Unfortunately, the rate of growth is still there. The Harvard environment was to prepare us for this. We were involved with the professors on a social level. Except they didn't prepare our superiors here," he noted wryly.

"The commitment of top management doesn't filter down to the middle manager. Unless he has been evaluated negatively, he will never change his attitude.

"For any young individual to get ahead, he must have a sponsor. Whether the black has a sponsor to the same degree the white has is a matter of question. That determines how far he will advance, given they both do the same quality of work.

"The black lacks the shoulder to cry on or sympathize with him. His white friend goes in to the manager's office and stays for an hour and a half. The black gets the bare essentials and no extra information. It's a very rough apprenticeship to prove himself over time. Initially, he may be evaluated poorly.

"Yet there's no overt prejudice in the trucking industry. The opportunity is there and I still am of that conviction. I've weathered the storm. My outlook looks promising."

Jim Nicholas is a sports enthusiast. He likes softball and football, golf and tennis, but the social opportunities for him to play have been slow in coming. He has taken up coaching Little League baseball, youth football, and hockey teams. "I've met a lot of interesting people and it's an extension into social life, mostly with Cummins people," he said.

Columbus is utopia for his children. "They can interact with friends both black and white. They have stayed overnight with white friends."

Yet Nicholas has reservations about what his children are exposed to here, especially in contrast with their previous lives in Boston and Baltimore.

"Some black adults have a tendency to become so amalgamated into white society that they accept all the white characteristics, good and bad. Many black traits that are considered negative by the white may actually be positive. They enable him to endure in all environments. They say the black child is rough in play. If we take away his defensive weapons, he will be vulnerable when he gets older.

"My kids tend to shed a cry over things where I never would have. If my son falls and skins his knee, he runs to his mother. If he ran to me, I'd send him back. This is where the little black ghetto kid has it over the white kid. These traits should be transferred to the white kid instead of the other way around. Unfortunately, we're not at the point in our socialization where we can teach the white kid.

"My kids have lost something. My little daughter has to be reminded she is black. She has no heritage to fall back on. I try to take her to Louisville and Indianapolis so she can see how black people live," he said.

Epilogue: November 1974

Two years after he joined the Cummins Engine Company, Rick Haynes appraised the situation again. "I'm still contented in Columbus," he said. Yolande had given birth to a son during the summer and Rick had just been reassigned to a job in international marketing as vice president—Mid-East Area which would involve a certain amount of foreign travel.

Bill Mays had moved after a year, as he had been promised, from presidential assistant to manager of marketing services.

The Seiferths had left Columbus. Jesse Seiferth had taken a job with General Electric in Virginia, and Irma had stopped working.

"The fact that you have Joseph, Haynes, and Barnes as officers doesn't serve the purpose of providing role models for young executives coming off the campus," Haynes said, confirming what Jesse Seiferth had believed. "Because we all came from outside. We didn't make it in the company."

He reflected further. "One of the reasons why the black professionals have a pervasive sense of powerlessness is because sometimes by choice and sometimes by exclusion we don't belong to the powerful institutions in the community. We don't belong to Kiwanis and Rotary and most of us would rather die than join the country club." He laughed at the irony that the black elite looked down on these pillars of the community. "It's not that we are excluded from them but that they are the traditional bastions of white racism and conservatism. So we don't enter the local power structure and it does intensify our feeling of powerlessness."

He ended on another note of paradox.

"But more and more the young white executive is turning his back on the same institutions which often leads him to leave the community," he said.

AMERICA'S CORPORATE LOVEBIRDS:
HARDING AND
MARY WELLS LAWRENCE

Fall 1974

They're the sweethearts of American business, the Mary Pickford and Douglas Fairbanks of the corporate realm. Mr. and Mrs. Harding L. Lawrence are probably the only two chief executives of Big Board companies who would dare suggest that love between corporate officers is a sound management strategy.

"I am stark staring in love with my husband and he with me," declared Mary Wells Lawrence, the forty-six-year-old chairman of Wells, Rich, Greene, Inc., in 1973 the most profitable among publicly held advertising agencies. "The reason all of this works is that we are crazy about each other. Otherwise it would be a disaster."

"We're happy," said Harding Luther Lawrence, the fifty-four-year-old chairman of Braniff International Corporation, a notable money-maker in the struggling airline industry.

"When you're happy, you see opportunities even in bad times," his wife said.

They were discussing the effect of their relationship on their businesses—a subject that has intrigued observers for years—on a Saturday afternoon in their Manhattan triplex apartment. Through the floor-to-ceiling windows of the living room fifteen stories above the East River they can sometimes see on a clear day the Braniff jets taking off for Dallas from La Guardia Airport.

The Lawrences were seated on a banquette plumped with enormous pillows of expensive chic. Mary Lawrence, leggy and slender and as radiant as a bride, did most of the talking.

Harding Lawrence, confident and smiling, controlled his restless energy by smoking a lot.

Their story began in 1965, with a plot predictable enough for an in-flight movie. Harding Lawrence, a dark-haired Texan who looked as though the Ashley Famous Agency had sent him over to play the part of a dynamic airline president, joined Braniff Airways. He had been the Number Two man at Continental Air Lines, whose president, Robert F. Six, is regarded as the last of the industry's pioneering swashbucklers.

Lawrence turned to Jack Tinker & Partners, the creative advertising agency unit within the Interpublic Group, to give Dallas-based Braniff sheen and national recognition.

A Tinker team headed by Mary Wells, an Ohio-bred, blonde copywriter with show-biz flair, did just that. Their "end of the plain plane" concept featured airplanes painted the colors of jelly beans and stewardesses peeling off the layers of their Pucci-designed uniforms as the planes headed south.

In 1966 Mary Wells and her team started their own agency, Wells, Rich, Greene, Inc. The Braniff account followed. In 1967 Harding Lawrence was divorced from his wife of fifteen years. He then married Mrs. Wells, who had been divorced from her husband, an advertising art director.

A planeload of guests attended the wedding in Paris. Mary and Harding Lawrence have lived happily ever after—although usually in different cities on weekdays.

Wells, Rich, Greene gave up the $7.5 million Braniff account in 1968 and took on instead $22 million in annual billings by Trans World Airlines—an optimal solution to a possible conflict of interest. Since then the Lawrences have tried to keep their companies apart.

"He never sees my accounts," she said.

"Neither of us has ever been to each other's meetings," he said. "I just know what I read in the papers about hers. I'm not even a stockholder."

"I spent six months preparing for my first stockholder meeting. He was very amused. But everything new to me he's done sixteen times," she said. Mary Lawrence asserted, "Harding hasn't taught me anything about the advertising business but absolutely everything about how to manage a business, the basic fundamentals. He's forever educating me."

Both of their companies are exceptionally profitable for their industries and operate with relatively low labor costs.

Braniff, for example, has used the computer to reduce the mounting cost of flight pay. Airplane crews are allowed eight hours flight pay for every twenty-four hours away from base. By scheduling the crews—with the help of the computer—so as to minimize the periods of time away from base, Braniff's bill for nonflying pay was cut from 26 per cent to 11 per cent of total crew costs.

Wells, Rich, Greene operates with fewer employees than most advertising agencies and they work harder for higher pay. "I provide the best advertising for selected kinds of accounts where talent is necessary," Mary Lawrence said.

"Some accounts need lots of advertising that runs once in trade journals. The companies that have such accounts have chosen to be very large and to set up training systems. My company is designed to be choice, to have nothing but the cream. My duty is not to run a school."

Wells, Rich, Greene specializes in large television accounts.

During the Lawrence administration, Braniff has had a 118 per cent increase in operating revenues and a 27 per cent rise in earnings. In the same period the U.S. airline industry as a whole (including Braniff) had a 108 per cent growth in revenues and a 78 per cent decline in earnings.

Wells, Rich, Greene's after-tax profit margin averaged close to 16 per cent from 1967 to 1972. This compares with 6 per cent profit margins averaged by the eight other major public advertising agencies.

"Whether she intended it or not, Mary was made for business," her husband said. "She would have been successful in any one she would have gone into because she has a grasp for all business principles. She has an uncanny feeling for what the consumer wants. Call it a sixth sense, I guess. She anticipates trends."

His wife has learned from his cool. "Harding never loses his head. He doesn't get carried away with short term crises or enthusiasms," she said.

"I didn't buy the large jets or engage in promotional fares to the extent that the other airlines did," he said. Aviation experts cite this restraint as a key factor in Braniff's performance because it thus avoided the overcapacity and financial drain suffered by other carriers.

The legacy that Juan T. Trippe, the founder of Pan American World Airways, left his international airline as he went into retirement was the decision to buy the Boeing 747. Without that commitment, Boeing could not have built the jumbo jet and the other United States and foreign airlines would not have felt competitively obliged to order it, too.

Trippe's rosy vision of the dawn of the era of truly mass air travel did not foresee the economic downturn of the 1970s which set in just as the 747 was introduced. Loaded down with massive debt to pay for the airplanes and with fewer passengers booked than they were designed to accommodate, Pan Am was driven on a course perilously close to bankruptcy. Other airlines suffered to varying degrees.

Lawrence refused to be stampeded into buying a jumbo fleet. His biggest competitor, American Airlines, was flaunting the appeal of the wide-bodied planes. American not only bought the Boeing 747 early on but was also the first customer for the McDonnell-Douglas version, the DC-10. Lawrence took delivery of one of the two 747s Braniff had ordered at $25 million each and asked Boeing to find a buyer for the other.

American put the 747 into service on the Dallas-New York run, when it had 80 per cent of that important market. Braniff countered by increasing the number of flights of its Boeing 727-200, a medium-size jet, and bringing it into all three of New York's airports (La Guardia can't accommodate the 747 or DC-10 jumbos).

Within three years Braniff had increased its share to nearly 50 per cent of the Dallas-New York market, using the weapon of scheduling to win the battle against the much-vaunted size and comfort of American's monster jets. About 70 per cent of Braniff's customers are business travelers; schedule frequency is what they appreciate most.

"There are certain fundamental business principles, laws that have to be recognized like gravity," Lawrence said. "The 747 is a fine, efficient airplane if properly used."

Braniff's sole 747 has an impressive fifteen-hour-a-day utilization on the Dallas-Honolulu run, an 8,000-mile round trip on which it completes two landings and two takeoffs, "the epitome for which that airplane was designed," he said.

Braniff is essentially a short-haul carrier with an average passenger flight of 488 miles. "The 727-200 is the epitome over the Braniff routes," according to Lawrence, and the backbone of Braniff's fleet. The plane has a built-in economic advantage: a direct operating cost of only about one cent a seat-mile. The DC-10's economics don't approach that advantage on flights of less than 2,000 miles.

Braniff uses only 727s (many of them new or refitted with "wide-bodied look" interiors) in its domestic system and McDonnell-Douglas DC-8s on its Latin-American operations.

"Airplanes are my business. I grew up with them," Lawrence said.

He also resisted wooing by the French and British manufacturers of the Concorde supersonic airplane. There are times when it's best not to be first, he said: "The original model would not perform the distance we would require." The minimum economic sense would be a 4,200-mile range for a Latin-American run. "The supersonic era is coming," he said. "But the public has a misconception about it. They think it will dominate travel. It won't carry a large percentage of the travel market for a long time."

Lawrence is not likely to make a major financial commitment just for publicity value, despite a contrary impression fostered by the "end of the plain plane" campaign.

"When we die, they'll put over our tombstones, 'They painted planes orange and green.' They won't say, 'He didn't buy the 747,'" Mary Lawrence moaned.

Harding Lawrence maintains that the campaign didn't really cost anything extra because the planes needed repainting and the stewardesses were due to get new uniforms anyway. And it did make people notice Braniff.

Nor was the ploy of having the artist Alexander Calder paint a Braniff plane in the fall of 1973 a costly gimmick either.

Everyone assumed this was another instance of Mary Wells pulling the strings at Braniff even though she doesn't have the account anymore. But they were wrong. George Gordon, a vice president of creative marketing for Foote, Cone & Belding was responsible. Ah, sweet irony . . . Foote, Cone & Belding is the agency that lost the TWA account to Wells, Rich, Greene when Mary Lawrence found it opportune to give up Braniff.

Gordon had thought for a long time that "it would be nice to have a Calder that flies—Calder is after all, the inventor of kinetic art."

He confided the idea to Arthur D. Lewis when they met on a flight from Arizona to New York. Lewis, then an investment banker, had been president of Eastern Airlines when Gordon was its marketing vice president. Gordon had directed the airline's Whisper Jet campaign. Lewis told Gordon to take the Calder idea to Harding Lawrence. Lewis would provide the introduction.

First, Gordon flew to France where Calder lives and got him to agree to paint a DC-8 for $100,000, a sum that Calder's New York representative later said was a steal—he would have asked half a million.

With the way paved by a letter from Lewis, Gordon then made a presentation to Lawrence who saw the idea as a "wonderful" symbol of Braniff's South American expansion and promptly signed a contract for Foote, Cone & Belding to help Braniff develop that route system with a theme of "South America with Flying Colors."

Mary Lawrence approved. "It's such a smiley plane, very bold, a very masculine-looking plane. It's simply smashing," she said.

Gordon didn't mind if the world gave credit to Mary for his idea. He was grateful for her encouragement and delighted to see his idea materialize. It brought a new account to his agency and inquiries from other companies.

As for Braniff, it got more than $100,000 worth of notice from the publicity.

At inaugural ceremonies for the plane, Harding Lawrence predicted that "More people will see this painting by a famous artist in a shorter time than perhaps any other in history." The Calder project for Braniff was solemnly likened to a rebirth of the cooperation between artists and businessmen of the Renaissance era.

Calder behaved with proper artistic lese majesty. Asked to identify the six-legged animal he had painted on an engine mount as a horse or a mule, he answered, "A horse-wolf, an animule." And someone neglected to brief the Braniff stewardesses, one of whom spoke up brightly to a reporter and said, "You can hardly miss it. It's the tackiest plane on the place." Meanwhile the eight toy-size models of the plane that Braniff sent on traveling exhibition to museums accrued thousands of dollars in value as art objects.

In 1967 Braniff's acquisition of Panagra, the airline jointly owned by Pan American World Airways and W. R. Grace & Company, stimulated revenues and strengthened Braniff as an international carrier with a Latin-American accent. The $30-million purchase made Braniff the dominant United States carrier to the West Coast of the South American continent.

Periodically, Lawrence held merger discussion with other domestic carriers, though none came to fruition during the next seven years.

In 1972 Lawrence, in a move to alleviate the cyclical nature of the airline business, turned the airline into a holding company, the Braniff International Corporation. It diversified into hotel operations (a natural tie-in with transportation) as well as training systems and security services for other airlines.

Through a subsidiary, Braniff International Hotels Inc., the airline operates a growing string of convention and resort hotels, including ones in Brownsville and Corpus Christi, Texas; Tucson, Arizona; Acapulco, Mexico; and Lima, Peru. Braniff provides technical and management services but does not invest in the properties.

In 1973 Braniff had net income of $23 million on operating revenues of $432 million. Its rate of return on shareholder investment was 19.7 per cent, in comparison with a 5.5 per cent average for the industry.

[One year later, Braniff announced new record profits. It was one of the few airlines to rise so blithely above the prolonged recession. Revenues for 1974 had increased 24 per cent to $552.4 million, net income nearly 13 per cent to $26.1 million.]

While Braniff was soaring in the airline industry, Wells, Rich, Greene winged its way in just seven years to thirteenth place on the advertising agencies' billings scoreboard in a ranking of 689 agencies compiled by *Advertising Age*. It had about $185 million in billings in 1973, including those of Gardner Advertising Company, Inc., a St. Louis agency acquired in 1972 in an exchange of stock. In 1973 Wells, Rich, Greene earned $3.4 million on revenues of $28.5 million.

Wells, Rich, Greene has drawn top clients such as Procter & Gamble, Westinghouse Corporation, and Miles Laboratories which want creative advertising for problem products. It gave Alka-Seltzer the "I Can't Believe I Ate the Whole Thing" TV commercial. Such clients also expect personal service which is why Mary Lawrence travels so often to Elkhart, Indiana, the home of Miles Laboratories.

Despite her reputation as a wordsmith, her distinction has been in what Madison Avenue calls "selling the work," rather than as a copy-writing genius.

"I'm more Mary Wells than she is," says Richard Rich, the copy writer of the founding triumvirate. He left the agency in 1969, wealthier but disenchanted. "All I want is my name off the agency."

Stewart Greene, the art director and the other founder, wound up his employment contract in April 1974. He left with a five-year consulting arrangement for a fee at the rate of $75,000 a year for the first two years and $52,500 for each of the next three.

A heady brew of sexuality (including wifeliness and mother-hood) and money runs through all of the Wells, Rich, Greene campaigns.

"I think of Mary as asexual in business and yet she's very sexy," said Joan Glynn, president of Simplicity Pattern Company, Inc., and a friend and former colleague from the days at Doyle Dane Bernbach where Mary Wells was a copy writer for seven years before Jack Tinker & Partners hired her away in 1964 at $60,000 a year. Mrs. Glynn was trying to explain why the formula has been more acceptable to male clients than to feminists.

Though Mary Wells Lawrence speaks of the distinction of being the highest-paid woman executive in America as "my little effort to-wards women's lib" and boasts that Wells, Rich, Greene has six women vice presidents, five of whom make more than $50,000 a year, she adds, "On the other hand, I'm not just in the business of promoting women."

If Mary Wells Lawrence's portrait does not appear among the icons of the women's rights movement, it may be because her buzz-words speak louder than her actions.

"Braniff's X-rated flight," as envious competitors called the Pucci airborne strip tease, catered to the tired businessman's fantasies about stewardesses. In a speech on marketing of the future, Mary Lawrence predicted that though women's liberation will affect women, they will still be anxious about looking pretty, "hanging on to their man," and their success with their children.

She was, as usual, selling Wells, Rich, Greene and making her statements sound authoritative with a few unsubstantiated statistics. But Mary Lawrence was also baring her soul.

Though women may change their lifestyles through work or by choosing to stay single, she said, "their vulnerabilities will remain the same for a time . . . The mother instinct is still powerful. The busier the mother, the greater her anxiety about her success with her children . . . another vulnerability to consider is that most women want to be married and are comfortable taking care of men. Yet the women's movement will lead women to feel they should be doing something important outside the home. Result: inner conflict. Add to that the fact that most women want very much to hang on to their man and the conflict grows. The married woman who makes any real effort to 'do her own thing' is usually also concerned that she is making things less comfortable and less attractive for her husband. Through the very process of becoming more *independent* of her husband, a married woman becomes more *concerned* about him. . . .

"Don't be fooled by the pantsuits and the militant libbers," she told the mostly male audience. She wasn't wearing one of her many Halston pantsuits that day. "Most women want to be sexually attractive and are not certain they are."

On another occasion, she confessed to an interviewer, "I never felt pretty until I fell in love with my husband. Harding made me feel pretty."

Similarly basic Mary Wells themes of money and service have been paired at various times for Braniff (paying customers if the flights were late), for TWA (rewarding employees who make customers happy), and for another client, Sunoco (the gas station owner who provides service because he has many mouths to feed).

"Harding and I are very interested in making money for our companies. There's a sense of responsibility as well as the game. It would be humiliating to run a company that didn't make money. What would be the point otherwise?" she said, trying to clarify her much-talked-about esteem for wealth.

Mary Lawrence says that one of the reasons her company has been so profitable as it has for its industry is that "I'd be so embarrassed not to live up to the standards Harding set, standards he set for himself.

"If I were not married to him, it would be a whole different story. I wouldn't know one one hundredth of what I do now. His influence over my business is enormous. I really don't think it would be true the other way."

The issue makes for sparkling debate because there are so many coincidences binding them together. Some are quirky and amusing.

For example, does it just *seem* that Braniff stewardesses all look like Mary Wells? Given the quick results that can be achieved with hair coloring, diet, and clothes and given the similar type casting of the secretaries at Wells, Rich, Greene, it's a toss-up between intent and the subconscious.

There are weightier examples, though.

For several years, Harding and Mary Lawrence were the highest-paid executives in their respective industries and that's more than a slight coincidence. She still is the best compensated in advertising, though he slipped to sixth place in 1972 as other airline chieftains succeeded in overtaking the coveted Harding Lawrence contracts, at least as far as salary is concerned.

Even Floyd D. Hall, chairman of chronically ailing Eastern Airlines, had boosted his base pay higher than Lawrence's, although his track record had been far less impressive. In a sense, Hall owed his job to Harding Lawrence, who had been the first choice of Laurance Rockefeller, Eastern's controlling stockholder, to run the airline. After Harding Lawrence declined—it was back in his pre-Braniff days when he was still Bob Six's man at Continental Air Lines—Hall was tapped.

The contracts of both Lawrences are strikingly similar, which is not surprising since they were drawn by the same lawyer, Arnold M. Grant, who happens to be a director of both Continental Air Lines and of Wells, Rich, Greene. (He is also on the latter's compensation committee.)

"Arnold Grant's philosophy has always been that when you sign a ten-year contract, you always think they are overpaying you," Lawrence said. "But ten years is a long time, and with inflation what it is and your responsibilities increasing, if you had not been a little luxurious, you would be upset. The purpose is to keep you happy and in place, to be inhibiting to another offer."

Mary Lawrence chimed in, "The price of getting a real executive should be a very small matter because you are talking of savings for the stockholders."

Harding Lawrence cut back in, "The cheapest thing we buy is our management. Yet it's one of the most important. The cost of our people to our total expenses is the lowest in our industries. And we think we produce a lot. One of the problems this country has is that it's losing productivity. In the past year, we had record profits.

That's true of Mary's company, too, I read somewhere." He laughed.

Arnold Grant drew Harding Lawrence's contract first. It gave him a base salary of at least $220,000 a year until 1980. In 1973 he also drew $121,000 under a 1968 incentive compensation plan. [The contract was amended in October 1974 to raise the base salary to $250,000 a year, with the possibility of further annual increases.] Mary Lawrence's base salary until 1981 is $225,000 a year, plus deferred compensation of $30,000 a year, plus incentive awards that brought her gross pay in 1973 to $440,595. If Braniff were to merge with another carrier, Harding Lawrence's pay will be adjusted to $300,000 a year.

Both Lawrences are insured by company policies that will pay $1 million to their estates should they die while employed. Grant conceded that the insurance provision "goes all the way back to picture days." A veteran movie industry lawyer, he once represented Mary Pickford and United Artists, the company she started with Douglas Fairbanks and Charlie Chaplin.

Despite Mary Pickford's reputation for insisting on high pay and a piece of the action, she doesn't compare to Mary Wells Lawrence in business acumen, Grant believes. "Mary Pickford never understood taxes," he said. "Mary Lawrence has been a source of total amazement to me. Her understanding, her instinct for business is remarkable. Her mind is constantly working, talking it out. She has the best mind of any man I know. Yet how totally feminine she is as a homemaker and mother."

Grant waxed rhapsodic, drawing on his considerable acquaintance with women who were—or appeared to be—clever about finances. He had been the lawyer in several real estate transactions for Marion Davies, the movie actress and companion of the publisher William Randolph Hearst. Miss Davies had been far more successful as a real estate investor than as a film star.

Grant speaks admiringly of the way in which Mary Lawrence signed a lease for two floors of office space in the General Motors Building right after it was constructed on what, in retrospect, were moderate terms. She also leased half of an additional floor in case the agency were to need it. If not (as it developed), the space could be subleased at a profit, thereby reducing the effective rental costs of Wells, Rich, Greene.

Grant had once been wed to Bess Myerson, the former Miss

America, who, toward the end of their marriage, was appointed New York City's Commissioner of Consumer Affairs by Mayor John V. Lindsay. During divorce proceedings in 1970, Grant refused to pay temporary alimony to Miss Myerson on the grounds that she was fully capable of supporting herself from her own funds. Eventually, she withdrew her claims for alimony and a property settlement and Grant won the divorce.

Though the Lawrences' employment contracts are similar, Mary Lawrence seems to have made more money from her company's stock than Harding Lawrence has from his. Those who know them both suspect that she cares more about money than he does.

"If I'd been interested in being terribly rich, I would have gone another route," he said.

Carl Spielvogel, executive vice president of Interpublic (whose offer of a ten-year, $100,000-a-year contract Mary Wells spurned to start her own company), recollects that she frequently spoke of wanting to make $2 million.

"She would look at me with those steely blue eyes," he recalled.

Mary Lawrence's eyes are brown. Spielvogel's mistaken impression is indicative of the image Mary Wells Lawrence has wrought for herself—that of the cool, determined (and sexy) blonde. Those who knew her as a copy writer going places in her late twenties and early thirties remember her as a prematurely graying brunette.

Mary Lawrence contests Spielvogel's version of her money motive. "Money never meant anything to me," she says over and over again.

"When they offered me a contract for $1 million over ten years at Tinker, I was so impressed I was almost teary. I thought it was more money than I'd ever make. I did not say I wanted to make $2 million.

"But that offer said to me that I was tied down for ten years. I had a need to do something my way, I had to find out if I could do something better than others could. They had promised me I could be president. But they never got around to letting me be president. They were terrific to me but I think my being a woman was hard for them to swallow. And so when they offered me the contract, I thought if I'm ever going to move—and do things my way—it had better be now."

In March 1966 Mary Wells, as she was then, resigned from Jack

Tinker & Partners and was followed by Richard Rich, a copy writer, and Stewart Greene, the art director. They had been part of the team that created the in-flight strip tease for Braniff.

The "Three Innocents Abroad," as she labeled them, opened their own advertising agency in a seven-room suite at the Gotham Hotel with Mary Wells's mother handling the telephone calls. Within a year and a half they had billings of $70 million which put them among the nation's top thirty agencies.

When Wells, Rich, Greene went public in October 1968, Mary Wells Lawrence owned 20.8 per cent of the common stock, or 301,000 shares, for which she had paid 10 cents a share two years before when the agency was founded. At the time of the public offering, she sold 75,250 of those shares at $17.50, netting herself a profit of $1.3 million. Then in a secondary offering in 1971, she sold another 110,850 shares at $21.75 and cleared $2.4 million more.

She sold 30,400 shares in small blocks during the next few years. Early in 1974, she had about 84,500 shares at a market value of about $8 a share. Advertising agencies had been stripped of their glamour in the bear market.

She then bought back almost the same number of shares, 30,500 at prices ranging from $8.50 to $9.25, increasing her holdings to 115,000 shares, or 7 per cent of the company. At that point, as will be seen, she announced a plan to turn the company private, a move from which she stood to gain still further.

She also held options for 150,000 shares at $20.50 a share that had been granted in 1968. Like so many other executives' options, they were worthless in 1974 because of the market tumble.

Harding Lawrence's profits from his Braniff stock were less than his wife had amassed from her interest in her agency. Or so it appeared when, in 1973, he whittled his stock ownership down to 413 shares.

From December 1972 to October 1973 he sold 225,000 shares in chunks, for $12 to $15 a share, for a total of $3.1 million.

His acquisition of 150,000 of those shares at an average cost of $12.41 a share in January 1968 was later viewed as a remarkable example of corporate solicitude by a House committee investigating conglomerates. Lawrence bought the stock with a note for $1.8 million bearing interest at the prime rate to be paid at maturity in January 1973. The stock was collateral for the note which was held by Greatamerica, Braniff's parent corporation, which had been merged with Ling-Temco-Vought, the conglomerate. L-T-V was forced by the government to divest itself of the airline in 1970.

Calculating the cost of the stock he had on loan, together with the five stock dividends and the rest of the stock which he had acquired at about $4 a share when he joined Braniff, it would appear that Lawrence made about $300,000 on the massive transaction.

Over-all, he said, "I made a substantial profit."

He gave "estate planning and the need to set a new tax base" as the reason for the sale. "I'm not a wealthy person," he said. "I incur debt from time to time. But I plan to reacquire stock."

Using debt as leverage is a cardinal Lawrence principle, he acknowledged. Including lease obligations, Braniff has a debt-equity ratio of about 2.2 to 1.

Lawrence also has options for 212,180 shares of Braniff common stock at $7.42 a share.

Harding Lawrence owed his unusual stock purchase deal—and, in fact, his job at Braniff—to Troy V. Post, the Dallas insurance entrepreneur who created Greatamerica.

Post is one of those Texas country boys on the big business landscape. Outwardly gentle, he has a fierce pride and gargantuan financial appetites. In 1933, at the age of twenty-eight, he had staked $130 to start his own life insurance company. It grew by his seat-of-the-pants daring—selling life insurance to soldiers during World War II without making them take physical examinations, then after the war buying up undervalued shares in other insurance companies.

Through Greatamerica, his financial holding company, Post bought control of Braniff, which had passed through several investors' hands after the accidental death of its founder, Tom Braniff.

Post hired Harding Lawrence to run the airline, with plenty of incentives to apply himself and feel content.

Post is a firm believer in such bait. "In the employment of key personnel, you have to get them so interested you can keep them. The only thing left to entice a person of that caliber is incentive," Post said in a discussion of why he had made the commitment (which James J. Ling ended up honoring) to lend Lawrence the money to buy his Braniff stock.

Post had indicated his esteem for Lawrence. "I'd have to rate him Number One," he said. "I think we stood a chance of losing him and he was too valuable to take that risk. He hasn't been a disappointment in any respect."

Post could not say the same about Ling, another Dallas kingfish whose name has become synonymous with the discredited corporate concept of the conglomerate.

Blinded somewhat by his friendship with Ling, Post sold his Greatamerica Corporation in 1968 to Ling-Temco-Vought Inc., which Ling had built in a decade into the nation's fourteenth largest industrial corporation.

The price was $500 million for which L-T-V issued 5 per cent debentures due in 1988. Post received one fifth of these $100-million face-value notes corresponding to the number of Greatamerica shares he held.

Post promised not to go back into the life insurance business in competition with L-T-V. Ling then sold off the life insurance companies as part of his strategy to acquire the Jones & Laughlin Steel Company.

Foreclosed from the insurance business he knew so well, Post struck out into unfamiliar territories. He pledged his L-T-V debentures to finance the building of Tres Vidas, a resort near Acapulco of hitherto unparalleled luxury and snobbism. "He tried to raid the *Almanach de Gotha* for his board of directors," a rival hotelman observed.

But Tres Vidas proved to need many more capital infusions than Post had planned. Simultaneously, his L-T-V debentures were developing pernicious anemia in the marketplace.

In the spring of 1970 Post was instrumental, among other disenchanted L-T-V investors, in pushing Ling out of his conglomerate sand castle. It was during those tempestuous months of doom for Ling that Harding Lawrence negotiated his enviable ten-year employment contract with Braniff. Some of Lawrence's supporters ascribe his audacity to an instinct for self-preservation. Lawrence never knew from one day to another to whom Ling might be selling Braniff. Ling had such discussions with representatives of Howard Hughes, the aviation-keen eccentric, and with David Mahoney, chairman of Norton Simon, Inc.

The toppling of Ling saved Lawrence and Braniff.

Post has survived his Ling wounds and his cash squeeze and is now concentrating his investments in resorts and insurance. Lawrence avoided any suggestions that Braniff take over Tres Vidas although the airline's hotel subsidiary collected some operating service fees from the resort.

So it is no mere coincidence that Troy Post is a director of Braniff and of Wells, Rich, Greene, as well as a member of the advertising agency board's incentive compensation committee. "I've never known anyone more accurate and precise in the handling of corporate affairs than she is," Post said of Mary Wells Lawrence.

Post's contribution as a director, Mary Lawrence has said, has been in the area of investments in real estate and oil and gas leases, areas "Troy knows a great deal about."

These investments have been more successful forms of diversification for Wells, Rich, Greene than those of other advertising agencies have been for them and better than Wells, Rich, Greene's foray into films. In 1973 the agency wrote off $652,000, or half of its investment in *Dirty Little Billy*, a movie it coproduced with Jack Warner in 1972. Critics were less than enthusiastic about it.

One of five profitable purchase and sales of real estate Wells, Rich, Greene made, after Troy Post scouted the deals, involved land near the new Dallas airport.

The oil and gas leases provided useful tax benefits and a lift for earnings when they were purchased. Eleven of the leases were bought from the King Resources Company, a since bankrupt empire built by John M. King, the Denver conglomerateur who was involved with Bernard Cornfeld, the dethroned mutual fund monarch.

Harding Lawrence served for a while on the King board. "That had nothing to do with Wells, Rich, Greene's oil and gas leases," he said.

Nor, he maintains, is there any connection between the presence of Joseph F. Cullman 3d, chairman of Philip Morris Inc., on the Braniff board since 1971 and the fact that Philip Morris is one of Wells, Rich, Greene's principal advertising accounts, the second after Braniff to join the agency's client roster back in 1966. "He's an outstanding businessman. We have one of the best outside boards," Lawrence said.

Gustave L. Levy, the ubiquitous corporate director, Wall Street investment banker, and business matchmaker, has been on the Braniff board since Lawrence took over. Levy got Mary Lawrence onto the board of the May Company for a while. When she went into business for herself, Levy, at Lawrence's request, was helpful in finding her a lawyer, Orville H. Schell, Jr., and giving her entrée to the Chemical Bank for a $100,000 loan. Levy also introduced her to White, Weld & Company, the underwriters for the Wells, Rich, Greene stock offering.

Levy's firm, Goldman, Sachs & Company, didn't do the underwriting although Mary Lawrence talked to him first about going public, because his partners took a dim view of advertising agencies' stocks. Ultimately, their judgment was proved correct.

Levy, by the way, is a director and investment banker for Norton Simon, Inc., as Hunt Foods and Industries Inc. was rechristened. Lawrence was on the Hunt board for a spell and Wells, Rich, Greene had Hunt for a client.

Then there's Emilio Pucci, the sportswear designer who's on the Wells, Rich, Greene board and still redesigning stewardesses' uniforms for Braniff. "Emilio is very knowledgeable about what is going on in Europe and sooner or later we have to get stronger in Europe," Mary Lawrence said, articulating the usefulness of the Italian marchese who helped Mussolini's daughter, Edda Ciano, escape into Switzerland in 1944.

Frank G. Colnar, Wells, Rich, Greene's senior vice president for financial planning, is definitely a Harding Lawrence contribution. He worked under him at Continental Air Lines. "I needed someone who was a sophisticated money kind of man and who had worked with the financial community," Mary Lawrence said. "When you start a company new, you want someone who is bright but also you want to be able to trust him. If Harding recommended him, I knew I could trust him."

Wells, Rich, Greene follows an accounting practice, unique in its industry, that gives earnings a boost. Costs of advertising and product development services for new accounts are deferred and amortized over a thirty-six month period. Because airlines defer training costs for new aircraft, it had been widely assumed that this accounting idea was Harding Lawrence's. "It was my idea," Mary Lawrence said, feigning hurt feelings.

"I don't know of any industry that doesn't defer. It's like chapter two in an accounting textbook. It's incredibly realistic," she said.

In the advertising agency business, when a new client signs on, the agency has incurred expenses of soliciting and usually doesn't get paid until ninety days after it officially starts servicing the account. At the other end of the relationship, the client gives ninety days notice of termination, and although the payments to the agency continue during that period, the agency reduces staff and other overhead on that account.

These customs tend to create abnormal peaks and valleys in quarterly earnings statements, something that concerns publicly listed companies more than privately held ones.

Some security analysts have been put off by the Wells, Rich, Greene accounting as they have been by those oil and gas leases. "Wells, Rich, Greene seems to play more games than other agencies," said Andrew Melnick of Drexel Burnham & Company.

But Jerry Levine of Moore & Schley, Cameron & Company termed the criticisms "much too belabored. I don't say the practices haven't influenced the stock," he said, "but they are prudent."

Besides, he was impressed with the agency's billings and earnings. "They do a unique job in a difficult business. They are not really comparable to other agencies because of the approach to the clients and the size of the accounts. The only important account they ever really lost was American Motors." So Levine was recommending the stock: "For the more speculative investor, I would think it could be an interesting vehicle," he said in January 1974.

That was Levine's opinion when the stock was selling around 9. It proved to be interesting, indeed, though not in a way he had in mind. Anyone who had followed his advice would have seen the price drift down to 5½ in early September when the Wells, Rich, Greene exchange offer was made.

Like every business move Mary Wells had ever made, it was an attention-getter. On September 4, 1974, she announced that Wells, Rich, Greene would buy back up to 1,405,008 of its 1,631,524 shares, or 86 per cent, of its common stock for cash and debentures.

This meant that she intended to turn Wells, Rich, Greene back into a private company. In itself this was not outrageous since, in the depressed climate of the market, more than a few companies were taking or contemplating the same step. It was the terms that caused heads to shake in anger or amazement. "While the situation isn't at all improper," the *Wall Street Journal* wrote, it "provides a glimpse of how an imaginative executive, whether by accident or design, might in six years more than double her interest in a company while, at the same time, sell off major portions of her stock for several million dollars." If all the shares sought by the company were exchanged, Mary Wells Lawrence's interest in the company would be increased from 7 to 43 per cent. She would more than double the 20.8 per cent interest she held when the agency went public in 1968. The 13 per cent she had sold off in the intervening years had brought her more than $3.5 million.

According to the terms of the offer, each common share would be exchanged for $3 in cash and $8 principal amount of new, ten-year subordinated debentures bearing an interest rate of 10 per cent a year.

Here was a way to go private without spending lots of cash to repurchase the stock.

Furthermore, the prospectus said that though an attempt would be made to have the debentures listed on the American Stock Exchange, "based on current market conditions, the debentures are likely to trade at prices significantly below their principal amount."

Similarly, White, Weld & Company, the underwriters, promised to make an over-the-counter market in the common shares that were not tendered, although here again, "if substantially all of the publicly held shares are exchanged, stockholders might encounter difficulty in obtaining prices they deem reasonable for their shares."

The stockholders were, in effect, being given little choice as to tender or to hold. If they held, the chances of their stock rising in price so that they could recoup what they paid in more effervescent markets was slight. On the other hand, they were being locked into the situation of lending the money to the company, on an unsecured basis, to turn them out since the debentures they were offered probably could not be cashed in at their face value.

At least one member of the Wells, Rich, Greene board that approved the offer, Troy Post, had had a similar opportunity with Ling's debentures and had been burned.

Investors in advertising agency stocks did not buy for income. They thought they had a piece of the future. Now that opportunity was being taken away from them.

In November a member of the Securities and Exchange Commission pointedly, though anonymously, criticized the deal. Commissioner A. A. Sommer, Jr., attacked the "fad of going private" trend in a lecture at the Notre Dame Law School. He called it "serious, unfair, and sometimes disgraceful—a perversion of the whole process of public financing."

By going private, a company frees itself from SEC rules of financial disclosure and its prohibitions against management conflicts of interest. Moreover, the company buys up at bargain prices what investors paid for at higher prices.

"These tender offers and these squeeze-outs usually benefit the insiders enormously . . . Is there not a clear conflict of interest when the shareholders are offered the empty choice of tendering or being forced out one way or another while the controlling shareholders reap benefits?" he asked.

The commissioner called no companies by name. But he referred to one that was bent on going private. If successful, the profit for the company's chairman and largest stockholder will increase sharply "without a single dime of additional investment by her. I would suggest there is something wrong with that," he said, adding, "I would further suggest that under well established legal principles such conduct may also be unlawful."

Since none of the chairmen of the thirty publicly listed companies then in the process of going private were women, there wasn't any doubt whom he meant.

"The spectacle of entrepreneurs inviting the public in when they can command high prices for their stock and then squeezing them out with little or no practical choice in the matter . . . at substantially reduced prices is hardly one to warm the soul of Thomas Aquinas or Aristotle," he declared.

Mary Lawrence didn't respond to his remarks. The agency's law firm issued a statement of its belief in the legality of the offer.

But when a stockholder brought suit to have the "squeeze-out" of shareholders enjoined, she testified in court that going private would enable Wells, Rich, Greene to improve employee compensation plans and make it easier to acquire other advertising agencies.

That, of course, had been one of the major reasons given for going public in 1968. The prospectus listed three incentive plans, two of them stock option and stock purchase plans designed "to attract new employees, to offer incentives to key employees, and to motivate them to continue in the employ of the Company."

Thousands of unexercised options would lose their value forever in a delisted company.

Mary Lawrence defended the action with more eloquent and graphic gloom. She resorted to her "government is moving in on business" theme. "Every little way it moves in, affects advertising. It's getting harder and harder to say anything. Clients more and more are concerned about standing out, about spending too much money," she said. "The ingredient problem is incredible. You don't know from month to month whether saccharine is in or out, whether aerosol is in or out.

"So the advertising industry will be fine as far as being a salary maker. It will be interesting, but it's not going to be a profitable business. Personally, I'm of the opinion we're on a road to nationalization of business, and advertising doesn't thrive down that road.

"My salaries for 1975 will be 25 per cent over what they were in 1973 and my billings are flat," she said in a non sequitur. Flat billings at that point were the consequence of a recession and the nationalization of industry seemed remote. [But indeed, billings had risen only 3 per cent in 1974 to $191 million, gross income a mere 2 per cent to $29.1 million, and most crushing of all, net income was down almost 5 per cent to $3.2 million. Lower earnings meant smaller contributions to the incentive compensation plan, so Mary's gross compensation for 1974 was reduced to $419,248 from $440,595 the year before.]

"If I could talk to every stockholder emotionally, I'd tell them to go buy Braniff. It has routes and planes. Or go buy Alcoa. At these bargain prices, get something that is real." She did not say what the stockholders were to use for money to pick up these bargains. Certainly not their proceeds from giving Wells, Rich, Greene back to Mary Wells Lawrence, since, as the prospectus had disclosed, the debentures with which they were lending the money for the purchase would not be easily marketable.

She declined to take sole credit for the ingenious idea, however. "There were about five of us, in my agency and on the board, looking for solutions. Our first hope was maybe through the acquisition of Doyle Dane Bernbach."

When reports of merger talks between the two agencies had surfaced in the spring of 1974, the industry had a juicy morsel upon which to chew. The notion of the blonde girl wonder of advertising taking over the great big agency for which she had once toiled as copy writer was a TV script writer's dream. If you could only get Mary Tyler Moore to play the lead. But the talks between Wells, Rich, Greene and Doyle Dane were broken off.

"It didn't work out," she said sadly. "We tried out 19,000 other ideas looking for a solution to the problem. This was one idea. It had something for it in dollars and cents and numbers on paper. But it was the least favorite.

"I loved being public. It's very classy. We'll disappear. The only agencies you hear about are public agencies."

As long as Mary Wells Lawrence is at its head, there isn't the slightest danger that Wells, Rich, Greene will lapse into obscurity. For not the least of Mary's gifts and according to some, the greatest, is that of being noticed and talked about.

Much has been made of her theatrical background. Her mother, Violet Berg, admits to being "a frustrated actress." Despite the family's meager resources during the depression years in Youngstown, Ohio, Violet Berg and her husband, Waldemar, a traveling furniture salesman, always found the means to give their only child, Mary Georgene, dancing and music lessons.

"When she was five, I noticed a little shyness so I took her to elocution class," Mrs. Berg related. "I guess she's been onstage from that day on. I always felt she would succeed in the theater."

The Bergs also encouraged their daughter, who was not a particularly distinguished student, to enter and win writing contests. Mary acted in the school plays and at fourteen became active in the Youngstown Playhouse. At seventeen she went off to the Neighborhood Playhouse School of Theatre in New York.

"I never really wanted to be in the theater but everybody thought I had this huge talent to act," Mary Lawrence said, looking back. "I wasn't that good and I really didn't want to do it." After a year, she transferred to the Carnegie Institute of Technology in Pittsburgh, which has a liberal arts program. "The idea was I'd get a degree and at least I could teach."

She didn't get to do either, but at Carnegie she met Burt Wells, an industrial design student. They married and she dropped out of college to go to work so he could finish his studies. The work to which she gravitated at McKelvey's Department store in nearby Youngstown was advertising.

"That huge talent was a great asset in advertising not in the theater," she says now.

It was very effective in September 1974, when President Gerald R. Ford convened a series of minisummit conferences, capped by a grand assembly in Washington, to make recommendations for tackling what he then perceived to be the nation's public enemy Number One, inflation.

Not surprisingly, the conferences were close to being stag reunions. The few women invited, such as Esther Peterson, the consumer expert, were eclipsed by Mary Lawrence as far as national television coverage went (though one of Mrs. Peterson's proposals for an inflation audit received serious consideration by the participants).

Secretary of Commerce Frederick B. Dent, who presided over the minisummit for business leaders in Pittsburgh, introduced Mary Lawrence with a tribute to her "beauty and intelligence."

At the summit conference in Washington, a television camera caught the Cabinet member watching her speak, with an expression of a moonstruck schoolboy. Senator Hubert Humphrey's regard was glum as he listened to her message.

Dressed in a gray suit with a white shirt and gray ascot tied like a necktie (with an effect that was vintage Marlene Dietrich), her blonde head shining amidst a sea of gray and balding pates, Mary Wells Lawrence offered her prescription for inflation.

She deplored the "antibusiness trend" in government, peppering her statement with a soupçon of selected statistics. "Since 1960 government has increased spending on programs other than defense 309 per cent," she declared. "In the same period, I've seen government's antibusiness feeling grow in almost direct proportion to increased government spending.

"Yesterday some congressmen and labor leaders spoke as though a socialized state and nationalization of business were their *goal*. This antibusiness trend is surprising when you consider that over 80 per cent of all taxes are generated by business—through corporate profits, social security taxes, taxes paid by people employed by business, and other business taxes.

"It's also surprising when you consider that people need business to prosper so that they can work in confidence—increase their wages—and improve their standards of living.

"The United States's first national priority should be to help its businesses succeed in world markets and to nourish them so they can provide high employment and higher salaries."

She denounced the "regulatory fever" in government. "With the Consumer Product Safety Commission and line-of-business reporting, government has gone too far in its passion to run business itself," she said. Government regulations in all industries are "one of the major factors in higher prices," she asserted. "In research we do, I've seen that the consumer does not want to pay for so much government in the way of higher prices . . . most people resented the *presumptuousness* of government attempting to force them to use seat belts. They were bitter when they had to pay for those belts."

She urged the President and Congress not to create any more agencies and controls for at least two years and to look for ways to eliminate legislation and agencies "that are obsolete or are a mistake and are adding to costs."

She referred to "studies" indicating that taxpayers feel "they are paying too many taxes for too many government programs" and recommended that the President hire a polling firm such as Daniel Yankelovich or George Gallup to hear "how much government involvement people really want to pay for in prices and taxes."

Later, she exulted to a friend for whom she replayed her performance from a video cassette, "What exposure I had." She had talked right over the heads of the participants and the TV audience to her clients, actual and prospective. Hark, ye automobile maker, drug manufacturer, or food account—Mary Wells is in your corner.

Once again she had used a lofty forum to sell herself and her agency.

Asked in 1973 to address a group of security analysts on "The Future of Marketing" (and, subliminally, to assure the disenchanted Wall Streeters that advertising agencies were solid investments), she laced her speech with videotape samples of Wells, Rich, Greene TV commercials. "I don't mean to suggest that Wells, Rich, Greene achieves humanness more often than any other agency," she told the audience after predicting that humanness will be an essential ingredient in consumer advertising of the seventies. "But to make my point, I need to show you five of our commercials," she added.

Invited by an association of bank executives to tell them what they might do to glamorize bank services, she also reviewed Wells, Rich, Greene campaigns (including the famous Alka-Seltzer "I Can't Believe I Ate the Whole Thing"). None of the campaigns were pertinent to banking. The audience went away no more informed about their marketing problem than when they came, but definitely under the spell of Mary Wells Lawrence and Wells, Rich, Greene.

"People listen to whatever she says," one of the members of the bank organization, a less-than-admiring Mary Wells watcher, said with some exasperation.

Some listeners at the inflation summit detected behind the hard sell a conservative economic and political philosophy. It made them wonder if, as one waggish friend of the Lawrences had said, "In the case of Harding and Mary, bedfellows make strange politics."

The friend remembered Mary "as a vague liberal, as all of the young ad crowd was in the fifties, though with no really developed political sense." By this account, Harding Lawrence had converted his wife to his southern Democratic conservatism.

The depth and breadth of his convictions had been manifested in 1953 when he had his youngest son christened "State Rights." (Now a student at Brown University, he is usually called "State.") "He was born at a time of national issues," Harding Lawrence said of his choice of the name. "It was a dividing line. I wondered, would anyone ever remember there had been such a thing as state rights."

Lawrence was schooled in Texas Democratic politics which meant that he has counted both Lyndon Baines Johnson and John Connally as his friends. In recent years the influence of Connally (who moved into the camp of Richard M. Nixon) would appear to have been stronger, though perhaps it was more expediency than ideology. The chairman of an airline seeking international routes must gain White House favor for his cause. During the same period, Pan American World Airways elected Connally a director.

In July of 1973 Braniff became the second airline (after American) to admit having made an illegal contribution of $40,000 to President Nixon's re-election campaign. On November 12, 1973, Harding Lawrence and Braniff pleaded guilty and were fined, respectively, $1,000 and $5,000.

In January 1974 Lawrence reimbursed Braniff for the fine it had paid, and he and other officers of the airline involved in the corporate contribution were billed $19,000 for legal fees to defend him and the company in court.

As Lawrence told investigators for the Senate Watergate Committee in 1973, he had first given Maurice Stans, former Secretary of Commerce and head of the Finance Committee to Re-elect the President, an unsolicited gift of cash in March 1972. It had been made from the personal funds of Harding and Mary Lawrence and of C. Edward Acker, president of Braniff, and his wife. Stans had thanked him and said he felt Braniff executives could do much more because "the company was doing much better than the rest of the industry." He suggested a $100,000 donation. Lawrence decided that $40,000 was fair enough and instructed a group of his executives to have the money "laundered" and delivered before the deadline of April 7, 1972, when public disclosure of donors would be required.

The "laundering" was done by voucher transmitted to Braniff's office manager in Panama and circulated back in cash to Dallas. From there it was carried by Lawrence to Stans.

There was another connection to the Nixon world, as yet not proved to be anything but tenuous. W. Sloan McCrea of Miami was elected to Braniff's board in February 1972. The reason Lawrence gave was that "Florida is more and more important to Braniff." As a gateway to Latin America, he presumably meant. McCrea is a Miami food broker, bank director, and partner in business and real estate deals of Charles G. ("Bebe") Rebozo, Richard Nixon's friend, confidant, and slush fund operator.

Despite the wide assumption that Harding Lawrence has made a convert to conservatism out of Mary Wells, she says he had nothing to do with her new convictions. "We happened to be going down the same road at the same time."

She traced her own path. "When I was a child, my parents were staunchly Democratic in a Republican community. We were quite poor and we felt that President Roosevelt had saved our lives and kept us from starvation. I had a strong feeling of being pro-Democratic.

"Politics were never my big thing. It just came on me. First at Doyle Dane when we did some advertising for LBJ. Then at Tinker when I put together a program for Nelson Rockefeller's second gubernatorial campaign and became quite familiar with state issues.

"When I married Harding, I got to know LBJ as a friend and wrote a couple of speeches for him and so did a couple of people at Wells, Rich, Greene. I kept picking up information. I was defining myself as a Democrat even though strongly pro-Rockefeller."

In 1974, after Nelson Rockefeller had resigned the governorship to devote himself to seeking the presidency under the guise of disinterested statesmanship, he formed the National Commission for Critical Choices for Americans, composed of Cabinet members, congressional leaders, academicians, and business personages, one of whom was Mary Wells Lawrence. (Among the other women: Bess Myerson, Clare Booth Luce, the right-wing playwright and former congresswoman and diplomat, and Marina Whitman, a former member of President Nixon's Council of Economic Advisers.)

"All those years, I felt the Democratic party represented me," Mary Lawrence said. "But the last few years, it's changed enormously. The Democrats have moved away from the middle- and upper-income people. I've been poor and struggling. When I was making $10,000 and $11,000 a year I felt the party represented me. I feel now it is more interested in people who are deprived. I'm pro-black, female, and doing things for the poor. I just don't like the methods of the party now. The poor need representation, but I don't think the party supports business and I am terribly enmeshed in business.

"Now I've become an independent. I'm probably righter than Barry Goldwater. I've read everything Milton Friedman has ever written. I think the basic intent of most of the Democratic programs are superb. The means to accomplish them are absurd."

If Harding and Mary Lawrence are attune in their political and economic thinking (as well as in everything else), it may be because their backgrounds are so similar. At least they think so.

"We both come from small towns west of the East Coast," he said.

He was born in Perkins, Oklahoma, in July 1920 and grew up in Gladewater, Texas; she was raised in Youngstown, Ohio, where she was born in May 1928.

His father, Moncey Luther Lawrence, was a minister of the Christian Church (Disciples of Christ); her father was a furniture salesman.

"At thirteen I started working in retail stores and in the oil fields," he said.

"At twelve I had my first actual job working evenings and weekends in a department store and I never stopped. Only since I met Harding have I taken a vacation," she said.

Mary's mother remembers her daughter going to work as a salesclerk at McKelvey's department store at the age of fifteen. It was during World War II, when the merchants went to the high schools to recruit employees to fill the gap caused by the departures for military service and the defense plants. It was to McKelvey's that Mary returned as a young working wife at twenty, but by then to the basement advertising department.

"It was an accident. I had to work. He had to get his degree. I decided it would be more interesting in advertising than selling. I fell in love with it. Here was this thing, this combination of writing and theater. Advertising put them all together," Mary Lawrence said.

The "he" was her first husband, Burt Wells. She seems to have difficulty mentioning his name—but then, she has difficulty remembering lots of people's names and has to be primed by her assistant. When Burt Wells died in 1973, after they had both been happily remarried to others for several years, she did not allude to his death even to mutual friends in the advertising business who had known them both. Those friends speak of Wells as a gentle person, the same description offered by Harding Lawrence's friends of his first wife.

In Mary Wells Lawrence's biography in Who's Who in America, there is no mention of Burt Wells. She is listed as having been married once, to Harding Lawrence, and as having five children. There is no indication that the first three (James, State, and Deborah) are Lawrence's. Or that Kathryn and Pamela are the daughters by adoption of her marriage to Wells (Katy is Hawaiian and Pamela is of Indonesian extraction). Harding Lawrence adopted the girls when he married Mary Wells. But her Who's Who description does not make these distinctions.

Harding Lawrence's does. His Who's Who listing identifies his first wife and mother of his children as Jimmie G. Bland, as well as his second wife, Mary Wells, and her children.

The name "Burt Wells," it seems, has been excluded from Mary Wells Lawrence's consciousness, even though he played a role in her life. "When my husband graduated from Carnegie, he wanted to go to New York, so we went and I went to work at Bamberger's," she said. From Bamberger's in Newark she moved rapidly into a series of retail advertising jobs, to the now vanished Wanamaker's and McCreery's department stores in New York, to Macy's (where she was named fashion advertising manager at the age of twenty-three), then on to the advertising agencies (McCann-Erickson, Lennen & Newell, Doyle Dane Bernbach for seven years, Jack Tinker & Partners), and then into her own business.

Even then, Burt Wells is mentioned without a name and in connection with a lack of money. "When I turned down the million-dollar contract from Tinker, I had $30,000 to my name from selling stock from Doyle Dane and Tinker. I had two kids and no alimony. My husband never came through with child support. I laid it all into

Wells, Rich, Greene. If there had been no Braniff account, God knows what would have happened."

So money or the absence of money figures in her memory, selective as it may be. "One of the things that's alike about Harding and me is that we both started early. Both of us have the work ethic like mad. We're very patriotic. Both of us also believe, not that the world is fair, but that you can do anything if you work hard enough. We're work oriented."

Violet Berg planted the work seed in Mary: "I always told her, nothing was impossible if she was willing to work. She believed it and I did." Mrs. Berg was a sportswear and a millinery buyer at McKelvey's, and after the Bergs moved to New York to be near their daughter, she took a job as an adjuster at Lord & Taylor to keep busy.

Harding interjects, "We all worked. My father and my brothers. That's the way we're raising our children. To assume responsibility, to be loyal and dedicated to the cause."

He worked his way through Kilgore College in Texas and the University of Texas. Then after serving with the Army Air Force during World War II and while working for Pioneer Air Lines in Houston, he managed to acquire a law degree from the South Texas College of Law.

He started at Pioneer in 1946 as a clerk in the operations department and one year later was promoted to general traffic and sales manager of the small, feeder airline. In another year, he had the title of vice president.

In 1955, when Pioneer merged with Continental Air Lines, he became vice president for traffic and sales. Three years later he was named executive vice president, a post he held until he went off to run Braniff in 1965.

Being Number Two to Continental's chief executive, Bob Six, was a slot that might have exhausted a lesser man. Six, a former pilot who built a minor regional airline into a major trunk carrier, is a demanding employer. But Lawrence performed for him with what one of Continental's directors described as "great grace and usefulness." He was also unquestionably loyal and it was assumed that if he were willing to wait around long enough (which he wasn't), he would be Six's heir in management.

Once Mary Lawrence said, "I learned early to listen. It got you everywhere. If you listen, they think you're awfully smart and by listening you get smarter. I learned how to do things to make people like me and want to help me."

Though the formula sounds feminine as well as communications industry-oriented, it is just as applicable to a rugged type like her husband. Men like Harding Lawrence. He is well-regarded by his colleagues and competitors in aviation because he has shown he can operate an airline profitably. Moreover, he seems to do so without leaving a trail of blood behind him. He is decisive and confident, but Lawrence is one chairman who lets other flowers bloom in his garden.

There is some dispute as to how willing Mary Lawrence is in this regard, particularly if the flowers grow too tall. Many have flourished with her—her belief in generous compensation extends to her employees—but many leave her, whether because they or she become disenchanted first is forever open to conjecture. Lawrence's team record seems to be more stable.

All along the way, Lawrence has always attracted the approval of older men who wanted to advance his career and from whom he was willing to learn. The finding of the patron may be the single most important factor in business success and no business school gives a course in it.

Lawrence learned a great deal from Six, not only about running an airline but, according to industry gossip, also about how to live grandly. Six married well-known performers. Ethel Merman, the brass-voiced singer, certainly taught him a thing or two about living with your name in lights. After they were divorced, he married Audrey Meadows, a quieter, prettier, and younger actress with a Hollywood gloss (despite the fact that she was a minister's daughter).

Some of the armchair psychologists of the airline confraternity theorize that in marrying Mary Wells, Harding Lawrence acted out the filial desire to surpass his father, i.e., Bob Six.

If lifestyle is the criterion, then the Lawrences have left the Sixes at the starting gate. Here, everyone agrees, the credit (or blame) belongs to Mary. After she and Lawrence met, his airline associates watched with fascination the evolution in his hair length and his tailoring and the number and manner of his abodes.

For though Bob Six and some of the other airborne entrepreneurs may have had their ducal urges, they were largely manifested in far-flung rustic retreats (airline executives and directors fly free of charge on complimentary passes) and monumental offices and staff (for which the stockholders ultimately pay).

The Lawrences' mode of living is straight out of *Vogue* magazine, *Women's Wear Daily,* and the gossip columns of Eugenia Sheppard and Aileen Mehle (who writes under the byline of "Suzy"), where indeed it is frequently reported. The style is totally alien to the aviation world which still carries the taste and tone of its military heritage.

Furthermore—shades of J. P. Morgan—it's not just the dwellings but the upkeep. As one Texas wheeler-dealer's wife commented in response to the rumor that the Lawrences' fairytale French Riviera property might be up for sale, "But who will she sell it to? Dallas people don't have that kind of money any more. She'll have to find a shah."

Curiously, too, the Lawrence lifestyle seems to contradict a basic tenet of their business philosophy: constantly reduce operating costs, deflate expenses, and run a tight ship.

Mary Pickford and Douglas Fairbanks (to pursue the America's-sweethearts analogy) had one palatial residence, Pickfair, in Beverly Hills. The Lawrences have four: a triplex on East End Avenue in Manhattan, where she and her two teen-age daughters live; a house in Dallas, where he is based (although more and more he is sleeping in New York); a cattle ranch near Tucson, Arizona; and La Fiorentina, one of the most luxurious estates at Saint-Jean-Cap-Ferrat, a 600-acre peninsula poking into the Mediterranean between Villefranche and Beaulieu that is believed to have the thickest density of millionaires of any territory in France.

"We have always found Cap Ferrat to be very soothing," Mary Lawrence told an interviewer from *Town & Country* magazine. "The privacy we have on the tip of the peninsula is precious."

Mary Lawrence bought La Fiorentina from the estate of Lady Kenmare at a reported price of $2 million. Since Mary Lasker, the advertising industry's dowager philanthropist, had been renting La Fiorentina for the month of August since 1957, the Lawrences permitted her to continue. Mrs. Lasker went on Braniff's board in 1971.

"I always admired Mary Lasker for all the good she does," Harding Lawrence said. "She has good judgment. I value her counsel and guidance. She is an extraordinary woman."

Mary Lawrence declared, "I admire her more than any woman I know."

All the Lawrence residences have been furnished by Billy Baldwin right down to the fingerbowls. "I didn't pick an ashtray—not a thing," Mary Lawrence asserts. She says she hires the best people to carry out her ideas, communicating with them by long memoranda before the work is begun. Because she spends as much time as she can in bed—reading, tearing stories out of newspapers and magazines, writing notes and eating—Baldwin has provided monarchial beds in all of the homes. Her New York bed is hung with silk draw curtains and lit for reading from the inside.

Baldwin is a society decorator who once whipped over to the Greek island of Skorpios to make it habitable for Aristotle Onassis' bride Jacqueline Bouvier Kennedy. His touch is recognizably stagey. Baldwin loves to swathe rooms in yards and yards of fabric. Among the clients whose dining rooms and foyers he has converted into Middle Eastern tents of fabric are the William Paleys of CBS.

Baldwin even curtained every inch of wall and closet in Harding Lawrence's study-dressing room on East End Avenue in French chintz. He put ruffles reminiscent of Turkish pantaloons on the chairs and banquettes of the living room. The mood of thirties' theatricality in the apartment is accentuated by a velvet-slippered butler who might be mistaken for a young Cesar Romero.

Lawrence is the he-man sort who looks as though he would be most comfortable in a saddle, a cockpit, or a Marlboro cigarette ad. He seems displaced in the Baldwin milieu, almost as though he were Clark Gable astray on the set of a Noel Coward comedy.

Mary Lawrence seems always to have had a craving for luxury. Her taste was champagne even when her income was Miller's High Life. She never seemed to worry about whether she could afford beautiful possessions. A friend recalls her impulsively buying a set of the expensive Porthault bed and bath linens back when she was earning a copy writer's salary and shrugging it off as an investment.

Now she dismisses the suggestion that she is keeping up with the Rockefellers. "We don't really spend a lot. We don't really earn a lot. We don't have cars or expensive jewelry," she said, overlooking the two blue company cars, one a Cadillac, the other a Mercedes 600 in which she and her assistant are driven to and from the offices of Wells, Rich, Greene and around New York.

"We don't have yachts or private planes," she said. But then most airline executives and their wives make do with courtesy passes that take them to almost any nook and cranny of the world.

"We can leave the houses and never be afraid there's anything to steal. You can't steal Billy Baldwin." A discriminating thief might want to make away with the immense Helen Frankenthaler and Milton Avery paintings and the African sculpture, though.

Furthermore, the Lawrences emphasize how hard they work and how seldom they occupy their various Billy Baldwin-decorated homes. They're at the Arizona ranch for the round-up on Labor Day and not much more. Harding considers the ranch as an investment since it turns a small profit as a cattle-raising venture and there's no point in being in a deal unless you make a profit, he says. They spend at most a total of one month during the year in France.

"Money never meant anything to me in the sense that there's no thing I really ever wanted except Fiorentina." Mary Lawrence sounds wistful when she says she'd like to be there more often. She notes that La Fiorentina would be a prize for a real estate developer, situated as it is on a peninsula, but of course she can't imagine selling it.

In the early years of their marriage, Mary had her daughters installed in the house in Dallas with Harding during the week. She joined them for three-day weekends. But as the girls approached adolescence, she transferred them to New York, and Dallas is seeing less and less of the Lawrences. (The family pets are divided between the two cities. The three French poodles are based in Dallas, the Burmese and Siamese cats in New York.)

"We really live in planes and motels and hotels," Mary said. One of her homes away from home is a Holiday Inn in Elkhart, Indiana.

"If you work as hard as we do and spend a lot of time with people during the week, when you finally grab a little bit of time for yourselves, the last thing you want to do is spend it in a hotel. With land, you get privacy. You can hole up. It's incredible to be able to disappear. Even though we don't get to these places very much," she said.

The Lawrences made a rule when they married that they would never go out with anyone else—not even to be paired harmlessly at dinners with other lone sheep or wolves. So they decline most invitations. Mary entertains clients at lunch or cocktails in her office and friends hardly at all. In the evening they get into whatever beds they

are using and talk to each other on the telephone (having probably
chatted half a dozen times by office tie line during the day).

"We give one or two parties in France. Our social life is maybe
ten times a year having two to four people by for dinner every two
or three months," Mary said.

"Not that we don't love people," Harding inserted. "But our
businesses are operating businesses."

"Also they're service businesses," she interrupted.

"You become part of your business," he said. "It's a way of life,
not a job."

On the rare occasions when the Lawrences do give parties, they
are eye-poppers. To celebrate the wedding of her assistant, Kathie
Durham, to Joseph Curran, vice president for marketing for RCA in
the spring of 1974, Mary invited the elite of the advertising industry
and a few members of the press such as Philip Dougherty, the
Times' advertising columnist, and Eugenia Sheppard, the fashion
and society writer, to a party at the East End Avenue penthouse.

They reported tubs of orchids everywhere, Dom Pérignon champagne flowing like rain, and dancing to an orchestra after dinner.

In 1972, when Mary Lawrence was named chairman of the Crystal Ball, Dallas' main charity event, she hired Earl Blackwell, the
party organizer and social quotient-lifter. Blackwell engaged Cecil
Beaton, the British photographer and stage designer, to turn one
ballroom of the Fairmont Hotel into a re-creation of Queen Victoria's Crystal Palace, and another into a *My Fair Lady* version of
Ascot.

Beaton and Blackwell imported celebrities from across continents
and seas, including a cousin of Queen Elizabeth, a London debu-
tante who had been escorted by Prince Charles, and Madame Hervé
Alphand, the wife of the French diplomat. These rare birds flapped
together with the Lyndon Johnsons, the John Connallys, and H.
Ross Perot, the computer millionaire. During dinner, forty dancing
girls in minimal silver lamé gyrated to rock music.

Dallas being, of course, the home base of the first Mrs. Harding
Lawrence, it was the most gorgeous case of social one-upmanship a
stranger had ever pulled off in Texas.

"The important thing about the Crystal Ball is that it earned
$250,000 for charity on the bottom line," Mary Lawrence said.

She had employed the same social means for strictly commercial
ends the year before when she commissioned Blackwell to stage a

party in Paris. Her client, the Menley & James Laboratories Division of Smith-Kline Corporation, whose cosmetics distribution had been in chain and drugstores, wanted to break into department stores with a new line of Love Cosmetics. "They needed awareness very fast," Mary said. Blackwell produced the Duchess of Windsor and Liza Minnelli for the occasion.

Though she relies on society minions like Blackwell, Baldwin, and Jo Hughes (the supersaleswoman at Bergdorf Goodman who selects most of the expensive, name-designer clothes Mary wears and says she doesn't care a whit about) and they pass the Lawrences' name to their allies, the gossip columnists, Mary and Harding Lawrence don't seem interested in social cachet. They have neither the time nor the desire to cultivate new friendships, little enough to maintain old ones. Mary Lawrence sends impetuous love notes and gifts to friends—like cases of wine and crates of French delicacies—as substitutes for her and Harding's presence.

"My mother and my kids. They're my greatest friends," she says. And her husband. She hankers for him in public, dispatching melting glances at him down the length of a dais or across a crowded banquet hall. In her pink-walled office overlooking Central Park from the twenty-eighth floor of the General Motors Building, she is surrounded by photographs of him and the children (hers and his). Her daughters' poems and notes are framed in lucite ("Momma, I love you," proclaims one of Katy's messages from the ranch).

She works at a highly polished Chippendale table that is really too small for a working desk. A new electric typewriter that she recently learned to operate, jettisoning her old Royal Standard because she feared it looked too old-fashioned, stands on a table beside it. The desk is one of the mistakes of the interior decorator, who did the Wells, Rich, Greene headquarters to look homey rather than officey.

But the effect is too feminine. Male clients have to be diverted from the pouffy, velvet-covered sofa in her office lest they sink in and feel foolish. She had ordered a restyling by Arthur Smith, the partner to whom Billy Baldwin had entrusted his clients when he retired, but Smith didn't get much further than slipcovering some conference rooms in chintz when the business downturn dictated a halt. Wells, Rich, Greene is an extension of her home just as Braniff's airplanes are of Harding's. "On a Braniff plane I'm not on a plane. I'm home," he says.

Mary moves through life as a royal person, never carrying money
or wearing a watch. Company cars or rented limousines chauffeur
her to and from airplanes. Arriving at hotels she goes directly to her
room. One of her three secretaries in New York makes arrangements by telephone for her to be checked in and out, for generous
tips to be left.

When she is in New York, Katherine Durham Curran, her lady-
in-waiting who has the title of a Wells, Rich, Greene vice president,
arrives at the East End Avenue apartment at 8 A.M. and takes her
dictation and directives for an hour until 9 A.M. The bed is already
covered with sheets of white bond paper containing Mary's scrib-
bled notes and with other scraps of intelligence.

At nine they are driven to the office, Mary Lawrence dictating en
route. "I had to learn to get over car sickness," says Kathie Curran,
a blonde and blue-eyed Katharine Gibbs graduate, who personifies
the Wells ideal of wholesome, bubbly sexiness. She also had to
master her boss's penmanship so she could produce the inimitable
Mary Lawrence hand-written notes.

Dictation continues in elevators and elsewhere, such as the salon
of Kenneth, the hairdresser. Having the secretary present and working while the boss is shampooed, set, and manicured is a mark of the
woman at the pinnacle of power. Mary Lasker is a pioneer example.
Lesser women go to the hairdresser alone and do their own note-
making under the dryer.

At midday, if she is not giving a luncheon address, or visiting, or
entertaining a client, Mary Lawrence has lunch on a tray in her
office. It's always the same lunch of broiled chicken, green salad,
and a sip of white wine, prepared by a chef and served by a man in
black butler's weeds.

At 7 or 7:30 P.M. she and Kathie Curran leave the office for
home. More dictation in the car. In the apartment, Mary takes a
Love lemon oil bath in her bathroom that has mirrored ceiling and
walls, gets into bed, eats on a tray, goes through her mail, and talks
on the telephone to Harding, wherever he is.

So where do they go from here?

There ought to be at least one more merger in Harding
Lawrence's future. The marriage that seems logical from an economic as well as a sentimental point of view is with Continental.
A Continental-Braniff merger would strengthen a trunk system
blanketing the Midwest and West and into South America. Bob Six

never did groom a successor at Continental after Harding Lawrence left.

Mary Lawrence can acquire another advertising agency. She can go on the boards of other companies, as she did in December 1974 when her client Sun Oil Company elected her a director without any questions being asked about arm's-length bargaining for its advertising account.

Anything is possible because, she once said, "It was never my intention to run a company. I never thought I would have a career. It happened because it was so enjoyable. It just kept growing and getting better and better."

As the man said in the Alka-Seltzer commercial, "I can't believe I ate the whole thing."

Postscript: April 1975

The exchange offer by Wells, Rich, Greene ended with the agency 57 per cent owned by its directors and officers. Stockholders had tendered 1,166,395 shares, about one quarter of a million less than the company had offered to buy back, and not enough to enable it to eliminate minority shareholders. Trading in Wells, Rich, Greene stock was suspended on the New York Stock Exchange, but the stock continues to be registered with the SEC and is traded over-the-counter. The stockholder who sued to have the exchange offer stopped lost his case in federal courts.

As of January 20, 1975 Mary Wells Lawrence owned 115,000 shares, or 24.7 per cent of the 465,463 shares of common stock, outstanding. She was unequivocally the largest stockholder in Wells, Rich, Greene.

At the annual meeting on March 6, earnings for the first quarter of the fiscal year 1975 were reported to have fallen 39 per cent compared with the same period the year before. Mary Lawrence said that salary raises and the addition of new employees last year accounted for about half of the profit decline. "I'm the only person in the agency who has not had a raise in seven years," she replied to a stockholder's question about the salary hikes.

On March 12, the Bureau of Enforcement of the Civil Aeronautics Board charged Braniff International Airways and American

Airlines with diverting moneys into secret political funds of greater size than had been disclosed in the Watergate affair.

American's concealed slush fund was said to be at least $275,000. Braniff and seven of its executives including Harding Lawrence were accused of drawing "off-the-books" income totalling $641,285 to $926,955 into a hidden account "for the use of Braniff management . . . at least in part for unlawful purposes."

The CAB report did not specify, however, how the alleged fund was used except for the gift to the Nixon campaign for which Lawrence and Braniff had already been penalized.

FINALE

WHAT NEXT?

Fattened and made cocksure by a decade of easy living and manic optimism, many businessmen lost their footing in the pounding surf of the 1970s. Many of the corporate sand castles they had so imaginatively constructed came tumbling down.

The 1960s, despite their social torment, the weakening of faith in institutions, the war far away, and the hostility between races and generations at home, had been good years for businessmen. Everything was going up—population, income, the stock market. The law of gravity seemed suspended. History was forgotten. Sodom and Gomorrah were construed as new markets. Everyone could have a piece of the shell game.

The 1970s arrived on an ominous note, with a recession and the rot beginning to show in Wall Street—a few smashing bankruptcies and consolidations amid the brokerage firms, the collapse of the Penn Central Railroad.

But the recovery was glorious for many businesses. Until the fourth quarter of 1973, ushered in with the Arab oil embargo, the auto industry was reveling in the best year in its history, and well into 1974 corporations in other sectors of the economy reported record profits.

From the middle of 1974 on, though, corporate mettle was to be tested. Though many in government and business couldn't bring themselves to pronounce the word "recession"—they debated it as though it were the number of angels dancing on the head of a pin—they had to suspect that the climate under which they had thrived, had changed. The combination of recession and inflation was totally unfamiliar, even to those who remembered their textbook lessons.

Apart from the economic slowdown per se, there was the fat, black cloud of the energy problem. One of the premises on which the American auto industry had been built was cheap gasoline. From that came the car culture and rippling out from that, the motel industry, the leisure industry in its myriad components, suburban real estate construction, for example. (And even the door-to-door selling of cosmetics and fragrances by housewives to other housewives on a commission arrangement, in which the sales representative bore such expenses as gasoline and upkeep of her automobile.)

There were so many other factors in the slowdown that many in business had never reckoned with before, singly or in combination. Sudden shortages and price escalations in commodities—flour (that could be traced to a massive sale of wheat to the Russians), sugar, coffee, soybean oil, plastics (a result of the petroleum crisis). These cost increases could not always be passed on to the customer, either because of government price controls (briefly and faintheartedly imposed) or because the customer was at the "choking point," as James L. Ferguson, the chairman of General Foods Corporation, called it.

And, of course, high interest rates. Taken alone, they need not have mattered, since interest is a cost of doing business and if the business is healthy enough, the interest cost is easily absorbed. But if the business is nourished largely by debt, the pressure of rising interest can be intolerable.

In the 1960s business had one creed, growth. Businessmen espoused the new math of synergism, otherwise known as two-plus-two-equals-five. In the 1970s a new, new math had to be devised to find the balance of two-minus-three. All creeds had to be reexamined, especially growth.

Writing in the *Wall Street Journal,* Alfred L. Malabre, Jr., reported that "the remarkably uniform conclusion is that economic expansion will be significantly slower than has generally been the case heretofore in the post-World War II era. The U.S. automobile industry, particularly, appears headed for sluggish growth."

Malabre quoted economic studies forecasting marked slowdowns in growth in the late 1970s that would continue into the 1980s. A decline in the nation's birth rate was mainly the cause, they said.

Already, the penalties for thinking only big were being exacted. Wall Street had chased away the small investor whom it had wooed into the market in the 1950s, with its campaign of "people's capitalism" presided over by Keith Funston, president of the New York Stock Exchange, a confidence-inspiring, ex-college president.

In the mid-1960s many in the Street turned their backs on "the little guy" and concentrated on the large institutional investors. These were the managers of portfolios running in the hundreds of millions and even billions of dollars, held by mutual funds, pension funds, college and university endowment funds, philanthropic foundations, insurance companies, and bank trust accounts. Wall Street brokerage firms and investment banking houses expanded their research departments, and some committed capital to operations for trading in huge blocks of stock.

The managers of those institutional portfolios became legends in their own time. Newsletters and magazines catered to them. They responded, for the most part, by believing their own press notices and following the herd instinct. The managers of the funds were addicted to growth. It was their cult. They tended to pursue it in the same companies, to become enamored of the same stocks. Their favorites earned the nickname "the nifty fifty."

The fifty were not, on the whole, speculative issues of pasteboard companies. The companies were shining examples of the best in American enterprise, technology, and business management— International Business Machines Corporation, Xerox Corporation, Avon Products Inc. But unlike the old "blue chip" companies such as the railroads, the steel companies, and the utilities that banks used to pack their widows-and-orphans clients into, the institutional investor favorites were slated for growth. Infinitely, it seemed.

Since most of the fund managers were young and dismissed the experiences of the 1930s as though they were a figment of fuddyduddy imaginations, they believed that companies and industries could keep on growing. The band would keep on playing, and if it ever stopped, they would be first off the merry-go-round.

Anyone who demurred from such a positive-thinking growth concept was ostracized. In 1969 McGeorge Bundy, a former Harvard dean and special assistant for national security affairs to Presidents Kennedy and Johnson, was then president of the Ford Foundation. A foundation report issued under his aegis urged managers of endowment funds to look for greater return in capital. It criticized them for erring on the side of caution. In 1974 the Ford Foundation announced that its assets had shrunk from $3 billion to $2 billion and that it would have to remeasure its grant-giving to fit its smaller bundle.

Merrill Lynch, Pierce, Fenner & Smith estimated that the market value of all stocks dropped about $500 billion between January 1973 and mid-September 1974. In 1974 twenty of the top stocks held by the funds lost $80.8 billion of their market value. The band had stopped, but the fund managers were stuck on the merry-go-round together.

Wall Street's passion for growth had also affected the managers of the corporations. Some of them spent inordinate amounts of time and energy fretting about the price of the company stock. Their own compensation was linked to it in the form of stock options. And it was apparent that the market, dominated by the stock-buying power of the fund managers, was only going to smile on companies that were sure to grow.

There were no Brownie points for managing a company to its reasonable size.

The men on the fourteenth floor at GM in Detroit drew down their mind-boggling rewards in a formula tied to big profits on big sales of big cars. Antitrust laws kept GM from growing any bigger through acquisitions or substantially increasing its share of the auto market.

With other companies, the only way to keep up the dizzying numbers game was by diversification. Either by buying up companies or internally adding new product lines or activities.

The fund managers considered some activities more glamorous than others, and their affections for glamour knew no limits. It was expressed in high multiples, the ratio of the price of the stock to the earnings of the company. With some of the glamour stocks like those of cable television companies and the world's largest cosmetic company, the ratio was the result of intellectual marijuana-smoking.

Cable television gave a peek at a rosy future. But it requires enormous capital investment, and no one had figured out the sticky details of who would pay for the services it promised and how much.

In the case of Avon, some simple basic questions must never have been asked—for instance, about the door-to-door system of selling the product and whether it might keep growing if lifestyles changed; whether beauty salons and mail-order clothing—two businesses chosen for diversification—could possibly generate the profits that lipsticks and fragrances can. Since neither beauty salons nor mail order are uncharted fields (as cable is), the answers were available if anyone wanted to ask or listen.

In an analysis of the new low ground the stock market had broken, Leslie M. Pollack, senior vice president of Shearson Hayden Stone Inc., wrote in October 1974:

"While the market may have been too high at its peak and some of these companies may have suffered from poor management, the total picture is devastating. The losers have been more than stock brokers and millionaires.

"They include 30 million individual Americans, universities, foundations, hospitals, charities, beneficiaries of profit sharing and pension plans, retired people, widows and orphans. Also, corporations that cannot raise equity capital for improvements and consumers and laborers who would benefit from such expansions.

"It is clear that wealth has been redistributed away from stockholders during the past fifteen years. The beneficiaries of this shift are hard to identify because much of this wealth seems to have vanished into thin air. However, their ranks include overpaid corporate chieftains with six-figure salaries and expense accounts, corrupt politicians in cahoots with organized special interest groups, movie stars, oil producers, and superathletes."

The aftermath of the period Pollack was analyzing yielded bizarre torture for many top corporate executives and their compensation consultants. The more business activity slackened and problems multiplied for their companies, the more distracted they were by the bursting of their personal financial bubbles. The fatal pinprick had been the stock market plunge.

Their plight was discussed at an executive compensation conference sponsored by *Dun's Review,* the business magazine, in November 1974. Pearl Meyer, executive vice president of Handy Associates, a management consulting firm, gave a candid review of the causes and effects of corporate avarice. "We induced or even seduced our executives to purchase stock on borrowed funds or to defer their earnings in stock," she said. "We called these seductions 'incentive plans.' Today these plans are acting as incentives in reverse.

"I hope that at the board level we are now recognizing the need to promote the real mutuality of interest between the executive and the company. Until recently, a board gave its chief executive and other officers some stock options. Or they otherwise induced him to become a shareholder. And they naïvely thought that this lure of speculative profit would bind the man to the company and its welfare. To the contrary, instead it induced him to greed," Mrs. Meyer said.

She mentioned an executive who became a millionaire through options in one company in the late 1950s. He then contacted Handy's executive searchers and made them aware of his "availability to enjoy another such golden opportunity."

"The last time I heard of him a few years ago," Mrs. Meyer said, "he was in pursuit of his third million with his sixth employer in fifteen years."

However, such golden opportunities had become nightmares of dross for many such executive prospectors in the 1970s. They had borrowed money to exercise the options the boards of directors had generously voted them. In some cases, banks extended loans that strained the limits of prudence. Though never spelled out, it was understood that the credit of the corporation, which was both the employer of the executive and a continuing source of new business for the bank, stood behind the loans.

One or more cruel turns of fate then occurred as the stock market sank and the executives found themselves deeply indebted for vanished profits. Interest payments on loans exceeded the income on their investments. Banks, which were anxious about their own solvency as more and more of the loans on their books began to look like terminal cases, issued margin calls for further collateral and pressed laggard debtors to keep up their interest payments. When executives pleaded inability to do so (and occasionally thumbed their noses at the banks and threatened to file for personal bankruptcy), the financial institutions turned to the corporations to make the executives comply, a ridiculous proposition since it was asking the members of the pinnacle club to tighten the screws on each other or on themselves.

Ring around the rosy was being played in a cupboard.

"I've seen executives who had interest in the millions and low-dividend income. Believe me that hurts," Mortimer M. Caplin, a Washington tax lawyer and a former Commissioner of Internal Revenue told the *Dun's* conference. "With the bankers breathing down his neck, obviously the executive's day-to-day effectiveness is impaired. What do you do for these people?"

Caplin sketched a few pitfalls. Some companies were making "soft loans" to the beleaguered executives, picking up their bank loans at low interest rates. But there were state and federal securities and tax laws that prohibited or penalized such thoughtful gestures.

A critical blow to stock options had been leveled by the Tax Reform Act of 1969 (which, on the other hand, by lowering the maximum tax rate on earned income from 70 to 50 per cent had made high salaries of more real value). Under provisions of that law, the executive incurred tax liabilities on the difference between his option price and the market value on the date of exercise. The spread is considered tax preference income and subject to a 10 per cent minimum tax. If the value of the stock shrank in a subsequent market decline, as so frequently happened in 1973 and 1974, the executive would be paying taxes on phantom profits. The only way to avoid the minimum tax was by selling the stock obtained by exercise of options within the taxable year.

Some executives rushed to do so even though it meant selling at a loss. Then they wanted restitution of their dashed expectations. All through the first half of the 1970s, stockholders were asked to vote new stock-option plans designed to make executives whole and insure that membership in the pinnacle club was a risk-free privilege. Never mind that it had been billed as an incentive proposition.

In some cases, indulgent boards rushed too quickly to vote fresh options. New options granted within thirty days of the sale of previous option stock is considered a "wash transaction" by the IRS, which reactivates the tax penalty the executive was trying to avoid.

So at least one board of directors voted to "reimburse" a chief executive "for the damages he had suffered" from their haste. The damage was an unanticipated increase in his 1973 tax liability which resulted "in a severe economic detriment" to him rather than the "economic incentive." In return for his relinquishing a claim for damages against the corporation, the company paid him $733,238, the amount of his increased tax liability and related expenses (which included his lawyer's fees). The company is entitled to take the sum as a tax deduction, but how many of those dollars it would still end up paying for would depend on the tax rate it eventually incurs for that year.

All of this came to light in a footnote on page 18 of the proxy statement of Norton Simon, Inc. It probably would have lain buried there had not Wilma Soss, the self-appointed detective for minority stockholders, appeared at the annual meeting in November 1974 wearing her Sherlock Holmes deerstalker's hat and carrying a magnifying glass, a costume she dons "whenever information in a proxy statement is obscure."

"I never heard of anything like this," she exclaimed. Mrs. Soss and her comrades, the Gilbert brothers, have been striving to curb stock-option excesses over the years, arguing that they do not serve the purpose of incentives.

The Norton Simon episode was considered embarrassing to its board and to David J. Mahoney, the chief executive who had been reimbursed. It caused chills and fever to break out in many executive suites where similar efforts at coddling corporate insiders had been made or contemplated.

At the Norton Simon meeting, stockholders ratified adoption of a 1974 stock-option plan, the third in six years, which canceled qualified stock options at $21.32 per share to make way for new nonqualified options at average prices of $14.25 a share. Mahoney has options for 534,930 shares under the new plan.

"I'm puzzled why you want a new option plan inasmuch as you still owe $1.3 million on old stock," Mrs. Soss declared. Here she was alluding to another plan approved in 1970. Under that executive stock purchase plan, Mahoney had purchased 75,000 shares of Series A convertible preferred stock with a secured loan from the company for $2.5 million payable over seven to ten years at 4 per cent interest. As of August 31, 1974, he still owed $1,379,000.

And in March 1974, two other officers of Norton Simon, Inc., were each given unsecured five-year loans for half a million dollars each to buy preferred stock.

"Is the board encouraging a lot of these people to become overextended," Mrs. Soss asked at the meeting. "Did the board push Mr. Mahoney into too high a tax bracket?"

In her speech to the *Dun's* conference, Pearl Meyer delineated a course for the future. "We need to write realistic business plans with measurable objectives. We need to hire the one best person for each job. And then—and only then—can we as compensation experts come in and do our thing: provide for equitable and motivational compensation programs that work both for the company and for the individual." She mentioned a large corporation that has nine different executive compensation plans in which its division managers participate. "This kind of compensation package inspires in me the image of the manager standing in front of a pinball machine," she said. "All he does at the beginning of the year is pull the plunger—and soon all kinds of red, blue, yellow, green, purple, and orange lights are lit. He doesn't understand exactly what he did, or what he is going to get for it—except that everyone tells him that he has been rewarded. The trouble is . . . he probably hasn't been rewarded. What he thinks he sees, he isn't going to get.

"We are going to have to rephrase some of our classic questions about compensation," Pearl Meyer asserted. "The first questions must get back to basics: what are we paying an executive for? . . . The old answer used to be: we were paying a chief executive and the managers under him to run the company for the welfare of the shareholders. In other words, to make the stock climb in price and to keep raising the dividend payout. Later, when we became more socially oriented, we said it was for the welfare of the shareholders, and the employees and the customers and the community—the society. But basically, management performance was still measured short-term and long-term and interim-term by the stock market."

Mrs. Meyer went on to say that in the climate of 1974–75 the stock market was not an accurate reflection of a company's performance. Moreover, some executives were occupied defending the company against take-overs. The lowered price of its stock in relation to its book value and earning power made it a sitting duck for raiders; sometimes management let the company be taken over in the shareholder's interest.

She then sketched what executives would be wanting for compensation under these changed business circumstances. Bonuses, tax shelters, protective benefits ("and not limited by blanket or artificial maximums such as $50,000 in life insurance and that sort of thing"), "no-fault" termination provisions in employment contracts, retirement income that won't be hacked away by inflation. Finally, bigger base salaries. "And without any substantial reduction in the over-all size of the compensation package," she said.

Since this trend will start at the lower and middle management

levels, Mrs. Meyer predicted, it will lead to base salary increases at
the top management level.

"Are you ready for this?" she asked the audience. "We are going
to see seven-figure salaries in the giant companies. Sooner or later,
surely by 1976, it's really going to happen: executives are going to
join the movie stars with million-dollar salaries."

The wide-awake audience uttered nary a murmur, an indication
they were indeed ready.

If a past is a record for the future, those who receive the raises
will continue to deplore the decline of productivity in American
industry, and the disappearance of the puritan work ethic. Among
the rank and file, that is.

It's worth noting how the board of directors keeps cropping up in
discussions of immoderate rewards for executives. The board votes
the stock options or the stock purchase loans. Actually, the board
approves the plan the chief executive has his executive compensation specialist prepare, to be just palatable enough for the board to
swallow. The corporation pays for the specialist's services.

"Sometimes I just gag when I hear what he's come up with," said
one compensation specialist, alluding to the chief executive of a
Fortune-500 company, famed for his well-publicized good looks
and management decisiveness and the whopping compensation he
succeeds in extracting from the directors of the several corporations
at which he has spent half a dozen years before moving to the next.

"On the days when I'm being honest with myself," said the exec
comp man mournfully peering into his glass of chablis at La Côte
Basque, "I say to myself, 'You're in the business of prostitution.'"

There is much that can and is being said about directors, that
inner circle of the pinnacle club, without casting aspersions on their
morals. Besides, some social theorists maintain that prostitutes are
oppressed workers in an industry created by a sick society.

It is more to the point to say that directors are often negligent,
inept, uninformed, lazy, past their prime, or observing the ethics of
the gentlemen's club and the fraternity. Since the director may owe
to the chief executive the prestige of his board appointment and
such perquisites as the increasingly substantial fees, free transportation, and, in the case of GM, the use of an automobile, is he
likely to contradict him or risk being dropped from the board?

A fascinating pastime is to comb the lists of boards of directors of
major corporations and cross-check them with other reference

sources such as directories and newspaper library files. American business begins to assume the outline of a genealogical chart.

For instance, as was glossed over during the confirmation hearings of Nelson A. Rockefeller for the vice presidency of the United States, there are interlocks between the Rockefeller Family and a hundred or so *Fortune*-500 corporations. "The family is not interested in control," said J. Richardson Dilworth, the family's chief financial adviser, himself a director of more than a dozen companies. Nonsense and evasions that would be inexcusable coming from a clerk are accepted at towering heights.

How quirky it seems that John L. Loeb, senior partner of Loeb, Rhoades & Company is not only a director but a member of the audit committee of the board (supposedly a watchdog group) of Distillers Corporation-Seagrams Limited, of which his former son-in-law, Edgar M. Bronfman, is president.

Or that Gustave L. Levy, senior partner of Goldman, Sachs & Company, was one of three members of the compensation committee of the Norton Simon board that voted the new options to Mahoney? Levy insists that one man can manage his own business and a slew of others at the same time. He has concurrently served on as many as twenty boards of directors.

It was Levy, by the way, who testified in a stockholder suit resulting from Goldman, Sachs's marketing of Penn Central commercial paper that he had lost almost $9 million for his friend Walter Annenberg, the Philadelphia publisher, then ambassador to the Court of St. James's, by investing part of Annenberg's account in the securities.

One might ask, as Wilma Soss did, where was the board of directors of General Foods when the millions of dollars of losses in hamburger restaurants were being accrued? What was the board of directors of General Motors doing when the imported cars were nibbling into its market, when American consumers were developing hate feelings toward auto manufacturers, when the alarms were being sounded about the shrinkage of energy resources? Collecting their five-figure directors' fees, sampling their Jell-O Pudding Treats, and test driving their GM automobiles for 3,000 miles.

Directors' seats have been one of the plushier sinecures of American corporate life, and only in recent years has there been a modest ground swell of demand for reform of the director system. Social ac-

tivists have wanted it broadened to take in representatives of previously excluded groups such as blacks, women, and consumers.

For a while, business frantically hunted for such untraditional
candidates, giving their executive search consultants welcome new
assignments which many were ill-fitted to execute since their pools
of talent were so shallow. A handful of blacks and women were
"overused and overcommitted," as Pearl Meyer tactfully put it. So
Aileen Mehle, the society gossip columnist; Dinah Shore, the singer;
the Reverend Theodore Hesburgh of Notre Dame University; the
Reverend Leon Sullivan of Zion Baptist Church in Philadelphia;
Mrs. Whitney Young, Jr., the widow of the civil rights leader; and
Mrs. McGeorge Bundy, wife of the head of the Ford Foundation,
became directors of mighty corporations. (The fact that Walter A.
Haas, Jr., chairman of Levi-Strauss was a director of the Ford
Foundation had nothing to do with Mary Bundy's election to the
jeans manufacturer's board, a spokesman said. It was because she
was a mother and Levi-Strauss sells a lot to mothers and because
her experience in nonprofit activities was impressive.)

Then there was Harry Gangloff, an engineering student at Drexel
University, appointed to the board of the First Pennsylvania Corporation as a youth representative (a pet idea of its chairman John
Bunting which was not widely copied by his corporate peers).
Gangloff fractured the clubman's code (a danger foreseen by many
chief executives who resisted the admission of outsiders). He confessed he didn't always understand what was going on at the
directors' meetings. "A business background would have helped
me understand the implications," he said.

Not necessarily, if we are to judge from the spate of lawsuits
against directors in some of the more outstanding recent insolven-
cies, such as those of the Penn Central and Franklin National Bank.

After the first round of grabbing for any token director in a
storm, corporate managements became critical of outsiders who did
what they were supposed to, namely, bring a new perspective to
the deliberations of the board.

Leon Sullivan was considered to be one-sided, harping mostly on
minority rights. "No question about it," he said. "And I am seeing
progress in GM." Another GM director, Catherine Cleary, president of First Wisconsin Trust Company and a member of the
boards of American Telephone & Telegraph Company, Kraftco
Corporation, Northwestern Mutual Life Insurance Company, and

the Kohler Company, angered feminists because she declined to consider herself their representative.

Patricia Roberts Harris, the lawyer who was a two-in-one selection (being black and female) at International Business Machines Corporation, the Chase Manhattan Corporation, and the Scott Paper Company, was told by a chairman after she expressed a criticism at a meeting that she should have raised the matter privately. Later the word was passed through the corporate grapevine that Mrs. Harris, an uncommonly ready talker, wasn't speaking up much at meetings. Conceding that she had been silent, she said, "I don't believe in taking positions and then regretting I didn't understand the ramifications. Part of it may be that sometimes people don't want to hear something critical from someone who isn't the chairman or their banker."

Myles Mace, a professor emeritus of the Harvard Business School is of the opinion that attempts to reform the corporation by changing the composition of the board are bound to fail because they merely accept "the great myth that boards do things when the reality is they don't." Boards are "creatures and agents of management," he says. They are inhibited from truly evaluating the chief executive's performance either because they are his cronies or they are unqualified to do so. They don't "manage" the corporation as most state corporation laws charge them with doing. According to Mace, they don't do much of anything except step in during a crisis.

But by then serious damage may have been done, as in the General Foods hamburger chain folly or as in the financial hemorrhage of Pan American World Airways. Donald Kendall, chairman of Pepsico, helped rally Pan Am's submissive board to get rid of chairman Najeeb Halaby. Morale picked up for a while under the successor the board approved, William Seawell, but he was unable to staunch the bleeding either.

Directors may be held accountable for a corporation's misfortunes, but those chosen for cosmetic reasons may not be fully cognizant of this harsh side of their newfound glory.

"A helluva lot of people are serving without having any knowledge of their legal liabilities," said Ulric St. Clair Haynes, Jr., a vice president of the Cummins Engine Company, a former minority management recruiter and a director of Marine Midland Banks, Inc.

"Some companies will insure their board members up to a couple of million dollars, but even if you're not going to lose all your worldly goods, your good name will be dragged through the mud and this is something the typical new board member doesn't realize," Haynes said.

The Securities and Exchange Commission and several federal courts have acted to hold directors personally liable for corporate mismanagement and fraud—in effect, demanding of them the active vigilance that custom has negated.

But confusion surrounds the law on director responsibility. In two cases involving the BarChris Construction Corporation, judges arrived at somewhat different conclusions. Two outside directors, a banker and an engineer, were held by one lower court liable for signing a registration statement that contained false material information that they failed to check independently. An appeals court absolved a third director of the duty to look behind the transaction before voting to authorize it. He was a partner in the investment banking firm that underwrote the issue though he didn't participate in it. But the two decisions involved different sections of the Securities Acts, and court decisions are made on individual cases of fact and legal interpretation.

The suggestion has come forth from several sources that so-called specialist directors (those with supposed expertise in areas of social concern) should have a limited role and limited liability like that of limited partners in law or brokerage firms. "They would only participate on those matters where their special knowledge would apply, but on complex problems, say, of compensation for executives, obviously they would disqualify themselves," says one proponent, Robert M. Estes, senior vice president and general counsel of the General Electric Company.

Different standards of accountability for directors strike some as likely to sow even more confusion. Certainly, the example Estes gives is a poor one. The most outrageous awards of executive compensation have been made by the most financially sophisticated directors. Voting on a billion-dollar capital expenditure for a new technology might be a more fitting example.

Numerous proposals have been made to address the reality that the outside directors, no matter how well intentioned, are usually not well informed about what goes on in the company and therefore have little choice but to approve what the chief executive puts before them at the monthly meetings.

Some of these would designate professional public directors with different areas of expertise. Outside board members would be given independent staffs of experts to help them to knowledgeably supervise company operations.

Former Supreme Court Justice Arthur Goldberg resigned from the board of Trans World Airlines, indignant at the director system. He offered such a prescription of staff support for a committee of overseers composed of outside directors.

Opponents say the staffs would only add to the already considerable bloat of the corporate bureaucracies and lead to divided authority. Lower levels of the organization would be subjected to double lines of reporting and uncertainty about where responsibility is lodged.

The questioning of the role of directors is a facet of a larger scrutiny of the American corporation, one that has been growing in intensity during the last decade. It has come from reformers like Ralph Nader, who has outgrown the label of consumer advocate, from a new generation of young, public interest lawyers both in and out of government, from older economists like John Kenneth Galbraith, always eager to shoot from the hip and infuriate business bureaucrats, and from churchmen and women with social concerns that they discover cannot be resolved without the assent and assistance of business.

Behind every query, the crybabies of big business see the specter of socialism, the loss of liberty (theirs). They keen over government usurpation of private prerogative, a fate worse than death unless it suits their convenience, such as in a bail-out of an aircraft manufacturer like the Lockheed Corporation. (By the rules of the free market they profess to hold so sacred, Lockheed might be judged unable to hack it in a competitive market.) Or as in the cause of trade with the Soviet Union, which would open up new markets for private American companies if only the United States Government would extend the foes of free enterprise the necessary credits in the form of loans at a lower rate of interest than American businesses pay. One can decry their inconsistency or admire their flexibility.

Business always fights with the ferocity of an endangered species against any disclosure of its operations. As businesses grow bigger and more diversified, stockholders are increasingly thwarted in their desires to know how the businesses are faring, since corporations have been allowed to shroud sales and profit figures and other pertinent information about individual divisions, subsidiaries, and activities in consolidated totals for the whole company.

If such information were spelled out in annual reports, stockholders might not be so surprised when the corporation suddenly announces a write-off in an acquired company that had been heralded a couple of years before as a profit gusher.

The largest companies that fight disclosure the hardest by financing the lobbying and propaganda campaigns against it are also those about whom industry trade intelligence is most informed. The auto industry can always produce figures about the individual divisions of GM. Only an average stockholder cannot.

Admittedly, the stockholder is not the only one who would like to know. Government antitrust lawyers, tax collectors, consumer groups, and other self-styled guardians of the public interest also need the information.

The Federal Trade Commission's attempt to compel 345 of the nation's largest industrial companies to submit such line-of-business reports on sales, profits, and amounts spent on plant and equipment, research, and advertising was protested with arguments that it violated privacy and due process and that it would give competitors unfair advantage. At the same time, corporate lawyers and accountants said the information sought was useless.

Similarly, Wall Street tried to stave off the Securities and Exchange Commission's determination to unfix commissions. The desperation of the financial community in this regard was hard to reconcile, on intellectual grounds at least, with unswerving devotion to free market philosophy.

The only consistency, then, that one ever sights in business is its self-serving steadfastness to what, at different times, it perceives to be its private interest. Yet business is continuously ambivalent about its privacy.

A recurring example for the mid-1970s was the trend for companies that had advantageously gone "public" in the 1960s to turn "private" when the price of their stock made the public exposure less attractive to the corporate insiders.

Between 1967 and 1972, years when the bulls went wild in Wall Street, 3,000 companies offered their stock to the public for the first time.

In October of 1974, when many were convinced the stock market would be in a prolonged slump, Bankers Trust Company pinpointed thirty publicly held companies that had started going private during the year. The bank offered its services to companies contemplating similar moves.

Two of the best known companies bent on retrieving their shares from the public were Wells, Rich, Greene and MGM which said it would go "semiprivate." Those who stood to gain the most were Mary Wells Lawrence, the chairman and a founder of the advertising agency, and Kirk Kerkorian, the West Coast wheeler-dealer who already owned more than half of the movie company.

"There's a very serious question whether a service agency like an ad agency or an accounting firm should ever be public," said Clinton Frank, head of the Chicago advertising agency bearing his name. Indeed there was, but Frank was late in recognizing it. He made the statement in late 1974, three years after he took his agency public. He changed his mind after twenty-three months.

In an address to the Notre Dame Law School in November 1974, A. A. Sommer, Jr., a Securities Exchange Commissioner vented his displeasure with the trend to go private, terming it "a perversion of the whole process of public financing, and a course that inevitably is going to make the individual shareholder even more hostile to America corporate mores and the securities markets than he already is.

"During the sixties and early seventies innumerable companies 'went public,' that is, publicly offered their securities. All of these companies invited the public to share in their fortunes . . . Corporate managers make their reputations and their fortunes by utilizing the money of others," he said, fixing on the questionable use of the public's money.

He mentioned a company whose "public offerings netted $696,000 for the corporation, over $12.5 million for the offering shareholders" through appreciation in the value of the stock they held. The company was Wells, Rich, Greene.

But when such a company goes private, the money to buy back stock from the public usually doesn't come from those insiders. "The money for the repurchase invariably comes from the corporate till," Sommer said. "There are mighty few instances in which a tender offer has been made by the controlling stockholders who gained from the corporation's going public."

With the proceeds of the public offerings "the corporation grew and prospered, then, with the power deriving from their managerial positions and shareholdings, the insiders take over the whole corporation for themselves," Sommer said.

The fuzziness of the line between private and public rights and interests and the audacity of some business opportunists stimulates the demands for protection of stockholders and consumers. It heightens the cries for more regulations of corporate disclosure, for environmental and safety controls, and for curbs on prices, wages, and executive compensation, too.

"The only thing that kills capitalism is capitalists," says Wilma Soss, who can't bear to think of it dying.

Considering his capacity to plunder and destroy corporations, which are not only legal fictions but sources of life and work for human beings, should the conglomerateur be permitted to operate as a private agent? Should the dinosaur companies, swollen, aged, and immobilized beyond their original economic purpose, be allowed to exist by and for their self-perpetuating bureaucrats?

As William R. Dill, dean of the New York University Graduate School of Business Administration, says, "We're going through a period of asking questions about a system of rewarding and controlling human greed. We're seeing a change from the concept of private enterprise, with secrecy and privacy of operation, to one of continual scrutiny."

The inspection of the business corporation and of the men and women at the top of it will become more searching. Not just because economic conditions compel it but because the more closely one looks inside the pinnacle club, the more there is to see.

INDEX